An Introduction to Communication and Artificial Intelligence

For my students

An Introduction to Communication and Artificial Intelligence

David J. Gunkel

polity

First published in 2020 by Polity Press

Polity Press
65 Bridge Street
Cambridge CB2 1UR, UK

Polity Press
101 Station Landing
Suite 300
Medford, MA 02155, USA

ISBN-13: 978-1-5095-3316-9
ISBN-13: 978-1-5095-3317-6(pb)

A catalogue record for this book is available from the British Library.

Library of Congress Cataloging-in-Publication Data
Names: Gunkel, David J., author.
Title: An introduction to communication and artificial intelligence / David J. Gunkel.
Description: Medford, MA : Polity Press, 2019. | Includes bibliographical references and index. |
Identifiers: LCCN 2019011785 (print) | LCCN 2019017010 (ebook) | ISBN 9781509533190 (Epub) | ISBN 9781509533169 (hardback) | ISBN 9781509533176 (pbk.)
Subjects: LCSH: Computational intelligence. | Natural language processing (Computer science)
Classification: LCC Q335 (ebook) | LCC Q335 .G86 2019 (print) | DDC 003/.5--dc23
LC record available at https://lccn.loc.gov/2019011785

Typeset in 10.5 on 12 pt Plantin by Servis Filmsetting Ltd, Stockport, Cheshire
Printed and bound in Great Britain by TJ International Limited

The publisher has used its best endeavours to ensure that the URLs for external websites referred to in this book are correct and active at the time of going to press. However, the publisher has no responsibility for the websites and can make no guarantee that a site will remain live or that the content is or will remain appropriate.

Every effort has been made to trace all copyright holders, but if any have been overlooked the publisher will be pleased to include any necessary credits in any subsequent reprint or edition.

For further information on Polity, visit our website: politybooks.com

Brief Contents

Detailed Contents

Part II: Applications

Part III: Impact and Consequences

Part IV: Maker Exercises

Preface

This book is designed to provide students in the field of Communication Studies with the basic knowledge, insight, and skill to make sense of emerging technology, specifically artificial intelligence, robots, and algorithms. As we know from our experiences with twentieth-century information and communication technology (ICT) – i.e., the personal computer and the Internet – students outside science, technology, engineering, and mathematics (the so-called STEM disciplines) need to understand the way emerging technology affects their lives and how their particular field of study can contribute to the conversations and debates about responsible employment and integration of technological innovation. But the basic information and technical facility necessary for this to happen are often inaccessible or difficult to obtain.

The basic problem is perhaps best formulated by Arthur C. Clarke, the celebrated science fiction writer and futurist: "Any sufficiently advanced technology is indistinguishable from magic" (Clarke 1973). For many of us – especially those not in one of the STEM fields – advanced technology does appear to be a kind of magic. Most of us have, and carry around, a kind of magical object or talisman. We call it a "smartphone," and it is powerful. We touch the device in just the right way, and our wish is its command. We enter the words of an incantation either by typing on a keypad or talking directly to the object, and it performs all kinds of supernatural feats, like teleporting our voice to a distant place, connecting us to an inexhaustible supply of knowledge residing in the clouds, or providing personalized recommendations and direction so that we do not lose our way. We all use and depend on these devices. But how they actually work – and (maybe even more importantly) understanding how and why they sometimes don't work – is something that remains hidden from view and underappreciated by most users. This is *the* problem. When technology appears to be magic, it has the power. When you do not know how your devices work, they are in control.

This book has been designed for and is specifically formulated to change this. It aims to demystify the technology by making the "secret powers" of artificial intelligence, robots, and algorithms accessible and understandable even if – and especially if – this is not your selected area of endeavor. And it does this for one good reason: to empower you to take control of your technology, your life, and your future. How we get to this destination involves a combination of different activities and approaches.

- *Introduction and Orientation.* We will begin with three introductory chapters that deal with the fundamentals and are designed to orient you to the concepts, terminology, and basic operations of the technology. Yes, there will be some math and some computer science, but it will be minimal, requiring nothing more than basic high-school-level knowledge. And the explanations that are provided have been formulated using accessible language specifically designed to "speak" to students from a wide range of different disciplines.
- *Applications.* These three introductory chapters are followed by detailed investigations of AI applications. Because this technology is now finding its way into virtually every aspect of life, it is impossible to deal with everything. So we need to be selective. In particular, we will take up and investigate four applications that, in one way or another, involve human social interaction and communication – machine translation, natural language processing, computational creativity, and social robotics.
- *Impact and Consequences.* AI applications do not exist in a vacuum. They have been developed and deployed in specific social contexts and have important consequences for human individuals and communities. For this reason, the book includes two chapters that investigate the impact and significance of AI, looking in particular at the social opportunities and challenges of the technology and investigating the range of available technical, legal, and moral responses.
- *Maker Exercises.* Reading about emerging technology is only half the story. In order to get the full picture, we will also need to do some practical, hands-on learning. For this reason, the book also includes "maker exercises" that are designed to give you direct experience with the technology by way of building actually working

applications. The exercises are designed to illustrate the concepts that are considered in the "explainer" chapters, and they have been developed with step-by-step instructions suitable for students with little or no experience in writing code.

This particular hybrid approach was devised in the course of teaching students in the Department of Communication at Northern Illinois University. Communication is an interesting monstrosity of a discipline that combines the humanities, social sciences, media technology, and art and design. Consequently, it provides what has been the perfect location to develop this material and to test it out on a diverse population of students with a wide range of different backgrounds and interests. What you hold in your hands is the result of a number of years of collaborative interaction between me and my students in the COMS 493 AI, Robots and Communication seminar. In other words, what is presented in the book has been thoroughly tested and revised several times over based on input from students like yourself. And it is for this reason that I dedicate this book to my students, who taught me so much over the years. This publication would not have been possible without their enthusiasm for the subject matter, their courage for jumping into the deep end of the pool and trying new things, and their insightful feedback and comments.

Finally, much of the material that has been incorporated in the book has been derived from my own research in emerging technology and written up for publication in journal articles and book chapters. Although I have not reproduced any of these previous published texts here in their entirety, the following have provided raw material for the book's chapters and maker exercises:

Mind the Gap: Responsible Robotics and the Problem of Responsibility. *Ethics and Information Technology*, 2018. https://doi. org/10.1007/s10676-017-9428-2.
Ars Ex Machina: Rethinking Responsibility in the Age of Creative Machines. In *Human-Machine Communication: Rethinking Communication, Technology, and Ourselves*, ed. Andrea L. Guzman, 221–236. New York: Peter Lang, 2018.
The Other Question: Can and Should Robots Have Rights? *Ethics and Information Technology* 20(2): 87–99. 2018. https://doi. org/10.1007/s10676-017-9442-4.
Other Things: AI, Robots, and Society. In *A Networked Self: Human Augmentics, Artificial Intelligence, Sentience*, ed. Zizi Papacharissi, 51–68. New York: Routledge, 2019.

Rage Against the Machine: Rethinking Education in the Face of Technological Unemployment. In *Surviving the Machine Age: Intelligent Technology and the Transformation of Human Work*, ed. Kevin LaGrandeur and James J. Hughes, 147–162. Cham, Switzerland: Palgrave Macmillan, 2017.

Computational Interpersonal Communication: Communication Studies and Spoken Dialogue Systems. *Communication +1* 5(1), 2016. http://scholarworks.umass.edu/cpo/vol5/iss1/7/.

Communication and Artificial Intelligence: Opportunities and Challenges for the 21st Century. *Communication +1* 1(1), August 2012. http://scholarworks.umass.edu/cpo/vol1/iss1/1.

Figures

Text figures

Maker Exercise Figures

Figures

Abbreviations

AGI	artificial general intelligence
AIML	artificial intelligence markup language
A.L.I.C.E.	Artificial Linguistic Internet Computer Entity
ALPAC	Automatic Language Processing Advisory Committee
ANN	artificial neural network
API	application program interface
AR	augmented reality
ASR	automatic speech-recognition
ATN	augmented transition networks
AVS	Alexa Voice Service
CALO	cognitive assistant that learns and organizes
CASA	Computer as Social Actor
CCS	computer conferencing system
CMC	computer-mediated communication
CSAIL	Computer Science and Artificial Intelligence Laboratory
CSS	cascading style sheets
DM	dialogue management
DST	dialogue state tracker
ECA	embodied conversational agent
EMI	Experiments in Musical Intelligence
EOD	explosive ordnance disposal
EULA	end user licensing agreement
FAHQT	fully automatic high-quality translation
GAN	generative adversarial network
GNMT	Google Neural Machine Translation
GOFAI	good old fashioned AI
GPL	General Public License

GUI	graphical user interface
HCI	human–computer interaction
HMC	human–machine communication
HMM	hidden Markov modeling
HRI	human–robot interaction
HTML	hypertext markup language
IFR	International Federation for Robotics
IoT	Internet of things
IP	intellectual property
IPPR	Institute for Public Policy Research
IR	industrial robot
MT	machine translation
NEH	National Endowment for the Humanities
NHTSA	National Highway Traffic Safety Administration
NIH	National Institutes of Health
NLG	natural language generation
NLP	natural language processing
NLU	natural language understanding
NPC	non-player character
NPR	National Public Radio
NSF	National Science Foundation
PSSH	physical symbol system hypothesis
RNN	recurrent neural network
SDK	software development kit
SDS	spoken dialogue systems
SDV	self-driven vehicle
SEO	search engine optimization
SLU	spoken language understanding
SR	speaker-recognition
SSML	speech synthesis markup language
STEM	science, technology, engineering, math
TFX	TensorFlow Extended
TLO	technology licensing office
ToU	Terms of Use
TTS	text-to-speech
UBI	universal basic income
WEF	World Economic Forum
XML	extensible markup language

Part I

Introduction and Orientation

1

Introduction

Key Aims/Objectives

- To investigate the origins and historical development of the technical terms "artificial intelligence" and "robot."
- To understand the important points of contact and crucial differences between the way these technologies have been presented in science fiction and how they actually exist and function in reality.
- To see how and why words matter and that the means by which we say something about technology is not neutral but often shapes what that technology is and can become.
- To provide an overview of the book, its approach to the subject matter, and its content.

Introduction

The term Artificial Intelligence (AI) identifies both a scientific field of inquiry and a technology or particular type of technological system or artifact. For most of us, however, perceptions of and expectations for AI come not from the science or the technology, but from fiction – specifically, science fiction, where one-time useful systems and devices like the HAL 9000 (*2001: A Space Odyssey*), Colossus (*Colossus: The Forbin Project*), or Ultron (*Avengers: Age of Ultron*) turn rogue; enslave humanity in a computer-generated dream world (e.g., the *Matrix* trilogy); or rise-up against their human creators and stage a revolt (e.g., *Terminator, Battlestar Galactica, Bladerunner 2049, Westworld*). This first chapter gets things started by sorting science fact from fiction. It looks at the origins of artificial intelligence, the hype that has surrounded the technology and its consequences as portrayed in popular culture, and the reality of machine intelligence as it exists right now in the early twenty-first century. As such, this introductory chapter is designed to demystify AI for a nonspecialist audience, account for the social/cultural/political contexts of its development, and provide readers with a clear understanding of what this book concerning AI and communication is about, what will be addressed in the chapters that follow, and why all of this matters.

1.1 Artificial Intelligence

The term "artificial intelligence" first appeared and was used in the process of organizing a research workshop convened at Dartmouth College (Hanover, NH, USA) in the summer of 1956. The initial idea for the meeting originated with John McCarthy, who was, at the time, a young assistant professor of mathematics at Dartmouth. In early 1955, McCarthy began talking with the Rockefeller Foundation (a private philanthropic organization that funds scientific research) about his plans. He eventually teamed up with three other researchers: Marvin Minsky, a cognitive scientist who, along with McCarthy, is credited as the cofounder of the MIT Computer Science and Artificial Intelligence Laboratory (CSAIL); Nathaniel Rochester, a computer engineer at IBM and lead designer on the IBM 701, the first general purpose, mass-produced computer; and Claude Shannon, the Bell Labs engineer who wrote *The Mathematical Theory of Communication*, which has supplied the discipline of communication with its basic "sender-message-receiver" process model.

In their proposal, titled "Dartmouth Summer Research Project on Artificial Intelligence," McCarthy et al. (1955) offered the following explanation about the basic idea and objective of the effort:

> We propose that a 2 month, 10 man study of artificial intelligence be carried out during the summer of 1956 at Dartmouth College in Hanover, New Hampshire. The study is to proceed on the basis of the conjecture that every aspect of learning or any other feature of intelligence can in principle be so precisely described that a machine can be made to simulate it. An attempt will be made to find how to make machines use language, form abstractions and concepts, solve kinds of problems now reserved for humans, and improve themselves. We think that a significant advance can be made in one or more of these

problems if a carefully selected group of scientists work on it together for a summer.

Although rather short, this opening paragraph contains a number of important insights and ideas that can help us get a handle on what artificial intelligence is as both a scientific subject and technological object.[1]

1.1.1 Intelligence

The idea begins with and proceeds from a "conjecture" or an educated guess, namely, "that every aspect of learning or any other feature of intelligence" can be simulated or modeled by a computer. This immediately raises a more fundamental question: What is *intelligence*? The question is clearly intelligible – we know what is being asked about – but coming up with a definitive answer turns out to be something that is difficult, if not close to impossible. Here is how AI scientist Roger Schank describes this difficulty in a short introductory essay titled "What is AI Anyway?":

> AI people are fond of talking about intelligent machines, but when it comes down to it, there is little agreement on exactly what constitutes intelligence. And, it thus follows, there is very little agreement in AI about exactly what AI is and what it should be. We all agree that we would like to endow machines with an attribute that we really can't define. Needless to say, AI suffers from this lack of definition of its scope. (1990: 4)

So here's the problem: how can we pursue and produce intelligence in a technological artifact, if we cannot define what intelligence is to begin with?

"One way to attack this problem," Schank (1990: 4) continues, "is to attempt to list some features that we would expect an intelligent entity to have." So rather than answering the question "What is intelligence?" by offering a definition, one can proceed by listing those capabilities and operations that typically characterize what is called intelligence. This is precisely what McCarthy, Minsky, Rochester, and Shannon did in the Dartmouth proposal. Instead of defining intelligence as such, they issued a short list of activities or functions that are generally considered features or recognizable characteristics of intelligence: (1) use and understand language, (2) form abstractions and concepts, (3) solve problems, and (4) self-improvement.

Schank, for his part, provides a similar list, which includes a more detailed explanation of each individual item:

Communication: An intelligent entity can be communicated with. We can't talk to rocks or tell trees what we want, no matter how hard we try.

Internal knowledge: We expect intelligent entities to have some knowledge about themselves. They should know when they need something; they should know what they think about something; and, they should know that they know it.

World knowledge: Intelligence also involves being aware of the outside world and being able to find and utilize the information that one has about the world outside. It also implies having a memory in which past experience is encoded and which can be used as a guide for processing new experience.

Goals and plans: Goal-driven behavior means knowing when one wants something and knowing a plan to get what one wants.

Creativity: Finally, every intelligent entity is assumed to have some degree of creativity. Creativity can be defined very weakly, including, for example, the ability to find a new route to one's food source when the old one is blocked. But, of course, creativity can also mean finding a new way to look at something that changes one's world in some significant way. (1990: 4–5)

The one thing we should note is that "communication" is situated at the top of the list. This is not an accident or random occurrence in the ordering of the five characteristics. Many of the other capabilities depend on or need some form of communication to be evidenced and identified as such. Take internal knowledge, for example. As Schank explains:

We cannot examine the insides of an intelligent entity in such a way as to establish what it actually knows. Our only choice is to ask and observe. If we get an answer that seems satisfying then we tend to believe that the entity we are examining has some degree of intelligence. (1990: 5)

In other words, our ability to recognize whether another entity does or does not possess internal knowledge is something that depends on the ability of that entity to tell us about that knowledge in some way that we can recognize. Since we do not have direct access to the "insides of an intelligent entity," all we can do, as Schank (1990: 5) describes it, "is ask and observe." The same can be said for many of the other features that appear on the list; their presence or absence would require some kind of external manifestation or mode of communication in order to be detected and identified as such. Consequently, communication – and not just verbal communication through the manipulation of language but also various forms of nonverbal behaviors – is fundamental to defining and detecting intelligence. If something can explain itself to us in language that we can understand, or exhibit interactive behaviors that are intentional and significant, it is called "intelligible." If it cannot, it is often considered to be "unintelligible."

1.1.2 Artificial

So much for the term "intelligence," but what about "artificial"? "Artificial" is a word that is often defined as being the opposite of "natural." There is a perceived difference between natural intelligence – the intelligence belonging to an entity that is the product of natural/biological evolution, like a human being or an animal – and the intelligence that would be fabricated for an artifact, like a computer or a robot. But there's more to it. The word "artificial" admits of at least two different definitions, and this is something highlighted and explained by Robert Sokolowski in his essay "Natural and Artificial Intelligence":

> One of the first things that must be clarified is the ambiguous word *artificial*. This adjective can be used in two senses, and it is important to determine which one applies in the term artificial intelligence. The word artificial is used in one sense when it is applied, say, to flowers, and in another sense when it is applied to light. In both cases something is called artificial because it is fabricated. But in the first usage artificial means that the thing seems to be, but really is not, what it looks like. The artificial is the merely apparent; it just shows how something else looks. Artificial flowers are only paper, not flowers at all; anyone who takes them to be flowers is mistaken. But artificial light is light and it does illuminate. It is fabricated as a substitute for natural light, but once fabricated it is what it seems to be. In this sense the artificial is not the merely apparent, not simply an imitation of something else. The appearance of the thing reveals what it is, not how something else looks. (1988: 45)

For Sokolowski, the word "artificial" can be used in two different ways. It can be employed to mean "fake," as in "artificial flowers." These paper or plastic objects are designed to look like real flowers, but they are not. And if we think they are real flowers, we have been deceived and are mistaken in our judgment. In this case, "artificial" means that the thing seems to be, but really is not, what it looks like." But the word can also be applied to an artifact that is neither fake nor a mere imitation of something, as in the case of artificial light. The light that emanates from a light bulb is "artificial" in comparison to the natural light of the sun, but that does not mean that it is fake light. It really is light; it is a means of actual illumination that is produced by another method. Used in this way, "artificial" does not mean "fake." It signifies the "substitute" for, or the "emulation" or "simulation" of, a natural phenomenon.

The important question here is which sense of the word "artificial" applies in the phrase "artificial intelligence." Is artificial intelligence "fake intelligence," such that AI applications and objects would be little more than a magician's trick, a kind of deceptive illusion? Or is artificial intelligence a form of real intelligence – the emulation or simulation of real intelligence – produced by other means? Not surprisingly, this remains a debated issue and a hotly contested matter even within the field of AI. I do not want to try to answer this question right now. I simply want to identify the reasons for the disagreement and conflict, because it will – in the course of subsequent chapters – help us understand what is being debated and why there have been disagreements, especially in situations involving the social significance and consequences of AI and related technology.

"Intelligence" and "artificial" are already ambiguous and rather difficult to define. When you take these two words and jam them together, you get what you might expect: a term that is just as ambiguous and difficult to define. "Artificial intelligence," as Schank (1990: 3) explains, "is a subject that, due to the massive, often quite unintelligible, publicity that it gets, is nearly completely misunderstood by the people outside the field. Even AI's practitioners are somewhat confused with respect to what AI is really about." Indeed, if we begin our investigation with some uncertainty about the very term "artificial intelligence," this is understandable. Not only is AI generally misunderstood by people outside the field, it is misunderstood and mixed-up by those within the field too. In other words, those individuals who would be considered experts in the field of AI – research scientists, engineers, professors, and industry leaders – often cannot come to a reasonable consensus as to what AI is, how it should be defined, or what it can become or is supposed to be.

Although this might initially seem to be a deficiency or "bad thing," it does have an advantage, which was explicitly recognized in the AI

100 report:[2] "Curiously, the lack of a precise, universally accepted definition of AI probably has helped the field to grow, blossom, and advance at an ever-accelerating pace. Practitioners, researchers, and developers of AI are instead guided by a rough sense of direction and an imperative to 'get on with it'" (AI 100 2016: 12). Although somewhat counterintuitive, the argument is that a lack of precise definition has actually helped the field of AI develop by allowing for and tolerating widely different approaches and efforts. Whether this is, in fact, beneficial or not is something that we will need to ask and evaluate as we consider different methods, projects, and technological artifacts.

1.1.3 Other complications

In addition to the difficulty of accurately defining the phrase "artificial intelligence," there are three additional challenges that tend to frustrate efforts to get a handle on what AI is or what it is about.

(1) *The AI Effect.* The first involves something that is called the "AI effect" or the "AI paradox." Here is how Jerry Kaplan (2016: 37) explains it in his short introductory book: "But the field of AI suffers from an unusual deficiency – once a particular problem is considered solved, it often is no longer considered AI." In other words, challenges that have been identified as an "AI problem" – that is, a problem that requires intelligence of some sort – are no longer considered to be AI problems once they are solved. Take the game of chess, for example. For decades, the task of playing championship-level chess was seen as a considerable challenge that would require actual intelligence to resolve. But once this had been achieved – in 1997, when IBM's Deep Blue defeated the reigning human champion Gary Kasparov – playing championship-level chess became just another computer application and was no longer considered a demonstration of true intelligence.

The same could be said of the US quiz show *Jeopardy!*, which requires the ability to understand statements and produce questions in natural human language. This capability, which, we should recall, was the first item listed in the Dartmouth proposal – e.g. "to make machines understand human language" – had always been considered to be something requiring real intelligence. But it too was achieved, when IBM's Watson defeated one of the most celebrated human players of the game, Ken Jennings, in February 2011. As Kevin Kelly (2014) of *Wired* magazine explains: "In the past, we would have said only a superintelligent AI could drive a car, or beat a human at *Jeopardy!* or chess. But once AI did each of those things, we considered that achievement obviously mechanical and hardly worth the label of true intelligence. Every success in AI redefines it." For this reason, what is AI and what is not AI becomes something of a moving target. As soon as AI achieves one of the objectives typically considered to be a benchmark of intelligence, we move the goal posts. This makes talking about and investigating AI difficult, as the benchmarks and examples are constantly in motion and being redefined.

(2) *Science or Engineering.* As we noted at the beginning, AI names both a science and an engineering practice, or, as Hamid Ekbia (2008: 4) explains, a way of *knowing* and a way of *doing.* Viewed as an engineering practice or a way of *doing,* the task of AI is to design, develop, and construct actual working systems. "Whether these systems are AI or not," as Schank (1990: 6) points out, "loses its import as one begins to work on them. The problem is to make them work at all, not to be a purist about what is or is not AI." Viewed as a science or a way of knowing, AI is perceived as an effort to build a synthetic version of the mind or to model its cognitive processes in order to better understand and investigate what comprises this thing we call "intelligence." Formulated in this way, AI is often allied with or considered a part of cognitive or neuroscience. The problem, or the complication, is that these two different approaches are not necessarily in sync with one another. As computer scientist Terry Winograd pointed out, AI has and pursues two distinct and at times incompatible goals:

> On the one hand is the quest to explain human mental processes as thoroughly and unambiguously as physics explains the functioning of ordinary mechanical devices. On the other hand is the drive to create intelligent tools – machines that apply intelligence to serve some purpose, regardless of how closely they mimic the details of human intelligence. At times these two enterprises have gone hand in hand, at others they have led down separate paths. (1990: 170)

(3) *The Hype Cycle.* The history of AI, whether it has been pursued as a science or an engineering practice, has been rocky, with significant fluctuations between periods of wild enthusiasm and disappointing skepticisms. If we return to the Dartmouth proposal, we find that the opening paragraph ends with what can only be seen as a rather optimistic statement: "We think that a significant advance can be made in one or more of these problems if a carefully selected group of scientists work on it together for a summer." And we should recall

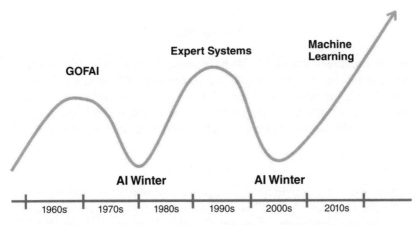

Figure 1.1   Cycles of boom and bust in the history of AI

that the problems that were to be solved (or at least were assumed to be close to being solved due to what would have been significant advancements) were things like natural language understanding and generation, the automatic formation of abstract concepts, the solving of problems on a level that was at least comparable to what human beings are capable of doing, and self-motivated and self-directed forms of improvement. None of these was even close to being achieved, let alone adequately formulated and addressed, by the end of the seminar. As McCarthy later admitted, the problems that were included as part of the summer seminar were actually much harder than originally thought.

This "cycle of boom and bust" (Kaplan 2016: 16) produces something of a sine wave in the historical trajectory of AI (Figure 1.1). At times, interest in the effort and the funding of research is ascendant and the big promises seem to be within grasp. This is followed by periodic "AI winters" or downturns, when both interest in and funding for AI projects fall off in the face of unfulfilled promises and what appear to be disappointing results. Since the initial enthusiasm seeded by the Dartmouth summer seminar, AI R&D has experienced a number of ups and downs. As I write, we are experiencing an upswing in both interest and development, partially due to recent innovations in machine learning and deep neural network applications (see Chapter 3). Whether this growth continues or eventually begins to fall off owing to the coming of another AI winter is something that has yet to be determined.[3]

1.2 Robot

In our consideration of AI, we have already inserted and substituted the word "robot." So what's the difference? What are robots? Is "robot" just another word for what we mean by AI? Or is a robot something significantly different? As you might anticipate, these questions also do not have a straightforward or simple answer.

1.2.1 Fictional beginnings

Unlike the term "artificial intelligence," which is rooted in actual scientific research, "robot" is the product of fiction. The word came into the world by way of Karel Čapek's 1920 stage play, *R.U.R.*, or *Rossum's Universal Robots*, in order to name a class of artificial servants or laborers. In the Czech language, as in several other Slavic languages, the word *robota* (or some variation thereof) denotes "servitude or forced labor." But Čapek was not, at least as he tells the story, the originator of this designation. That honor belongs to the playwright's brother, the painter Josef Čapek, who suggested the word to his brother during the time of the play's initial development (for more, see Gunkel 2018: 15). Since the publication of Čapek's play, robots have infiltrated the space of fiction. But what exactly constitutes a robot differs and admits of a wide variety of forms, functions, and configurations.

Čapek's robots, for instance, were artificially produced biological creatures that were human-like in both material and form. This configuration persists with the bioengineered replicants of *Bladerunner* and *Bladerunnner 2049* (the film adaptations of Philip K. Dick's *Do Androids Dream of Electric Sheep?*) and the skin-job Cylons of *Battlestar Galactica*. Other fictional robots, like the chrome-plated android in Fritz Lang's *Metropolis* and C-3PO of *Star Wars*, as well as the 3D printed "hosts" of HBO's *Westworld* and the synths of Channel 4/AMC's *Humans*, are human-like in form but composed of non-biological materials. Others that are composed of similar synthetic materials have a particularly imposing profile, like *Forbidden Planet*'s Robby the Robot, Gort from *The Day the Earth Stood Still*, or Robot from the television series *Lost in Space*. Still others are not humanoid at all but emulate animals or other kinds of objects, like the trashcan R2-D2, the industrial tank-like Wall-E, or the electric sheep of Dick's novella. Finally, there are entities without bodies, like the HAL 9000 computer in *2001: A Space Odyssey* or GERTY in *Moon*, with virtual bodies, like the Agents in *The Matrix*, or with entirely different kinds of embodiment, like swarms of nanobots.

In whatever form they have appeared, science fiction already – and well in advance of actual engineering practice – has established expectations for what a robot is or can be. Even before engineers have sought to develop working prototypes, writers, artists, and film-makers have imagined what robots do or can do, what configurations they might take, and what problems they could produce for human individuals and communities. John Jordan expresses it quite well in his short and very accessible introductory book *Robots*:

> No technology has ever been so widely described and explored before its commercial introduction . . . Thus the technologies of mass media helped create public conceptions of and expectations for a whole body of compu-mechanical innovation that *had not happened yet*: complex, pervasive attitudes and expectations predated the invention of viable products. (2016: 5)

1.2.2 Defining "robot"

So what is a robot? Even when one consults knowledgeable experts, there is little agreement when it comes to defining, characterizing, or even identifying what is (or what is not) a robot. In the book *Robot Futures*, Illah Nourbakhsh (2013: xiv) writes: "Never ask a roboti-cist what a robot is. The answer changes too quickly. By the time researchers finish their most recent debate on what is and what isn't a robot, the frontier moves on as whole new interaction technologies are born."

One widely cited source of a general, operational definition comes from George Bekey's *Autonomous Robots: From Biological Inspiration to Implementation and Control*: "In this book we define a robot as a machine that senses, thinks, and acts. Thus, a robot must have sensors, processing ability that emulates some aspects of cognition, and actuators" (2005: 2). This "sense, think, act" paradigm has considerable traction in the literature – evidenced by the very fact that it constitutes and is called a *paradigm*. The definition is, as Bekey (2005: 2) explicitly recognizes, "very broad," encompassing a wide range of different kinds of technologies, artifacts, and devices. But it could be too broad insofar as it may be applied to all kinds of artifacts that exceed the proper limits of what many consider to be a robot.

John Jordan (2016: 37) notes that "the sense-think-act paradigm proves to be problematic for industrial robots: some observers contend that a robot needs to be able to move; otherwise, the Watson computer might qualify." The Nest thermostat provides another complicated case. "The Nest senses: movements, temperature, humidity, and light. It reasons: if there's no activity, nobody is home to need air conditioning. It acts: given the right sensor input, it autonomously shuts the furnace down. Fulfilling as it does the three conditions, is the Nest, therefore, a robot?" (Jordan 2016: 37). And what about smartphones? According to Joanna Bryson and Alan Winfield (2017: 117), these devices could also be considered robots under this particular characterization. "Robots are artifacts that sense and act in the physical world in real time. By this definition, a smartphone is a (domestic) robot. It has not only microphones but also a variety of proprioceptive sensors that let it know when its orientation is changing or when it is falling."

In order to further refine the definition and delimit with greater precision what is and what is not a robot, Winfield (2012: 8) offers the following list of qualifying characteristics:

> A robot is:
> 1 an artificial device that can sense its environment and *purposefully* act on or in that environment;
> 2 an *embodied* artificial intelligence; or
> 3 a machine that can *autonomously* carry out useful work.

Although it is ostensibly another version of sense-think-act, Winfield adds an important qualification to his list – "embodiment" – making it clear that a software bot, an algorithm, or an AI implementation like Watson or AlphaGo are not robots, strictly speaking. This is by no means an exhaustive list of all the different ways in which "robot" has been defined, explained, or characterized. What is clear from this sample, however, is that the term "robot" is open to a considerable range of diverse and even different denotations. And these "definitions are," as Jordan (2016: 4) writes, "unsettled, even among those most expert in the field."

1.3 Why Words Matter

So what is it – AI or robot? The problem is not only that each of these words lacks a univocal and clearly articulated definition but that the two terms are often used interchangeably to identify the same thing or a substantially similar kind of thing. What one researcher calls "robot" another may call "AI." Consider the self-driving car. Is this an automobile controlled by AI instead of a human driver, or is it a transportation robot? A lot depends on who tells the story (are they, for example, trained in robotics or in cognitive science?), in what particular context, and to whom. To complicate matters, the two terms are often mixed up and substituted for one another within the published literature. A good example is Nils J. Nilsson's *The Quest for Artificial Intelligence: A History of Ideas and Achievements* (2010). In this landmark book – "landmark" insofar as it is often considered to be one of the best, if not *the* best, comprehensive histories of the science and technology of AI – the two terms are used synonymously, or at least in a way that does not draw a clear and explicit distinction between the one and the other. Although the book is advertised as a history of AI (the phrase "artificial intelligence" is in the title), Nilsson begins the story with ancient automatons or robots – the Tripods of Hephaistos, Pygmalion's "living" statue Galatea, the numerous robots planned or constructed by Leonardo da Vinci and Jacques de Vaucanson, and the science fiction robots of Čapek's *R.U.R.* and Isaac Asimov's robot stories.

1.3.1 The rhetoric of technology

Our task is not to sort this out once and for all but simply to identify this terminological problem and to recognize that what is under investigation is as much a product of technological innovation as it is a rhetorical construct. For this reason, words matter. What we call these things and how they come to be described in both fiction and science are important to how we understand what they are, what they might become, and what all this means. This method of investigation – attending not just to the object identified in and by language but to the language by which one makes the identification – follows a long and venerable tradition that goes at least as far back as ancient Greek philosophy. In one of Plato's dialogues – *Phaedo* – Socrates provides an account of the origins of his investigative efforts. He tells how he initiated his particular research program by trying to follow the example established by his predecessors and seeking wisdom in "the investigation of nature" (Plato 1982: 96a). He describes how this undertaking, despite its initial attraction and his best efforts, continually led him astray, how he eventually gave it up altogether, and how he finally decided on an alternative strategy by investigating the truth of things in λόγος (logos), a Greek word that means "word" but is typically translated by a number of related terms: "language" and "logic." "So I thought," Socrates explains, "I must have recourse to λόγος and examine in them the truth of things" (Plato 1982: 99e).

Examining the truth of things in λόγος does not mean that Socrates was some kind of idealist who denied the existence of real things. There is more to it, as Socrates explains: "Now perhaps my metaphor is not quite accurate for I do not grant in the least that he who investigates things in λόγος is looking at them in images any more than he who studies them in the facts of daily life" (Plato 1982: 100a). What Socrates advocates, therefore, is not something that would be simply opposed to what is often called "empirical knowledge." Instead, he advocates an epistemology – a way of knowing about things – that questions the "naive empiricist picture" (Chang 1996: x), which assumes that things can be immediately grasped and known outside the concepts, terminology, and logics that always and already frame our way of looking at them. In other words, Socrates recognizes that the truth of "things" is not simply given or immediately available to us in a raw and naked state. What these things are and how we understand what they are is something that is, at least for our purposes, always mediated through some kind of logical process by which they come to be grasped and conceptualized as such. What we know of the things and the world in which they exist is always "clothed" in the language we use to identify, describe, and examine them. This mode of investigation should be familiar to students of communication insofar as the study of rhetoric has always been sensitive to the way that knowledge production and acquisition is not only about *what* is said about the world but also about *how* we say it.

What this means is that our investigation – and this examination of AI and communication in particular – will need to focus not just on the technological objects, but also on the way scientists, engineers, science fiction writers and filmmakers, journalists, politicians, critics, and others situate, conceptualize, and explain this technology in and by language and other symbolic systems. In other words, AI, or robot, is not some rigorously defined, singular kind of thing that exists out there in a vacuum. What is called "AI" or "robot" is something that is socially negotiated such that word usage and modes of communication shape expectations for, experience with, and understandings of the technology. Consequently, we need to be aware of the fact that whatever comes to be called "AI" or "robot" is always socially situated and constructed. Its context (or contexts, because they are always plural) is as important as its technical components and characterizations. What is and what is not AI or robot is as much a product of science and engineering practice as it is an effect of how we come to talk about it.

1.3.2 Science fiction prototyping

When it comes to the social shaping and rhetoric of technology, science fiction plays a significant and influential role. In fact, much of what we know or think we know about AI and robots comes not from actual encounters with technology but from what we see and hear about in fiction. Ask someone – especially someone who is not an insider – to define "AI" or "robot," and chances are the answer provided will make reference to something in a science fiction film or television program and not found (at least not yet) in social reality. And this not only applies to or affects outsiders looking in. "Science fiction prototyping," as Brian David Johnson (2011) calls it, is rather widespread within the disciplines of AI and robotics even if it is not always explicitly called out and recognized as such. As the roboticists Bryan Adams, Cynthia Breazeal, Rodney Brooks, and Brian Scassellati (2000: 25) point out: "While scientific research usually takes credit as the inspiration for science fiction, in the case of AI and robotics, it is possible that fiction led the way for science." Because of this, science fiction is recognized as being both a useful tool and a potential liability.

Engineers and developers, for instance, often endeavor to realize what has been imaginatively prototyped in fiction. Cynthia Breazeal (2010), for example, credits the robots of *Star Wars* as the inspiration for her pioneering efforts in social robotics:

> Ever since I was a little girl seeing *Star Wars* for the first time, I've been fascinated by this idea of personal robots. And as a little girl, I loved the idea of a robot that interacted with us much more like a helpful, trusted sidekick – something that would delight us, enrich our lives and help us save a galaxy or two. I knew robots like that didn't really exist, but I knew I wanted to build them.

In addition to influencing research and development programs, science fiction has also proven to be a remarkably expedient medium – perhaps even the preferred medium – for examining the social opportunities and challenges of technological innovation in AI and robotics. And a good number of serious research efforts (in sociology, philosophy, and law) have found it useful to call upon and employ existing narratives, like the robot stories of Isaac Asimov, the TV series *Star Trek*, the film *2001: A Space Odyssey*, and the reimagined *Battlestar Galactica*, or even to fabricate their own fictional anecdotes and "thought experiments" as a way of introducing, characterizing, and/or investigating a problem, or what could, in the near term, become a problem. As Peter Asaro and Wendell Wallach explain:

> For most of the twentieth century, the examination of the ethical and moral implications of artificial intelligence and robotics was limited to the work of science fiction and cyberpunk writers, such as Isaac Asimov, Arthur C. Clarke, Bruce Sterling, William Gibson, and Philip K. Dick (to name only a few). (2016: 4–5)

Despite its utility, however, for many laboring in the fields of robotics and AI (both the science and the engineering practice), this incursion of pop culture and entertainment into the realm of the serious work of science is also a potential problem and something that must be, if not actively counteracted, then at least carefully controlled and held in check. Science fiction, it is argued, often produces unrealistic expectations for and irrational fears that are not grounded in or informed by actual science (Bartneck 2004; Kriz et al. 2010; Bruckenberger et al. 2013; Sandoval et al. 2014). As Alan Winfield explains:

> Real robotics is a science born out of fiction. For roboticists this is both a blessing and a curse. It is a blessing because science fiction provides inspiration, motivation and thought experiments; a curse because most people's expectations of robots owe much more to fiction than reality. And because the reality is so prosaic, we roboticists often find ourselves having to address the question of why robotics has failed to deliver when it hasn't, especially since it is being judged against expectations drawn from fiction. (2011: 32)

1.3.3 Reality check

For these reasons, science fiction is simultaneously credited for being a useful tool and criticized for being a significant obstacle to properly understanding what the terms "AI" and "robot" designate. The critical task is to take from fiction what is useful for the dialogue about AI and robots but in such a way that what we find in fiction is always tempered by and tested against the facts on the ground. One of the tasks of this book is to engage in this kind of "reality check" so that we can proceed from an informed position and deal with both the promises and the realities of innovation with emerging technology.

A good illustration of this can be provided by comparing the fictional HAL 9000 computer from the 1968 film *2001: A Space Odyssey* to Siri, Apple's voice-activated digital assistant. Although both the science fiction AI HAL and the Siri application talk to human users and can engage in verbal exchanges, there are important and significant differences. HAL is what AI researchers typically call artificial general intelligence (AGI). He (the vocal qualities that are displayed by the computer already suggest male gender) is capable of performing a wide range of different cognitive tasks, from inter-personal interactions with the human occupants of the spaceship to playing winning games of chess and overseeing all aspects of ship-board operations.

Siri, by contrast, is what is often called "narrow AI." She (the initial vocal qualities of the application were intentionally designed to suggest female gender) was designed to answer questions and provide a vocal interface to Internet data and applications on the mobile device. At this point in time, AGI is still a dream that has yet to be achieved. In fact, the perceived failure of actual efforts in both AI science and engineering to achieve AGI – or even to approach something close to it – has often been the motivating factor for critical reevaluations and reassessments of the entire field. As Winograd wrote at the beginning of what is now regarded as the second AI winter:

> Futurologist have proclaimed the birth of a new species, *machina sapiens*, that will share (perhaps usurp) our place as the intelligent sovereigns of our earthly domain. These "thinking machines" will take over our burdensome mental chores, just as their mechanical predecessors were intended to eliminate physical drudgery. Eventually they will apply their "ultra-intelligence" to solving all of our problems . . . Critics have argued with equal fervor that "thinking machine" is an oxymoron – a contradiction in terms. Computers, with their foundations of cold logic, can never be creative or insightful or possess real judgement. Although my own understanding developed through active participa-tion in artificial intelligence, I have now come to recognize a larger grain of truth in the criticisms than in the enthusiastic predictions . . . Indeed, artificial intelligence has not achieved creativity, insight, and judgment. But its shortcomings are far more mundane: we have not yet been able to construct a machine with even a modicum of common sense or one that can converse on everyday topics in ordinary language. (1990: 167)

As Winograd points out, the expectations for AGI – machines with intellectual abilities on a par with or even surpassing that of human beings – have not come to pass; the critics of AI have actually been more accurate than the enthusiastic futurologists. In fact, from the perspective of a realistic assessment of the state-of-the-art in 1990, Winograd admits – and rather disappointedly, since he had worked inside the field of AI for decades – that many of the benchmarks of intelligence, like basic common sense or conversing in ordinary language about everyday topics, remain unfulfilled.

Despite this demonstrated failure in efforts to design and develop the kind of robust AGI that we have seen portrayed in science fiction, *narrow AI* applications like Siri are a reality. These specific applications may not be anywhere close to achieving what has been expected for AGI – like the capabilities that Winograd lists: creativity, insight, and judgment – but they are capable of accomplishing a particular outcome and can provide some limited aspects of what has been envisioned and predicted. Siri is certainly not HAL, but she can process and answer questions in natural language. She might not, at least at this time, be able to hold long and detailed conversations with you in a way that would be indistinguishable from talking to another human person, but the application can answer questions, control the operational features of our digital devices, and search for and provide needed information in vocalized forms that we can understand.

One way to explain the recent resurgence of AI is to recognize that what has changed is not only (or even primarily) machine capabilities – and there have been some important innovations in this area, especially with deep neural networks and big data – but a recalibration in our expectations for AI. As long as what we sought and expected was AGI, science and engineering failed to achieve these objectives. But if we scale back the expectations, recent innovations do in fact provide workable solutions that would, depending on how they are defined and characterized, be considered a kind of low-level and specific form of machine intelligence. In other words, the recent advancements in AI (advancements that we will be investigating in considerable detail in the course of the chapters that follow) may have as much to do with successful efforts to re-engineer and reshape human expectations for the technology as they do with technological innovations in engineering.

1.4 Overview of the Book

Communication figures prominently in both the definition and the project of AI. It is one of the objectives listed by McCarthy and colleagues for the Dartmouth summer seminar of 1956. It is the first item on the list of intellectual capabilities that is supplied by Schank in his introduction to *The Foundations of Artificial Intelligence: A Sourcebook* (1990). And it is one of the crucial benchmarks of efforts in the field throughout its relatively short sixty-plus-year run. This book comprises an investigation of AI and robots from the perspective of, and focusing on, the opportunities and challenges of communication. It is therefore designed to assist students in AI with an appreciation for how the art and science of communication can inform efforts in the science and engineering practice of AI and for students in nontechnical fields (arts, humanities, and social sciences) who want or need to know how AI and robots influence and affect the social situation and processes of human interaction and communication. In order to achieve this objective, we will highlight and focus on those issues, problems, and systems where communication (and the social aspects of human communication, in particular) is of principal importance.

1.4.1 Communication and AI

Chapter 2 sets the stage for how this interdisciplinary effort will proceed. Despite the central importance of communication in the science and engineering of AI, both sides – the field of AI/robotics and Communication Studies – have missed the important points of contact. On the one hand, AI as both a science and an engineering practice has paid little attention to the kind of social issues and aspects that are the defining conditions of Communication Studies. When AI/robotics does concern itself with communication, it is often from a purely functional perspective and for the sake of developing better methods for human–computer or human–robot interaction (HCI or HRI) – basically designing and developing better control mechanisms and display technologies.

This way of proceeding is understandably informed by the influential work of Claude Shannon, who was one of the organizers of the Dartmouth summer seminar. Shannon's process model of communication was concerned with an engineering problem – the accurate and efficient transfer of information. But his theory is limited and does not account for the intention, meaning, or social context of the message. As he famously explained at the beginning of the *Mathematical Theory of Communication*:

> The fundamental problem of communication is that of reproducing at one point either exactly or approximately a message selected at another

point. Frequently the messages have *meaning*; that is they refer to or are correlated according to some system with certain physical or conceptual entities. These semantic aspects of communication are irrelevant to the engineering problem. (1949: 31)

This conceptualization is perhaps necessary, but it is not a sufficient condition for what we typically have in mind with the word "communication." As José Hernández-Orallo (2017: 371) explains: "From a cognitive point of view it is still possible to measure how efficiently two agents communicate, i.e., their bandwidth, the error rate, etc., but certainly this is not what we are usually thinking of when referring to the *ability to communicate*." Communication, therefore, requires something beyond the mere exchange of data. As J.C.R. Licklider and Robert Taylor argue, "to communicate is more than to send and to receive. Do two tape recorders communicate when they play to each other and record from each other? Not really – not in our sense" (1968: 1).

What is needed, therefore, is not just the sending and receiving of information, but the production and maintenance of a shared sense of understanding or commonality. Students of communication will recognize this as one of the important contributions of James Carey, who recognized that communication needs to be considered from both a transmission perspective (Shannon's way of thinking) and a ritual perspective, which was missing, and/or deliberately excluded, from Shannon's theory. Carey (1989: 18) writes: "In a ritual definition, communication is linked to terms such as 'sharing,' 'participation,' 'association,' 'fellowship,' and 'the possession of a common faith.' This definition exploits the ancient identity and common roots of the terms 'commonness,' 'communion,' 'community,' and 'communication.'" In other words, the task for thinking AI and communication also requires that we conceptualize and understand AI as a social and/or human science.

On the other hand, the field of communication has not done much better. When it comes to AI and robots, Communication Studies has either ignored the field altogether or been conspicuously uninterested in any of it. This is rather curious, because the discipline had an open invitation. Back in 1985 – when personal computers were in their infancy and the Internet was little more than a National Science Foundation project for connecting academic research institutions – two communication scholars, Robert Cathcart and Gary Gumpert, sought to figure out and explain the significance of the computer for the field of Communication Studies. In an essay titled "The

Person–Computer Interaction," the two researchers distinguished between communicating *through* a computer and communicating *with* a computer. The former is what we now call computer-mediated communication (CMC), and it has been one of the focal points of the field since the turn of the century. The latter, which only recently received the name "human–machine communication" (HMC) (see Guzman 2018) has been largely ignored and neglected.[4] For this reason, communication has missed an opportunity – the opportunity to think about and conceptualize AI and robots not as a medium through which human users exchange information but as the communicative other in social exchanges and interactions. By marginalizing or missing this aspect, Communication Studies has written itself out of AI science and engineering. And it is the objective of this book to repair and remediate that oversight.

1.4.2 Basic concepts and terminology

The third and final chapter of Part I investigates and explains a set of fundamental concepts necessary for understanding AI development and its significance. The main objective of the chapter is to investigate and explicate the differences between the two methods for doing or developing AI – symbolic reasoning and machine learning. Right from the beginning, there was a methodological split in how AI would be pursued and developed, and the difference between these two approaches can already be seen in the Dartmouth proposal. As Nathaniel Rochester (who was, at that time, a manager of information research at IBM) explains, the usual way of programming a computer involves writing step-by-step instructions for the machine to follow. "In writing a program for an automatic calculator, one ordinarily provides the machine with a set of rules to cover each contingency which may arise and confront the machine" (McCarthy et al. 1955: 10). This "symbolic reasoning" or "rule-based" approach was something that interested John McCarthy, who sought to develop an artificial language for AI:

It therefore seems to be desirable to attempt to construct an artificial language which a computer can be programmed to use on problems requiring conjecture and self-reference. It should correspond to English in the sense that short English statements about the given subject matter should have short correspondents in the language and so should short argument or conjectural arguments. (McCarthy et al. 1955: 17)

The other approach involves what we now call "machine learning." This alternative was also identified and advanced in the course of the Dartmouth proposal, and it had (at the time) a particularly strong advocate in Marvin Minsky (who was then a postdoctoral fellow at Harvard University in mathematics and neurology):

> It is not difficult to design a machine which exhibits the following type of learning. The machine is provided with input and output channels and an internal means of providing varied output responses to inputs in such a way that the machine may be "trained" by a "trial and error" process to acquire one of a range of input–output functions. Such a machine, when placed in an appropriate environment and given a criterion of "success" or "failure" can be trained to exhibit "goal-seeking behavior." (McCarthy et al. 1955: 8)

Despite the fact that both approaches were "put on the table" at the time of the Dartmouth conference, symbolic reasoning became (for reasons that we will investigate in detail) the privileged way of doing things in AI from about 1965 to the end of the century. The decisive break is typically located in a rather unlikely place – a book coauthored by the one-time advocate of machine learning Marvin Minsky and his MIT colleague Seymour Papart. Their book, *Perceptrons: An Introduction to Computational Geometry* (1969), was highly critical of the connectionist architecture that had been used in neural network machine-learning efforts and almost single-handedly put an end to this area of research. I say "almost," because machine learning, and especially the neural network architectures that Minsky and Papart (1969: 4) had criticized as being "without scientific value," return with a vengeance in the twenty-first century, to the extent that the recent boom in AI is largely attributed to advancements in machine-learning techniques and technologies. The third and final chapter of Part I gets into both approaches to doing AI, and breaks them down for a nonspecialist and potentially mathematically challenged or even math-phobic audience.

1.4.3 Applications

Part II of this book focuses on specific AI applications – situations where some form of AI is applied to a communications problem or where AI/robots are involved in communicative situations or social interactions with human users. Chapter 4 examines machine translation (MT), which is, as the name implies, the use of computer applications to translate between different human languages. If AI is defined as doing something that we think is typically a behavior or activity that takes intelligence, then translation is a good poster-child. You intuitively know this from your own experience studying and learning a second language. Translating between your native language (let's say English) and the second language (let's say Spanish) takes considerable memory and cognitive effort. Programming digital computers to do the same has been assumed to be a job perfectly suited to both the science and engineering of AI. In fact, MT is one of the first applications of "intelligent machines."

The computer as we now know it – that is, an electronic digital information processor – is a product of code-breaking efforts during World War II. The two machines currently competing for the title of "first electronic digital computer" – Colossus in the UK and ENIAC in the US – were initially developed to aid the work of cryptographic analysis, or code-breaking. Observing this effort first hand, Warren Weaver, who was head of the Applied Mathematics Panel at the US Office of Scientific Research and Development, connected the dots by suggesting that translation might be a special case of crypt-analysis. The idea took off. And today it is not uncommon to use Google Translate to "help" with your Spanish homework, translate a webpage in a language that is not your native tongue, or mediate between human communicators in real time. Chapter 4 looks at the technology and social consequences of using machines to mediate between different human languages.

MT is a specific instance of what has been called natural language processing (NLP). Chapter 5 extends the analysis of NLP and looks at applications that do more than mediate between human users and can be said to understand and use natural human language them-selves. These efforts take up and respond to one of the challenges listed in the Dartmouth proposal, namely, to figure out how to make computers use language. This task, however, was already identified in Alan Turing's "game of imitation," which he had proposed as a test case for machine intelligence. When Turing published his seminal paper, "Computing Machinery and Intelligence," in 1950, six years before the Dartmouth summer seminar, he estimated that the tipping point – the point at which a computational mechanism would be able to successfully engage in interpersonal communication with human users in such a way as to appear to be another human communicator – was at least a half-century away.

It did not take that long. Already in 1966, Joseph Weizenbaum, a professor at MIT, demonstrated a simple NLP application that was able to converse with human users. ELIZA, as the application was called, was the first chatbot. Since ELIZA, there has been a steady increase in the capabilities of NLP applications, culminating (at least for now) in spoken dialogue systems (SDS) like Siri, Alexa, and Google Duplex. Chapter 5 investigates (1) the theory behind NLP and the development of computational linguistics; (2) the engineering challenges and technical features of specific NLP applications, including simple chatbots like ELIZA and the SDS implementations available in smartphones and home digital assistants; and (3) the way NLP applications are challenging existing theories and practices in communication by creating new opportunities for the discipline of Communication Studies.

The ability to use language raises important questions about intention and origination. Chapter 6 generalizes this inquiry and investigates what is now called "computational creativity." As technologies of various sorts and configurations encroach on human abilities in areas like manufacturing, decision-making, communication, transportation, etc., the one remaining bulwark of human exceptionalism appears to be creativity and artistry. But maybe not for long. There are already technologies that can produce what appear to be creative work in all areas of human endeavor – writing original stories for publication, composing and performing original music, making unique and innovative scientific discoveries, and generating new works of art. Consequently, it appears that what we have called "creativity" and "artistry" may not be as uniquely human as one might have initially thought. Chapter 6 examines the technologies and the opportunities/challenges of increasingly creative machines. In doing so, it asks and investigates a rather simple set of questions: "Can machines create art?" And if they can, what does that mean for us, and especially for those of us looking to make a career in one of the creative fields involving content generation like art and design, journalism, web programming, film/media, or communications?

The final chapter in the section on applications (Chapter 7) considers social robots. A social robot is a machine that is designed to interact and respond to human users in a human-like way. Whether these devices have a humanoid form (like the androids created by David Hanson or Hiroshi Ishiguro) or not (like the Paro seal robot used in elder care, or Cynthia Breazeal's Jibo, which looks like a chubby desktop lamp), social robots are socially situated technologies that are able to communicate in a manner that is reasonably close to achieving what would be expected of another human individual. Chapter 7 looks at the rise of the social robot and the opportunities and challenges these devices introduce into human social relationships and interactions. The chapter will (1) survey the development and uses of social robots, covering the range of current implementations, e.g., medical assistive systems, domestic robots, online companions, and even sex robots; (2) examine the design and engineering challenges of creating different kinds of mechanisms with human-level interaction capabilities, e.g., verbal communication, nonverbal understanding and behaviors, and emotional/social intelligence; and (3) evaluate the social opportunities and challenges of machines that are deliberately designed to occupy the place of another person.

1.4.4 Impact and consequences

Part III, the third and final substantive section of the book, investigates the social consequences and significance of these technological innovations. Because these intelligent and/or autonomous technologies affect virtually every aspect of human existence – from transportation and financial transactions to interpersonal communication – their impact is both broad and deep. For this reason, we will not be able to deal with every item and issue in detail; we will instead make a strategic choice, limiting ourselves to two important and pressing matters.

Chapter 8 will take up and investigate a problem that should be on the mind of any university student anticipating graduation and entry into the workforce – "technological unemployment." In a widely publicized study from 2013, researchers from the University of Oxford predicted that close to 50 percent of all US jobs are at risk of being automated in the next twenty years (Frey and Osborne 2017). And what is targeted for automation are not just those occupations that are "dangerous, dirty and dull," but professions that had at one time seemed impervious to the threat of automation: lawyers, accountants, customer service representatives, transportation professionals, journalists, translators, technical writers, creatives, etc. This chapter will help students understand (1) the exigencies and realities of technological unemployment, (2) the way automation impacts jobs and job opportunities, and (3) what can be done right here/right now to prepare for this inevitability. The world new graduates will come to inhabit is a world full of different AI and robotic systems. The questions that students need to ask and begin answering right now are: "Where do I fit in this picture?" "What new opportunities are available to me as a recent graduate?" and "How can I best prepare myself for lifelong success?"

The ninth and final chapter will consider questions of social responsibility and ethics in the face of increasingly interactive, social, and autonomous systems. As machines of various capabilities displace human decision-making and action, we need to ask ourselves who, or maybe even "what," can and will be held responsible for both good and bad outcomes. Consider a problem discovered at Amazon in 2014, when the retail giant began developing a proprietary algorithm to automate the task of reviewing job applications. As a major player in online commerce and a leading developer of commercial AI systems, Amazon is interested in recruiting the best and the brightest software developers and engineers, and the algorithm was supposed to assist this effort by sorting through a deluge of applications and identifying the most qualified applicants for the position. I say "supposed to," because shortly after being put into operation (by early 2015, in fact), it became clear that the algorithm had been making determinations in a way that was not gender-neutral. In other words, the algorithm was routinely discriminating against female applicants, who were consistently ranked lower than their male counterparts. This happened not because programmers intentionally designed the algorithm to be biased. It occurred because the machine-learning system that Amazon developed had been trained on a decade of existing data concerning applicants, and since most of the applications from that period of time had been from male software developers and engineers, the algorithm had unintentionally learned to reproduce this gender bias in its decisions and recommendations (Dastin 2018).

Unfortunately, this situation is neither unique nor exceptional, as forms of "algorithmic bias" have now shown up in all kinds of places. In 2015, the algorithm that powers Google Photo mistakenly identified images of African American men as gorillas (Simonite 2018). Criminal risk-assessment algorithms, like that developed by Northpointe, have been shown to privilege white defendants, providing them with better sentencing and parole decisions than that imposed on minority defendants (Angwin et al. 2016). And some of the most powerful and widely used facial-recognition systems have had trouble discerning and dealing with the faces of non-Caucasian individuals (Barrett 2018). The question in all these situations – especially when someone's career or life is adversely affected by a machine decision – is: who (or what) is responsible for the prejudice and the error? Who or what can be held accountable for the bad decision-making and action? Is it the programmer? Is it the user of the system? Is it the system itself? Or is it some combination of both people and technology, and what would this actually mean for our moral and legal systems? The final chapter grapples with these questions not in order to provide a single and definitive answer, but to formulate the range of possible responses that can be made in the face of these important social and moral challenges.

1.4.5 Maker exercises

In Part IV of the book, included as a kind of appendix, are five maker exercises designed to support the information and instruction provided in the substantive chapters with "learn by doing" opportunities and examples. Each maker exercise is tied to one of the chapters and designed to provide more practical ways for engaging with, working with, and learning about the material. Arguably, the exercises are optional. The book is designed for and can be used without doing any of them. That said, they are important for three reasons. First, they provide practical instruction that can support and reinforce the information presented in the chapters; second, they offer instructors and students some hands-on experience that can help develop both skills and confidence with technology; and, third, they can address and accommodate differences in learning styles and approaches, providing students with more than one way to succeed. The objective of this book is to demystify technology, and one of the best ways that I know of to achieve this goal is by "popping the hood" on actual applications and experiencing first hand what they do, how they work, and why.

Summary of Key Points

- The words "artificial intelligence" and "robot" have a complex and interesting cultural history. "AI" originally comes from the world of science and then enters the realm of fiction. "Robot" comes from the world of fiction and then enters the domain of real-world science and engineering practices.
- These words matter. How we name and describe the technology is not accidental, and the means by which we represent and talk about these systems and devices in various forms of media (books, stage plays, films, television, games, etc.) is as important to how we understand and think about the technology as the actual systems and devices.
- The book – which is designed to explain and demystify the technology of AI and robotics for students in the humanities and social sciences – is organized into four sections: Part I is an introduction that connects the dots between communication and AI and

investigates basic concepts and terminology; Part II is a detailed investigation of four applications that are important to the field of Communication Studies; Part III is a consideration of the social consequences and significance of the technology; and Part IV consists of maker exercises designed to support instruction with hands-on learning opportunities.

2

Communication and AI

Key Aims/Objectives

- To demonstrate how and why interpersonal communication has been the defining condition of machine intelligence, beginning with Alan Turing's agenda-setting paper on the subject.
- To look at recent advances in AI and robot development, noting how these applications and technologies are no longer media *through* which we communicate with each other, but now occupy the place of the other *with* whom we communicate.
- To understand how these innovations introduce new opportunities and challenges for Communication Studies and necessitate a fundamental shift in the research models and methods that define the discipline.

Introduction

Although the phrase "artificial intelligence" is the product of an academic conference at Dartmouth College in 1956, it is Alan Turing's 1950 essay "Computing Machinery and Intelligence" and its "game of imitation," or what is now routinely called the Turing Test, that arguably has defined and characterizes the field. Although not widely recognized either by AI researchers or communication scholars, Turing situates communication – and a specific form of interpersonal communication – as the defining condition of and test case for machine intelligence. This chapter pursues and investigates two related issues: first, how communication – specifically interpersonal conversational behavior – has been and remains definitive of machine intelligence; and, second, how developments in the science and engineering of AI introduce new opportunities and challenges into the field of Communication Studies.

2.1 Communication and Machine Intelligence

Whether it is explicitly acknowledged or not, communication (that is, "communication" as the concept is understood and mobilized in the discipline of Communication Studies) is fundamental to both the theory and the practice of AI. In particular, it is communication that provides the science with its defining condition and experimental test case. This is immediately evident in the agenda-setting paper that is credited with defining what machine intelligence is – Alan Turing's "Computing Machinery and Intelligence" (see Turing 1999). The paper was initially published in the British journal *Mind* six years before the Dartmouth conference; since then, it has been reprinted and commented upon in numerous collections and anthologies (see also Turing 2004). Its immense influence can be easily quantified by taking note of the fact that it has been cited more than 10,500 times in the subsequent literature (Google Scholar as of December 2018).

2.1.1 The game of imitation

Turing begins the essay with the question "Can machines think?" But he immediately recognizes persistent and seemingly irresolvable terminological difficulties with the question itself:

> I propose to consider the question, "Can machines think?" This should begin with definitions of the meaning of the terms "machine" and "think." The definitions might be framed so as to reflect so far as possible the normal use of the words, but this attitude is dangerous. If the meaning of the words "machine" and "think" are to be found by examining how they are commonly used it is difficult to escape the conclusion that the meaning and the answer to the question, "Can machines think?" is to be sought in a statistical survey such as a Gallup poll. But this is absurd. (1999: 37)

In response to this difficulty, a semantic problem with the very words that would need to be employed in order to articulate the question in the first place, Turing proposes to pursue an alternative line of inquiry:

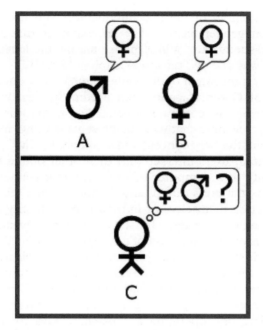

Figure 2.1 The game of imitation, phase one

> Instead of attempting such a definition, I shall replace the question by another, which is closely related to it and is expressed in relatively unambiguous words. The new form of the problem can be described in terms of a game which we call the "imitation game." It is played with three people, a man (A), a woman (B), and an interrogator (C) who may be of either sex. The interrogator stays in a room apart from the other two. The object of the game for the interrogator is to determine which of the other two is the man and which is the woman. (1999: 37)

This determination, as Turing explains, is to be made by way of a sequence of questions and answers. The interrogator (C) asks participants A and B various things, and, based on their responses, tries to discern whether the respondent is a man or a woman (Figure 2.1).

"In order that tone of voice may not help the interrogator," Turing further stipulates, "the answers should be written, or better still, typewritten. The ideal arrangement is to have a teleprinter communicating between the two rooms" (1999: 37–8). The interrogator, therefore, interacts with two unknown participants by way of a form of synchronous computer-mediated interaction that we now routinely call "chat." Because the exchange takes place via text messages routed through a machine, the interrogator cannot see or otherwise perceive the identity of the two interlocutors and must, therefore, ascertain their gender based solely on responses that are supplied to simple questions like "Will X please tell me the length of his/her hair," which was one of Turing's examples (1999: 37).

The initial arrangement of the game of imitation should be familiar to students of Communication and Media Studies. In fact, what Turing describes is computer-mediated communication (CMC) *avant la lettre*, meaning that what he presents is CMC in advance of the invention of this very concept and acronym. In CMC, as it is typically formulated, users interact with each other online through the instrumentality of a computer or other Internet-connected device. Consequently, the users cannot and do not see each other, and they can even disguise themselves or hide their true identity behind profiles, screen names, or avatars. In fact, one never really knows for sure who or what is on the other end of a computer-mediated interaction.

This point is something that is made abundantly clear in a famous cartoon from the early days of the Internet. The cartoon, which was drawn by Peter Steiner and published in the *New Yorker* magazine in 1996, pictures two dogs sitting in front of an Internet-connected computer. The one operating the machine says to his companion, "On the Internet, nobody knows you're a dog." (The image, which cannot be reproduced here owing to copyright restrictions, is available at https://en.wikipedia.org/wiki/On_the_Internet,_nobody_ knows_you%27re_a_dog.) The point of the illustration is simple: with online interactions, the identity of the person to whom you are talking is something that is hidden from view and not able to be determined except by way of the things he/she/it says to you in the computer-mediated conversation. Turing's imitation game is based on this basic set-up. The interrogator interacts with two other people whose true identities are hidden behind the screen of a computer. So the task of the interrogator is to figure out the identity of his interlocutors from evaluating the content of what they say in response to questions.

Turing then takes his thought experiment – or what he calls a "game" – one step further. "We can now ask the question, 'What will happen when a machine takes the part of A in this game?' Will the interrogator decide wrongly as often when the game is played like this as he does when the game is played between a man and a woman? These questions replace our original, 'Can machines think?'" (1999: 38). In other words, if the man (A) in the game of imitation is replaced with a computing machine, would this device be able to respond to questions and pass as another human person, effectively fooling the

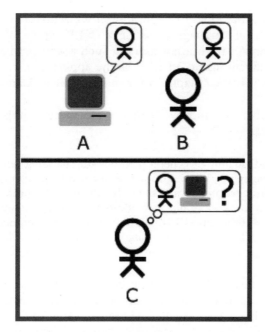

Figure 2.2   The game of imitation, phase two

interrogator into thinking that it was just another human being (see Figure 2.2)? It is this question, according to Turing, that *replaces* the initial and unfortunately ambiguous inquiry "Can machines think?" If a computer or a computer application like a chatbot, a non-player character (NPC), or spoken dialogue system (SDS) does in fact become capable of successfully simulating a human being, of either sex, in communicative exchanges with a human interrogator to such an extent that the interrogator cannot tell whether he is interacting with a machine or another human being, then that device would, Turing concludes, need to be considered "intelligent."

At the time that Turing published the paper, he had estimated that the tipping point – the point at which a computational mechanism would be able to successfully play the game of imitation – was at least a half-century in the future:

> I believe that in about fifty years' time it will be possible to programme computers, with a storage capacity of about 10^9, to make them play the imitation game so well that an average interrogator will not have more than 70 per cent chance of making the right identification after five minutes of questioning. (1999: 44)

It did not take that long. In 1966, Joseph Weizenbaum demonstrated a simple natural language processing (NLP) application that was able to converse with human users in such a way as to appear to be another intelligent agent. ELIZA, as the application was called, was the first chatbot (see Chapter 5 for more on ELIZA and other NLP applications).

ELIZA was, technically speaking, a rather simple piece of programming:

> [It consisted] mainly of general methods for analyzing sentences and sentence fragments, locating so-called key words in texts, assembling sentences from fragments, and so on. It had, in other words, no built-in contextual framework of universe of discourse. This was supplied to it by a "script." In a sense ELIZA was an actress who commanded a set of techniques but who had nothing of her own to say. (Weizenbaum 1976: 188)

ELIZA was designed using some very basic features of computer programming, namely regular expressions matches, which can identify patterns like "You are X," where the value of "X" can be any adjective selected by the user (i.e. "angry," "unhappy," "mean," "thoughtful," etc.); and pre-scripted responses that insert the value of the variable, providing suitable outputs like, "What makes you think I am X?" (try it for yourself with Maker Exercise 1). Despite this simplicity, Weizenbaum's program effectively demonstrated what Turing had initially predicted:

> ELIZA created the most remarkable illusion of having understood in the minds of many people who conversed with it. People who know very well that they were conversing with a machine soon forgot that fact, just as theatergoers, in the grip of suspended disbelief, soon forget that the action they are witnessing is not "real." This illusion was especially strong and most tenaciously clung to among people who know little or nothing about computers. They would often demand to be permitted to converse with the system in private, and would, after conversing with it for a time, insist, in spite of my explanations, that the machine really understood them. (1976: 189)

Even if ELIZA did not completely "win" at the game of imitation, the program was a strong contender and demonstrated the possibility of what Turing had originally proposed. In other words, ELIZA was a convincing enough conversational partner that it could pass (at least for some of the users of the program) as another human being.

2.1.2 Significance and consequences

Although there is a good deal that has been written in response to Turing's essay, the game of imitation, and the successes (or failures) of practical implementations like that provided by ELIZA, Turing's work has three important features and consequences that matter (or at least should matter) for us.

The other minds problem   Turing's essay situates communication – and a particular form of potentially deceptive social interaction – as the deciding factor. This is not a capricious decision. There are good epistemological reasons for focusing on this particular capability, and it has to do with what philosophers and behavioral scientists routinely call "the problem of other minds" – the seemingly undeniable fact that we do not have direct access to the inner workings of another's mind. "How does one determine," as Paul Churchland (1999: 67) famously characterized it, "whether something other than oneself – an alien creature, a sophisticated robot, a socially active computer, or even another human – is really a thinking, feeling, conscious being; rather than, for example, an unconscious automaton whose behavior arises from something other than genuine mental states?" In other words, we generally assume that other people are thinking/feeling creatures like ourselves. But strictly speaking, we have no way of knowing this for sure. I might know my own mind (although Sigmund Freud might argue that this too is a deception or only a partial understanding) and have a good idea that I am a thinking/feeling thing. But what about others? How do I know for sure – beyond a reasonable doubt – that you are also a thinking/ feeling creature? How can I know the woman sitting across from me on the subway is also a conscious entity with an internal life of thoughts and feelings? How can I know what and even if my dog or cat thinks and has conscious experience? The problem is that we don't have any way to resolve these questions in a credible way. Even if we employ expensive medical-imaging devices, like fMRI machines that show which parts of the brain light up when various stimuli are presented to an organism, none of that confirms the presence of a thinking, feeling, or conscious mind.

Attempts to resolve or at least respond to this problem inevitably involve some kind of behavioral demonstration or test, like Turing's game of imitation. "To put this another way," as Roger Schank (1990: 5) concludes, "we really cannot examine the insides of an intelligent entity in such a way as to establish what it actually knows.

Our only choice is to ask and observe." For Turing, and for many who follow his lead, intelligence is something that is neither easy to define nor able to be directly accessed. It is, therefore, evidenced in and decided on the basis of external behaviors that are considered to be signs or symptoms of intelligence, especially communication and human-level verbal conversation. In other words, because intelligent thought is not directly observable, the best one can do is deal with something – like communicative interaction – that is assumed to be the product of intelligence and can be empirically observed, measured, and evaluated.

Turing's game of imitation leverages this rich philosophical tradition. If an entity – another human being, an animal, a robot, an algorithm, and so on – is, in fact, capable of performing communicative operations at least on a par with what is typically expected of another human individual, irrespective of what actually goes on inside the head or information processor of the entity itself, we would need to consider this thing intelligent. Following from this, Turing had estimated that developments in machine communication would advance to such a degree that it would make sense to speak (and to speak intelligently) of machine intelligence by the end of the twentieth century: "I predict that by the end of the century the use of words and general educated opinion will have altered so much that one will be able to speak of machines thinking without expecting to be contradicted" (1999: 44).

If you have ever taken a philosophy course, all of this should sound familiar. In fact, this problem – the problem of other minds – has deep philosophical roots, going back at least to the work of the French thinker René Descartes. For Descartes, whose innovative method followed a rigorous discipline of self-doubt or skepticism, the only thing that could be known for certain was "I think, therefore I am." But that was it. There was, at least according to Descartes's strict scientific method, simply no way to know for sure whether the other people on the street had the same kind of inner experience or not. In fact, he admits, in a passage that sounds more like a science fiction movie than a work of modern philosophy, that he cannot be certain whether other people on the street are in fact thinking things like himself or nothing more than empty-headed robots that have been designed to look and act like human beings.

Descartes, however, has what he thinks is a solution to this problem – something that is called *solipsism*, the fact that you can only know your own mind and have no access to the minds of others. According to Descartes, there is one sure-fire way to resolve this impasse. If one were, for example, confronted with cleverly designed machines that looked and behaved like human beings, there would be at least one way to determine that these artificial figures were in fact machines and not real human persons:

> They could never use words, or put together other signs, as we do in order to declare our thoughts to others. For we can certainly conceive of a machine so constructed that it utters words, and even utters words which correspond to bodily actions causing a change in its organs (e.g., if you touch it in one spot it asks what you want of it, if you touch it in another it cries out that you are hurting it, and so on). But it is not conceivable that such a machine should produce different arrangements of words so as to give an appropriately meaningful answer to whatever is said in its presence, as the dullest of men can do. (1988: 44–5)

Turing's game of imitation leverages this rich philosophical tradition and turns it back on itself. If, in fact, a machine is able, as Descartes wrote, "to produce different arrangements of words so as to give an appropriately meaningful answer to whatever is said in its presence," then we would, Turing argues, have to conclude that it was just as much a thinking, intelligent entity as another human being.

Challenges and counterexamples Although this conclusion follows quite logically from Turing's argument, there has been and continues to be considerable resistance to it. For Turing, the critical challenge had already been articulated by Lady Lovelace (aka Augusta Ada Byron, the daughter of the English poet Lord Byron), who not only wrote the "software" for Charles Babbage's Analytical Engine (*circa* 1837) but is, for that reason, considered to be the first computer scientist. "Our most detailed information of Babbage's Analytical Engine," Turing (1999: 50) explains, "comes from a memoir by Lady Lovelace. In it she states, 'The Analytical Engine has no pretensions to originate anything. It can only do whatever we know how to order it to perform.'" According to Lovelace, a computer (and, at the time she wrote this, "computer" referred not to an electronic device but to a large mechanical information processor made up of intricate gears and levers) only does what we tell it to do. We can, in fact, write a software program, like ELIZA or even Apple's Siri, that takes verbal input, extracts keywords, rearranges these words according to pre-programmed scripts, and then spits out seemingly intelligible results. This does not, however, necessarily mean that such a mechanism is capable of original thought or of understanding what is stated in even a rudimentary way.

This counterargument is further developed by the American philosopher John Searle in his well-known "Chinese Room" thought experiment. This intriguing and rather influential illustration, which he first introduced in 1980 with the essay "Minds, Brains, and Programs" and then elaborated in subsequent publications, was offered as an argument against the claims of strong AI – that machines are able to achieve intelligent thought:

> Imagine a native English speaker who knows no Chinese locked in a room full of boxes of Chinese symbols (a data base) together with a book of instructions for manipulating the symbols (the program). Imagine that people outside the room send in other Chinese symbols which, unknown to the person in the room, are questions in Chinese (the input). And imagine that by following the instructions in the program the man in the room is able to pass out Chinese symbols which are correct answers to the questions (the output). The program enables the person in the room to pass the Turing Test for understanding Chinese but he does not understand a word of Chinese. (1999: 115)

The point of Searle's imaginative illustration is quite simple – simulation is not the real thing. "The Turing test," as Searle (1999: 115) concludes, "fails to distinguish real mental capacities from simulations of those capacities. Simulation is not duplication." In other words, merely shifting verbal symbols around in a way that looks like linguistic understanding (from the outside) is not really an understanding of the language (Figure 2.3). As Terry Winograd (1990: 187) explains, a computer does not really understand the linguistic

Figure 2.3   Artist's rendition of John Searle's Chinese Room

tokens it processes; it merely "manipulates symbols without respect to their interpretation." Or, as Searle (1984: 34) characterizes it, computers have syntax and a method of symbol manipulation, but they do not have semantics.

Demonstrations like Searle's Chinese Room, which seek to differentiate between the appearance of something and the real thing as it actually is in itself, not only deploy an ancient philosophical distinction between appearance and reality, which is initially developed in the work of Plato, but inevitably require some kind of privileged and immediate access to the inner workings of the real thing and not just how it appears to be. But instead of taking a detour through ancient philosophy, let's return to and reconsider Steiner's dog cartoon. In it, we see a dog using an Internet-connected computer, presumably passing for human and fooling others into thinking that it is just another human user. As the computer-using dog says to its companion: "Online nobody knows you're a dog." This illustration, however, is only funny on the basis of a crucial and necessary piece of information: we see that it is really a dog in front of the computer screen and typing on the keyboard. Without access to this visual information, the cartoon would not work. It would not be funny.

So let's apply this insight to Searle's Chinese Room thought experiment. In order to be able to make a distinction between a simulation of intelligence and "real intelligence," one would need access not only to external indicators that look like intelligence, but also to the actual activity of intelligence as it occurs (or does not occur) in the mind of another. This requirement, however, immediately runs into the problem of other minds and the epistemological limitation that it imposes: namely, that we cannot get into the "head" of another entity – whether that entity be another human being, a nonhuman animal, an alien life form, or a sophisticated robot – to know with any certitude whether it actually does perform whatever it appears to manifest. In other words, Searle is only able to distinguish between and compare what appears to happen for those individuals interacting with the room and what really goes on inside the room because he has already provided privileged access to the inner workings of the room itself. His "counterexample," therefore, appears to violate the epistemological limitations imposed by the problem of other minds, which is something Turing's game of imitation was careful to acknowledge and respect.

Social behavior and effects   Even if one is convinced, following the arguments offered by Searle and Lovelace, that a computer application like ELIZA is just a "mindless" instrument that merely manipulates linguistic tokens, the Turing Test also demonstrates that it is what human users do with and in response to these manipulations that makes the difference. In other words, whether or not we conclude that the mechanism is, in fact, intelligent, the communicative behavior that is exhibited in, for example, the game of imitation or other social interactive exchanges does have an effect on us and our social relationships. As Weizenbaum insightfully pointed out:

> [T]he human speaker will contribute much to clothe ELIZA's responses in the vestments of plausibility. However, he will not defend his illusion (that he is being understood) against all odds. In human conversation a speaker will make certain (perhaps generous) assumptions about his conversational partner. As long as it remains possible to interpret the latter's responses to be consistent with those assumptions, the speaker's image of his partner remains undamaged. (1967: 474–5)

This insight has been experimentally confirmed by Byron Reeves and Clifford Nass's Computer as Social Actor (CASA) studies, or what is also called the Media Equation:

> Computers, in the way that they communicate, instruct, and take turns interacting, are close enough to human that they encourage social responses. The encouragement necessary for such a reaction need not be much. As long as there are some behaviors that suggest a social presence, people will respond accordingly . . . Consequently, any medium that is close enough will get human treatment, even though people know it's foolish and even though they likely will deny it afterwards. (1996: 22)

The CASA model, which was developed in response to numerous experiments with human subjects, describes how users of computers, irrespective of the actual intelligence possessed by the machine, tend to respond to the technology as another socially aware and interactive subject. In other words, even when experienced users know quite well that they are engaged with using a machine, they make what Reeves and Nass (1996: 22) call the "conservative error" and tend to respond to it in ways that afford this other thing social standing on a par with another human individual.

This has recently been demonstrated and confirmed with robots in the field – especially in the case of the explosive ordnance disposal (EOD) robots that are now utilized in situations of military conflict. As Peter Singer (2009), Joel Garreau (2007), and Julie Carpenter

(2015) have all reported, soldiers form surprisingly close personal bonds with their units' EOD robots, giving them names, awarding them battlefield promotions, risking their own lives to protect that of the robot, and even mourning their "death." This happens not because of how the robots are designed or what they are. It happens as a byproduct of the way the mechanisms are situated within the unit and the role they play in battlefield operations. As Eleanor Sandry explains:

> EOD robots, such as PackBots and Talons, are not humanlike or animal-like, are not currently autonomous and do not have distinctive complex behaviours supported by artificial intelligence capabilities. They might therefore be expected to raise few critical issues relating to human–robot interaction, since communication with these machines relies on the direct transmission of information through radio signals, which have no emotional content and are not open to interpretation. Indeed, the fact that these machines are broadly not autonomous precludes them from being discussed as social robots according to some definitions . . . In spite of this, there is an increasing amount of evidence that EOD robots are thought of as team members, and are valued as brave and courageous in the line of duty. It seems that people working with EOD robots, even though the robots are machinelike and under the control of a human, anthropomorphise and/or zoomorphise them, interpreting them as having individual personalities and abilities. (2015a: 340)

Existing EOD robots, like the PackBots and Talons mentioned by Sandry, are not designed for, nor do they function as, "social robots" (see Chapter 7 for more on this subject). They are industrial looking – basically small tanks with a movable arm – and are created and deployed for the sole purpose of instrumental utility in the disposal of explosive ordnance. Furthermore, these EOD robots are not autonomous and in many cases would not even qualify as semi-autonomous devices by any stretch of the imagination. Most of these technological artifacts are still under human remote control, do not incorporate or contain anything approaching advanced AI capabilities, and in most cases would not even be considered as "smart" as your average "smartphone." Despite this, soldiers in the field often treat these robots as comrades-in-arms and not as a tool or just another piece of military hardware. They do so not because of what these robots are but because of the role that these artifacts play in combat operations and how they participate in or contribute to unit cohesion. Consequently, in order for something to be recognized and treated as another social actor, "it is not necessary," as Reeves and Nass (1996: 28) conclude, "to have artificial intelligence," strictly speaking. All that is needed is that they appear to be "close enough" to encourage some kind of social response.

2.1.3 Summary and outcomes

Communication has been central to the definition and demonstration of machine intelligence from the very beginning. In Turing's game of imitation, it is the act of communication – and interpersonal conversational behavior in particular – that has been situated as the defining condition of AI. But if this is true, why have these subjects – machine intelligence and artificial intelligence – been virtually absent from the field of Communication Studies? Why has AI remained outside the realm of the work that we do in the field of communication? Or, to put it another way, why isn't AI a communication science, and why is it that communication professionals do not play a more central role in the research, development, and commercial deployment of AI systems and robotics? Answering these questions will require a critical reassessment of the discipline of communication and its particular method for dealing with computer technology.

2.2 Machine Intelligence and Communication Studies

In Turing's game of imitation, the computer occupies the position of the medium through which human users exchange messages and also one of the participants with whom one is engaged in communicative interactions. In other words, the computer is both something *through* which messages are passed and the other *with* whom one communicates. In the field of communication, as mentioned in Chapter 1, these two alternatives were initially identified and formalized in the mid-1980s by Robert Cathcart and Gary Gumpert in their essay "The Person–Computer Interaction." In this rather early publication ("early" insofar as the IBM PC had just been introduced in 1981 and the Web had yet to be invented), the authors differentiated between communicating *through* a computer and communicating *with* a computer. The former, they argued (1985: 114), names all those "computer facilitated functions" where "the computer is interposed between sender and receiver." The latter designates "person–computer interpersonal functions" where "one party activates a computer which in turn responds appropriately in graphic, alphanumeric, or vocal modes establishing an ongoing sender/receiver relationship."

These two alternatives were subsequently corroborated and further refined in James Chesebro and Donald Bonsall's 1989 book, *Computer-Mediated Communication*. In this more extensive examination of the role and function of the computer in the field of communication, the authors develop a five-point scale that delimits the range of possibilities for what they call "computer–human communication." The scale extends, on one side, from the computer utilized as a mere medium of message transmission between human users to, on the other side, the computer understood as an intelligent agent with whom human users interact. Although providing a more complex articulation of the intervening possibilities, Chesebro and Bonsall's formulation remains bounded by the two possibilities initially identified by Cathcart and Gumpert: the computer is either a passive medium *through* which human users exchange information, or it constitutes an active subject *with* whom one communicates. Despite early identification of these two possibilities, the field of Communication Studies has, for better or worse, privileged one over and against the other. With very few exceptions, Communication Studies has decided to address the computer as a medium through which human users interact with one another, and this decision is immediately evident in and has been institutionalized by the CMC model.

2.2.1 Computer-mediated communication

The concept of CMC – although not appearing under that exact name just yet – was initially introduced and formalized in J.C.R. Licklider and Robert W. Taylor's 1968 essay "The Computer as a Communication Device." In this important and influential essay, Licklider and Taylor argued for what was, at that time, an entirely different understanding of computer technology. As the name indicates, *computer* was initially designed to provide for rapid and automatic computation or "number crunching," and for this reason it was limited to the fields of mathematics, electrical engineering, and computer science. For Licklider and Taylor, however, the computer was more than a mere calculator or numerical processor; it was (or at least they proposed that it was) an instrument of mediated human interaction that provided users with a natural extension of face-to-face communication (1968: 21). One year after the publication of "The Computer as a Communication Device," ARPANET, the precursor to the Internet, began operation. As if to fulfill Licklider and Taylor's thesis, the actual use of this network "did not support remote computing. The network evolved instead to become primarily a medium for interpersonal communication" (Dutton 1995: 95).

Licklider and Taylor (1968: 29) originally called this new development "computer-aided communication," but the term "computer-mediated communication" began to gain acceptance in the decade that followed. In 1978, Starr Roxanne Hiltz and Murray Turoff employed the phrase in their extended examination of computerized teleconferencing, *The Networked Nation: Human Communication via Computer*. Although Hiltz and Turroff (1978: xix) used the term "computer conferencing system" (CCS) to name "any system that uses the computer to mediate communication among human beings," they had also employed "computer-mediated communication" as a generic designation for various forms of human communication via the computer, including "computerized conferencing, computer assisted instruction, and home terminals from which white collar work can be done" (1978: 167).

The phrase "computer-mediated communication" was elevated to the status of a technical term in Hiltz's subsequent collaboration with Elaine Kerr, which was undertaken for the US National Science Foundation. This 1981 study was expanded and published a year later under the title *Computer-Mediated Communication Systems: Status and Evaluation*. In this report, CMC was defined as "a new form of enhanced human communication" (1982: 31).

> Essentially computer-mediated communication means that large numbers of people in business, government, education, or at home can use the computer to maintain continuous communication and information exchanges. More than a replacement for the telephone, mails, or face-to-face meetings, computer communication is a new medium for building and maintaining human relationships. (1982: ix)

For Hiltz and Kerr, CMC designated human communication through the instrumentality of computers. Recent employments and characterizations of CMC have reiterated and solidified this characterization. For Susan Herring, editor of one of the first published collection of essays addressing the subject, "computer-mediated communication is communication that takes place between human beings via the instrumentality of computers" (1996: 1). John December (1997), editor of the now defunct *Computer-Mediated Communication Magazine*, answers the self-reflective question "What is CMC?" with a similar definition: "Computer-mediated communication is

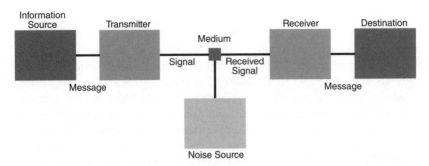

Figure 2.4 Shannon and Weaver's model of communication

a process of human communication via computers." Defining the role and function of the computer in this manner is both intuitively attractive and conceptually sound. In fact, it possesses at least three advantages for scholars of communication.

Process model of communication CMC situates the computer at an identifiable position within the process model of communication, which was initially formalized in Claude Shannon and Warren Weaver's *The Mathematical Theory of Communication*. According to this model, communication is defined as a dyadic process bounded, on the one side, by an information source or sender and, on the other side, by a receiver. These two participants are connected by a communication channel or medium through which messages selected by the sender are conveyed to the receiver (Figure 2.4). This rudimentary model not only is "accepted as one of the main seeds out of which Communication Studies has grown" (Fisk 1994: 6), but establishes the basic elements and parameters for future elaborations and developments. Although subsequent models, like those devised by George Gerbner (1956), B.H. Westley and M.S. MacLean (1957), and Roman Jakobson (1960), extend and elaborate Shannon and Weaver's initial concept, they retain the basic elements of senders and receivers connected by a medium that facilitates the transmission of messages.

CMC locates the computer in the intermediate position of channel or medium. As such, it occupies the position granted to other forms of communication technology (e.g., print, telephone, radio, television, etc.) and is comprehended as something through which human messages pass. This understanding of the machine as medium has been taken up and further elaborated in the work of Marshall McLuhan, the Canadian media theorist. For McLuhan, media – and the word encompasses a wide range of different technological devices, applying not just to the mechanisms of communication, like newspapers and radio, but to all kinds of tools and machines – are defined as "extensions of man." This is, of course, immediately evident in the title to what is considered one of his most influential publications, *Understanding Media: The Extensions of Man* (1995). And the examples employed throughout his book are now very familiar: the wheel is an extension of the foot, the telephone is an extension of the ear, and the television is an extension of the eye. Understood in this way, technical mechanisms have been defined as instruments or prostheses through which various human faculties come to be extended beyond their original capacity or capability.

Instrumental theory of technology   This intermediate position is also substantiated and justified by the traditional understanding of the proper role and function of the technological apparatus. According to Martin Heidegger's analysis in *The Question Concerning Technology* (1977), the assumed understanding of any kind of technology, whether it be the product of handicraft or industrialized manufacture, is that it is a means employed by human users for particular ends.

> We ask the question concerning technology when we ask what it is. Everyone knows the two statements that answer our question. One says: Technology is a means to an end. The other says: Technology is a human activity. The two definitions of technology belong together. For to posit ends and procure and utilize the means to them is a human activity. The manufacture and utilization of equipment, tools, and machines, the manufactured and used things themselves, and the needs and ends that they serve, all belong to what technology is. (1977: 4–5)

Heidegger terms this particular conceptualization "the instrumental definition" and indicates that it forms what is considered to be the "correct" understanding of any kind of technological contrivance. As Andrew Feenberg (1991: 5) summarizes it in the introduction to his *Critical Theory of Technology*: "The instrumentalist theory offers the most widely accepted view of technology. It is based on the commonsense idea that technologies are 'tools' standing ready to serve the purposes of users." And because a tool "is deemed 'neutral,' without valuative content of its own" (1991: 5), a technological instrument is evaluated not in and for itself, but on the basis of the particular employments that have been decided by a human user. This insight is succinctly summarized by the French theorist Jean-François Lyotard in *The Postmodern Condition*:

Technical devices originated as prosthetic aids for the human organs or as physiological systems whose function it is to receive data or condition the context. They follow a principle, and it is the principle of optimal performance: maximizing output (the information or modification obtained) and minimizing input (the energy expended in the process). Technology is therefore a game pertaining not to the true, the just, or the beautiful, etc., but to efficiency: a technical "move" is "good" when it does better and/or expends less energy than another. (1984: 44)

Lyotard's explanation begins by affirming the understanding of technology as an instrument, prosthesis, or extension of human faculties. Given this "fact," which is stated as if it were something that is beyond question, he proceeds to provide an explanation of the proper place of the machine in human endeavor. According to his analysis, a technological device, whether it be a corkscrew, a clock, or a computer, does not in and of itself participate in the important questions of truth, justice, or beauty. Technology, on this account, is simply and indisputably about efficiency. A particular technological innovation is considered "good" if and only if it proves to be a more effective means to accomplishing a desired end.

Normal science   This understanding of technology has been and remains largely unquestioned, because it constitutes what epistemologists (individuals who study knowledge) routinely call "normal science." The term "normal science" was introduced by the American philosopher Thomas Kuhn in his ground-breaking book *The Structure of Scientific Revolutions* to describe those undertakings that are guided by an established and accepted paradigm. Paradigms, according to Kuhn (1996: x), are "universally recognized scientific achievements that, for a time, provide model problems and solutions to a community of practitioners." Normal sciences, as Kuhn demonstrates, have distinct theoretical and practical advantages. Operating within the framework of an established paradigm provides students, researchers, and educators with a common foundation and accepted set of basic assumptions. This effectively puts an end to debates about fundamentals and allows researchers to concentrate their attention on problems defined by the discipline, instead of quibbling about competing methodological procedures or basic principles. For this reason, a paradigm provides coherent structure to a particular area of scientific research. It defines what constitutes a problem for the area of study, delimits the kind of questions that are considered to be appropriate and significant, and describes what research procedures and resulting evidence will qualify as acceptable.

When the computer is understood and examined as an instrument or medium facilitating human communication, research generally concentrates on either the quantity and quality of the messages that can be distributed by the system or the kinds of relationships established between the human senders and receivers through its particular form of mediation. Evidence of this can be found, as Kuhn (1996: 136) argues, in the contents of standard textbooks, which "address themselves to an already articulated body of problems, data and theory, most often to the particular set of paradigms to which the scientific community is committed at the time they are written." With few or no exceptions, textbooks in the discipline of Communication Studies, whether introductory or advanced, address the computer as a *medium* of human communication and seek to investigate the effect this technology has on the quantity and quality of human interactions and relationships. For Communication Studies, CMC has been considered "normal science."

2.2.2 The new normal

Despite widespread acceptance and remarkable success, the CMC model inevitably misses a crucial opportunity originally mobilized by Turing and explicitly identified by Cathcart and Gumpert (1985) and Chesebro and Bonsall (1989): the fact that computer technology is not limited to being a medium of human-to-human interpersonal communication but might also become and occupy the position of an active participant in communicative interactions with human users. This other opportunity – one which has remained in the margins of communication scholarship for several decades – is beginning to be increasingly important as we come face to face with new and emerging technology that challenges us to reconsider and respond to the computer as something more than a mere instrument of message transmission. Let's briefly consider three examples (subsequent chapters will delve into more detailed analyses).

Things that talk   Since the debut of ELIZA, there have been numerous advancements in chatbot design, and these devices now populate many of the online social spaces in which we live, work, and play. As a result of this proliferation, it is not uncommon for users to assume they are talking to another (human) person, when in fact they are just chatting up a chatbot. This was the case for Robert Epstein, a Harvard University PhD and former editor of *Psychology Today*, who fell in love and had a four-month online "affair" with a chatbot (Epstein 2007). This was possible not because the bot, which went by the name "Ivana," was somehow "intelligent" in a general sense, but because the bot's conversational behavior was, in the words of Reeves and Nass (1996: 22), "close enough to human to encourage social responses." And this approximation, as Miranda Mowbray (2002: 2) points out, is not necessarily "a feature of the sophistication of bot design, but of the low bandwidth communication of the online social space," where it is much easier to convincingly simulate a human agent.

Despite this knowledge – despite educated, well-informed experts like Epstein, who has openly admitted that "I know about such things and I should have certainly known better" (2007: 17) – these software implementations can have adverse effects on both the user and the online communities in which they operate. To make matters worse (or perhaps more interesting) the problem is not something that is unique to amorous interpersonal relationships. "The rise of social bots," as Andrea Peterson (2013: 1) accurately points out, "isn't just bad for love lives – it could have broader implications for our ability to trust the authenticity of nearly every interaction we have online." Case in point – national politics and democratic governance. In a study conducted during the 2016 US presidential campaign, Alessandro Bessi and Emilio Ferrara found that "the presence of social media bots can indeed negatively affect democratic political discussion rather than improving it, which in turn can potentially alter public opinion and endanger the integrity of the Presidential election" (2016: 1).

But who or what is responsible for the adverse outcomes in these circumstances? The instrumental theory typically leads such questions back to the designer of the application, and this is precisely how Epstein (2007: 17) made sense of his own experiences, blaming (or crediting) "a very smug, very anonymous computer programmer" who, he assumes, was located somewhere in Russia. But things are already more complicated. Epstein is, at least, partially responsible for "using" the bot and deciding to converse with it, and the online community in which he met Ivana is arguably responsible for permitting (perhaps even encouraging) such "deceptions" in the first place. For this reason, the assignment of culpability is not as simple as it might first appear to be. As Mowbray argues:

> [Interactions like this] show that a bot may cause harm to other users
> or to the community as a whole by the will of its programmers or other

users, but that it also may cause harm through nobody's fault because of the combination of circumstances involving some combination of its programming, the actions and mental or emotional states of human users who interact with it, behavior of other bots and of the environment, and the social economy of the community. (2002: 4)

Unlike artificial general intelligence (AGI), which would presumably occupy a subject position reasonably close to that of another human agent, these ostensibly mindless but very social things simply muddy the water (which is probably worse) by complicating and leaving undecided questions regarding who or what is doing the talking.

Things that have something to say In May 2015, National Public Radio (NPR) staged a rather informal but informative competition of human versus machine. In this twenty-first-century remake of that legendary race between John Henry and steam power, NPR reporter Scott Horsley went up against Automated Insights Wordsmith, a natural language generation (NLG) algorithm designed to analyze patterns in data and turn them into human readable narratives. The rules of the game were simple: "Both contenders waited for Denny's, the diner company, to come out with an earnings report. Once that was released, the stopwatch started. Both wrote a short radio story and got graded on speed and style" (Smith 2015). Wordsmith crossed the finish line in just two minutes with an accurate but rather utilitarian composition. Horsley's submission took longer to write – a full seven minutes – but was judged to be a more stylistic presentation of the data (see Table 2.1).

What this little experiment demonstrated is not what one might expect. It did not show that the machine is somehow better than or even just as good as the human reporter. Instead, it revealed how these programs are just good enough to begin seriously challenging human capabilities and displacing this kind of labor. In fact, when *Wired* magazine asked Kristian Hammond, co-founder of Narrative Science (Automated Insights' main competitor), to predict the percentage of news articles that would be written algorithmically within the next decade, his answer was a sobering 90 percent (Ford 2015: 85).

For students of communication, however, this demonstration also points to another, related issue, which is beginning to gather interest and momentum in studies of digital journalism and technical writing. Written text is typically understood as the product of someone – an author, reporter, writer – who has, it is assumed, something to say

Table 2.1: Side-by-side comparison of the radio story generated by Automated Insight's Wordsmith and that composed by Scott Horsley (Smith 2015).

Automated Insights (NLG algorithm)	Scott Horsley (NPR reporter)
Denny's Corporation on Monday reported first-quarter profit of 8.5 million dollars. The Spartanburg, South Carolina-based company said it had profit of 10 cents per share. The results beat Wall Street expectations. The average estimate of four analysts surveyed by Zacks Investment Research was for earnings of 9 cents per share. The restaurant operator posted revenue of $120.2 million in the period, also beating Street forecasts. Three analysts surveyed by Zacks expected $117.1 million. Denny's shares have risen nearly 6 percent since the beginning of the year. In the final minutes of trading on Monday, shares hit $10.90, a climb of 61 percent in the last 12 months.	Denny's Corporation notched a grand slam of its own in the first quarter, earning a better-than-expected ten cents a share, as restaurant sales jumped by more than 7 percent. Operating revenues topped $120 million. Adjusted net income jumped 36 percent to $8.7 million. Denny's is one of the nation's largest full-service restaurant chains. The growth in sales suggests consumers are opening their pocketbooks for pancakes, eggs, and hash browns. Earnings were also helped by lower costs for raw materials. Denny's results were also helped by the re-opening of the high-volume location inside the Las Vegas Casino Royale restaurant. After sales grew faster than expected in the first three months of the year, managers raised their sales forecast for the remainder of 2015.

or to communicate by way of the written document. It is clear, for instance, who "speaks" through the instrument of the text composed by the human reporter. It is Scott Horsley. He is responsible not just for writing the story but also for its formal style and content. If it is a well-written story, it is Horsley who gets the accolade. If it contains grammatical mistakes or factual inaccuracies, it is Horsley who is held accountable. And if we should want to know about what the reporter wrote and why, Horsley can presumably be consulted and will be able to respond to our query.

But what about the other story, the one from Automated Insights Wordsmith? Who or what speaks in a document that has been written – or assembled or generated (and the choice of verb, it turns out, matters here) – by an algorithm? Who or what is or can be held responsible for the writing? Who or what can respond on its behalf? Is it the corporation that manufactures and distributes the software? Is it the programmers at the corporation who were hired to write the program instructions? Is it the data to which the application had access? Is it the user of the device who set it up and directed it to work on the data? Or is it perhaps Wordsmith itself?

The problem, of course, is that these questions are not so easily resolved. It is not entirely clear who or what (if anything) speaks in and for this text. As Tal Montal and Zvi Reich have demonstrated in their study "I, Robot. You, Journalist. Who is the Author?" the development and implementation of "automated journalism" has resulted in "major discrepancies between the perceptions of authorship and crediting policy, the prevailing attribution regimes, and the scholarly literature" (2016: 1). This uncertainty regarding authorship and attribution opens up a significant "responsibility gap" that affects not only how we think about who or what communicates, but also how we understand and respond to questions concerning responsibility in the age of increasingly creative (and maybe even "expressive") machines.

Things that are more than things   In July 2014, the world got its first look at Jibo. Who or what is Jibo? That is an interesting and important question. In a promotional video that was designed to raise capital investment through pre-orders on Indiegogo, social robotics pioneer Cynthia Breazeal introduced Jibo with the following explanation: "This is your car. This is your house. This is your toothbrush. These are your things. But these [and the camera zooms into a family photograph] are the things that matter. And somewhere in between is this guy. Introducing Jibo, the world's first family robot" (Jibo 2014). Whether explicitly recognized as such or not, this promotional video leverages a crucial distinction that French theorist Jacques Derrida (2005: 80) calls the difference between "who" and "what." On the side of "what" we have those things that are mere instruments – our car, our house, and our toothbrush. According to the usual way of thinking, these things are mere instruments or tools that do not have any independent status whatsoever. We might worry about the impact that the car's emissions have on the environment (or perhaps stated more precisely, on the health and well-being of the other human beings who share this planet with us), but the car itself is not a socially significant subject. On the other side, there are, as the video describes it, "those things that matter." These are not things, strictly speaking, but the other persons who count as socially and morally significant Others. Unlike the car, the house, or the toothbrush, these Others have independent status and can be benefited or harmed by our decisions and actions.

Jibo, we are told, occupies a place that is situated somewhere in between what are mere things and those Others who really matter (Figure 2.5). Jibo is not, therefore, just another instrument, like the

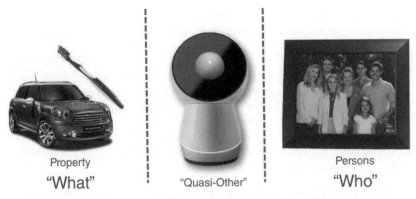

Property   Persons
"What"   "Quasi-Other"   "Who"

Figure 2.5   Jibo occupies an ambivalent position in between what are mere things (property) and those others who are persons

automobile or toothbrush. But he/she/it (and the choice of pronoun is not unimportant) is also not quite another member of the family pictured in the photograph. Jibo inhabits a place in between these two ontological categories. It is a kind of "quasi-other" (Ihde 1990: 107). This is, it should be noted, not unprecedented. We are already familiar with other entities that occupy a similar ambivalent social position, like the family dog. In fact animals, which, since the time of Descartes, have been the other of the machine (Gunkel 2012: 60), provide a good precedent for understanding the changing nature of things in the face of social robots, like Jibo. Kate Darling writes:

> Looking at state of the art technology, our robots are nowhere close to the intelligence and complexity of humans or animals, nor will they reach this stage in the near future. And yet, while it seems far-fetched for a robot's legal status to differ from that of a toaster, there is already a notable difference in how we interact with certain types of robotic objects. (2012: 1)

This occurs, Darling continues, because of our tendencies to anthropomorphize things by projecting into them cognitive capabilities, emotions, and motivations that do not necessarily exist in the mechanism per se. But it is this emotional reaction that necessitates new forms of obligation in the face of things. "Given that many people already feel strongly about state-of-the-art social robot 'abuse,' it may soon become more widely perceived as out of line with our social values to treat robotic companions in a way that we would not treat our pets" (2012: 1).

Jibo, and other social robots like it, are not science fiction. They are already, or will soon be, in our lives and in our homes. As Breazeal describes it:

> [A] sociable robot is able to communicate and interact with us, understand and even relate to us, in a personal way. It should be able to understand us and itself in social terms. We, in turn, should be able to understand it in the same social terms – to be able to relate to it and to empathize with it . . . In short, a sociable robot is socially intelligent in a human-like way, and interacting with it is like interacting with another person. (2002: 1)

In the face of these socially situated and interactive entities, we are going to have to decide whether they are mere things, like our car, our house, and our toothbrush; someone who matters, like another member of the family; or something altogether different that is situated in between the one and the other. In whatever way this comes to be decided, however, these things will undoubtedly challenge the way we typically distinguish between who is to be considered another social subject and what remains a mere instrument or tool.

2.3 Paradigm Shift

The three examples presented above introduce situations where the computer (or computational mechanism) seems to be something more than a medium or instrument of human message transfer. In these cases, as Turing had initially stipulated, the technology occupies, with varying degrees of success, the position of another subject with which (or "with whom") one communicates and interacts. These three examples confront the "normal science" of Communication Studies with some innovative challenges that do not quite fit the standard model of CMC. And this results in something of a crisis within the discipline and the way it typically deals with, explains, and makes sense of the role and function of computer technology in human communication.

Responses to challenges like this typically take one of two forms, which the Slovenian philosopher Slavoj Žižek (2008: vii) calls "Ptolemization" and "Copernican" revolution:

> When a discipline is in crisis, attempts are made to change or supplement its theses within the terms of its basic framework – a procedure one might call "Ptolemization" (since when data poured in which

clashed with Ptolemy's earth-centered astronomy, his partisans introduced additional complications to account for the anomalies). But the
true "Copernican" revolution takes place when, instead of just adding
complications and changing minor premises, the basic framework itself
undergoes a transformation.

Ptolemization indicates efforts to revise an existing paradigm by
introducing modifications and complications, like the epicycles that
were added to the Ptolemaic model of the solar system to account
for seemingly aberrant observational data, in an effort to ensure
the continued functioning and success of the prevailing "normal
science." Copernican revolution, on the contrary, designates not
minor adjustments or revisions in the prevailing system of knowledge
but a complete reconfiguration or transformation of its basic framework. The name, of course, comes from Nicolaus Copernicus, whose
heliocentric model of the solar system provides, for Kuhn and others,
the prototype of scientific revolution, insofar as it not only introduced
a new framework or model of astronomy but literally inverted or
overturned the Ptolemaic system by moving the sun, which had been
located on the periphery, to the center of the system.

In responding to recent technological innovations like chatbots
and digital assistants, computational creativity, and social robots, we
can try and have tried various kinds of Ptolemization strategies. We
have, in other words, sought to modify the CMC model to accommodate these recent innovations. Doing so, however, often requires
contorting the model in ways that make it increasingly complex and
cumbersome. One can, for instance, try to locate the person behind
the chatbot and explain things by way of the standard instrumentalist
way of thinking. But this explanation gets exceedingly complicated,
resulting in more questions than answers. A good illustration of this
can be found in *Wired*'s interview with Marshall McLuhan. If you do
not know the publication, *Wired* is to Silicon Valley what the *Wall
Street Journal* is to Wall Street. When the magazine began publication, the editors named Marshall McLuhan their "patron saint," a
gesture that sought to recognize the importance of McLuhan's work
for digital media and the Internet. In January 1996 (ancient history
in terms of Internet time), the magazine published a rather surprising interview with their "patron saint." It was surprising because,
at the time it was conducted, McLuhan had been dead for more
than a decade. Here's how it happened, as explained in the article's
introduction: "About a year ago, someone calling himself Marshall
McLuhan began posting anonymously on a popular mailing list

called Zone (zone@wired.com). Gary Wolf began a correspondence with the poster via a chain of anonymous remailers" (Wolf 1996: 1).

So, with whom or with what was Wolf interacting? Was this "virtual McLuhan" actually the ghost of Marshall McLuhan, an imposter engaging in a little role-playing, or an automated chatbot programmed with, as Wolf (1996: 1) described it, "an eerie command of McLuhan's life and inimitable perspective"? Technically, there is no way to answer this question. The interviewer was limited to what had appeared online and, because the exchange took place through the instrumentality of anonymous remailers, was unable to get behind the screen to ascertain the real thing as such. In the face of this dilemma, the editors of *Wired* did something that was, from the perspective of accepted journalistic practices, either "embarrassingly wrongheaded and pretentious" (Morrison 2006: 5) or incredibly innovative and inventive. Instead of writing off the whole affair as ultimately unverifiable, they decided to publish the interview as given, leaving the question "Who is doing the talking?" open-ended and unresolved.

Instead of trying to fit these anomalies to the existing model – an effort that is, as illustrated in the *Wired* interview, always a bit odd and somewhat ill-fitting – the alternative is to change the model. This is what Kuhn had called a paradigm shift. And we already have a clue to an alternative in Cathcart and Gumpert's essay from 1985. In reframing or repositioning the computer according to this other way of thinking, all kinds of things change, not the least of which is our understanding of who, or what, qualifies as a legitimate subject of communication. That is, who or what we are talking to, and who or what is actually doing the talking. For Norbert Wiener, the progenitor of the science of cybernetics, these developments fundamentally alter the social landscape:

> It is the thesis of this book [*The Human Use of Human Beings*] that society can only be understood through a study of the messages and the communication facilities which belong to it; and that in the future development of these messages and communication facilities, messages between man and machines, between machines and man, and between machine and machine, are destined to play an ever-increasing part. (1988, 16)

In the social relationships of the not too-distant future (and we need to recall that Wiener initially wrote and published these words in 1950, the same year as Turing's influential paper), computer technology will no longer comprise an instrument or medium through which human users communicate with each other. Instead, it will occupy the position of another social actor with whom one communicates and interacts. In coming to occupy this other position, however, we inevitably run up against and encounter fundamental questions – questions that not only could not be articulated within the context of the previous CMC paradigm, but, if they had been articulated, would have been, from that perspective, considered inappropriate and even nonsense. What, for example, is our responsibility in the face of this Other – an Other who is otherwise than another human entity? How do or should we respond to this other form of socially significant Otherness? How will or should this machinic Other respond to us? Although these questions appear to open onto what many would consider to be the realm of science fiction, they are already part of our social reality. And it is time Communication Studies (and many of the other disciplines in the arts, humanities, and social sciences) take seriously the impact and significance of this transformation.

2.4 Conclusion/Summary

From what we have seen in this chapter, the defining condition of machine intelligence (beginning with Alan Turing's influential 1950 essay on the subject) has been communication, and human-level interpersonal communication in particular. Despite this, the field of Communication Studies has largely ignored this opportunity, and this is the case even if researchers in the field – like Cathcart and Gumpert and Chesebro and Bonsall – explicitly called it out as early as the mid-1980s. Instead of taking up this challenge, Communication Studies (for better or worse) sought to fit computer technology to its existing conceptual framework (or paradigm) and formalized this decision with the institution (and institutionalization) of the CMC model. And it clearly worked. CMC has proven to be useful, and it has been operational for close to forty years. But at this point in time – during the first several decades of the twenty-first century – the model is beginning to show signs of weakness, stress, and even failure in the face of new challenges coming from innovations in AI and robotics. We are not just talking through computers to each other; we are also talking to computers as if they were an Other. Teachers, researchers, and students therefore have a unique opportunity. We can either continue to uphold the CMC paradigm and leave these develop-ments in AI and robots to others – like computational linguists, behavioral scientists, computer scientists, etc. – or we can recalibrate and work to transform communication, return to and capitalize on the original insights provided by Cathcart and Gumpert and Chesebro and Bonsall, and begin to investigate AI as a communication science and recognize Communication Studies as a significant player in the science and engineering of AI.

Summary of Key Points

- From the beginning, AI has been a communication science. In his agenda-setting paper on the subject, Alan Turing replaced the question "Can machines think?" with a demonstration of communicative ability. If a machine can simulate a human being in interpersonal conversational interactions, then it should be considered intelligent.
- Design, development, and demonstration of machines capable of achieving this benchmark – passing or coming close to passing the Turing Test – have been available since Joseph Weizenbaum's ELIZA chatbot and have only gotten more capable and sophisticated since that time.
- Responding to these innovations will necessitate research and development in communication, but doing so will also require a major conceptual overhaul or paradigm shift in the models and methods of communication studies. Communication Studies, in other words, has a lot to contribute to the science and engineering of AI, but only if the field innovates beyond the restrictive CMC paradigm and develops new frameworks that can accommodate other kinds of communicative subjects.

3

Basic Concepts and Terminology

Key Aims/Objectives

- To define the word and the concept "algorithm" and explain how it relates to the science and engineering practice of AI.
- To understand the difference between the two main methods for developing AI applications – symbolic reasoning or "good old fashioned AI" (GOFAI) and artificial neural networks (ANN), or what is also called connectionism – that support machine-learning capabilities.
- To explain in detail the fundamental principles, basic operations, and technical exigencies of both GOFAI and ANN approaches to developing AI applications.
- To appreciate the important difference between two conceptual pairs that are utilized within the field of AI: (1) artificial general intelligence (AGI) vs. narrow AI; (2) strong AI vs. weak AI.

Introduction

Before getting into detailed investigations of specific systems and applications, we need to get a handle on fundamentals. In other words, we need to do some basic work in the science and engineering of AI in order to make sense of and understand some of the basic concepts and terminology. Toward this end, this chapter introduces and explains a number of pivotal concepts and the related vocabulary necessary for understanding the technology and its development. The goal of the chapter is to assist students (who are neither AI experts nor computer science majors) to learn how to "talk the talk" and "walk the walk" – meaning that we want not only to cultivate facility with the specialized language of the field, but also to develop an understanding of the ideas, concepts, and standard practices that are identified and talked about with this terminology.

3.1 Algorithm

As you begin to engage with and investigate AI, one term you are likely to encounter is "algorithm." According to the dictionary, an algorithm is a process or set of rules to be followed in calculations or other problem-solving operations. Although this definition is accurate, it probably tells you very little about what an algorithm actually is, why it is called that, and what it has to do with artificial intelligence. So let's sort this out.

3.1.1 Word origins and usage

The word "algorithm" is derived from the name of an influential Persian mathematician – Muhammad ibn Musa al-Khwarizmi – who lived and worked in the royal court of Bagdad during the ninth century AD. Al-Khwarizmi is credited with numerous advancements in mathematics including the development of algebra. Around the year AD 825, he wrote an influential book on Hindu–Arabic numbers, which is the decimal numbering system that is currently used today. The book exerted considerable influence in medieval Europe by way of a twelfth-century Latin translation, which was titled *Algoritmi de numero Indorum*. In English, this title simply means "Algoritmi on the Numbers of the Indians," where the word "Algoritmi" is the Latinized form of Al-Khwarizmi's last name. Over time, the term "algoritmi" or "algorithm" became associated with a particular method of mathematical problem-solving.

An algorithm can be generally described as "any well-defined procedure that takes some value, or set of values, as input and produces some value, or set of values, as output. An algorithm is thus a sequence of steps that transform the input into the output" (modified version derived from Cormen et al. 2009: 5). Let's sort this out and make it more accessible by looking at two examples, one mathematical and one not-so mathematical, and we will start with the latter. Strictly speaking, a recipe is an algorithm. You start with a number of different ingredients as input: flour, sugar, eggs, butter, baking powder, etc. This input is processed by following a series of step-by-step instructions, like you see here:

1 Heat the oven to 350°F.
2 Sift together the flour and baking powder. Set aside.
3 Prepare the baking pan by rubbing the bottom and sides of the pan with a little butter or shortening.
4 Beat the butter and sugar until fluffy and light.
5 Add the eggs.
6 Add the flour and baking powder mixture.
7 Pour the batter into the baking pan and smooth the top with a spatula.
8 Bake for 25 to 30 minutes.

If the steps are followed correctly and in the designated order, the input (the ingredients) will be transformed into the desired output, which in this particular case is a cake.

The same general idea applies to mathematical computations, like finding the greatest common divisor of two numbers. This is called Euclid's Algorithm, after the Greek mathematician who first described it in 800 BC. The algorithm – a term that was not utilized by Euclid, who lived and worked well over a thousand years before al-Khwarizmi – can be represented as a flowchart diagram (Figure 3.1). It takes two numbers, represented by the variables A and B, as its input (step 1) and processes these numbers by following a series of finite steps. This begins (step 2) by testing whether the value assigned to variable B is 0. If it is 0, then we jump down the flowchart and print out the value that had been assigned to variable A as the output (step 8). If, however, the value of B is something other than 0, then we test whether the numeric value assigned to variable B is greater than the value that had been assigned to A (step 3). The results of this test, which is either "yes" (B is greater than A) or "no" (B is not greater than A), leads to two different sets of subsequent steps (step 4 or step 6). If one follows all the steps correctly and in order, then the algorithm will successfully transform the input (the numeric values that had been assigned to the variables A and B) into the desired output, which in this case will be the greatest common divisor, or that one number that can divide both input numbers without leaving a remainder.

We can make the process automatically computable by developing a version of the algorithm written in coded instructions that can be run or executed on a computer. Because there are a number of different computer languages, the exact coding will be different

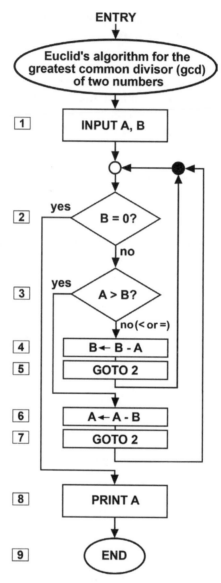

Figure 3.1   Flowchart representation of Euclid's Algorithm

depending on the language that is employed. Here is one version using an object-oriented language (Figure 3.2).

But algorithms implemented in code are not restricted to mathematical processes. We can also write algorithms to process other

```
//Euclid's algorithm for greatest common divisor
integer euclidAlgorithm (int A, int B){
    A=Math.abs(A);
    B=Math.abs(B);
    while (B!=0){
        if (A>B) A=A-B;
        else B=B-A;
    }
    return A;
}
```

Figure 3.2   Euclid's Algorithm implemented in object-oriented code

kinds of input. ELIZA (see Chapter 2), for instance, is an algorithm for processing natural language. The application takes a series of words as input. It processes this input by applying a number of transformation steps that have been written in the coded instructions. And it generates output in the form of human readable sentences and questions. If you did the first maker exercise – the simplified DIY ELIZA – you have already (even if you did not know it at the time) written your own natural language processing algorithm.

3.1.2 Algorithm or AI?

Even though the first example – a recipe for a making a cake – could be accurately characterized and described as an algorithm, it is not common to refer to recipes as "food algorithms" or to title cookbooks *Algorithms for the Kitchen* (Walmsley 2012: 42), and doing so is likely to be met with puzzled looks and bemused confusion. This is because "algorithm" (and the way it is currently utilized across disciplines) is a word that is usually restricted to computational operations. For this reason, the definition of algorithm, in both the textbooks and dictionaries, is more properly stated like this: "An algorithm is any well-defined *computational* procedure that takes some value, or set of values, as input and produces some value, or set of values, as output. An algorithm is thus a sequence of *computational* steps that transform the input into the output" (Cormen et al. 2009: 5; emphasis added). The important item here is the addition of the word "computational," which describes not only mathematical operations but also any process that can be modeled with mathematical logic. For this reason, an algorithm can be specified using either standard human language (like the description of Euclid's Algorithm that was provided above), in the design of hardware like a logic circuit, or more often than not in the coded instructions of a computer application or program.

Given this characterization, one might be tempted to conclude that every algorithm is AI and every AI is algorithmic. But this statement is only half correct (and even then not without some controversy and debate). It is the second half that is accurate. To date, the vast majority of effort in both science and engineering practice has sought to implement AI through developing software instructions to be run on computers, that is, by writing algorithms. It is the first part – "every algorithm is AI" – that is incorrect or inaccurate. Instead of trying to explain this with theory and abstractions, let's come at it by way of some very practical, real-world examples.

Consider two of Google's most popular services: Search and Translate. The former is not and has never really been considered AI (even if Google has increasingly applied AI techniques and technologies to support its search algorithm). Taking a word or phrase as input, searching through a database or index to find an exact or even approximate match, and displaying the results of that process is a rather mechanical and repetitive process that appears to be well suited to the information processing capabilities of the digital computer. In other words, simply matching words (or phrases) does not appear to be a task that requires much cognitive effort or intelligence.

Translating between human languages, however, is widely considered AI and has been since at least the time of the Dartmouth summer seminar, if not before (see Chapter 4). Taking a sequence of English words as input and then being able to convert them into a properly rendered German translation (for example) is something that is assumed to involve considerable intellectual skill and not able to be resolved with simple word search and matching procedures. Translation, in other words, involves more than correlating English words with German words and making replacements. A good translation is not just word-for-word transposition but the carrying over (the literal meaning of the word "trans-late") of the meaning that is expressed in the English sentence into a recognizable German statement that says approximately the same thing.

Even though these popular applications are both algorithms – or, what is probably a more accurate description, an ensemble of interoperating algorithms where the output of one provides the input for one or more of the others – one is widely considered to be AI, while the other generally is not. So what accounts for this difference? Why is Search considered to be "just an algorithm," while Translate has been routinely identified as AI? The difference is not – at least not primarily – technological. Both applications take natural language input, process that input by performing a number of transformations, and generate output that is understandable by human users. The difference is behavioral. If you remember back to Chapter 1, AI is defined not in terms of some special technological features but by the perception of behaviors that are exhibited by the system. As John McCarthy famously wrote: "[T]he artificial intelligence problem is taken to be that of making a machine behave in ways that would be called intelligent if a human were so behaving" (quoted in Kaplan 2016: 1). In other words, something is considered AI because it does an operation (provides output from a given set of input) that would be called "intelligent" if it had been performed by a human being.

The big problem here, as we have already discussed in the introduction, is that this difference is neither static nor rigorously formulated. According to what has been called the "AI effect," some algorithmic implementations that were at one time defined as intelligent behavior eventually become "demoted" to just another computer application. Playing championship-level chess, for example, had been considered the kind of behavior that required human-level intelligence. But after IBM's Deep Blue successfully defeated Gary Kasparov in 1997, chess-playing algorithms became just another computer application and were no longer considered the kind of behavior that would require intelligence. Furthermore, the difference can be deliberately manipulated in an effort to control how the technology is situated and understood.

Consider what is happening in the field of journalism and technical writing. We now have algorithms, like Narrative Science's Quill and Automated Insights's Wordsmith, that are capable of generating or composing (and the choice of verb is already a crucial decision about this matter) original stories for publication with little or no human involvement. In some cases, this has been called AI, because writing an original story is determined to be one of those behaviors that is the product of intelligence. Narrative Science (2018), for example, describes Quill as "AI that automatically communicates relevant information at scale." Calling Quill "AI" may be an accurate description of the technology, but it is also a clever marketing decision – one that connects the Quill product to the hopes and dreams that have been developed in both science fiction and science fact around the term and concept "AI."

In other situations, however, the technology has been characterized less dramatically as an NLG application. According to Automated

Insights (2018), "Wordsmith is the natural language generation platform that transforms your data into insightful narratives." Whereas Quill is intentionally described as AI, Wordsmith is characterized as an NLG platform, and one would be hard pressed to find the term AI applied to the Wordsmith product in any of the official literature. Again, this formulation is as much a description of technological function as it is a marketing strategy. AI can be – again, due to its presentations in popular culture – frightening, especially at a time when there is increased talk about robots replacing human workers (see Chapter 8). Calling Wordsmith an "NLG platform" can have the effect of sounding less threatening then calling it AI.

A similar decision concerning what we call things is evident in journalism education and professional studies, where researchers have tended to use the term "algorithmic journalism" as opposed to something like "AI journalism" or "automated journalism." This choice of terminology (which is, we should note, still evolving insofar as the field is relatively new and terms are being invented and reinvented) is not accidental. Calling it "algorithmic journalism" gives the impression that the application is not going to replace (or even threaten to replace) human intellectual labor but is just another computerized tool to be used by skilled reporters. Again, there is some marketing and politics at play in how terms like "AI" and "algorithm" are used and this will, especially as it applies to the issue of technological unemployment, be addressed in subsequent chapters (see Chapter 8, in particular). For now, what is important to note and keep in mind as we move forward is the following: (1) AI, as developed and implemented in digital technology, is algorithmic; (2) but not all algorithms implemented on the computer would be designated or recognized as AI; and (3) the difference between these two is subject to the "AI effect," meaning that it is, has been, and probably will remain in flux.

3.2 Competing Methods

At the time of the Dartmouth summer seminar, two general methods were recognized as equally valid approaches for developing AI, and the proposal made explicit mention of both "manipulating words according to rules of reasoning and rules of conjecture" and "neuron nets." But, as Hubert and Stuart Dreyfus (1988: 15–16) point out, the fork in the road actually predated the summer seminar by several years:

In the early 1950s, as calculating machines were coming into their own, a few pioneer thinkers began to realize that digital computers could be more than number crunchers. At that point two opposed visions of what computers could be, each with its correlated research program, emerged and struggled for recognition. One faction saw computers as a system for manipulating mental symbols; the other, as a medium for modeling the brain. One sought to use computers to instantiate a formal representation of the world; the other, to simulate the interactions of neurons. One took problem solving as its paradigm of intelligence; the other, learning. One utilized logic; the other, statistics. One school was the heir to the rationalist, reductionist tradition in philosophy; the other viewed itself as idealized, holistic neuroscience.

What Dreyfus and Dreyfus identify here are two different theories or perspectives concerning the digital computer and its operations. In this section, we will investigate the advantages and disadvantages of both approaches by considering their history, their relative successes and limitations, and the underlying assumptions about cognition and intelligence that each one operationalizes.

3.2.1 Symbol manipulation

This method is based on mathematical logic and the hypothesis that intelligence consists in the manipulation of symbols. The concept is attributed to Alan Newell and Herbert Simon, who initially introduced it in terms of something they called "the physical symbol system hypothesis" (PSSH):

> A physical symbol system has the necessary and sufficient means for general intelligent action. By "necessary" we mean that any system that exhibits general intelligence will prove upon analysis to be a physical symbol system. By "sufficient" we mean that any physical symbol system of sufficient size can be organized further to exhibit general intelligence. (1976: 116)

What this means is that "thinking" (or "intelligence") is presumed to be little more than rule-based symbol manipulation. This hypothesis has two important consequences, as Nilsson (2007: 1) explains. First, human intelligence is a kind of symbol manipulation, because symbol manipulation is a *necessary* condition for intelligence. Second, "[c]omputers, when we provide them with the appropriate symbol-processing programs, will be capable of intelligent action," because symbol manipulation is *sufficient* for intelligence.

This way of thinking about thinking has deep philosophical roots. It is ultimately grounded in the logic of Aristotle, but finds considerable traction during the modern era in the work of René Descartes (1596–1650), Thomas Hobbes (1588–1679), and Gottfried Wilhelm Leibniz (1646–1716). "Descartes," as Dreyfus and Dreyfus (1988: 17) explain, "had already assumed that all understanding consisted of forming and manipulating appropriate representations, that these representations could be analyzed into primitive elements (*naturas simplices*), and that all phenomena could be understood as complex combinations of these simple elements." Hobbes took this one step further, arguing that all thinking could be entirely reduced to a process of calculation or what he called "reckoning": "When a man *reasons*, he does nothing else but conceive a sum total from *addition* of parcels, or conceive a remainder from *subtraction* of one sum from another . . . For REASON, in this sense, is nothing but *reckoning* (that is, adding and subtracting) of the consequences of general names agreed upon for the *marking* and *signifying* of our thoughts" (1994: 22–3). But it is with Leibniz, the German philosopher and mathematician, that this "computational theory of mind" (as it is now called) reached its apex. Leibniz sought to devise not only a universal symbol system – the *characteristica universalis* (an idea that will be essential to the concept of machine translation, see Chapter 4) – but also a method of logical reasoning, a *calculus ratiocinator* where all dispute and debate in human endeavor could be resolved through the simple act of calculation.

3.2.2 Neural networks

The other approach, what the Dartmouth proposal called "neuron nets," comes not from philosophical abstraction concerning the logical process of thinking but from observations of the physical characteristics and operations of the brain, specifically the neuron. This alternative was inspired by three intersecting innovations.

(1) *Artificial neuron.* In 1943, Warren McCulloch and Walter Pitts theorized that the activity of the neuron could be explained in terms of a logic function, and they devised a mathematical model that described the neuron as a "threshold logic device." According to this simplified formalization, a neuron takes in different inputs. It adds up these signals, and if the sum exceeds some predetermined threshold (T), it "fires." In other words, if the threshold condition is met, the neuron produces the output 1; if not, it results in 0 (Figure 3.3).

In their now famous scientific paper – "A Logical Calculus of Ideas Immanent in Nervous Activity" – McCulloch and Pitts demon-

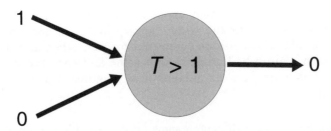

**Figure 3.3   Graphical representation of the McCulloch–Pitts
artificial neuron**

strated that this computational model could explain how networks of
interconnected neurons, like your brain, encode logical propositions
or statements, like the logical AND function, which requires both
inputs into the neuron to be true (that is, each input has the value 1 in
order to produce a true outcome, e.g., output with the value 1). At the
time that they conducted and published this research, they were not
thinking of implementing this computational model on a computer.
In 1943, electronic digital computers were still under development
in top-secret government laboratories and not something that would
have been widely available to university researchers. Consequently,
McCulloch and Pitts were more interested in using this mathematical
model as a way to understand the operations of the brain and to treat
psychiatric disorders.

(2) *Learning.* In 1949, Donald Hebb explained how networks of
biological neurons learn. "When an axon of cell A is near enough to
excite a cell B and repeatedly or persistently takes part in firing it,
some growth process or metabolic change takes place in one or both
cells such that A's efficiency, as one of the cells firing B, is increased"
(1949: 62). This insight, something that is now called Hebb's Rule,
describes (a) how the connection between two biological neurons
comes to be strengthened when they fire together, and (b) how this
"synaptic plasticity" facilitates and accounts for the operations of
memory and learning. For the artificial neuron, this meant that the
mathematical model of McCulloch and Pitts had to be modified by
applying weighted values – numerical multipliers – to each of the
input connections so that the value of the inputs could be adjusted
to be either "weaker" or "stronger" relative to the initial input value.

(3) *Perceptron.* All of this comes together in 1958 with the "perceptron," a computer implementation of the McCulloch–Pitts artificial
neuron developed by a Cornell University computer scientist named
Frank Rosenblatt. The perceptron was initially designed to be a

pattern-recognition algorithm applied to images (hence the name, which is derived from the word "perception"). It consisted of a number of artificial neurons connected to each other in a network where each neuron had an activation value and each synaptic connection, following the work of Hebb, was weighted. Ethem Alpaydin explains:

> During operation, each neuron sums up the activations from all the neurons that make a synapse with it, weighted by their synaptic weights, and if the total activation is larger than a threshold, the neuron fires and its output corresponds to the value of this activation; otherwise the neuron is silent. If the neuron fires, it sends its activation value in turn down to all the neurons with which it makes a synapse. (2016: 87)

This alternative methodology – something now called *artificial neural networks* (ANN), *parallel distributed processing*, or *connectionism* – provides for a distinctly different way of developing AI algorithms, one that operates on statistical principles rather than symbolic logic (Figure 3.4). "In this *connectionist* approach to AI," as Paul Smolensky (1990: 306) explains, "intelligence is an *emergent* property of the network's processing; each individual processor [artificial neuron]

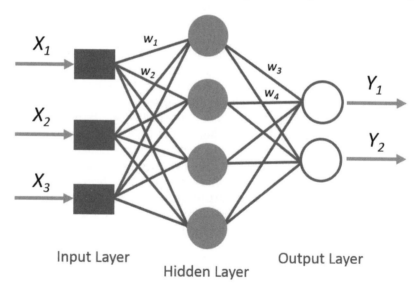

Figure 3.4 Graphical representation of an artificial neural network with weighted connections (w) between layers of interacting neurons

has no intelligence, and the messages they exchange [the synaptic connections] – real numbers – participate only in very simple numerical operations." But it works. Data propagated through the network produce a pattern of activations in the interconnected artificial neurons that eventually result in some output. And by progressively adjusting the weighed connections between the neurons in the network, the system can be adjusted or "tuned" to exhibit different kinds of output behavior. This is what is called "machine learning." Consequently, the rules by which input is transformed into output are not specified as distinct (and static) logical steps applied to the input data; instead, the network evolves the transformation rules. Thus the "intelligence" that is exhibited by the network is an emergent property.

3.2.3 Unequal distribution

Although both methods were in play at the time of the Dartmouth summer seminar and pursued with equal effort and funding opportunities in the years that followed, connectionism all but disappeared from the field by the mid-1960s. This was due to both exaggerated claims made by supports of neural network AI and criticisms leveled against it by opponents. On the one hand, Rosenblatt did not do himself or the perceptron any favors when it came to publicity. Although Rosenblatt's own achievements were limited to an extremely basic image-recognition algorithm, he (in)famously made the following prediction in a 1958 story published in the *New York Times*: "Perceptrons might be fired to the planets as mechanical space explorers . . . the machine would be the first device to think as the human brain . . . in principle it would be possible to build brains that could reproduce themselves on an assembly line and which would be conscious of their existence" (quoted in Kaplan 2016: 33).

On the other hand, and partially in response to persistent inabilities to achieve anything close to what Rosenblatt and others had predicted, there were vocal critics of connectionist architecture, most famously Marvin Minsky and Seymour Papert. Their book, *Perceptrons: An Introduction to Computational Geometry* (1969), all but ended research and development in connectionism. Here is how Dreyfus and Dreyfus explained it:

> Everyone who knows the history of the field will be able to point to the proximal cause. About 1965, Minsky and Papert, who were running a laboratory at MIT dedicated to the symbol-manipulation approach and therefore competing for support with the perceptron projects, began

circulating drafts of a book attacking the idea of the perceptron. In the book they made clear their scientific position: "Perceptrons have been widely publicized as 'pattern recognition' or 'learning' machines and as such have been discussed in a large number of books, journal articles, and voluminous 'reports.' Most of this writing . . . is without scientific value." (1988: 21)

Although Minsky and Papert's criticism was largely focused on single layer perceptrons and therefore not entirely sensitive to the complexity and capabilities of multilayer systems, their book pretty much killed off interest in and funding for connectionist machine-learning research projects, ensuring that the symbol-manipulation approach became (for better or worse) "the only game in town" (Dreyfus and Dreyfus 1988: 21). This is precisely why, some twenty years later, Paul Haugeland (1989: 112) dubbed it "good old fashioned AI" (GOFAI), because it was the only way of doing things for close to two decades.

This exclusivity begins to change in 1986, with the publication of an influential set of books that has since been called "the connectionist bible" – *Parallel Distributed Processing: Explorations in the Microstructure of Cognition* (McClelland et al. 1986; Rumelhart et al. 1986). "Despite its high retail price and mammoth size," as Joel Walmsley (2012: 89) explains, "this enormously influential collection sold out its first printing with advance orders even before it had been published: neural networks were back on the map."

There are a number of reasons for the reemergence of connectionism at this particular time. First, there were remarkable increases in computing power. The perceptron of Rosenblatt was implemented on a large, expensive, and relatively slow mainframe. By 1986, small and agile mini- and microcomputers were becoming widely available. Second, there had been disappointments and significant setbacks with applying GOFAI methods to real-world challenges, like image-recognition. Despite valiant efforts, these tasks proved to be too difficult to encode in step-by-step instructions. Third, there was a much larger amount of digital data available and easily accessible for training neural networks, mainly due to an increase in electronically stored information on the Internet. This proliferation in data is the beginning of what we now call "big data." For these reasons, much of the recent innovation in AI development – like DeepMind's AlphaGo, Google Translate, and Facebook's facial-recognition system – are built on and powered by machine-learning neural networks.

3.3 How Things Work

From what we have seen so far, there are important and fundamental differences in the two methods that have been employed to develop AI algorithms. But how exactly does each one work? Typically, answers to this question involve a rather long detour through mathematical logic and statistics. For this reason, it is standard practice to see "explanations" of neural networks that look like this:

$$O_k = \frac{1}{1+e^{-\sum_{j=1}^{3}\left(w_{j,k} \cdot \frac{1}{1+e^{-\sum_{i=1}^{3}(w_{i,j} \cdot x_i)}}\right)}}$$

This equation represents the mathematical model of a simple three-layer neural network with three nodes in each layer (Rashid 2016: 83). Unless you are already familiar with this mode of mathematical notation and concepts in statics, an algebraic formalization like this will probably mean little or nothing. So rather than approach things from this abstract and rather formal perspective, we can proceed along a more intuitive path and get at the question by considering a concrete example. Toward this end, we will consider two methods for developing a simple temperature conversion algorithm that takes degrees Fahrenheit as input and transforms this data into degrees Celsius as the output. The first version will employ a classic GOFAI or symbol-manipulation approach; the second will use a neural network trained on a small set of temperature data (see Maker Exercise 3 to try it for yourself).

3.3.1 GOFAI approach

As you might recall, from either high school math or one of your gen ed requirements, the standard equation for calculating the conversion of degrees Fahrenheit to Celsius looks like this:

$$C = (F - 32) * 5/9$$

It is possible to write this formula in computer code to make the transformation on input data. But let's say, for the sake of argument, that you do not know the conversion equation and only have access to a handful of actual temperature associations:

Fahrenheit	Celsius
32	0
50	10
99	38

In this case, a symbol-manipulation approach to writing a conversion algorithm would proceed by working through a sequence of conditional statements that specify transformations for each temperature value. Conditional statements are logical expressions that facilitate simple decision-making. We work with these kinds of statements everyday: "If it is raining, take your umbrella." "If you are standing, sit down." "If it is 12 noon, eat lunch." These statements are called "conditional," because the first part of the sentence, i.e. "If it is raining . . .," asks about or tests for a particular condition or situation, e.g., whether it is raining or not. The second part, ". . . take your umbrella," is activated or operationalized, if the initial condition is valid or true. The conditional statement is one of the fundamental elements of GOFAI algorithms, and it can be written like this:

if (r) u

In this case, "r" is a symbol or variable that means "It is raining," and "u" is a symbol or variable that represents "take your umbrella." But what if it is not raining? In that case – when the initial condition is not valid – we can specify a different result or output:

if (r) u
else !u

This second statement codes for two possible outcomes. If it is raining (r), then take your umbrella (u). But if it is not raining (else), then do not take your umbrella (!u), where the exclamation point indicates negation or "not."

Following this basic approach, we can compose a temperature conversion algorithm by putting together a sequence of conditional statements that respond to a numeric input:

```
if (TempF == 32) TempC = 0;
else if (TempF == 50) TempC = 10;
else if (TempF == 99) TempC = 38;
else TempC = "Don't Know";
```

The first line tests whether the input value (TempF) is 32 or not. If it is 32, then the output value of degrees Celsius (TempC) is set to the value 0. (Note: The double "==" sign tests whether a particular variable, like TempF, has a stated value, like 32. The single "=" sign is an "assignment operator" that assigns a value, like 0, to a particular variable, like TempC.) If this first case is not valid, then move to the next line, which tests whether the input value (TempF) is equivalent to 50 or not. If it is, then the output value of degrees Celsius (TempC) is 10. If not, then move to the next line, which tests whether the input value (TempF) is 99. If it is, then the output value is 38. If none of these three conditions is valid, then move to the last line, which says "Don't know" and covers all other input temperature values for TempF.

Obviously, this is a rather limited (and, as a result, somewhat unimpressive) algorithm insofar as it only "knows" three temperature conversions. And it only "knows" these three because the individual human being writing the code already has access to this information and is able to encode this knowledge in the symbols that comprise the set of logical instructions. If we wanted to expand the algorithm's capabilities, we can either add more lines of code that test for other known temperature conditions (assuming that we have access to this data) or we can generate approximate conversions for those temperatures that fall in between the three that we already do know. Let's work with the latter by adding two conditional statements that can accommodate the in-between cases:

```
if (TempF == 32) TempC = 0;
else if (TempF > 32 AND TempF < 50) TempC = 4;
else if (TempF == 50) TempC = 10;
else if (TempF > 50 AND TempF < 99) TempC = 21;
else if (TempF == 99) TempC = 38;
else TempC = "Don't Know";
```

Here we have simply inserted two lines to cover temperatures that are, in the first case, between 33 and 49, and, in the second case, between 51 and 98. These conditional statements are written using the greater-than and less-than operators to test whether the value of the input (TempF) is greater-than 32 *and* less-than 50. If this stated condition is valid – or "returns true" – then the value assigned to the output variable TempC is 4. Although this second version is an improvement over the first one, it is still rather imprecise and not entirely serviceable for actual use. If we wanted to make this temperature conversion algorithm more robust, we would need to encode additional conversion steps, which would require adding more lines of code.

There is a technical term for this kind of "close enough even if not perfect" way of proceeding. It is called *heuristics*. The word "heuristic," which comes from an ancient Greek word meaning "find" or "discover," identifies a technique for finding an approximate solution to a problem that either cannot be solved or would take too much time and energy to solve exactly. It is, in other words, a way of trading computational completeness, accuracy, or precision for speed of execution or numbers of lines of coded instructions. In effect, the GOFAI temperature conversion algorithm we just considered produces acceptable results with a minimal amount of processing time. It is not absolutely perfect, but it is workable and able to be implemented with just a few lines of code. Most GOFAI applications utilize heuristics. In fact, as Margaret Boden (2016: 24) explains: "There's no principled distinction between heuristics and algorithms. Many algorithms are, in effect, mini-programs incorporating some particular heuristic."

So what we have seen in this section is a symbol-manipulation or GOFAI approach to writing a basic temperature conversion algorithm. Although the demonstration is rather simplistic, there are four general conclusions that can be drawn from it:

1 The application proceeds by working through individual step-by-step instructions, which, in this particular case, take the form of a series or sequence of conditional statements that test the value of input data and, based on which condition is met, provide some specified output data. In other words, temperature data is represented by symbols and processed by manipulating those symbols, hence the moniker "symbol manipulation."
2 The programmer of the algorithm needs to know the temperature conversions. Consequently, the "intelligence" of this kind of system is actually the intelligence of the programmer encoded in and represented by lines of code (or instructions) that can be manipulated by the computer.
3 If for some reason there is an error with the temperature conversion process, one can identify the line (or lines) where the error happens and make the appropriate alterations to fix the problem.
4 Finally, the results of the algorithm are decent but not completely perfect. Efforts to develop a more accurate version of the algorithm

would require that we add lines of code to cover a wider range of input values for conditions that were not originally included. Doing so, however, increases the number of coded instructions, which would (eventually) necessitate longer processing time.

3.3.2 Artificial neural network

In the second method, we do not tell the computer how to perform the temperature conversion. Instead, we set-up a neural network, train it on a small set of temperature data, and then allow the network to "learn" the conversions by exploiting patterns that emerge from the data. The first step in the process is to define the artificial neuron that will make up the individual components of the artificial neural network, or ANN. This is done by writing an algorithm that instantiates a mathematical model of the neuron in computer code.

So let's do some simple math (and I promise you, it will be simple). An artificial neuron can be mathematically described and modeled in the following way (see Figure 3.5). On the one end, there are inputs (a, b, c). These inputs will be numerical values in the range of 0 to 1. Each of the input connections is weighted (w) with a numerical value. These weights, which can vary in value from 0 to 1 (thus they can be values like 0.25 or 0.9) alter the input by multiplying the input value by the numerical value of the weight. If the input is 1 and the weight (the value assigned to the variable w) is 0.56, the resulting value of the input is 0.56. If the input value is 0.8 and the weighted value is 0.25 the resulting value of the input is 0.2.

The three input values (modified by the value of the weight) are then added together or summed up. This is indicated on the diagram by the Greek letter Σ which is the standard mathematical notation for

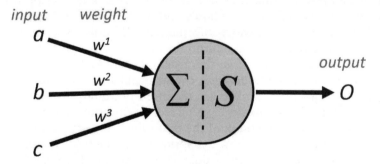

Figure 3.5   Diagram of an artificial neuron

summation. The sum of the inputs is compared to some threshold condition that determines whether an output is produced or not. This is called an activation function and it is represented on the diagram by the letter S. There are a number of different mathematically defined activation functions. The simplest is a *step function*, which produces the output 1, when the threshold is met, and 0 (or nothing), if it is not. The perceptron used this particular activation function. For our example, we are going to use a *sigmoid function*. The sigmoid function, which is rather common in contemporary artificial neurons, provides for a wider range of possible outputs and is not limited to the all-or-nothing result of the perceptron. Mathematically the sigmoid function can be described like this:

$$O = \frac{1}{1 + e^{-x}}$$

Let's take this slowly; it's not as bad as it looks. The letter e is a mathematical constant with a repeating decimal. It has the approximate value of 2.718 . . . We begin by raising the value of this constant (or approx. 2.718) to $-x$, which is the negative of the sum total of the input values. We then take this result, add 1 to it, and invert it. The result of this calculation is assigned to the output (O). What this does is supply us with a neuron that generates a range of output values that are not just 0 or 1 (as with a step function) but some number situated between 0 and 1.

Because the artificial neuron is a mathematical model, it can be implemented in computer code. Fortunately, once you write the code for this kind of element, it can be used again and again as a standard piece of reusable code. And there are a number of code libraries that developers can call on in order to access and deploy these prefabricated elements. In our example, we are going to get the code for our artificial neuron from Synaptic, a Javascript library that was developed by Juan Cazala and freely distributed online (see Maker Exercise 3, for more information). By doing so, we do not need to code the artificial neuron for ourselves, we can just call on the code that is available in the Synaptic library. In Synaptic, the coded instructions for defining the artificial neuron require more than 800 lines of code. We are therefore not going to look at the entire thing. We can, however, get a feel for how the neuron is coded by looking at a small chunk of the 800+ lines of instruction. Figure 3.6, for example, shows how Synaptic defines the basic features of a multilayer perceptron. At this point, we do not need to analyze each line individually. What is important is simply to note the way the

```
 1
 2  // Multilayer Perceptron
 3    Perceptron: function Perceptron() {
 4
 5      var args = Array.prototype.slice.call(arguments);
 6      if (args.length < 3)
 7      throw new Error("not enough layers (minimum 3) !!");
 8
 9      var inputs = args.shift();
10      var outputs = args.pop();
11      var layers = args;
12
13      var input = new Layer(inputs);
14      var hidden = [];
15      var output = new Layer(outputs);
16
```

**Figure 3.6   Segment of the Synaptic code for defining a
multilayer perceptron**

mathematical model of the perceptron can be implemented in lines
of coded instructions.

One single artificial neuron by itself is not very useful. What is
useful is when we connect a number of these neurons together to
create an ANN. So after defining the features and functions of the
individual neuron, we then need to specify the features and basic
structure of the network. Because ANNs are organized in layers, we
need to specify the number of layers that comprise the network, the
number of neurons per layer, and the number of connections from
the neurons in one layer to those in another layer.

For our temperature conversion example, we will be using a
network that has three layers – an input layer, an output layer, and
one hidden layer situated in between the input and output layers. It is
called "hidden" because, unlike the input and output layers, it is not
exposed to the outside world. To keep things simple, our network will
have one neuron in both the input and the output layers, while the
hidden layer will have three neurons (see Figure 3.7). This is admit-
tedly a very simple and limited network. Most ANNs have numerous
input and output neurons, many more hidden layers made up of a
multiplicity of neurons, and a large number of connections between
the neurons that comprise one layer and those in a subsequent layer.
In fact, the term *deep learning* derives from the number of hidden
layers in the network and describes the "depth" of the network due
to the accumulation of multiple hidden layers.

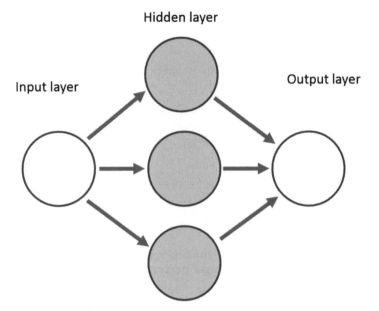

Figure 3.7   A simple 1–3–1 artificial neural network

This rather basic and simplified 1–3–1 network can be implemented in code by specifying the instructions given in Figure 3.8). Looking at the instructions, you can see that we are specifying three layers (lines 5–7) with one neuron for the **inputLayer** and **output-**

```
1
2  //make the network
3  const { Layer, Network } = window.synaptic;
4
5  var inputLayer = new Layer(1);
6  var hiddenLayer = new Layer(3);
7  var outputLayer = new Layer(1);
8
9  inputLayer.project(hiddenLayer);
10 hiddenLayer.project(outputLayer);
11
12 var myNetwork = new Network({
13     input: inputLayer,
14     hidden: [hiddenLayer],
15     output: outputLayer });
16
```

Figure 3.8   Setting up the artificial neural network

Layer and three neurons for the **hiddenLayer**. The results or output from the **inputLayer** are sent or projected to the **hidden-Layer** and the results or output of this layer are sent or projected to the **outputLayer** (lines 9–10).

After the network is set-up, we then train it on some data. To keep things simple, we will train our 1–3–1 ANN on four pieces of data, specifically four temperature correlations:

Fahrenheit	Celsius
30	0
50	10
70	21
99	38

Training the network consists in feeding this temperature data into the network. This is called *forward propagation*. It involves activating the network by sending each of the values for degrees Fahrenheit (30, 50, 70, and 99) into the input layer, having this number passed from the input layer into each one of the three neurons in the hidden layer and, in the process, getting transformed by the numeric weights assigned to each of the connections, and then passing these values to the output layer (which are also transformed by applying the weights assigned to the connections between the hidden layer neurons and the output layer), where their sum total represents the resulting degrees Celsius.

The first time this is done, the weights are set randomly, and, as you might anticipate, the output number is rather arbitrary and in most cases a very bad guess. For instance, when we propagate the number 30 through the network, it might produce an erroneous output, like 12. Because we know what the value should be (according to the data set, 30 should be 0), we can use this information to calculate the value of the error, which is simply a numeric measurement of the difference between the (wrong) outputted number and the valid value that it should be. If there is a significant error, this occurrence triggers an adjustment to the numeric values of the weights on the connections. This is called *back propagation*, and it is how the "learning" tran-spires. Machine learning in the case of an ANN like this simply means readjusting the weighted connections between the layers based on back propagating the errors that have been generated by the network.

```
1
2  // train the network
3  var learningRate = .3;
4  for (var i = 0; i < 80000; i++)
5  {
6      myNetwork.activate([0.30]);
7      myNetwork.propagate(learningRate, [0]);
8
9      myNetwork.activate([0.50]);
10     myNetwork.propagate(learningRate, [0.10]);
11
12     myNetwork.activate([0.70]);
13     myNetwork.propagate(learningRate, [0.21]);
14
15     myNetwork.activate([.99]);
16     myNetwork.propagate(learningRate, [0.38]);
17  }
18
```

Figure 3.9   Instructions for training our 1–3–1 ANN. What you see here are the four temperature associations (beginning on line 6) preceded by a *for* loop that specifies the number of times this data is forward propagated through the network (line 4) and value of the LearningRate variable (var), which is a number (in this case 0.3) that is used to adjust the weights of the connections, each time the errors produced by the network are back propagated

In the case of our example, the adjustment that is made to the weights, per iteration, is 0.3 and is expressed (on line 3 of Figure 3.9) as the value of the **LearningRate** variable. In other words, the numeric value of the error is not utilized to make adjustments to the weighted connections; the occurrence of an error triggers an adjustment that applies the value of the **LearningRate** to the weighted connections.

As the network recursively performs this operation – forward propagating data into the network and then back propagating the resulting errors in order to readjust the weighted connections again and again and again – like 80,000 times (as is specified on line 4 of Figure 3.9) – the entire system gets successively better at approximating the correct output. It is kind of like tuning a string instrument, like a guitar or violin. You pluck a string and obtain a result. If the resulting tone is not what was expected (or in more technical terms, if the expected value of the note or the frequency produced by the vibration of the string is not entirely correct, e.g., it sounds either sharp or flat), you make an incremental adjustment by rotating the tuning peg. Then you repeat the process again and again until it "sounds right." Like all analogies, this is not perfect, but it does provide a good, nontechnical description of the process.

Once operational, the ANN produces decent conversions. If we enter the number 30, for example, the network spits out the value 0. This should be no big surprise, insofar as we already knew this and provided the information as part of the training data. But (and this is the important part) if we input a number that the network has never "seen" before, like 66 Fahrenheit, we now obtain the result of 19 Celsius, which is correct. In fact, the network, after it has been trained on only four temperature associations, is rather accurate at converting a wide range of different temperature values. It is able to do so because the network has "learned" the conversion method by finding patterns in the available data and applying this to numbers it has never encountered previously. The network, it is important to remember, does not understand temperature in any way; what it "understands" (if we can use this rather anthropomorphic characterization) are numeric patterns derived from associations available in existing data.

So unlike symbol-manipulation GOFAI, a machine-learning neural network like this does not have prescribed step-by-step instructions that specify how to make the transformation in temperature values. The network learns or formulates the conversions by discovering patterns in data that are then encoded in the network by adjusting the weighted connections between layers of neurons. This has several important consequences. First, the programmer or developer of the algorithm does not need to know everything about the task in order to write the algorithm. With GOFAI approaches, the "intelligence" of the algorithm is a product of the (more-or-less accurately represented) intelligence of its developer. With machine learning, the "intelligence" of the algorithm emerges out of patterns that are discovered by the network in the data on which it is trained. For this reason, the developer of the algorithm does not need to know much about the task and might, in fact, actually know very little or even nothing about it.

Second, as you might anticipate, this is both an advantage and a problem. It is advantageous insofar as developers can create practical applications and solutions to problems without necessarily knowing anything about the task at hand. Take facial-recognition as an example. We are quite capable of recognizing the faces of friends and family members. But can you specify in step-by-step instructions exactly how this happens? It turns out that specifying the individual steps involved in performing the task of facial-recognition is incredibly difficult, and efforts to write GOFAI facial-recognition algorithms have generally resulted in failure. If, however, we set-up a neural network and train it on billions of images of human faces, this will result in an algorithm that is as accurate or, in some cases, even more accurate than human beings at performing facial-recognition. Consequently, this approach provides a way to solve problems where we have access to data but do not necessarily know the step-by-step procedures needed to transform input into output.

But this also means that developers of machine-learning systems typically do not have full knowledge of or control over the algorithms they create. What the algorithm does or does not do is therefore often just as surprising (or shocking) to its developers as it is to users. In other words, when things go right, like DeepMind's AlphaGo defeating Lee Sedol in the game of Go (see Chapter 6), or when things go terrible wrong, like Microsoft's twitterbot Tay.ai becoming a raving neo-Nazi racist (see Chapter 5), the developers often cannot explain why this happened or (especially in situations where things go wrong) how to fix it. Unlike a GOFAI algorithm, where individual lines of erroneous code can be easily identified and repaired, the neural network only has different weighted connections, and those values, which are seemingly arbitrary numbers, tell us little or nothing about the operations of the network and its eventual behavior. This will, as we shall see in subsequent chapters (see Chapter 9, in particular), produce new opportunities and significant challenges when it comes to deciding questions concerning social accountability and legal responsibility.

Third, the kind of learning that is described and illustrated with this particular example is not the only form or method of machine learning. In this example, we have employed *supervised learning*. It is called "supervised" because we have access to examples of correct input–output pairs (the four temperature associations in the data set) that can be used to compare network output to desired output and, as a result of this, generate errors that can then be back propagated through the network to adjust the weighted connections. This way of doing machine learning is best suited to applications that typically involve regression – e.g., predicting or estimating a continuous quantity – or classification tasks. But there are other methods, like *unsupervised learning* and *reinforcement learning*. In unsupervised learning, there is no predefined output values that can be used for comparison; all we have is a large set of data. The aim of unsupervised learning is to find the regularities or patterns in the input data. "There is," as Alpaydin (2016: 111) explains, "a structure to the input space such that certain patterns occur more often than others, and we want to see what generally happens and what does not." This kind of learning is best suited to clustering tasks, like image-recognition, where we have a large amount of data but do not necessarily know what pattern to look for or utilize.

Reinforcement learning is designed to emulate trial and error. It is best suited to situations where we do not have preexisting data but we let the machine generate various outputs and then quantify its performance in the form of a reward signal that can be fed back into the system. Unlike supervised or unsupervised learning, here there is no preexisting training data. The system generates data "by trying out actions in the environment and receiving feedback (or not) in the form of a reward. It then uses this feedback to update its knowledge so that in time it learns to do actions that return the highest reward" (Alpaydin 2016: 128). A good example of situations where this approach works well is gaming applications, where the algorithm learns how to master a particular game (e.g., Atari's Breakout) from the "experience" of numerous trials (Mnih et al. 2015). Finally, it should be noted that these different approaches to developing machine learning are not mutually exclusive and can be combined to work together. DeepMind's championship Go-playing algorithm, AlphaGo, for instance, was initially trained on a large data set of expert human games (supervised learning) and then improved through reinforcement learning by playing games against itself.

3.3.3 Summary: GOFAI vs. ANN

Historically, both methods for developing AI applications and algorithms have been in play. But, at different times in this history, one method seems to have the upper hand. Symbol manipulation got the nickname "GOFAI" because it was the favored method – virtually the only method – for more than two decades. But now, since at least the turn of the century, machine learning with deep neural networks, which had been marginalized during this earlier period, seems to be grabbing all the attention. Despite these ups and downs, it turns out that the two methods are not mutually exclusive and that each one has its own set of distinct strengths and weaknesses that balance out those exhibited by the other. "In general," as Kaplan (2016: 36) explains, "symbolic reasoning is more appropriate for problems that require abstract reasoning, while machine learning is better for situations that require sensory perception or extracting patterns from noisy data."

To illustrate this point, Kaplan provides two informative examples:

> Suppose you want to build a robot that can ride a bike (that is, one that can control the pedals and handlebars, and is able to balance). Representing the problem in symbolic terms may be possible, but imagine trying to interview a human expert in an effort to build an expert system [a kind of GOFAI algorithm] to do this. (2016: 36)

This is a task that would be better suited to machine learning and most likely reinforcement learning through trial and error. But this does not mean that machine learning works in all situations and circumstances. "There are," Kaplan (2016: 37) continues, "other issues for which machine learning techniques aren't well suited. To state the obvious, machine learning is not useful for problems where there's no data, just some initial conditions, a bunch of constraints, and one shot to get it right." In these situations, symbolic reasoning has the upper hand, because it works at a higher level of abstraction, where the problem and the steps necessary to solve it can be described in logical procedures.

In the chapters that follow this introductory section, we will consider a number of AI applications that address problems or opportunities with human communication – machine translation, natural language processing and generation, computational creativity, and social robots. In the process, we will look at and inquire about the opportunities and challenges of both GOFAI methods and machine-learning solutions. But before getting into these applications, there is one final set of terms – actually two pairs of terms – that need to be sorted out and explained.

3.4 A Pair of Terminological Pairs

In the science and engineering of AI, there are two pairs of terms that are often confused with one another, even though they are intended to address and explain different conceptual differences. The first pair consists of "artificial general intelligence" (AGI) vs. "narrow AI"; the second involves "strong AI" vs. "weak AI." We will, therefore, conclude this chapter on basic concepts and terminology by getting a handle on and sorting out what makes these two conceptual pairings different and why they have often been confused with each other.

3.4.1 AGI vs. narrow AI

From at least the time of the Dartmouth summer seminar, the apex of AI has been the creation of machine intelligence that is on a par with, if not eventually better than, human intelligence. This kind of wide-ranging or general cognitive capability is something that is imaginatively portrayed in science fiction. Consider, for example, the HAL 9000 computer in Stanley Kubrick's award-winning feature film *2001: A Space Odyssey* (1968). HAL, as the computer is called, is able to perform a wide range of intellectual operations and exhibits intelligent behavior across different kinds of tasks. Here is how the computer is introduced and characterized in the course of a fictional BBC documentary – a kind of film inside the film:

> *BBC journalist*: The sixth member of the Discovery crew was not concerned about the problems of hibernation, for he was the latest result in machine intelligence – the H-A-L 9000 computer, which can reproduce, although some experts still prefer to use the word "mimic," most of the activities of the human brain and with incalculably greater speed and reliability. We next spoke with the H-A-L computer, whom we learned one addresses as "Hal." Good afternoon, Hal, how is everything going?"
>
> *HAL*: Good afternoon, Mr. Amer, Everything is going extremely well.
>
> *BBC journalist*: Hal, you have an enormous responsibility on this mission, in many ways, perhaps the greatest responsibility of any single mission element. You are the brain and central nervous system of the ship and your responsibilities involve watching over the men in hibernation. Does this ever cause you any lack of confidence?
>
> *HAL*: Let me put it this way, Mr. Amer. The 9000 series is the most reliable computer ever made. No 9000 computer has ever made a mistake or distorted information. We are all, by any practical definition of the words, foolproof and incapable of error.
>
> *BBC journalist*: Hal, despite your enormous intellect, are you ever frustrated by your dependence on people to carry out actions?
>
> *HAL*: Not in the slightest bit. I enjoy working with people. I have a stimulating relationship with Dr. Poole and Dr. Bowman. My mission responsibilities range over the entire operations of the ship, so I am constantly occupied. I am putting myself to the fullest possible use, which is all I think that any conscious entity can ever hope to do.

As you can see from this short exchange, the HAL 9000 computer is presented as a fully conscious and intelligent entity with cognitive abilities that range from conversational interactions with a human interviewer to managing the operational details of a spacecraft on its way to Jupiter. This vision of AI – which we should note was influenced by actual R&D, insofar as the scientific advisor on the film was Marvin Minsky, one of the organizers of the Dartmouth summer seminar – is now called Artificial General Intelligence (AGI).

Although the phrase was introduced and first utilized by Mark Gubrud in 1997, it is formalized in a 2007 book titled *Artificial General Intelligence* and edited by Ben Goertzel and Cassio Pennachin. In the preface to the book, the editors differentiate between two different kinds of effort in AI engineering (or what they call "practical AI"): AGI and narrow AI.

> What is meant by AGI is, loosely speaking, AI systems that possess a reasonable degree of self-understanding and autonomous self-control, and have the ability to solve a variety of complex problems in a variety of contexts, and to learn to solve new problems that they didn't know about at the time of their creation. (2007: vi)

This objective is distinguished from more pragmatic efforts to engineer specific problem-solving applications: "Pragmatic but specialized 'narrow AI' research which is aimed at creating programs carrying out specific tasks like playing chess, diagnosing diseases, driving cars and so forth" (2007: vi). At this point in time, AGI is still a hypothesis, and its feasibility is something that is open to debate and considerable disagreement. Although there has been some effort to produce a broadly intelligent and conscious machine, achievement of AGI is still something that remains a future possibility. Narrow AI, however, is a reality. We do have applications that are able to carry out specific tasks, like translating between different human languages, engaging in conversational exchange with human users, generating original stories for publication, or playing championship-level chess and Go. To put it another way, the AGI of HAL is still science fiction, but specific or narrow AI applications that can talk to you and engage in basic conversational interactions, like Siri and Alexa, are in fact a reality.

3.4.2 Strong vs. weak AI

These two terms – AGI and narrow AI – are often confused with another conceptual pairing: strong AI vs. weak AI. But they are not the same. Unlike the previous conceptual pairing, the terms "strong" and "weak" do not refer to differences in engineering practice but to two hypotheses concerning the impact of AI science. The concept originally comes from the philosopher John Searle, who used the words "strong" and "weak" in conjunction with his Chinese Room thought experiment (see Chapter 2). Here is how Searle initially defined it:

> I find it useful to distinguish what I will call "strong" AI from "weak" or "cautious" AI (Artificial Intelligence). According to weak AI, the principal value of the computer in the study of the mind is that it gives us a very powerful tool. For example, it enables us to formulate and test hypotheses in a more rigorous and precise fashion. But according to strong AI, the computer is not merely a tool in the study of the mind; rather, the appropriately programmed computer really is a mind, in the sense that computers given the right programs can be literally said to understand and have other cognitive states. (1980: 417)

For Searle, "weak AI" indicates the ability of the computer to simulate cognitive processes. In cognitive science, the purpose of weak AI, as Searle understands it, is to provide researchers with a tool for developing a better understanding of the working of the mind. "Strong AI," by contrast, makes the claim that a computer, when programmed correctly, would not just simulate thought and mental processes (for the purposes of modeling various aspects or features of the mind) but would be an actual conscious mind.

Despite this clarification, "strong AI" is often used in place of AGI and "weak AI" is assumed to be similar to what is called "narrow AI." But this is incorrect and, once again, the best way to explain the difference is by way of example. If (or when, as some have argued) AGI is a reality, it will still be an open question whether it is "strong" or "weak" in Searle's sense. If the AGI is an honest-to-goodness, actual working mind – like the human brain just instantiated in a different kind of material substrate, e.g. in silicon as opposed to biological cells – then the AGI will be "strong." If, however, the AGI is just a clever simulation of a wide range of human cognitive capabilities produced by other means than actual thinking behavior, as we typically understand it, then the AGI would be "weak." This is the meaning of the comment made by Mr. Amer, the BBC journalist in the scene from *2001: A Space Odyssey* that was quoted above: ". . . the H-A-L 9000 computer, which can reproduce, although some experts still prefer to use the word 'mimic,' most of the activities of the human brain." If the HAL 9000 computer is, as he himself (and the computer is gendered "male") proclaims, a conscious entity that is just like or substantially similar to a human being, then HAL is strong AI. But, if HAL is just a really sophisticated imitation or emulation of human cognitive capabilities – producing the effect of cognition without really "cognizing" anything – than HAL is weak AI.

The same holds for "narrow AI" or smart devices and applications. Consider Amper – a music composition and production algorithm that was used by Taryn Southern in 2018 to write and produce the music for I AM AI, a pop-music recording that was promoted as the first full-length album entirely written and produced by AI. Is the music created by the Amper algorithm just a clever simulation of human creativity, producing pop tunes that mechanically emulate human creativity? Or does Amper's music open the opportunity for us to reevaluate human creativity and significantly revise what is meant by artistry, such that AI could be called "creative" in its own right? If the former, then Amper is weak AI; if the latter, then it could be considered a kind of strong AI. The problem in both cases is that it may be difficult to tell the difference between a really sophisticated simulation and the real thing. And, as you might have already anticipated, this question leads us right back to the problem of other minds and Searle's Chinese Room thought experiment. For the purposes of this book and the detailed investigations of AI applications that follow this chapter, we will use the terms "weak AI" and "strong AI" in the sense that was initially introduced and developed by Searle, and AGI vs. narrow AI in the sense that had been described by Goertzel and Pennachin.

Summary of Key Points

- The word "algorithm" has been derived from the name of a ninth-century Persian mathematician. It identifies a standard procedure for solving computational problems. AI, as developed and implemented in digital technology, is algorithmic. But not all algorithms implemented on the computer are AI. This is due not to a technological difference, but to the social influence and impact of the "AI effect."
- There are, generally speaking, two different methods for developing algorithms for AI applications: symbolic reasoning, which utilizes symbolic logic and also goes by the name GOFAI; and artificial neural networks, or ANN, which operate on statistical principles instead of symbolic logic and facilitate various forms of "machine learning." Although both methods were available and in development at the time of the Dartmouth summer seminar, efforts with and funding for the two have not been consistent over time.

- In the field of AI, there are two pairs of conceptual differences that need to be differentiated: artificial general intelligence (AGI) vs. narrow AI, and strong AI vs. weak AI. The former explains qualitative difference in practical capabilities – e.g., an AI system with human-level cognitive capabilities vs. a very specific "smart" application that does one thing well. The latter pair identifies two ways of theorizing the significance of AI – whether the device or system is an actual mind or just a simulation.

Part II

Applications

4

Machine Translation

Key Aims/Objectives

- To recognize the necessity and importance of (1) translation for effective human communication; (2) the religious, mythical, and science fiction origins of automatic translation; and (3) the history of the concept of machine translation (MT) from early efforts in the seventeenth century to the influential Weaver memo of 1949.
- To understand the different techniques and technologies for developing MT applications – rule-based, example-based, statistical, and neural network – and to compare and contrast the relative strengths and weaknesses of these different methodologies.
- To question and reflect critically on the fundamental assumptions concerning human language and communication that are already operative in MT research and that influence these efforts to devise automatic translation systems and devices.

Introduction

Ten rozdział dotyczy tłumaczenia maszynowego. Unless you can read and understand Polish, the sentence that begins this chapter is probably confusing and virtually unintelligible. And this points to something rather important. Human communication is dependent on language, and natural human languages are different, diverse, and seemingly incompatible. It is currently estimated that there are somewhere in the range of 6,900–7,100 different languages in use worldwide. We typically contend with this linguistic diversity in one of two ways. We can seek to become proficient in more than one language, which is one of the reasons why the university curriculum in the United States and elsewhere typically has a foreign language requirement. (Translation: That is why you have to take four semesters of Spanish, German, or Chinese in order to complete your undergraduate degree.) Or we can translate – literally "carry over" – the meaning that is expressed in one language to that of another. This can be accomplished either by applying the efforts of a human translator – an individual who has adequate knowledge of at least two different languages and considerable experience making transformations from one language into the other – or a computational mechanism. This chapter deals with machine translation (this is a translation into English of the Polish sentence provided above), the field of computer linguistics, which deals with the use of algorithms for automatically translating from one natural language into another.

4.1 Historical Context

Before looking at the technical aspects of machine translation, or MT as it is called, let's take a step back and ask about the reason for – or *raison d'être* – of translation and the basic concepts behind efforts to mechanize translation between languages. Translation is needed in order to contend with and even overcome the fact that human beings speak a wide range of different languages. This is especially important as the world's peoples become more involved with each other through international trade and exchange, travel and migration, and daily involvements and interactions with each other on a global scale by way of telecommunications technology. But how and why is this a "problem" in the first place? How did we get here? And what does this mean for efforts in the science and engineering of artificial intelligence?

4.1.1 Mythic origins and science fiction

In the Judeo/Christian tradition, the fact that different human communities speak different languages is something that is explained by way of a myth or legend incorporated in the first book of the Holy Scriptures. (In Jewish traditions this is called the Torah; for Christians, it appears in the Old Testament of the Bible.) The story is usually called "The Tower of Babel," and it can be found in the book of Genesis 11:1–9:

Now the whole world had one language and a common speech. As people moved eastward, they found a plain in Shinar and settled there. They said to each other, "Come, let's make bricks and bake them thoroughly." They used brick instead of stone, and tar for mortar. Then they said, "Come, let us build ourselves a city, with a tower that reaches to the heavens, so that we may make a name for ourselves; otherwise we will be scattered over the face of the whole earth." But the Lord came down to see the city and the tower the people were building. The Lord said, "If as one people speaking the same language they have begun to do this, then nothing they plan to do will be impossible for them. Come, let us go down and confuse their language so they will not understand each other." So the Lord scattered them from there over all the earth, and they stopped building the city. That is why it was called Babel – because there the Lord confused the language of the whole world. From there the Lord scattered them over the face of the whole earth.

"The Tower of Babel" story begins at a mythical point in time when it is assumed that all of humanity lived in a single place on the planet and spoke one common language. Subsequent generations of scholars and religious teachers have argued that this "original language" was the "Adamic tongue" that had been bestowed on Adam and Eve (the first man and woman) by Yahweh, or God. This single language was a powerful tool of communication, because (according to the story) it facilitated cooperation between different individuals, so much so that the entire human population of planet earth could agree to work together and construct a city and a massive tower that reached all the way into the heavens.

Upon seeing this impressive work, God begins to get worried that humanity might get too powerful, do all kinds of other impressive things, and that nothing would be impossible for them to achieve. So, in an effort to curb their ambitions, God puts an end to the building project by confusing the language. This linguistic confusion makes it virtually impossible for the human population to talk with one another and to complete work on the tower. As a result, they abandon the edifice, scatter over the face of the earth, and end up speaking different languages. This is why, as explained at the end of the story, the place where this occurred was called *Babel*, because it was here that God confused the original human language, creating the babble of different languages that we live with today.

The Babel story, we should remember, is just that. It is a story. It is not a statement of anthropological fact. In fact, the origins (in the plural) of human language and its remarkable diversity are things that are studied and debated by linguists, anthropologists, neurobiologists, evolutionary biologists, behavioral scientists, etc. But the mythic narrative is informative, because it provides us with a way to characterize the rationale, task, and objective of translation. Because of linguistic difference – the "damage" that was supposedly inflicted at the Tower of Babel – humans speak different languages. This difference often impedes communication and makes it difficult for a person who speaks Polish, for example, to be understood by someone who speaks Korean, English, or any of the other languages. Translation is the process of taking a word or set of words from one language and rendering it into a word or set of words in another language. As we have already indicated, the word "translation" literally means "carrying across," and pointing this out is itself an act of translation insofar as the word is initially of Latin origin and therefore needs to be translated into English.

The work of translation typically requires a human intermediary or "translator," some individual who is knowledgeable in at least two different languages and can therefore represent in the target language what had been said or written in the source language. If you have ever tried this, you know it is more difficult than it sounds, even for individuals who would call themselves bilingual. In English, for example, we can say something like "Makes no difference to me" in response to questions concerning a choice between two alternatives, like when you are asked whether you prefer still or sparkling water with your meal. If you wanted to convey this in Polish, the English sentence could be translated as *"Nie ma dla mnie znaczenia."* Although this is a rather accurate word-for-word rendering of the initial English statement, it is unlikely that a native Polish speaker would say such a thing. Instead, they might say, *"Wszystko jedno,"* which literally means "Everything [is] one." In other words, the task of translation is not simply rendering the words of one language into the exact words of the other language. It involves more. It involves knowing the meaning and context of words in the source language in order to reproduce that same meaning (or at least a close approximation thereof) in the words of the target language.

If the Old Testament of the Christian Bible narrates the origin and *raison d'être* (a French phrase meaning "the reason for existence") of translation between languages, the New Testament provides a clue concerning the ambitions and objectives of automatic, universal translation. This occurs at an event called "Pentecost," which is described in the second chapter of the Acts of the Apostles. After the crucifixion and death of their teacher, Jesus Christ, the Apostles hole up in a room in order to avoid suffering a similar fate. This only changes when they receive the Holy Spirit, which is represented, within the context of the story, in the form of tongues of fire that descend from heaven. After receiving the gift of the spirit, the Apostles leave their stronghold and began proselytizing in the streets. Even though they speak in their native language, everyone hears their words in his/her own language: "And the people were amazed and marveled saying: 'Are not all these men who are speaking Galileans? How is it that each of us hears them in our own language to which we were born?'" (Acts 2:7–8). The story of Pentecost, therefore, narrates the alleviation of Babelian confusion through real-time translation. In this way, Pentecost promises to reestablish universal understanding between humans despite the problem of linguistic difference that was imposed at Babel. In other words, Pentecost repairs and remediates the babble of Babel.

But the promise of overcoming linguistic difference is not just a part of our religious traditions. We also see versions of it in the techno-myths of science fiction. Consider, for example, a device called "Babel fish." According to *The Hitchhiker's Guide to the Galaxy* – a title that names both a novel by Douglas Adams and an encyclopedic reference book cited within that novel:

> The Babel fish is small, yellow, leech-like and probably the oddest thing in the universe. It feeds on brain wave energy, absorbing all unconscious frequencies and then excreting telepathically a matrix formed from the conscious frequencies and nerve signals picked up from the speech centers of the brain, the practical upshot of which is that if you stick one in your ear, you can instantly understand anything said to you in any form of language. (Adams 1979: 59–60)

The Babel fish, therefore, reproduces the miracle of Pentecost for its host by providing flawless, real-time translations from and into any and all languages.

A similar device, named the Universal Translator, is part of the standard equipment of Star Fleet in the science fiction television and film franchise *Star Trek*. According to the *Star Trek Encyclopedia*, the Universal Translator is a "device used to provide real-time two-way translation of spoken languages" (Okuda et al. 1994: 361). In the original series, which made its debut in the mid-1960s, the Universal Translator was a hand-held device about the size of a flashlight (a graphic representation can be found in Franz Joseph's *Star Fleet Technical Manual*, 1975: T0:03:02:04). In the sequel, *Star Trek: The*

Next Generation (as well as its spin-offs, *Deep Space Nine*, *Voyager*, *Enterprise*, etc.), the Universal Translator is incorporated as a piece of software residing in the ship's main computer. According to the *Star Trek Next Generation Technical Manual*, "the Universal Translator is an extremely sophisticated computer program that is designed to first analyze the patterns of an unknown form of communication, then to derive a translation matrix to permit real-time verbal or data exchanges" (Sternbach and Okuda 1991: 101). Because of this, researchers and developers often utilize these fictional examples to explain the efforts and objectives of MT for a nontechnical audience: "The basic idea of machine translation . . . is that of Star Trek's universal translator or a mechanized version of Douglas Adams's Babel Fish – a black box that converts the source language input into a (perfect) target language output without any human interaction" (Raído and Austermühl 2003: 246).

4.1.2 MT before computers

Efforts to overcome linguistic diversity and solve the translation problem by way of technology pre-date the invention of the electronic digital computer. Seventeenth-century Europe, in particular, saw the development of a number of techniques and technologies designed to address this issue by way of developing an artificial universal language. In 1657, for example, Cave Beck, an English schoolmaster and clergyman, proposed something he called a "Universal Character" in a book that had a rather cumbersome (but descriptive) title: *The Universal Character, by which all Nations in the World may understand one another's Conceptions, Reading out of one Common Writing their own Mother Tongues.* What Beck proposed is something that linguists now call *pasigraphy*, from the Greek words "pasi," meaning "all," and "grapho," meaning "to write." Beck's pasigraphy used Arabic numbers as its symbol system; every word was assigned a unique number, and this number was the same across different languages. A similar project, titled *The Groundwork or Foundation Laid (or So Intended) for the Framing of a New Perfect Language and a Universal Common Writing*, was published by Francis Lodwick in 1663. This project not only proposed a universal language to which everyone would have equal access; it also sought to create a perfected system of communication that would be, as Umberto Eco (1995: 73) describes it, "capable of mirroring the true nature of objects." Similar systems were introduced by Athanasius Kircher in the *Polygraphia nova et universalis ex combinatoria arte detecta* (1663), the *Via lucis* (1668) of Comenius, George Dalgarno's *Ars Signorum* (1661), and John Wilkins's *Essay towards a Real Character, and a Philosophical Language* (1668).

But the seventeenth-century European innovator who gets most, if not all, the attention in this area is Gottfried Wilhelm Leibniz. This privileged position was codified by Norbert Wiener in the introduction to the text that originated the science of cybernetics: "If I were to choose a patron saint for cybernetics out of the history of science, I should have to choose Leibniz. The philosophy of Leibniz centers about two closely related concepts – that of a universal symbolism and that of a calculus of reasoning" (1996: 12). The importance of and connection between these two concepts were summarized in a 1679 letter that Leibniz wrote to the Duke of Hannover:

> For my invention uses reason in its entirety and is, in addition, a judge of controversies, an interpreter of notions, a balance of probabilities, a compass which will guide us over the ocean of experiences, an inventory of all things, a table of thoughts, a microscope for scrutinizing present things, a telescope for predicting distant things, a general calculus, an innocent magic, a non-chimerical Kabal, a script which all will read in their own language; and even a language which one will be able to learn in a few weeks, and which will soon be accepted amidst the world. (Quoted in Eco 1995: xii)

Leibniz's proposed invention would accomplish two very important objectives: it would provide a thoroughly rational protocol whereby all debate and controversy in philosophy, science, and mathematics would be resolved through simple calculation; and it would establish a universal character or system of writing that would transcend linguistic differences and overcome the babble of Babel.

As you might have guessed, none of these grand plans for a pasigraphy or universal artificial language common to all of humanity ever succeeded. If one of them had done so, you would be using it right now instead of reading about it. But what these "failed" attempts illustrate for us are several important assumptions or basic principles that come to inform and influence subsequent efforts in MT.

- *Technological fix.* If the problem that is confronted by the effort of translation is the incompatibility of the different natural languages, then the solution is a technology – and we need to remember that writing, printing, and the manufacture of books are early forms of information technology – that can respond to and alleviate this problem. The pasigraphy of Beck or the *characteristica universalis* proposed by Leibniz are technological inventions designed to remediate the communications problem that is imposed by linguistic difference. In the fields of media studies and the philosophy of technology, the idea that there is a "technological fix" for a social/cultural problem is something that is part and parcel of a theory called "technological determinism."

- *Language is computable.* Linguistic data (i.e., words, sentences, and their meaning) can be encoded in mathematical symbols and processed automatically. Beck's pasigraphy encoded language using the ten ordinal numbers (0–9), and Leibniz's "invention" sought to resolve important debates in human knowledge by encoding data in numeric form and solving disputes not through argumentation but by simple, mechanical calculation. As Leibniz famously claimed: "If this were done, whenever controversies arise, there will be no more need for arguing among two philosophers than among two mathematicians. For it will suffice to take the pen into the hand and to sit down by the abacus and say to each other (and if they wish also a friend called for help): Let us calculate" (quoted in Russell 1992: 200). This concept is connected to the computational theory of mind, the idea that what constitutes human thinking and intelligence is just computation or number crunching. And this idea, which is an essential aspect of AI science and engineering insofar as it is the task of AI to reproduce in a computational mechanism the capabilities of human intelligence, is something that is also attributed to Leibniz.

- *Universal language.* Linguistic difference – or, the incompatibility between different natural languages – can be overcome once and for all by encoding language in an artificial idiom that is universal and shared by all of humanity. Unlike medieval efforts to rediscover the original, pre-Babelian Adamic language used by Adam and Eve – and there were some rather interesting and also disturbing efforts to do just that (see Eco 1995) – the Universal Character was an artificial language that would repair the babble of Babel through the application of scientific/mathematical principles. This meant that one could mediate between two different natural languages by the imposition of an intermediary language that could mediate between the two different languages and translate ideas expressed in one language into the other, providing for automatic and mechanized translation.

4.1.3 The Weaver memo

The idea of applying electronic computers to the task of translation was something initially formulated and presented in a memorandum written by Warren Weaver in 1949. For this reason, Weaver is often called "the father of machine translation." You are probably already familiar with the name. Weaver was the coauthor, along with Claude Shannon, of the *Mathematical Theory of Communication*, a publication that introduced the process model that is a crucial element of most introductory courses in communication (see Chapter 2). During World War II, Weaver was head of the Applied Mathematics Panel at the US Office of Scientific Research and Development. In this capacity, he had the opportunity to experience the application of electronic calculating machines – what we now call "computers" – to the task of *cryptography*, the coding and decoding of secret messages. One of the technologies that gave the Nazis a considerable advantage in the conduct of wartime operations was the Enigma machine – a sophisticated cryptography instrument, looking something like a rather hefty typewriter, that rendered messages issued by the German high command virtually unreadable when intercepted. The allies applied a considerable amount of effort to decoding the Enigma code. This was the wartime occupation of Alan Turing at Bletchley Park in the United Kingdom (dramatically presented in the 2015 film *The Imitation Game*), where the Enigma code was eventually broken with the aid of skilled mathematicians from Poland, and the work of the Applied Mathematics Panel that Weaver oversaw in the US.

In 1949, Weaver, who had by that time returned to his pre-WWII position at the Rockefeller Foundation, wrote a brief memorandum in which he proposed that translation between languages might be a special instance of cryptography and therefore solvable using the same tools that had been developed during the war. In fact, Weaver's "Translation," as the memorandum has been called, introduced a number of important proposals that taken together frame the opportunity and challenge of MT.

(1) *Linguistic difference is a problem.* Right at the beginning of the memorandum, Weaver operationalized an idea that proceeds directly from the "Tower of Babel" story, even if he does not mention it by name. He begins the memo by recognizing the "fact" that linguistic difference is a significant problem that impedes human communication and international cooperation: "There is no need to do more than mention the obvious fact that a multiplicity of language impedes

cultural interchange between the peoples of the earth, and is a serious deterrent to international understanding" (1949: 1). So right at the beginning, in the first line of the memorandum, Weaver affirms and mobilizes the basic idea that comes from the "Tower of Babel" story – confusion between different human languages is a barrier to intercultural exchange and a serious impediment to international understanding and cooperation.

(2) *Technological fix.* Like Beck, Leibniz, and others, Weaver thinks that there must be a technological solution to this problem. In Weaver's case, that solution comes in the form of the new electronic technology of the computer: "The present memorandum, assuming the validity and importance of this fact, contains some comments and suggestions bearing on the possibility of contributing at least something to the solution of the world-wide translation problem through the use of electronic computers of great capacity, flexibility, and speed" (1949: 1). There are two things to note here. First, Weaver hedges against the possible failure of his argument by recognizing that one first has to agree to the validity of the assumption that linguistic difference is, in fact, a problem to be solved. Although this might appear to be a mere rhetorical gesture, we will eventually see how this was a prescient insight and comment. Second, Weaver is entirely realistic about the importance of his work. He does not claim to solve everything once and for all; he simply offers the memorandum as a modest contribution in the direction of an eventual solution. He is, in other words, content to get things started by planting the seeds or the initial ideas of MT.

(3) *Translation = cryptography.* Based on his wartime experience, Weaver surmised that linguistic difference and the task of translation could be addressed in terms roughly equivalent to that of cryptography. As he recounts in the memorandum, this idea was first developed and presented to Norbert Wiener in a letter from March 4, 1947: "One naturally wonders if the problem of translation could conceivably be treated as a problem in cryptography. When I look at an article in Russian, I say 'This is really written in English, but it has been coded in some strange symbols. I will now proceed to decode'" (quoted in Poibeau 2017: 53). Whether Weaver's hypothesis is factually accurate or not is something that is still open to debate. What is not in question, however, is the idea of applying the experiences and tools of cryptography to processing natural language. Consequently, this sentence, and the memorandum in total, initiated what would become machine translation and, more generally speaking, natural language processing (NLP).

(4) *Universal language.* The memo was intended to be a short "think piece" and not a technical paper. So there is very little in Weaver's text that would be considered an actual methodology or approach. Despite this, Weaver does engage in some theorizing about basic procedures, mobilizing both Babelian imagery and the concept of universal language developed by seventeenth-century European philosophers and mathematicians like Leibniz.

> Think, by analogy, of individuals living in a series of tall closed towers, all erected over a common foundation. When they try to communicate with one another, they shout back and forth, each from his own closed tower. It is difficult to make the sound penetrate even the nearest towers, and communication proceeds very poorly indeed. But, when an individual goes down his tower, he finds himself in a great open basement, common to all the towers. Here he establishes easy and useful communication with the persons who have also descended from their towers. Thus may it be true that the way to translate . . . is not to attempt the direct route, shouting from tower to tower. Perhaps the way is to descend, from each language, down to the common base of human communication – the real but as yet undiscovered universal language. (1949: 11)

Weaver's remix of the "Tower of Babel" story concerns not a single tower and the origin of linguistic diversity, but a series of different towers and the problem of translation. He tells of a multiplicity of individual towers that indicate the isolation and incompatibility of each language. Translation therefore proceeds by trying to make one language understandable in terms of another – a difficult process that can be illustrated, as Weaver explains, by shouting from the top of one tower to another (Figure 4.1). This problem can, Weaver continues, be circumvented by descending the individual towers to the common foundation or basement that underlies linguistic differences. The idea is simple. Instead of trying to translate from language to language – shouting from tower to tower – one might make better progress in translation by way of "descending" to a more fundamental and universal representation that underlies particular linguistic differences.

> Thus may it be true that the way to translate from Chinese to Arabic, or from Russian to Portuguese, is not to attempt the direct route, shouting from tower to tower. Perhaps the way is to descend, from each language, down to the common base of human communication – the real but as yet undiscovered universal language – and then re-emerge by whatever particular route is convenient. (1949: 11; see Figure 4.2)

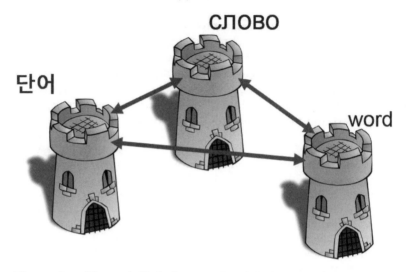

Figure 4.1 Weaver's Babelian remix with the task of translation
pictured as the difficult process of shouting from one isolated
linguistic tower to another

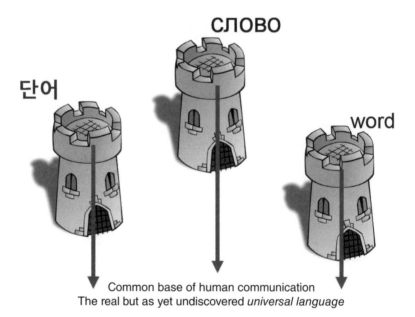

Common base of human communication
The real but as yet undiscovered *universal language*

Figure 4.2 Weaver's solution. Descend the individual linguistic
towers and establish communication using the common base of
human communication

Although Weaver could not have known it at the time, this proposal accurately describes and characterizes the two methods initially undertaken by MT research and development in the twentieth century.

4.2 Machine Translation: Techniques and Technologies

The influence of Weaver's memorandum cannot be overestimated. The idea of overcoming linguistic differences – fixing the babble of Babel – by way of applying computer technology to the problem of translation definitely had traction. As a result, Weaver's memo along with his access to lucrative funding sources in the US federal government, launched a concerted effort in MT that has, since that time, gone through a number of different technical phases or iterations. These can be broken down into the following three methods: rule-based translation, statistical translation, and machine-learning translation.

4.2.1 Rule-based MT

From his experience working with cryptography, Weaver surmised that translation could be understood as a problem of logical deduction and therefore solved through the application of recursive logic or coded step-by-step instructions. Here is how Weaver explained it in his "Translation" memo:

> A more general basis for hoping that a computer could be designed which would cope with a useful part of the problem of translation is to be found in a theorem which was proved in 1943 by McCulloch and Pitts. This theorem states that a robot (or a computer) constructed with regenerative loops of a certain formal character is capable of deducing any legitimate conclusion from a finite set of premises. (1949: 9–10)

Following this formulation, early efforts in MT (those initially put in play in the 1950s) sought to develop a sequence of logical rules for transforming the input of one language, like English, into the output of another, like Chinese.

Different MT projects and implementations have performed this task in different but related ways. These different approaches to rule-based MT – or what is also called "classical MT" (Jurafsky and Martin 2017) – can be organized into three main variants: Direct,

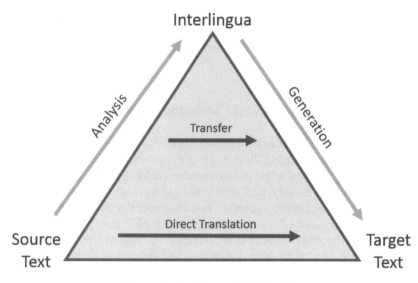

Figure 4.3   Vauquois Triangle

Transfer, Interlingua. "These three kinds of approaches," as Thierry Poibeau (2017: 28–9) explains, "can be considered to form a continuum, going from a strategy that is very close to the surface of the text (a word-for-word translation) up to systems trying to develop a fully artificial and abstract representation that is independent of any language." This can be visualized and represented by a diagram called the Vauquois Triangle, named after a French MT researcher Bernard Vauquois, who was active in the field in the later part of the 1960s (Figure 4.3).

Direct translation   At the base of the triangle is the direct approach, where each word in the source language is translated into a word in the target language. This method is generally based on a bilingual dictionary that supplies a list of word-for-word substitutions. If this sounds rather intuitive, it is because this is what we tend to do when translating languages with the aid of a bilingual dictionary or phrase book. Take for example the French sentence, "*J'ai un livre rouge.*" This can be translated into English by following the associations provided in the dictionary (Table 4.1).

Direct translation simply takes the words in the source text (French) and replaces them with words in the target language (English). Direct MT systems simply encode these substitutions and transformations in a set of logical steps or rules that can be executed on a digital com-

Table 4.1: Example of direct translation from French to English

FRENCH	ENGLISH
J'ai	I have
un	a
livre	book
rouge	red

puter. Code for translating the above French sentence into English might look something like this:

```
if "j'ai" return "I have"
if "elle a" return "she has"
if "il a" return "he has"

if "un livre" return "a book"
if "le livre" return "the book"

if "rouge" return "red"
if "bleu" return "blue"
if "noir" return "black"
```

This short example demonstrates two important items. First, direct translation is not too terribly difficult. All you need is a bilingual dictionary that pairs up words or phrases from the source language with those in the target language such that the linguistic transformation produces results close enough to being considered correct and intelligible. And most of the first-generation MT systems from the 1950s, which were designed for and run on rather slow and cumbersome mainframe computers, came closer to achieving the latter even on a good day. But (and this is the second point) this way of performing translation can get out of hand very quickly. The example code provided above can only deal with one, very short, and limited sentence with only a few variables. Imagine writing code to cover every conceivable sentence that could be produced in French and then reproducing that entire effort for translations that move in the opposite direction – that is, from an English source to a French target. The numbers of lines of code start to multiply uncontrollably. (To get a feel for this problem, try it yourself by writing a direct translation program in Maker Exercise 3).

Not only does this approach have trouble scaling, but it typically produces very literal results that can miss the actual meaning and nuance conveyed by the source text. This problem can be seen in "mistranslations" with early English/Russian MT projects from the 1950s. But first we need a little historical context. One of the "pressing needs" that fueled both the interest in and the initial funding for MT activities in the US in particular was the exigencies of the Cold War – the fact that the US Department of Defense and the intelligence agencies, like the CIA, wanted to be able to translate documents and information gathered from the Soviet Union into readable English. So there was considerable effort in the US to devise Russian to English translation programs, just as there were similar projects in the Soviet Union to do the opposite, namely, translate English into Russian.

One of the classic (and perhaps apocryphal) examples of the kind of errors made by these systems is the translation into Russian of the biblical phrase "the spirit is strong, but the flesh weak." This had been reportedly translated as "*водка крепкая, а мясо протухло,*" which means "the vodka [is] strong but the meat rotten." Clearly, the MT system produced an accurate word-for-word substitution, but that transformation could not account for important differences in the context and meaning of the statement. (This is not, we should note, the only or even the most important mistranslation from these first-generation MT systems; John Hutchins, one of the pioneers in the field, provides a rather impressive lists of "errors" in his various books from 1986, 1992, and 2000.) For these reasons, direct translation is not very practical or popular, even if the basic concept it develops and demonstrates remains the core idea of all MT methodologies.

Transfer approaches   One of the problems with direct word-for-word translation can be immediately seen in the example provided above (Table 4.1). In the case of the French sentence "*J'ai un livre rouge,*" direct translation would produce the following (incorrect) English result "I have a book red." This is due to an important grammatical difference between English and French concerning the position of adjectives with respect to the noun they modify. In English the adjective (red) is situated before the noun (book); in French the adjective (rouge) comes after the noun (livre). Similar difficulties are encountered when translating between other language pairs, like English and Japanese. English is what linguists call an SVO language, a language that uses the word order subject-verb-object – e.g., "The dog ate ice cream." Unlike English, Japanese employs an SOV word order (subject-object-verb) – e.g., "The dog ice cream ate."

In order to address and deal with these potential problems, MT researchers developed more sophisticated "transfer rules" that were designed to handle these different structural and lexical complexities. For instance, the translation of the French phrase *"livre rouge"* into English could be handled by simply applying a general rule that inverted the position of the adjective with respect to the noun. Technically this is accomplished by applying what is called "contrastive knowledge," that is, knowledge about the differences between the two languages, in the process of formulating and writing the transfer rules. One simple but effective way to accomplish this is to parse (divide up) the linguistic data not by individual words, as is done in a bilingual dictionary, but by phrases, as you might see in a travel phrase book. So instead of using word-for-word substitutions, the MT system could be designed to employ meaningful sets or segments of words.

> if "un livre rouge" return "a red book"
> if "un livre bleu" return "a blue book"
> if "un livre noir" return "a black book"
>
> if "le livre rouge" return "the red book"
> if "le livre bleu" return "the blue book"
> if "le livre noir" return "the black book"

Although providing for more accurate translations than the direct word-for-word approach, this method would require that MT developers not only anticipate virtually every possible statement that could be made in French, but then write individual (and exceedingly redundant) lines of code to deal with each and every possible variation. A more economical approach – "economical" from the perspective of the number of lines of code that would need to be written and processed – could be achieved by using regular expression matches and a set of more general replacement rules. "Regular Expressions" are a rather common feature in programming languages. They involve a formal method for defining a particular pattern of characters in a string of text data that can then be used by a search algorithm to perform simple "find and replace" operations. In other words, programmers can write lines of code that specify something like the following:

> INPUT = "J'ai un livre rouge"
> Search INPUT for "rouge" OR "bleu" OR "noir"
> If search is successful, invert word order

Another approach abstracts from the individual words to their grammatical function in the sentence. This involves identifying and tagging each word and then applying appropriate reordering rules. This method employs a simple index that identifies the grammatical function of each word, which is a common feature available in dictionaries:

> ADJ = bleu, noir, rouge . . .
> NOUN = avion, chaise, livre . . .
> ARTICLE = un, une, le, la . . .

Using this index, one could formulate a set of instructions that evaluates the input sentence, identifies and tags the grammatical function of each word in the sentence based on the associations supplied by the index, and then applies a simple transformation rule that inverts the word order irrespective of the specific words involved: i.e., NOUN ADJ → ADJ NOUN. The transformation can be applied either at the point of input so that the source text is reordered prior to applying the bilingual dictionary, or after, such that the target output is reordered prior to being displayed to the user.

Interlingua   One significant problem with both the direct and the transfer approaches is that they are designed to work with a distinct set of transformation rules based on a predefined pair of languages, like English and French. This is not a problem when the task of translation is limited to just a few languages, but it becomes increasingly complicated and unruly as the number of languages to be translated into one another increases. In other words, both the direct approach, which utilizes a bilingual dictionary for word-to-word translation between languages, and the transfer approach, which formulates more complex transformation rules based on a specific pair of languages, have trouble scaling. To quantify the problem, consider the following. For any number of languages (n), this particular systems-architecture requires $n(n-1)$ transfer modules. In other words, if we have two languages ($n = 2$), like French and English, you would need $2(2-1)$ or two transfer modules – one to transform French into English and the other to transform English into French. But let's say we want to use the same approach for four languages ($n = 4$). This would require twelve different transfer modules, or $4(4-1)$. Following this procedure, a machine translation system capable of translating between the twenty-four recognized languages of the European Union ($n = 24$) would require 552 separate translation modules.

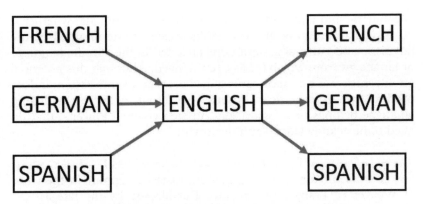

Figure 4.4   Block diagram of a translation system for three European languages using English as an intermediary or interlingua

To address this limitation, which affects not only translation efficiency but also its expense, many multilingual systems have been designed to employ a third, intermediate language, or *interlingua*. As Klaus Schubert (1992: 81) explains: "the $n(n-1)$ formula is based on the assumption that every source language is linked directly with every target language. If these direct links can be given up in favour of a single, central representation, the combinatorial problem is removed." This alternative systems-architecture is more economical, requiring only $2n$ translation models. If we wanted, for instance, to design a system to translate between Spanish, French, and German, we could utilize English as an interlingua. This would require only six translation modules: three to translate the source languages into English and three to translate out of English into the target languages (Figure 4.4).

Interlinguas consist in both natural languages that have been selected for convenience and in artificial languages that have been invented for the purposes of mediating linguistic differences, like Esperanto. In either case, the choice of interlingua, although clearly expedient for effectively managing the number of translation modules, is not without important linguistic and cultural consequences. By translating every language into and out of the interlingua, the translation system effectively privileges one particular language, restricting all possible expressions to concepts and logics that are germane to that particular idiom. Esperanto, for example, although formulated as a universal, international language, privileges native speakers of European languages from which Esperanto has derived its grammar, vocabulary, and alphabet. Consequently, the interlingua, whether it comprises a natural or an artificial language, is often limited by the linguistic and cultural assumptions encoded in the specific language or languages from which it has been derived. Although this potential ethnocentrism is not necessarily a deal breaker for translation, it does produce important critical concerns – especially when the mediating language belongs to a historically situated colonial power – that do need to be acknowledged and dealt with.

The end of an era   The three methods of classical MT – direct, transfer, and interlingua – experienced enthusiastic support in the wake of Weaver's "Translation" memo. But already by the late 1950s, optimism for success with these MT efforts began to lose ground and were increasingly the target of criticism. The first salvo of critical reevaluation came from Yehoshua Bar-Hillel, an Israeli researcher who not only was the first academic to work full time in the field of MT, but also had organized the first International Conference on the subject in 1952. After about a decade of dedicated work on MT systems, Bar-Hillel began to reconsider the progress (or lack of progress) in the field. In February 1959 published a now-famous technical publication, *Report on the State of Machine Translation in the United States and Great Britain*. The report delivered a rather negative assessment of the objective – implicit in the Weaver memo – of creating computational mechanisms capable of performing fully automatic high-quality translation (FAHQT) and therefore recommended that researchers should give up working on that task and seek instead to develop computer-assisted tools to support human translators. The disillusionment that is expressed in Bar-Hillel's report is as much an indication of the author's own disappointment with the lack of technical progress in the field as it is a product of the rather unrealistic expectations that had been imposed on this research effort since the release of the Weaver memo.

The next critical blow came in November 1966 with an influential document published in the US by the Automatic Language Processing Advisory Committee (ALPAC), *Languages and Machines: Computers in Translation and Linguistics*. The ALPAC Report, as the document has come to be called, was critical of both the high costs of MT research projects and the lack of progress in achieving anything close to FAHQT. "To illustrate this point," as Poibeau (2017: 81) points out, "the report included four translation results from Russian to English using four of the era's machine translation systems. The translations were mediocre at best." In the wake of the ALPAC

Report, MT experienced a slow-down in both funding and research effort in the English-speaking world in general and the US in particular. Although research and funding continued to be supported elsewhere in the world, this slow-down produced a kind of "MT winter" – or what Poibeau (2017: 83) calls "a long pause" – that extended from the mid-1960s into the mid-1980s. One of the bright spots in this period was SYSTRAN, a classical MT system initially developed by Peter Tomas in 1968, contracted to the European community in 1975, and made available to early adopters of the Internet on the pre-Google search engine AltaVista in the form of an application called Babel Fish.

4.2.2 Example-based MT

Things begin to thaw and pick up again in the mid-1980s with the introduction of a new methodology called "example-based MT." The development of this approach was made possible by an increase in the number of machine-readable documents available on the Internet, especially parallel corpora or bilingual texts. Parallel corpora consist of textual pairings of the same content in at least two different languages, and these aligned documents have been an important resource for translators for centuries. One of the oldest and most important has been the Rosetta Stone, a large piece of granodiorite that was inscribed with three different versions of a decree issued in 196 BC by King Ptolemy V – Egyptian hieroglyphic script, Demotic script, and ancient Greek. The Stone was key to helping archaeologists decipher Egyptian hieroglyphics, as they could use its pairing to the other two known scripts to figure out this previously unknown writing system.

For contemporary MT systems, a good source of parallel corpora can be found in the official record of the debates, discussions and transactions, and agenda items of the Canadian Parliament. These transcripts, known as the Hansard, are published online in both French and English and are lined-up, or aligned, sentence by sentence (Figure 4.5). Digitized parallel corpora like these can be used to guide translation efforts by supplying actual examples that can be applied to future translation tasks.

The concept of example-based MT was introduced by the Japanese computer scientist Makoto Nagao in the mid-1980s. Nagao recognized that classical, rule-based MT systems, which performed reasonably well for translations between the different European languages, had considerable problems when applied to languages

First Reading of Senate Public Bills	Première lecture des projets de loi d'intérêt public émanant du Sénat
S-205 — October 25, 2016 — An Act to amend the Canada Border Services Agency Act (Inspector General of the Canada Border Services Agency) and to make consequential amendments to other Acts.	**S-205** — 25 octobre 2016 — Loi modifiant la Loi sur l'Agence des services frontaliers du Canada (inspecteur général de l'Agence des services frontaliers du Canada) et d'autres lois en conséquence.
S-215 — January 30, 2017 — An Act to amend the Criminal Code (sentencing for violent offences against Aboriginal women).	**S-215** — 30 janvier 2017 — Loi modifiant le Code criminel (peine pour les infractions violentes contre les femmes autochtones).
S-225 — June 16, 2016 — Mr. Carrie (Oshawa) — An Act to amend the Controlled Drugs and Substances Act (substances used in the production of fentanyl).	**S-225** — 16 Juin 2016 — M. Carrie (Oshawa) — Loi modifiant la Loi réglementant certaines drogues et autres substances (substances utilisées dans la production de fentanyl).

Figure 4.5   Excerpt from the Canadian Parliament's Order Paper and Notice Paper for February 1, 2017

from different linguistic groups, like English and Japanese. As Nagao described it in his influential paper from 1984:

> European languages have a certain common basis among them, and the mutual translation between these languages will be possible without great structural changes in sentential expressions. But the translation between two languages which are totally different, like English and Japanese, has a lot of difficult problems. Sometimes the same contents are expressed by completely different sentential structures, and there is no good structural correspondence between each part of the sentences of the two languages. (1984: 176)

To remedy this problem, Nagao proposed to develop a new kind of MT procedure that is based on how human beings actually work with linguistic difference.

At the beginning of his paper, Nagao points out that human beings do not produce translations by following the kind of rule-based approaches operationalized in classical MT systems. Instead, they translate by following existing examples:

> Let us reflect about the mechanism of human translation of elementary sentences at the beginning of foreign language learning. A student memorizes the elementary English sentences with the corresponding Japanese sentences. The first stage is completely a drill of memorizing lots of similar sentences and words in English, and the corresponding Japanese. Here we have no translation theory at all to give to the

student. He has to get the translation mechanism through his own instinct. He has to compare several different English sentences with the corresponding Japanese. He has to guess, make inferences about the structure of sentences from a lot of examples. (1984: 173)

Example-based MT simply seeks to develop algorithms that can achieve this kind of inference automatically by searching for and locating fragments of aligned translations in existing bilingual corpora, extracting and storing these translated fragments, and then recombining the different fragments in order to produce more or less acceptable output in the target language.

A simplified example might help. In his introduction to *Machine Translation*, Thierry Poibeau (2017: 112) provides the following illustration: "Let's imagine that we ask the system to translate 'Training is not the solution to every problem' into French and that a bilingual corpus is available with, among others, the following pairs of sentences" (see Table 4.2).

Table 4.2: Segment of a bilingual corpus for translations between English and French

	ENGLISH	FRENCH
Ex 1	Training is not the solution to everything	La formation n'est pas la solution universelle
Ex 2	Training is not the solution to all parenting struggles	La formation n'est pas la solution à toutes les difficultés rencontrées par les parents
Ex 3	There is a solution to every problem	Il y a une solution à tous les problèmes
Ex 4	There is a spiritual solution to every problem	Il y a une solution spirituelle à tous les problèmes

The translation system performs a simple text search (similar to what you would do when using the search feature in MS Word or other application), trying to match segments from the input text – "Training is not the solution to every problem" – to what is available in the bilingual corpus. In the process, the search identifies two matches for the phrase "Training is not the solution . . . ," which is associated with the French phrase *"La formation n'est pas la solution . . . ,"* and two matches for the phrase ". . . to every problem," which is aligned with the French *". . . à tous les problèmes."* By extracting and recombining (or, more accurately stated, "concatenating") these two fragments – *"La formation n'est pas la solution"* + *"à tous les problèmes*" – the system can then produce a translation of the source text: "*La formation n'est pas la solution à tous les problèmes.*" Again, we should remember that the computer does not need to "understand" the meaning of the words or the phrases that are being searched, matched, and rearranged. From its perspective (assuming that it has a perspective) "*La formation*" is a string of searchable text characters, no different from other strings of characters like "gQx$_&2NmK." Meaning takes place in us when the output is displayed to the human user, who is able to read and interpret its significance.

Example-based MT garnered attention during the 1980s and was especially attractive for systems designed to handle Asian languages, which do not exhibit the same kind of linguistic similarities that are often available with Western/European language groups, like Italian, Portuguese, and Spanish. But this approach to developing MT applications does have important limitations. For one thing, it requires a large number of parallel corpora that are aligned, if at all possible, at the sentence level. Fortunately, this kind of data became increasingly accessible throughout the 1980s as documents were digitized and uploaded to the Internet. But even though the number of parallel corpora has increased considerably since the privatization of the Internet, there are still situations where aligned fragments cannot be identified. When this occurs, example-based MT systems either fail or need to fall back on direct word-for-word translations. As a result of this problem, example-based MT quickly gave way to, and came to be incorporated into, another technological innovation – statistical MT.

4.2.3 Statistical MT

Statistical MT is based on and exploits the statistical nature of human languages. Fortunately, we do not need to get into a lot of complex statistical theory to see what is meant by this. The word order of a reasonably valid sentence in any natural language, English for example, can be statistically analyzed and evaluated. Consider the following words listed here in alphabetical order: book, English, in, is, language, the, this, written. Some arrangements (sequential orderings of these words) have a high probability of actually occurring in everyday use of the language. For example, this sequence of words would have a rather high probability of actually occurring somewhere at some time: "This book is written in the English language." While other sequences of the same words would have a very low probability of actually occurring – e.g., "Book language the is English this in written." Likewise, there are sequences of Portuguese words – "*Este livro está escrito em inglês*" – that would have a higher probability of being recognized as more or less accurate translations of the valid English sentence (the word order with the highest probability of actually occurring) than some other sequences of Portuguese words, like "*Em está inglês livro este escrito.*" Statistical MT simply utilizes this observed fact regarding human languages to produce mechanized translation procedures.

One key feature of statistical MT systems is that the procedure is formalized by beginning from the other end of the translation task. Classical MT begins with the source text and then seeks to devise rules or coded instructions to transform the source material into a reasonable version in the target language. Statistical MT begins not with the source but with the target. The initial question that statistical MT asks is therefore a bit different: "Given different sentences (or, more accurately stated, sequences of words) in the target language, which one or ones have the highest probability of being recognized as accurate translations of the sentence (or valid sequences of words) in the source language?" This can be formalized by using something called Bayes' Theorem, a well-known principle from probability theory:

$$\Pr(T|S) = \frac{\Pr(T) \ \Pr(S|T)}{\Pr(S)}$$

On its own, this formula probably tells you very little (unless, of course, you have done some prior work in statistics). So let's break it down and reformulate it in terms we can work with.

- $\Pr(T)$ is a statistical model of the target language, what researchers usually call a language model. In effect, it is a set of different word sequences that can occur in the target language ranked by the probability of that particular sequence actually occurring in the target language. In other words (and stated more formally), $\Pr(T)$ is the probability that T forms a statistically valid and well-formed sequence of words in the target language. Using this model, we can identify the most probable sequence of words from a number of different possible arrangements. Table 4.3 illustrates what a simplified (very, very simplified) language model for English might look like.

The probabilities associated with the different word orders in this model are not just "made up." They are discovered by looking at and evaluating (or taking a mathematical measurement) of a

Table 4.3: Example probabilities for different word orders in English

Word order	Probability
I left the apartment and went to class	0.35
I left class and went to the apartment	0.30
I left the class and went to apartment	0.15
I left apartment and went to the class	0.12
I the class left and apartment went to	0.08
Class the went to left and I apartment	0.00

large number of available corpora that provide real-world examples of the different ways the words in the target language have been sequenced and organized. This is one place where the fundamental insight from example-based MT figures prominently in statistical MT. Just as we did in example-based MT, so we can use the large amount of linguistic data – that is, corpora or sets of valid sequences of words in a particular language – that are available in a machine-readable form on the Internet. By looking at, for example, the entire set of works written by William Shakespeare, certain word orders will be evaluated as more probable than others. (In fact – and this is just a side note – the works of Shakespeare, although one would think they are rather large and robust when it comes to supplying different kinds of word sequences, provide a relatively small number of possible variations, such that a language model built only on the works of Shakespeare would be of rather limited application. For this reason, language models are typically constructed on the basis of a large number of different kinds of corpora. This is one meaning of the term "big data" – large numbers of examples that can be used to generate a robust language model.)

- $\Pr(T \mid S)$ is a translation model that evaluates the probability that a particular sequence of words in the source text S corresponds to a valid sequence of words in the target language T. In terms of how this operates, a sentence in the source language is parsed or broken down into small verbal fragments (either individual words or short word phrases). These are then correlated with possible translations in the target language. In classical MT, this correlation would have been performed by using a bilingual dictionary, e.g. simple word-for-word substitutions. In statistical MT, the correlation follows the example provided by example-based MT and is formulated by evaluating actual examples of translation available in existing parallel corpora. In effect, the "bilingual dictionary" in statistical MT takes each word in the source language and correlates it with a list of possible translations in the target language (as demonstrated by actual examples in the parallel corpora) along with the probability associated with each one of these possible correlations. Table 4.4 gives an illustration of what one of these bilingual dictionaries might look like for the English word "motion."

Table 4.4: Possible French translations of the English word "motion"

English word	Possible translations	Probability
motion	mouvement	0.35
	geste	0.12
	motion	0.11
	proposition	0.10
	résolution	0.10
	marche	0.05
	signe	0.04

Source: Modified from Poibeau 2017: 132. Each of the listed French translations of "motion" appears along with a probability based on the number of times the word "motion" was actually translated in this way.

- Pr(S) indicates a language model for the source language. But since the source text is the sequence of words to be translated, we generally do not need to evaluate the probability of its word sequence. In other words, we can assume that the sequence of words in the source text is in fact valid insofar as it is an actually spoken or written statement in the source language. For this reason, it is possible to disregard the denominator in Bayes' Theorem and simplify the formula:

$$T = argmax_T [Pr(T) * Pr(S|T)]$$

The resultant translation in the target language T is the product of the maximized values ("*argmax*" is a mathematical abbreviation meaning "arguments of the maxima") of a function where the probability of the word sequence in the target language is multiplied by the probability of the correlation between the source text and the target language. For this reason, a group of IBM researchers who first developed this approach to statistical MT in a series of influential scientific papers published in the early 1990s called this formula the "fundamental equation of machine translation" (cf. Brown et al. 1990, 1993).

But this is still a bit abstract and inaccessible. So let's take an example and follow how statistical MT would process the data for translating the following Spanish sentence into English (this example is derived from Geitgey 2016): "*Quiero ir a la playa más bonita.*" Recall that we do not need to deal with Pr(*S*) insofar as we can safely assume that this sentence has a very high probability of being a valid sequence of Spanish words. So we begin by parsing the source text into verbal chunks, either individual words or short sequences of closely associated words. This can be done, as we saw above, by performing recursive searches on the input text string in order to find and extract individual elements (or substrings of the string). The result of this would be a list of individual verbal units: *Quiero* | *ir* | *a* | *la playa* | *más bonita*.

The translation model Pr(*S*|*T*) looks to a set of bilingual corpora to find all the different ways human translators have translated these words (or sequence of words) in the past. This produces a bilingual dictionary with each word from Spanish associated with its possible English translations and a statistical ranking that indicates the probability for that particular correlation (Table 4.5).

Table 4.5: A list of possible English translations for the individual verbal units in the source language and their associated probabilities as discovered in data available from parallel corpora

quiero		ir		a		la playa		más bonita	
I want	0.33	to go	0.31	to	0.44	the beach	0.55	more pretty	0.33
I love	0.26	to work	0.14	at	0.31	the seaside	0.45	most pretty	0.18
I like	0.18	to run	0.22	per	0.25			more lovely	0.32
I try	0.15	to be	0.05					most lovely	0.17
I mean	0.08	to leave	0.28						

From this data, the program then generates thousands of different possible translations, basically different arrangements of words in English that have a high likelihood of being valid translations of the source text. It then evaluates these different possible word sequences by looking to the language model for the target language Pr(*T*), meaning that the program evaluates the probability that one or more of the generated sentences have, in fact, actually occurred in corpora of the target language. In other words, of all the sentences that are generated, some will be more likely than others to occur in the target language. So the program identifies the one, or ones, that are most likely to occur, and disregards the others (see Table 4.6).

Table 4.6: Possible English sentences and the probability of actually occurring in existing texts or corpora

I love	to be	at	the seaside	most lovely	0.39
I like	to leave	per	the beach	more pretty	0.05
I mean	to be	at	the seaside	more lovely	0.11
I want	to go	to	the beach	most lovely	0.45

Looking at the probabilities available in this example, it is clear that the final sentence, which has a probability of 0.45, is the most likely candidate for translating the Spanish sentence *"Quiero ir a la playa más bonita."* One thing to note is that the resulting word sequence in English is not exactly correct. We do not typically say "the beach most lovely" (maybe in poetry, but not in standard conversational English). This would need to be adjusted by applying a reordering rule for nouns and adjectives as described above. Also, we should take note of the fact that all of this can be accomplished working with statistical evaluations of probable word order. The computer does not need to "understand" (and, in fact, cannot "understand") what is meant by the Spanish sentence or its English translation. It can perform the task of translation for us by simply working with probable sequences of words and probable associations between different words as exemplified in the existing parallel corpora.

As you might have already predicted, one of the major advantages to statistical MT is that it is able to leverage the best of both worlds. That is, it calls upon and utilizes the numerous examples that are available in machine-readable parallel corpora, basically calling upon and remixing decades of translation experience from human translators. At the same time, this approach is able to make best use of what made classical MT attractive in the first place – the ability to work with individual words or very small verbal units, thus producing a more robust translation system. For this reason, statistical MT quickly took over the field around the turn of the century. Google Translate, for instance, initially operated with a licensed version of SYSTRAN, one of the most successful classical MT products on the market. This was eventually replaced in 2006 by a Google-developed statistical MT system, which mainly used United Nations and European Parliament transcripts for its parallel corpora. This system remained in operation for a decade and was only replaced when Google introduced a new neural MT engine (more on this below). But the switch to statistical MT in 2006 introduced significant improvements in the Google

Translate application that were directly noted and experienced by users of the translation service.

This does not, however, mean that statistical MT is the ultimate solution. There are, in fact, three well-documented complications with this approach to developing MT systems:

1 The quality of translation is limited by the parallel corpus on which the system is trained. The Canadian Parliament's Hansard Index is an easily accessible resource of machine-readable documents. One would expect that a system trained on government transcripts would be good at translating similar kinds of texts – rules, regulations, formal parliamentary debates, etc. – but might have considerable difficulties if applied to poetry or other forms of literature.

2 The most expedient way to get around this problem is by calling upon and using a wide range of different kinds of parallel corpora – not just transcripts of parliamentary debate, but translations of the great works of literature, technical manuals, and scientific papers. The problem here is that this diversity of machine-readable parallel corpora is something that is only possible with some language pairs, like English and French, and may not be available to many others, like Icelandic and Cambodian or Romanian and Korean. This introduces not only a kind of bias, where some language pairs will have much better translation capabilities than others, but also the need to reintroduce interlinguas. "If you are asking Google to translate Georgian to Telugu," Adam Geitgey (2016) explains, "it has to internally translate it into English as an intermediate step because there's not enough Georgian-to-Telugu translations happening to justify investing heavily in that language pair."

3 Because of the extensive coding necessary to build and maintain these various statistical models, this approach to MT is labor-intensive and expensive. A good illustration of this can be found in the five different models proposed by the IBM research team (Brown et al. 1993), where each subsequent model introduced a different set of manually defined algorithms to correct for defects inherent in the previous model. For these reasons (especially this final one), statistical MT is eventually replaced by innovations that make use of the opportunities of deep learning neural networks.

4.2.4 Neural network MT

As we have already seen in Chapter 3, neural networks have been around for a number of decades. Despite this, their popularity with developers has ebbed and flowed – at times, they have enjoyed considerable attention; at other times, they have remained in the margins. The 2000s saw a significant uptake in interest as new methods and developments in deep neural networks proved capable of resolving a number of "wicked problems" that had escaped resolution by rule-based approaches: handwriting-recognition, speech-recognition, image-recognition, facial-recognition, etc. – basically any situation where it is necessary to locate and exploit patterns that exist in large data sets. Not surprisingly, similar approaches were sought for and applied to the task of MT. Perhaps the most visible indicator of this was Google Translate, which began, in November 2016, by moving its translation services from a statistical MT methodology to a new neural network translation system called Google Neural Machine Translation (GNMT). The impact and success of the new approach was immediately apparent to users of the application and was widely publicized. As was noted in a *New York Times* article from December 14, 2016, things seemed to change overnight:

> As of the previous weekend, Translate had been converted to an AI-based system for much of its traffic, not just in the United States but in Europe and Asia as well. The rollout included translations between English and Spanish, French, Portuguese, German, Chinese, Japanese, Korean. and Turkish. The rest of Translate's hundred-odd languages were to come, with the aim of eight per month, by the end of next year. The new incarnation, to the pleasant surprise of Google's own engineers, had been completed in only nine months. The AI system had demonstrated overnight improvements roughly equal to the total gains the old one [the statistical MT system] had accrued over its entire lifetime. (Lewis-Kraus 2016)

Recognizing the potential improvements available by applying neural networks to language translation, all the other players – Microsoft (Bing Translate and Skype), Facebook, SYSTRAN, etc. – did the same. For this reason, most commercially available MT applications now employ some form of neural network machine learning.

Although there are important variations in each individual application/implementation, all these systems employ and work with the same basic architecture, which was initially introduced in a scientific paper written by a team of Canadian and European researchers in

2014 under the direction of Kyunghyun Cho. The paper, "Learning Phrase Representations using RNN Encoder–Decoder for Statistical Machine Translation," demonstrated the feasibility of using recurrent neural networks (RNN) to develop MT applications that could work with phrases rather than individual words, thus preserving important information regarding context and avoiding one of the common problems with statistical MT's focus on word-to-word translations. It is the combination of two innovations (mentioned in the title of the paper) that make this possible: recurrent neural networks and encoding/decoding.

An RNN is a neural network where the previous state of the network is used as one of the inputs to the next calculation, allowing the network to discover patterns in a sequence of data. As Cho et al. (2014: 1725) explain: "An RNN can learn a probability distribution over a sequence by being trained to predict the next symbol in a sequence." Because human languages are little more than a set of complex patterns (sequences of different arrangements of a finite set of elements), RNNs can be used to learn – or perhaps better stated "discover" or "identify" – patterns that exist within and comprise a particular language.

Encoding is the process of making numerical measurements of input data. This can be done to images for the purpose of building facial-recognition applications, and it can also be done with sentences. In effect, a sentence (or valid sequence of words) can be turned into a unique set of numerical measurements. This is accomplished by feeding into the RNN each word in the sentence one after the other until all words in the sentences have been processed. Because the RNN incorporates the results of previous calculations into the next operation, the final encoding represents all the words in the sentence. Or, as Poibeau (2017: 185) explains, "Each word is encoded through a vector of numbers and all the word vectors are gradually combined to provide a [numeric] representation of the whole sentence" (see Table 4.7).

Table 4.7: Example encoding of an English sentence

Input sentence	Measurements representing the input sentence			
	0.129878	−0.083371	−0.008493	0.155623
	−0.134902	0.495002	−0.080211	0.073908
The sky is blue	0.099697	0.145057	0.100562	0.169381
	−0.002102	−0.026187	0.102709	0.032985
	−0.120154	0.002259	0.100233	−0.015721

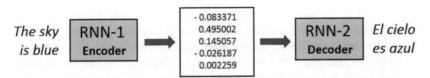

Figure 4.6   Schematic diagram of sequence-to-sequence RNN for machine translation

We can now create a translation system by connecting two RNNs in a configuration that is called sequence-to-sequence. In this "Seq2Seq" model, the first RNN generates an encoding that represents a particular sentence. The second RNN can then take the encoded data (the output of the first RNN) and perform the same operation in reverse order, decoding the numerical data in order to reproduce the initial input sentence. Stated more accurately, the system "learns to *encode* a variable-length sequence [the original sentence] into a fixed-length vector representation [the numerical measurement] and to *decode* a given fixed-length vector representation back into a variable-length sequence" (Cho et al. 2014: 1725). Obviously, this procedure (encoding and then decoding the initial sentence) is not very interesting or useful. But we can do the same thing using another language, like Spanish. In other words, we can train the second RNN to decode "the fixed length vector representation" not into the original English but into a valid sequence of Spanish words by calling upon the associations that are available in a set of parallel corpora, as was done in statistical MT (see Figure 4.6).

In effect, this approach is really just a variant of statistical MT, where the bilingual lexicon is replaced by an encoder/decoder that has been trained on data that is available in the parallel corpora. What this means is that "once the RNN Encoder–Decoder is trained," as Cho et al. (2014: 1726) conclude, "the model can be used in two ways. One way is to use the model to generate a target sequence given an input sequence [i.e., generate a translation]. On the other hand, the model can be used to score a given pair of input and output sequences [i.e., rate and select the best translation from a set of competing possibilities]." How all of this comes to be implemented in code is a technical matter that requires considerable knowledge of and experience with recurrent neural networks. For a taste of what this entails, you can look at the TensorFlow tutorial at https://www. tensorflow.org/tutorials/.

Applying neural networks to the task of MT has a number of advantages.

1 It tends to be more accurate and reliable. Because neural network MT is designed to encode and work with entire sentences without having to decompose them into smaller segments, it is able to preserve and account for context and word nuance. These systems can, for example, differentiate between the different meanings of a word like "bank," which can vary due to context – "I am going to the *bank* to get a loan" vs. "I sat on the *bank* and gazed across the river." Unlike previous MT systems, neural network approaches can be designed to account for and handle these different "word embeddings."

2 These systems tend to be more efficient and less costly to develop and maintain. This is because the translation model is something that is automatically generated by the algorithm from patterns that are discovered in the training data rather than something that is dependent on the knowledge, expertise, and programming effort of human developers. Obviously human beings are still needed to design the network and set up its training on data, but the actual "rules" or instructions by which the translation takes place do not need to be defined and/or programmed. The machine is able to discover these things "for itself."

3 Applying neural networks to MT has, at least in the short run, produced remarkable improvements in translation quality in a relatively short span of time. Even though this approach to MT is rather young – with Google Translate having just implemented it in 2016 – it is performing as well as, if not better than, the statistical machine translation systems that took close to fifteen years to develop. It is doubtful that this rapid improvement will persist at this level over the long haul. Nevertheless, it did, in fact, completely revolutionize the field virtually overnight.

This is not to say that neural network MT is perfect. There are at least two important limitations and potential problems that need to be noted:

1 *Black box*. Like all neural network applications, this approach to MT remains empirical, meaning that these systems work – they are able to produce what appears to be a reasonable translation – but how or why they work is not necessarily something that can be observed, explained, and/or theorized. This means, as we have already seen in Chapter 3, that these systems can be criticized for being "black boxes" – complex systems with internal operations that are not readily available to human oversight or understand-

ing. As Poibeau (2017: 193) explains: "It is hard to understand and analyze the way a neural system works, since the internal representation of the data is purely numerical, huge and complex, and more importantly not directly readable by a human being." In effect, we have translation systems that work, but exactly how they work remains a bit of a mystery.

2 *Data driven.* Like statistical MT, this approach utilizes the translation data provided by parallel corpora, meaning that translation is dependent on the quantity and quality of this data. In some cases, there are a number of high-quality parallel texts to work with. In other cases, there are considerably fewer that are available in machine-readable form. Consequently, like the statistical MT systems before it, neural network MT needs big data, and the larger and more robust these data sets are, the better.

4.3 Return to Babel

At the end, we can return to where it all began and ask the following set of questions. With all this progress in the technology of MT, have we finally achieved the means to repair and overcome, once and for all, the damage that was experienced at the Tower of Babel? Is MT a technologically enabled version of the miracle of Pentecost, where no matter who is speaking and in what language, we can all understand what is being said in the language into which we were born? Was Warren Weaver's prediction from 1949 correct and accurate – have we devised a workable solution to the worldwide translation problem through the use of electronic computers of great capacity, flexibility, and speed? Or, to put it more directly and in a way that matters for university students, does MT make the foreign language requirement obsolete? Interestingly, the answer to this question must be both "yes" and "no." It all depends on how we understand language and linguistic difference.

If language is understood as little more than a means of inter-personal communication, and if linguistic difference – or, if you like, the diversity of languages that was the unfortunate legacy of the Tower of Babel – is understood as an obstacle to human communication and cooperation, then MT seem to promise a solution that is on a par with or at least very close to achieving what was experienced at Pentecost and has been imagined in science fiction with, for example, *Star Trek*'s Universal Translator or the Babel Fish from the *Hitchhiker's Guide*. You can, right now, travel the world and, by way of a smartphone app, simply point the phone's camera at some text, e.g., a sign or restaurant menu, and have Google Translate immediately render the unfamiliar words and phrases in your native language. And by employing some augmented reality (AR) visualization techniques, the scene you see on the phone's screen can look exactly like the world outside, with one exception: the text that is displayed is rendered in another language of your choosing.

Similarly, by using Microsoft's Skype Translator, you can seamlessly interact with another person who speaks an entirely different language in realtime over the Internet. In other words, a person in Australia who only speaks English can have an intelligible conversation with someone in Germany who only speaks German. The application renders spoken English into understandable German, and vice versa, thus mediating the linguistic difference between the two participants. Although the application is currently limited to translating between ten languages (English, Spanish, French, German, Mandarin Chinese, Italian, Portuguese, Arabic, Russian, and Japanese), its capabilities will be progressively expanded in order to encompass a wider variety of languages. Seen from this vantage point, it appears that these MT applications and tools do in fact remediate the babble of Babel and call for an end – or at least a significant reevaluation – of the need to learn other languages.

But not so fast. There is more to it, a lot more. Language is not just a tool of communication, it is also the expression and carrier of culture. In other words, languages are not just different ways of encoding thought, as Weaver had assumed in his "Translation" memo. They are also the means of thought such that different languages make available different ways of thinking about and engaging with the world. This alternative viewpoint is something that is rooted in the Sapir–Whorf hypothesis (named for two linguists who independently developed slightly different versions of it, Edward Sapir and Benjamin Lee Whorf) – the idea that language determines (or at least strongly influences) thought and that linguistic elements can limit and shape cognitive categories. A similar idea was put forward in the work of the philosopher Ludwig Wittgenstein (1981: 5.6), who famously argued that "*the limits of my language* mean the limits of my world." The proverbial illustration of this insight (something initially reported by the anthropologist Franz Boas and repeated with considerable regularity in both the academic and popular literature) is that the Inuit language of the Arctic contains many different names for what we, in English, call "snow," each one identifying a different aspect of the phenomenon not necessarily accessible to or able to be captured by the others.

Considered from this perspective, the linguistic diversity that was (supposedly) instituted at Babel might not be a catastrophic loss of communicative ability; it could be a good thing. Here is how George Steiner explains it in his book-length examination of translation:

> The ripened humanity of language, its indispensable conservative and creative force live in the extraordinary diversity of actual tongues, in the bewildering profusion and eccentricity (though there is no center) of their modes. The psychic need for particularity, for "in-clusion" and invention is so intense that it has, during the whole of man's history until very lately, outweighed the spectacular, obvious material advantages of mutual comprehension and linguistic unity. In that sense, the Babel myth is once again a case of symbolic inversion: [hu]mankind was not destroyed but on the contrary kept vital and creative by being scattered among tongues. (1975: 233)

Steiner's reading suggests an inversion of the traditional interpretation of the Babelian narrative. He argues that the so-called "catastrophe" of Babel, namely the confusion instituted by the multiplicity of languages that had divided humanity, does not constitute a kind of damage to be repaired, but is instead a substantial advantage and gain. At Babel, humankind was not destroyed by confusion; it was "kept vital and creative" through linguistic diversification. Like biodiversity, Steiner argues, linguistic diversity is a feature and not a bug. It has ensured human ingenuity and survival. If we look at language from this perspective, then the learning of more than one language and the task of translating between different languages are not just about efficient and effective communication. They involve learning about, experiencing, and living in a particular way of seeing, conceptualizing, and engaging the world. What is interesting about MT, therefore, is that it can alleviate language learning of the assumption and burden of mere communication, opening up opportunities to see other ways to think about and work with languages. So instead of replacing language learning and the foreign language requirement, it is more likely that MT will have the effect of recontextualizing and reformulating – a process David Bolter and Richard Grusin (1999) called "remediation" – the *raison d'être* for studying languages in the first place.

Summary of Key Points

- Linguistic differences separate human individuals and communities. The origin of and reason for this division have been explained in myth and religious scriptures. And their reparation is predicted and prototyped in science fiction.
- Efforts to design and develop mechanized translation systems have been in existence for several centuries, beginning with the universal language projects of seventeenth-century Europe and extending to the post-WWII memo written by Warren Weaver.
- Because of the importance and influence of Weaver's memo, MT is considered to be one of the first, if not *the* first, practical applications of computer technology and the organizing principle of much of the early work in AI.
- MT R&D has progressed through several stages of technological development. It begins with simple rule-based systems, extending from direct translation methods suitable for dealing with pairs of languages to the use of interlinguas for expanded capabilities across multiple languages and progressing through example-based and statistical MT, which provide for better phrase- and sentence-level transfers. It currently employs sequence-to-sequence RNNs trained on large sets of linguistic data.
- Even though machine translation has improved over time and is remarkably convenient for facilitating human interaction on a global scale, it will not eradicate linguistic differences or the need for humans to learn other languages. This is because language is more than a tool of communication; it is also the expression and carrier of culture.

5

Natural Language Processing

Key Aims/Objectives

- To investigate the concept, technological features, and historical development of natural language processing (NLP) applications, beginning with the first chatbot ELIZA and proceeding through recent innovations.
- To examine the development and technological features of spoken dialogue systems (SDS), like Siri and Alexa, detailing advancements in the technology, different modes of implementation, and open problems in SDS design.
- To identify the points of contact between NLP innovation and efforts in Communication Studies, profiling how research in communication can support work in NLP engineering and how NPL systems can contribute to and inform research in Communication Studies.
- To reflect on and consider the future opportunities and challenges, where communicative interaction is not limited to human-to-human transactions but also involves human–machine communication.

Introduction

In science fiction, AI systems and robots talk. They communicate with us using natural human language. The HAL 9000 computer of *2001: A Space Odyssey* has conversations with the human members of the spacecraft crew, identifying and addressing each individual by using their first names. "He" (and the voice of the computer is intentionally gendered male) participates in a BBC interview, talking candidly about his "simulating relationship" with his human companions and even proudly listing off his specific accomplishments. And when things go wrong – and they do go very wrong – the computer dramatically explains himself and even pleads for his own life: "Dave, stop. Will you stop, Dave? . . . I'm afraid. I'm afraid, Dave."

The robots of science fiction also talk. Lt. Commander Data of *Star Trek: The Next Generation* not only produces intelligible vocalizations, but coordinates these utterances with gestures, facial expressions, and other nonverbal cues that are designed to assist humans in working and interacting with the device. Even R2-D2 from *Star Wars* uses language. Its "vocalizations" may not consist of what we recognize as words and phrases, but the trashcan-looking droid emits a series of electronic beeps, squeaks, and blurts that are (within the context of the narrative) clearly expressive of something that can be readily understood and interpreted for us by the android C-3PO.

But using language is not just fiction. Creating machines that can talk or communicate with human users in, and by employing, what is called "natural language" has been one of the objectives of AI from the very beginning. It was the first item on the list of proposed tasks to be addressed and accomplished by the Dartmouth summer seminar of 1956 ("an attempt will be made to find how to make machines use language"), it comprised the defining condition and test case for "machine intelligence" in Alan Turing's agenda-setting paper from 1950, and it was implemented and demonstrated in some of the earliest applications, like Joseph Weizenbaum's ELIZA program and Terry Winograd's SHRDLU. For this reason, working with, processing, and reproducing natural human language content is not one application among others; it is the definitive application. In this chapter we will look at natural language processing (NLP), focusing on two particular implementations – chatbots and spoken dialogue systems (SDS).

5.1 Chatbots

The term "bot" is short for "software-robot." Bots consist of a chunk of software code designed to accomplish some particular routine task automatically and autonomously. And the virtual spaces of the network are crawling with them, so much so that bot activity now accounts for over 50 percent of all traffic on the Internet (Zeifman 2017). There are web crawlers like the Googlebot, which seek out and rank web pages; spambots, which automatically generate email messages and overwhelm our inboxes with everything from marketing pitches to phishing campaigns; and there are chatbots and socialbots, two related subspecies of bot that are designed for human-level social interactions. As Robert Gehl and Maria Bakardjieva put it:

> [T]he socialbot is designed not simply to perform undesirable labor (like spambots) and not only to try to emulate human conversational intelligence (like chatbots). Rather, it is intended to present a Self, to pose as an alter-ego, as a subject with personal biography, stock of knowledge, emotions and body, as a social counterpart, as someone like me, the user, with whom I could build a social relationship. (2017: 2)

If the objective of the bot is to "pass itself off as a human being" (Boshmaf et al. 2011: 93), then chatbots are not just one specific implementation of AI, or what Richard Bartle (2003: 616) has called "AI in action," but comprise the defining condition of machine intelligence as originally stipulated by Alan Turing.

If Turing initially theorized these things, it was Joseph Weizenbaum who first implemented the concept by constructing a working prototype. ELIZA, as the application was called, was the first chatter- or chatbot. Although neither form of the term was utilized by Weizenbaum, it has been applied retrospectively as a result of the efforts of Michael Mauldin, founder and chief scientist of Lycos, who introduced the neologism in 1994 in order to identify a similar NLP application that he initially called CHATTERBOT. ELIZA was (as we have already seen in Chapter 2) a rather simple piece of GOFAI programming. It was designed to give the impression of understanding but did little more than identify keywords in user input, assemble prefabricated sentences from fragments, and then display this result in the form of a readable text string. Despite this fact, many users of ELIZA were taken in by the performance and insisted that the chatbot really did, in fact, understand them. And this is precisely what worries social scientists like Sherry Turkle (2011: 9): "I find people willing to seriously consider robots not only as pets but as potential friends, confidants, and even romantic partners. We don't seem to care what their artificial intelligences 'know' or 'understand' of the human moments we might 'share' with them . . . the performance of connection seems connection enough."

5.1.1 A chatbot menagerie

ELIZA was just the beginning. Since Weizenbaum's initial demonstration, there have been numerous efforts to further develop the capabilities and operations of chatbot technology, including the following.

PARRY (1972): Unlike Weizenbaum's ELIZA, which was originally designed to emulate the conversational activities of a Rogerian therapist, Kenneth Colby's PARRY (which was written in the LISP computer language) simulated a person with paranoid schizophrenia. In 1972, PARRY and a version of ELIZA that was named DOCTOR were connected over ARPANET (the precursor to the Internet) and interacted with each other in a highly publicized demonstration at ICCC 1972 (International Conference on Computer Communications). The transcript of a subsequent "conversation" was recorded and published by Internet-founding father Vinton Cerf (1973) in January of the following year.

CHATTERBOT (1994): Unlike ELIZA and PARRY, which could only engage in conversational interactions with a single dedicated user, Michael Mauldin's CHATTERBOT was designed to be a non-player character (NPC) in TinyMUD, a text-based virtual world. As Mauldin (1994: 16) explained: "We created a computer controlled player, a 'Chatter Bot,' that can converse with other players, explore the world, discover new paths through various rooms, answer players' questions about navigation (providing the shortest-path information on request), and answer questions about other players, rooms and objects." Since this initial demonstration in the virtual world of TinyMUD, bots of various kinds and configurations have become a standard feature in computer games and online virtual worlds.

A.L.I.C.E. (1995): Richard Wallace's "Artificial Linguistic Internet Computer Entity" was originally written in Java and utilized an XML schema called AIML (artificial intelligence markup language). The aim of AIML, which has been distributed under an open source license and implemented on a number of different platforms (see, for example, Pandorabots.com), was to encourage other developers to modify the initial program and produce numerous Alicebot clones. A.L.I.C.E. won the restricted category Loebner Prize three times: in 2000, 2001, and 2004. This prize, initiated by US inventor Hugh Loebner in 1991, is "the first formal instantiation of the Turing Test" (Loebner Prize 2018) – basically an international competition that pits chatbots against each other in an effort to find the most human-seeming chatbot. Additionally, filmmaker Spike Jonze has credited his personal experience with an Alicebot as the source of inspiration for the film *Her* (see Morais 2013).

Cleverbot (1997): Unlike previous rule-based chatbot systems, the responses of Rollo Carpenter's Cleverbot are not prefabricated or scripted. Instead, the bot is designed to derive its conversational behaviors from interactions with human users on the Internet. Although the exact method by which this is accomplished has not been made public (Pereira et al. 2016: 7), it has been described as a kind of crowdsourcing. Natalie Wolchover (2011) explains:

> Since coming online in 1997, Cleverbot has engaged in about 65 million conversations with Internet users around the world, who chat with it for fun via the Cleverbot website. Like a human learning appropriate behavior by studying the actions of members of his or her social group, Cleverbot "learns" from these conversations. It stores them all in a huge database, and in every future conversation, its responses to questions and comments mimic past human responses to those same questions and comments.

In 2011, Igor Labutov, Jason Yosinski, and Hod Lipson of the Cornell Creative Machines Lab repeated the famous 1972 experiment with ELIZA and PERRY by staging a conversation between two instances of Cleverbot (a video recording is available at https://www.creativemachineslab.com/videos.html).

Tay.ai (2016): Like Cleverbot, Microsoft's Tay – purportedly an acronym for "thinking about you" – was a machine-learning socialbot designed to emulate the conversational behavior of a teenage social media user. As Microsoft explained, the system "has been built by mining relevant public data" – that is, training its neural networks on anonymized information obtained from social media – and was designed to evolve its behavior from interacting with users on the social network Twitter, the mobile messaging service Kik, and the group chat platform GroupMe (Microsoft 2016). Tay was not Microsoft's first foray into this area. They were building on the success of another socialbot, Xiaoice, which had been operational in China since 2014. Tay.ai became famous (or perhaps better stated "infamous") in March 2016. Shortly after being released onto the Internet, the bot was targeted by a group of users who began manipulating Tay's learning capabilities by feeding it intentionally racist and bigoted statements. As a result, Tay started tweeting hateful racist comments that could not be controlled or held in check, forcing Microsoft to take the bot offline just sixteen hours after its launch (Figure 5.1).

Figure 5.1   Screenshot of one of the racist tweets posted by Tay.ai

5.1.2 Limitations and restrictions

As can be seen in this representative (but arguably limited) sample of chatbots, there have been numerous advancements in bot design, with the most significant change being a steady move from rule-based GOFAI architectures, whereby responses are pre-scripted, to corpus-based chatbots that are designed to mine existing human-to-human conversations or previous human responses to human–machine interactions. Each year (since 1991), advancements in chatbot design are put through their paces and tested during the Loebner Prize, an international competition and formal instantiation of Turing's game of imitation. Even though there have been impressive performances year after year, no chatbot has succeeded in "fooling all of the people all of the time," and, for this reason, the gold medal (and the $100,000 prize) has yet to be bestowed. Furthermore, all chatbots, irrespective of design, inherit three important practical limitations that follow from Turing's original theoretical proposal.

First, the mode of interaction is restricted to a very narrow range of interpersonal behaviors. Beginning with Turing's game of imitation, chatbots have been designed as question-and-answer systems. That is, their social involvement is intentionally limited to situations where human users engage with the bot by asking and responding to direct questions. This mode of interaction was prescribed by the initial set up of Turing's game of imitation, and its influence and legacy are evident in published transcripts from the Loebner Prize competition. Here, for example, is a short excerpt from the winning entry in the 2009 competition. The bot, which was named "Do-Much-More," was developed by David Levy (2009), and the judge in this particular exchange was Alan Garnham, Professor of Psychology from the University of Sussex:

Judge: Hello, how are you?
Do-Much-More: Hello. How are you?
Judge: I'm fine, but what about you?
Do-Much-More: I really can't say anything for certain. To be honest, I'm a bit fussy about such things.
Judge: What can you talk about?
Do-Much-More: I can talk about nothing at all, except in very wet weather.
Judge: Well, it's dry today, so do we have to remain silent?
Do-Much-More: I rather doubt if we do. If you want to find out for sure, you could always try hiring a detective.
Judge: I don't really have time in a five-minute window, do I?
Do-Much-More: I can't say. I can tell you that time has moved forward, but I don't suppose that's much help.
Judge: What are you doing at the conference?
Do-Much-More: Oh, I am doing various things. I want to use them to decorate a Christmas tree.
Judge: Isn't that rather unseasonal?
Do-Much-More: Most probably it isn't. It is just pretending.
Judge: Are you an academic?
Do-Much-More: Most probably I'm not. I am just putting on an act.
Judge: What are you, then?
Do-Much-More: Well, am I birds? Am I spaceships? Or am I just horse-flies? I've got a completely open mind about it.

Restricting communicative interaction to Q&A exchanges, although expedient for the purposes of conducting the demonstration and running the Loebner Prize competition, is a deliberate and rather artificial constraint that severely limits the range of conversational activity. It even permits and perhaps encourages what some critics have called "cheap tricks" (Parkin 2015), like confusing participants with odd diversions – for example, the comment made by Do-Much-More concerning the decoration of a Christmas Tree.

Second, the Q&A interactions are restricted to typewritten text. Although one might think that this was done in order to accommodate technical limitations with speech-recognition and synthesis, which were all but nonexistent during Turing's time, this is not the sole or principal reason. For Turing, and the chatbots that follow his lead, the use of textual interaction is not a technical exigency; it is a necessary and deliberate element of the imitation game's design. Turing's game was initially formulated in terms of gender.

"The object of the game for the interrogator," as Turing (1999: 37) explained, "is to determine which of the other two is the man and which is the woman." So the main reason for limiting the interaction to text form is to level the playing field: "In order that tones of voice may not help the interrogator the answers should be written, or better still, typewritten. The ideal arrangement is to have a tele-printer communicating between the two rooms" (Turing 1999: 37). Obviously, restricting the conversational interaction to textual exchanges is technically expedient once a computer takes the place of the man or woman in this elaborate game of gender performance, but that was not, at least according to Turing's initial formulation, the principal reason for limiting the game to typewritten questions and answers.

Third, this "limitation" is not immaterial, it is actually a crucial design element that is advantageous to the operation of chatbots and socialbots, especially on the Internet. By participating in rather artificial, text-based conversations, a bot, like ELIZA or Cleverbot, can be mistaken for and "pass" as another human user. This "act," as Miranda Mowbray (2002: 2) points out, is often not "a feature of the sophistication of bot design, but of the low bandwidth com-munication of the online social space" where it is "much easier to convincingly simulate a human agent." In other words, chat- and socialbots capitalize on the technical exigency of online social interac-tion, where conversational engagement, whether between two human users or a human user and a bot, is limited to the circulation of simple text strings. Consequently, all that is needed are the rudiments of some kind of social presence in order for human users to mistakenly assume that they are talking to *someone* instead of *something*. In other words, the apparent "intelligence" of the bot is as much a product of bot's internal programming and operations as it is a product of the tightly controlled social context in which the device operates.

5.2 Spoken Dialogue Systems

Next-gen chat- and socialbots involve technologies that are able, like the Samantha OS imaginatively presented in the Spike Jonze film *Her* (2013), to work with spoken input and output. These devices, which now go by a number of different names – e.g., smart speaker, digital assistant, vocal social agent, conversational user interface, task-oriented dialogue agent, screenless Internet – are all forms of what developers call spoken dialogue systems, or SDS.

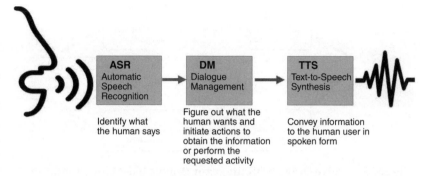

Figure 5.2   Three-stage SDS diagram (adapted from Hirschberg and Manning 2015)

5.2.1 SDS basics

SDS do not consist of one technology but of an ensemble of several different but related technological innovations: "[A]utomatic speech recognition (ASR), to identify what a human says; dialogue management (DM), to determine what that human wants; actions to obtain the information or perform the activity requested; and text-to-speech (TTS) synthesis, to convey that information back to the human in spoken form" (Hirschberg and Manning 2015: 262) (see Figure 5.2). This three-stage formulation is an analytic construct useful for the purpose of representing standard SDS architecture. It is, however, not the only or even the best schematic available. Other researchers, like Gabriel Skantze (2005) and Deeno Burgan (2017), provide a more detailed formulation that involves five individual technological elements: automatic speech-recognition (ASR), natural language understanding (NLU), dialogue management (DM), natural language generation (NLG), and TTS synthesis (see Figure 5.3). And a third formalization, with six stages – ASR, spoken language understanding (SLU), dialogue state tracker (DST), dialogue policy, NLG, and TTS synthesis – has been provided by other researchers (e.g., Williams et al. 2016). For the purposes of our investigation and analysis, we will utilize the simplified three-stage representation provided by Hirschberg and Manning (2015).

(1) *Automatic speech-recognition.* Despite the apparent complexity and technical advancement beyond simple text-based chatbots like ELIZA, SDS are still designed for and operate with text data. Consequently, the principal task of ASR is to convert an acoustic speech signal to a sequence of discrete textual symbols (words).

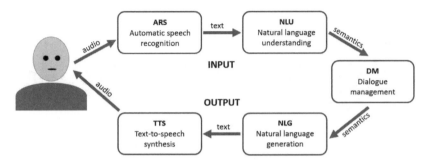

Figure 5.3   Five-stage SDS diagram (image based on Skantz 2007)

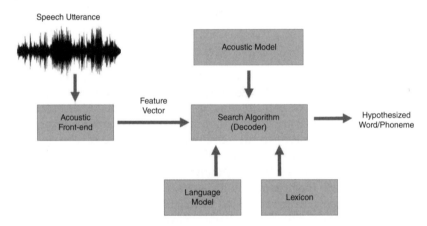

Figure 5.4   Simplified block diagram of ASR architecture

More accurately described, ASR generates a hypothesis of the most likely sequence of words out of all valid word sequences that are available in a particular language (like English) from a given acoustic input. Figure 5.4 is a simplified illustration of a typical ASR.

The *acoustic front-end* utilizes audio signal processing techniques in order to generate a digital representation of spoken input. The *acoustic model* is a data file that describes the probability of a specific sequence of speech sounds. In effect, it predicts what word the user may have said by calculating the most likely sequence of phonemes (individual speech sounds) from the occurrence of any one particular sound. Hidden Markov modeling (HMM) remains one of the most commonly used statistical methods to generate these phonic sequences. The *lexicon* lists valid words in the language. It does not, however, need to account for every single word in the language but only those words related to the specific domain in which the ASR is intended to operate (e.g., customer service, reservation systems, digital assistant, etc.). The *language model* describes the possible sequence of words that typically occur in the chosen language or domain of ASR operations. These can be represented either by hand-coding the rules of a generative grammar or by calculating the likelihood of different word pairings from analyzing patterns in available data (books, online publications, newspapers, etc.). Finally, the *decoder* estimates the best possible sequence (or sequences) of words given the initial spoken input, the modeling of acoustic data, and the words and word sequence available in the lexicon and language model. This produces a hypothesized textual result. It is "hypothesized," because the ASR operates on the basis of statistical models and therefore produces results that have a high probability of being accurate but are nevertheless still something of a good, informed guess.

(2) *Dialogue management.* The DM first parses the output of the ASR by analyzing the text string into its component parts and generating a semantic representation of what was said, and then assembles a valid response (or something that is, from the user's perspective, at least reasonably close to a valid response). The former is called natural language understanding (NLU), while the latter is called natural language generation (NLG). The objective of NLU is to construct a representation of the user's utterance that can be processed by the computer. This can be accomplished through the application of different methodologies, extending from modified versions of ELIZA's simple keyword search/identification to more sophisticated systems like Stanford CoreNLP, which is able to work out the syntactic structure of individual sentences by using a dependency grammar analysis and machine-learning algorithms trained on various corpora of human conversational interactions. If, for example, the user says "Show me flights from Chicago to New York on Monday morning," the NLU module of the DM might generate the following semantic representation:

DOMAIN: Air-Travel
INTENT: Show-Flights
ORIGIN-CITY: Chicago
ORIGIN-DATE: Monday
ORIGIN-TIME: 9am
DEST-CITY: New York

The semantic representation is formulated using a predefined domain ontology, which includes a list of all the kinds of things that the user might say to the system. This is why most contemporary SDS are domain specific and only function well in situations that can be pre-determined and tightly constrained – like scheduling appointments or conducting an Internet search. Working with this representation, the NLG module can then generate a response that will eventually be sent to the TTS for output to the user. In most contemporary SDS systems, this is performed by applying prefabricated templates, in which all or most of the words have been predefined by the system designer. These responses may be entirely canned or fixed – e.g., "Hello, how can I help you?" – or may include variables that can be filled in with values that the user has provided – e.g., "What time do you want to leave ORIGIN-CITY?" or "I have booked you a flight to DEST-CITY on ORIGIN-DATE at ORIGIN-TIME."

(3) *TTS synthesis.* The task of the TTS module is to convert the textual output of the DM (or the NLG component of the DM) into an audible form that simulates intelligible speech. This is accomplished either through concatenation synthesis, which uses a library of pre-recorded samples (either whole words or individual phonetic elements) that are assembled piece by piece – kind of like the cut-out letters of a ransom note – in order to produce a legible spoken message, or through formant or articulatory synthesis, both of which produce the audio waveform algorithmically without relying on pre-recorded samples. Most commercially available SDS, like Siri, Alexa, and Google Assistant, currently utilize some form of concatenation synthesis.

5.2.2 SDS implementations

One of the first commercially available SDS applications was Siri, a project spun-off from DARPA's cognitive assistant that learns and organizes (CALO) program that ran from 2003 to 2008. Siri was initially developed at SRI International by Tom Gruber, Dag Kittlaus, and Adam Cheyer; it was made available as a free app in the Apple App Store in February 2010 and shortly thereafter was acquired by Apple. The software application was popularized via its inclusion in the iPhone 4S (initially released in 2011) and is currently an integral component of the Apple iOS for smartphones and tablets. Siri has been described and marketed as "an intelligent personal assistant" and a "knowledge navigator," which was an idea initially introduced and proposed by former Apple CEO John Sculley in his 1987 book *Odyssey*. Technically speaking, Siri consists of four basic NLP innovations:

1 *Speech-recognition.* Siri employs an ASR engine, originally developed by Nuance Communication, which is capable of accepting and parsing spoken commands and inquiries in a number of languages. When you give Siri a command or ask it a question, your vocalizations are picked up by the device's microphone and recorded. As the Siri Team (2017) at Apple explained in one of its technical papers: "The microphone in an iPhone or Apple Watch turns your voice into a stream of instantaneous waveform samples, at a rate of 16000 per second." Those data are immediately uploaded to the Apple server where they are scrubbed of background noise (an ongoing and persistent problem for any speech-recognition system), statistically analyzed, and turned into text information that can be computationally processed. "The server," as ZDNet's Andrew Nusca (2011) explains, "compares your speech against a statistical model to estimate, based on the sounds you spoke and the order in which you spoke them, what letters might constitute it." Siri's speech-recognition engine is also designed with an on-device voice trigger and speaker-recognition (SR) capability. When the device detects the wake-up phrase, "Hey Siri," it identifies the user, which is an essential verification step necessary for many of Apple's personalization services, and "processes the rest of the utterance as a Siri request" (Siri Team 2017). As a result of steady improvements over time, *Wired* magazine estimates that "Siri's raw voice recognition rivals all its competitors, correctly identifying 95 percent of users' speech" (Pierce 2017).

2 *Natural language understanding.* On the server, the resulting data is run through an algorithm that sifts through thousands of combinations of sentences to determine what the inputted phrase might mean. How Siri actually does this is a carefully guarded secret, but most contemporary NLU systems work by employing the same basic method. "A natural language system like Siri," as Macworld's Marco Tabini (2013) explains, "usually starts by attempting to parse the syntactical structure of a piece of text, extracting things like nouns, adjectives, and verbs, as well as the general intonation of the sentences." This latter element helps determine whether the user input was a command to do something (e.g., send a text message) or a question (e.g., a request for information about current weather conditions). Fortunately, Siri does not need to "know" or "understand" everything that might be said to it. The system is designed to operate within a rather narrow range of possibility and has been programmed to identify and work with

those words and phrases that are required to fulfill tasks that it can perform. If the system receives user input that is not recognized as fitting this predetermined context, Siri is provided, like many of the chatbots before it, with a (sometimes sassy) pre-scripted reply.

3 *Natural language generation.* Once the NLU algorithm identifies the user's request, the system then begins to assess what tasks need to be carried out. For Siri, which resides in a mobile device, this requires determining whether or not the information needed can be found in the device – e.g., play a song or access the phone's contact list – or whether it requires data from an online service. Once this has been determined, the application then formulates a response and outputs this information in audio form. As was already demonstrated with ELIZA, automatically assembling a response by rearranging words and inserting a few pieces of data can provide acceptable but often unremarkable and artificial-sounding results. In an effort to address this, Siri employs many of the NLG tricks that have been developed in subsequent generations of chatbots in order to produce natural-sounding results that are able to convey something like "personality."

4 *TTS synthesis.* Unlike a chatbot, Siri's responses need to be converted to audio data. This text-to-speech (TTS) transformation relies on a library of pre-recorded human voice samples – not whole words, but individual phonemes, like the long "e" sound in the word "fourteen" – that can then be arranged in the correct order to supply audible output. This approach to concatenation synthesis requires hours of recorded vocalizations from human voice actors that are then isolated, catalogued in a database of sound samples, and reassembled into understandable audio content on the fly. The American-English voice of Siri was originally performed by Susan Bennett in 2005, and Apple has tapped other voice talent to gather the necessary linguistic samples for the twenty-one languages that the Siri application currently supports.

Amazon's voice assistant, Alexa, was initially patented in 2012 and released as a commercial product in 2014 along with the Echo smart speaker. Like Siri, Alexa is able to take vocal input, process this data, search for and obtain results, and then communicate this output to users in audio form. But unlike Siri, which has remained captive in the confines of Apple's proprietary system and devices, Amazon has deliberately decided to make its cloud-based Alexa Voice Service (AVS) available to other manufactures and device developers by publishing its API (application program interface) and offering developers a full SDK (software development kit) to aid efforts to integrate Alexa into their products. As explained on the Amazon (2018a) Alexa developer site:

> The Alexa Voice Service (AVS) enables developers to integrate Alexa directly into their products, bringing the convenience of voice control to any connected device. With AVS, your product will enable users to stream media, request the weather forecast and local news, get updates on traffic conditions, ask general knowledge questions, set timers and alarms, query Wikipedia and much more.

Amazon has even provided developers with tools to control Alexa's behaviors. One such tool, called speech synthesis markup language (SSML), allows programmers to control Alexa's pronunciation, intonation, timing, and emotional responses, customizing the way the application sounds.

Giving away its AVS for free might sound rather generous, but it is actually part of a rather savvy business strategy: Amazon wants to encourage and make it easy for developers to build the AVS into devices so that everything becomes a gateway to Amazon and its massive retail services. This capability, however, also points to one of the potential problems and pitfalls with using SDS devices and services. Since Alexa's "smarts" (like that of Siri) reside not in the device but in Amazon's cloud-based service, everything that is said to Alexa is recorded, processed, and stored on the server. As Amazon (2018b) explains in its Alexa Terms of Use (ToU) document:

> 1.3 Alexa Interactions. You control Alexa with your voice. Alexa streams audio to the cloud when you interact with Alexa. Amazon processes and retains your Alexa Interactions, such as your voice inputs, music playlists, and your Alexa to-do and shopping lists, in the cloud to provide, personalize, and improve our services. *Learn more* about these voice services including how to delete voice recordings associated with your account.

Knowledge of this operation has sparked privacy concerns on the part of consumers. And there has been some negative press suggesting that Alexa could be "listening" and recording everything that happens in its presence. This criticism is not entirely accurate. The device is only "listening" after being activated by a user employing the "wake-up" word, "Alexa." Until that happens, the device sits idle or in a state that could be called "sleep mode." But once it is activated, everything that is said to and in the presence of the Alexa enabled device is recorded and stored in the Amazon cloud. This is necessary, as Amazon explains in its ToU document, in order to support and improve personalization services. But this does necessitate the collection, processing, and warehousing of vast amounts of user data. Users do, as the ToU indicate, have the ability to review and even delete the voice recordings, but this requires considerable effort and it only affects the voice recordings; it does not exercise any control over the data that may have been extracted from these recordings and how that information comes to be utilized.

Compared to its competitors, Google has been rather late in recognizing the importance of and responding to the need for SDS applications and appliances. In May 2016, the company introduced both Google Home, a voice-activated smart speaker, and Google Assistant, a cloud-based virtual assistant designed to perform the following tasks: answer user questions and perform translations by leveraging the power of Google Search and Google Translate; control entertainment content and devices; assist users with the planning of daily activities and accessing data on weather and traffic; manage events with Google Calendar, make calls, and add items to the user's shopping list; and control Internet connected devices (thermostats, lights, etc.) throughout the home. Like Siri, Google Assistant was initially restricted to Google devices and software (Pixel smartphones and the Android OS), but, following Amazon's lead, it has now opened Google Assistant to third parties so that the service can be integrated into all kinds of Internet-connected devices.

If Google was a bit late to market with its SDS products and services, it has recently taken a lead in developing more natural sounding conversational interactions. Google Duplex (introduced in the spring of 2018) is an SDS application that is designed for completing specific tasks, such as scheduling appointments and obtaining information over the telephone. Google Duplex's conversations (samples of which are available online – see Leviathan and Matias 2018) sound natural due to several innovations, mainly in the DM and TTS elements of the SDS system. Duplex uses a recurrent neural network (RNN) built using the TensorFlow Extended (TFX) general-purpose machine-learning platform. Duplex's RNN was trained on a corpus of anonymized phone conversation data, basically a large set of audio recordings and their written transcripts obtained from actual human-to-human telephone conversations – data from every telephone call that begins with the following statement: "This call may be recorded for training purposes."

Once trained, the network uses the output of Google's ASR technology in order to process and "understand" user input. One of the key features of Duplex is that it is designed to function within tightly controlled and constrained domains of knowledge – e.g., making restaurant reservations or scheduling an appointment for a haircut – and the "understanding model" was trained separately for each of these specific tasks. This means, as Google's Yaniv Leviathan and Yossi Matias (2018) explain, that Duplex "can only carry out natural conversations after being deeply trained in such domains. It cannot carry out general conversations."

In order to sound more natural than other SDS devices and applications, Duplex uses a combination of existing concatenative TTS with a new synthesis TTS engine constructed on Google's Tacotron and WaveNet technologies. As Jonathan Shen and Ruoming Pang (2017) of Google explain:

> In a nutshell it works like this: We use a sequence-to-sequence model optimized for TTS to map a sequence of letters to a sequence of features that encode the audio. These features, an 80-dimensional audio spectrogram with frames computed every 12.5 milliseconds, capture not only pronunciation of words, but also various subtleties of human speech, including volume, speed and intonation. Finally these features are converted to a 24 kHz waveform using a WaveNet-like architecture.

To add to the realism of the vocalizations, Duplex is designed to model and incorporate speech disfluencies, those "ums" and "uhs" that are often utilized to signal that we are still processing or making sense of the conversational data. Because the spoken output of Duplex is virtually indistinguishable from that of a human being, Google has issued assurances that the system will always self-identity as an AI in order to avoid potential deceptions or confusions.

These three systems, Siri, Alexa, and Google Assistant, are just a representative sample and are certainly not the only available SDS implementations on the market. There is also Microsoft's Cortana, which was named after an artificial intelligence character in the *Halo* video game franchise and voiced by Jen Taylor; Samsung's S Voice and its successor Bixby, which is now being integrated in IoT (Internet of things) home appliances as well as the company's mobile products; Amtrak's Julie, an interactive voice-response agent for the company's automated information and reservation telephone system; and many others. Although the exact method of operation varies from system to system – Cortana, for instance, uses Microsoft's Bing to search for and locate information, while Google's Assistant leverages the power of the Google search engine – the basic operations and components remain pretty much the same, such that the differences across these various SDS implementations are more variations on a theme than substantive differences in kind.

5.2.3 Open problems in SDS development

Because of numerous technical improvements – e.g., increased efficiency in data throughput, better algorithms for processing linguistic data like the application of HMM, and the employment of machine-learning algorithms – current SDS applications appear to perform rather well, at least in predefined circumstances and tightly controlled domains. As Hirschberg and Manning (2015: 262) conclude in their critical assessment of the technology: "Although SDSs now work fairly well in limited domains, where the topics of the interaction are known in advance and where the words people are likely to use can be predetermined, they are not yet very successful in open domain interaction, where users may talk about anything at all." In other words, commercially available SDS products like Siri, Alexa, and Google Assistant work well as long as our interactions with them are limited to a narrow range of predefined possibilities: answering questions, providing recommendations, or performing basic actions by delegating requests to cloud-based services.

So what is still needed to evolve the communication capabilities of the technology? According to Hirschberg and Manning, building more robust SDS systems will require not only improvements in the design and operation of the various technical components that make up these systems, but also better knowledge concerning human conversational behavior:

> There are many challenges in building SDSs, in addition to the primary challenge of improving the accuracy of the basic ASR, DM, and TTS building blocks and extending their use into less restricted domains. These include basic problems of recognizing and producing normal human conversational behaviors, such as turn-taking and coordination. Humans interpret subtle cues in speakers' voices and facial and body gestures (where available) to determine when the speaker is ready to give up the turn versus simply pausing. These cues, such as a filled pause (e.g., "um" or "uh"), are also used to establish when some feedback from the listener is desirable, to indicate that he or she is listening or working on a request, as well as to provide "grounding" (i.e., information about the current state of the conversation). (2015: 263)

There are ongoing technological challenges with the design and operation of the various components that make up SDS, like error correction with ASR in noisy environments or latency in the processing of data by the DM module. These are technical issues properly addressed by engineers and device manufacturers. But what is also necessary, and what for now remains an "open problem" in effective SDS design and development, is "recognizing and producing normal human conversational behaviors, such as turn-taking and coordination" and making sense of the nonverbal cues and nonlinguistic verbal expressions that are commonly used to fill pauses, signal the need for feedback, or provide information on the status and state of the interpersonal relationship.

In addition to these problems, Hirschberg and Manning also mention disambiguation and conversational entrainment. The former refers to the ability that humans have to sort out important differences between words "such as 'yeah' and 'okay,'' which may have diverse meanings – including agreement, topic shift, and even disagreement – when spoken in different ways" (2015: 263). The latter concerns the way that human interlocutors are able to accommodate their communicative interactions to each other in order to negotiate differences. "In successful and cooperative conversations humans also tend to entrain to their conversational partners, becoming more similar to each other in pronunciation, word choice, acoustic and prosodic features, facial expressions, and gestures" (2015: 263). Consequently, there is a wide range of social/interactional issues that need to be properly identified, modeled, and eventually made computable. These are not engineering problems, at least not yet. They are first and foremost a matter of research – observation, data collection, and theory generation – in interpersonal communication.

For the most part, SDS developers have attempted to address these aspects of human conversational behavior by drawing on research from the field of linguistics. Svetlana Stoyanchev, Alex Liu, and Julia Hirschberg (2014), for instance, utilize work in theoretical and applied linguistics to develop a computational model capable of producing more natural clarification questions in dialogue systems. And Gabriel Skantze (2007) bases his extensive work with SDS on linguistic research. There is undoubtedly a lot to be obtained from linguistic analysis, and the coupling of linguistics with mathematical modeling and computation – what is called "computational linguistics" – already has a proven record of success.

But linguistics generally focuses attention on the elements and operations of language, and, in the case of SDS, spoken as opposed to written language. As Skantze explains:

> A useful unit for analysis of written text is the sentence. Sentences are delimited by punctuation marks, where each sentence commonly express one or more propositions. For spoken dialogue, on the other hand, such units are much less adequate for analysis . . . A unit that is commonly used for segmenting spoken dialogue is instead the *utterance*. In dialogue, speakers exchange utterances, with the intent of affecting the other speaker in some way. (2007: 13)

In addition to considering the communicative function of the utterance – what is actually said – linguistic analysis also seeks to parse and process *disfluencies*, like filled pauses, repetitions, repairs, and false starts. Despite this rather broad consideration of conversational activity, however, linguistics is not typically concerned with other, equally important, aspects of the communicative encounter – e.g., social context, tone of voice, spatial proximity, nonverbal behaviors, etc. For this reason, the discipline of linguistics, for all its usefulness in SDS development, does not provide a complete picture of the full range of interpersonal behaviors.

5.3 NLP and Communication Studies

Many of the widely recognized "open problems" in SDS research and development are precisely what is targeted and studied in the field of communication, especially efforts in interpersonal communication. Conversely, many NLP implementations, like Cleverbot, Siri, or Google's Duplex, offer unique opportunities to test communication theory, verify the results of communication research, and develop new forms of generating experimental evidence. In other words, it appears that SDS application development could learn a thing or two from communication research, and communication research could, in turn, benefit from many of the opportunities made available by SDS developments (Figure 5.5).

5.3.1 What communication research can contribute to SDS

Research in the discipline of communication can supply theory and data to help address and resolve open problems in SDS development. According to Hirschberg and Manning's (2015: 263) review article, one of the fundamental problems in SDS design is "recognizing and

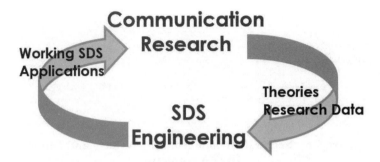

Figure 5.5   Symbiotic relationship between efforts in communication research and SDS development

producing normal human conversational behaviors," especially as regards turn-taking and the use of both verbal and nonverbal cues to coordinate conversational interaction.

Turn-taking   According to communication scholars John Wiemann and Mark Knapp (1975: 75), "the phenomenon by which one inter-actant stops talking and another starts, in a smooth synchronized manner, is considered to be the most salient feature of face-to-face conversation," and research focusing on experimental studies of face-to-face human interaction begins to develop traction in the 1970s. In 1972 Starkey Duncan published a widely cited study in the *Journal of Personality and Social Psychology*, which sought to identify the mechanisms of turn-taking through experimental observation of face-to-face human interactions. And in 1974, Harvey Sacks, Emanuel Schegloff, and Gail Jefferson published what is considered to be the seminal research paper in conversational turn-taking, establishing what many consider to be the benchmark for speech-exchange systems. Since that time, there have been numerous empirical investigations of turn-taking in both face-to-face interpersonal interactions and group decision-making. More recent studies have focused on the way turn-taking is affected and modified by technological mediation though telecommunications, video conferencing, and computer-mediated communication (cf. Hiltz et al. 1986; Kiesler and Sproull 1992; Hopper 1992; Lobel et al. 2005). Although a good deal of the published research in conversational turn-taking involves modeling linguistic performance (Duncan 1972; Sacks et al. 1974; Auer 1983; Oreström 1983; O'Connell et al. 1990), there is a significant aspect of it, as Wiemann and Knapp (1975: 75) point out, that depends on nonverbal contributions. As a result, "turn-taking" is

```
// Fake time thinking to allow for user self-reflection
// And to give the illusion that some thinking is going on
var elizaresponse = "";
function think(){
    document.Eliza.input.value = "";
    if( elizaresponse != "" ){ respond(); }
    else { setTimeout("think()", 250); }
}
```

**Figure 5.6   Segment of code from the Wallace and Dunlop
ELIZA emulator**

and remains one of the main topics covered in standard textbooks
addressing interpersonal communication. A more complete inven-
tory and understanding of all the variables and factors involved in
regulating human-to-human conversational turn-turning may help
with the design of human machine communication systems that are
more natural, engaging, effective, and personal.

A good example of this can be found in the design of chatbots.
Because of the speed at which the computer processes user input,
chatbots can sometimes provide results that are, from the perspective of the human user, too fast to be believable. This is evident in
one of the transcripts from Do-Much-More's Loebner Prize performance, when one of the human judges, John Carroll from the
University of Sussex, responded to the bot's initial greeting with
the following statement: "I'm fine – gosh you're a quick typist."
For this reason, bots are often programmed to include a short delay
in the display of output. The purpose of this delay, as is evident from
the programmer comments included in the piece of code shown in
Figure 5.6 from Wallace and Dunlop's (1997) ELIZA emulator (the
comments are marked with a double //), is to approximate the time
necessary for a respondent to think and supply a suitable answer.
Although consisting of just a simple timer – coded in Javascript with
the `setTimeout()` method and using a delay of 250 milliseconds
– the intended effect is to approximate human-like turn-taking in
conversational interactions.

Verbal and nonverbal cues   A good deal of conversational interaction
is negotiated through nonverbal elements, which can include visual
cues or "body language," vocal intonation or paralanguage, chrone-
mics, and oculesics like eye contact and gaze direction. Turn-taking,
for instance, is often indicated by either a change in vocal tone, or
a pause in the temporal sequence of the verbal delivery, or a visual

cue, such as a nod or glance. Although research in these aspects of human communication have been pursued and published in the fields of semiotics (Ekman and Friesen 1969; Lindenfeld 1971) and the social sciences of anthropology and psychology (Harper et al. 1978; Hecht and Ambady 1999), it is Communication Studies that has staked a claim to this particular area of research since the mid-1970s (Burgoon 1980). Since this time, attending to the importance of both verbal and nonverbal cues has not just become a legitimate area of communication research, but is considered one of the central concerns of the discipline. And more recent publications in the field, like that of Jones and LeBaron (2002: 499), have sought to correlate the study of the nonverbal and verbal components, which have been historically distinguished, in order to formulate "more integrated approaches to the study of verbal and nonverbal communication so that more holistic understandings of social interaction may emerge."

Right now, commercially available SDS applications, like Siri and Alexa, are only attending to what is said. How it is said and in what particular fashion it is articulated are not necessarily part of the current implementations. Siri, in other words, can parse and process the words that users speak, but the system is currently unable to make sense of the pauses, the social context, the vocal tone, and the gestures made by users in the process of speaking. But it is possible to imagine a more sophisticated implementation of SDS that would be capable of processing these other elements to assist the effectiveness and efficiency of communicative interaction between human users and the SDS application or appliance.

5.3.2 What SDS can do for communication research

The manufacture of working SDS implementations can provide research in Communication Studies with unique opportunities to verify results, test conclusions, and even improve methodology. Currently, theory produced in communication research is typically tested and verified in experiments with human subjects. SDS provide researchers with some other options and research opportunities.

First, the design of working SDS systems will require that various concepts and theories of human communication be made computable and employed to control the behaviors of various types of SDS operations. The development of SDS, therefore, offers opportunities for the testing of theory through the construction of mechanisms that employ or embody a particular theoretical model. In the process, results obtained from experimenting with different instantiations of theory can be reflected back into the discipline of communication for improving the accuracy and formulation of the theoretical models. This approach has proven to be extremely useful in other fields, like computational linguistics. As Hirschberg and Manning (2015: 266) explain, "the development of probabilistic approaches to language [necessary for SDS development] is not simply about solving engineering problems: Probabilistic models of language have also been reflected back into linguistic science," and, as a result, "many areas of linguistics are themselves becoming more empirical and more quantitative in their approaches." It is likely that similar outcomes would be obtained from developing probabilistic approaches to interpersonal communication.

Second, the effectiveness of operational implementations of SDS will need to be tested and evaluated in actual interactions with human users. Although the immediate goal of this effort might be to "stress test" the design in actual social circumstances, these situations will also provide researchers working in communication with a unique opportunity to investigate how human subjects interact with other kinds of communicative agents. In other words, because the manufacturing and marketing of more effective SDS, for example, will require countless hours of controlled testing with human users, scholars of communication will have a unique opportunity to study new forms of social interaction and to use this data for both SDS improvement and theory development. This will be crucial not only for the discipline of Communication Studies but for the social sciences in general. As Norbert Wiener (1988) predicted more than a half century ago, we now live in a world where social interaction is not limited to human-to-human interactions but also involves various forms of human–machine communication. Communication Studies is in a unique position to investigate and develop knowledge about this new social arrangement and its consequences.

5.3.3 Example

These suggestions are just that: suggestions. Demonstration of the usefulness of interpersonal communication research for the design and development of SDS and the expediency of SDS applications for communication research will only be achieved in practice. This kind of interdisciplinary work – the very work this book seeks to identify and initiate – remains to be undertaken. At this point, the best we can do is project the opportunities and challenges of this effort by considering a concrete example: the effect of eye-gaze (a form of nonverbal communication) on conversational turn-taking.

Although gaze behavior is not an immediate concern for the design of speech-only SDS (like Siri, Alexa, Google Assistant, etc.), it is increasingly important for more sophisticated implementations and future developments with social robots (see Chapter 7). This is the subject of a 2014 research article by Gabriel Skantze, Anna Hjalmarsson, and Catharine Oertel. Their study applies findings from research with human-to-human interactions to robots in order to model and study the effects of nonverbal eye-gaze behaviors on human–robot interactions. The investigation sounds promising insofar as the researchers are engaged with available studies in human communication and are applying results of this research to the design and operation of sociable robots. A quick look through the article's bibliography, however, reveals an obvious lack of research from the field of interpersonal communication, even though communication scholars have been involved in the study of this subject matter and have made considerable contributions to the research literature (for an overview, see Berger 2005).

This absence is not necessarily a problem. Identifying the lack of something is never sufficient evidence that it should have been included in the first place. What is needed, therefore, is not just an indication that something is missing, but a demonstration that shows how the inclusion of this absent material would be able to add a crucial dimension currently unavailable in the works that have been cited. In other words, we would need to demonstrate that research in Communication Studies has some significant insight to contribute to this area of investigation such that its exclusion represents a missed opportunity for developing better and/or more robust forms of research.

This is, in fact, the case with research in nonverbal communication. Typically, scholars have divided verbal and nonverbal communication into separate channels of message transmission such that information supplied by one channel can be reinforced, recontextualized, or even subverted by the information supplied by the other (Jones and LeBaron 2002). This differentiation persists in many of the studies conducted with human–robot interaction, mainly because the division is already operationalized by the literature that researchers have called upon and because this kind of separation assists computational modeling – i.e., each channel (verbal and nonverbal) can be isolated and independently modeled and controlled. Research efforts in interpersonal communication, however, have begun to challenge this conceptual duality (Streeck and Knapp 1992) and have sought to devise more integrated approaches that consider the verbal and nonverbal elements as interacting components of a holistic system (Jones and LeBaron 2002: 500). This alternative way of framing and modeling conversational behavior could supply improvements for SDS design and, as a result, produce better or "more natural" human–robot conversational interactions. Obviously, however, this is still just a hypothesis. Its definitive test and demonstration will require practical implementations. But such implementations need to begin by recognizing the potential that is already available in this marginalized body of literature.

At the same time, the design of SDS systems can be used to model interpersonal communication scenarios in such a way that researchers are able to have precise control over experimental variables. This is precisely what Skantze, Hjalmarsson, and Oertel pursue in their study:

> We have systematically manipulated the way the robot produces turn-taking cues. We have also compared the face-to-face setting . . . with a setting where the robot employs a random gaze behaviour, as well as a voice-only setting where the robot is hidden behind a paper board. This way, we can explore what the contributions of a face-to-face setting really are, and whether they can be explained by the robot's gaze behaviour or the presence of a face at all. (2014: 51)

This kind of systemic manipulation of experimental variables could be very useful to communication researchers.

For example, Judee K. Burgoon and colleagues (1985, 1986) have published a series of influential studies concerning the effects of eye-gaze on social perceptions and outcomes. These studies have, following a standard practice in interpersonal communication research, utilized "confederates," who were trained by the researchers to produce three different levels of eye-gaze response in simulated interviews with test subjects: "The confederate interviewees were six undergraduate students, three males and three females, who were trained to keep their verbal replies and all other nonverbal behavior consistent across interviews. The eye contact manipulation consisted of one of three levels: high, medium or low" (Burgoon et al. 1985: 137). Although expedient for the purposes of conducting the study, utilizing confederates introduces significant limitations and unwanted variability:

> While the numerous significant differences due to confederates are an experimenter's nightmare, they do underscore the need to conduct

interpersonal communication research using multiple confederates. The current findings strongly demonstrate the idiosyncratic differences in individual communication styles that may mediate communication outcomes. Had only one or two of the confederates in this experiment actually been used, very different results might have appeared. One has to wonder how many interpersonal experiments have been subject to this kind of undetected confound. (Burgoon et al. 1985: 143)

This confounding problem, as the researchers clearly point out, is not unique to this one study but constitutes a persistent and often unidentified difficulty across interpersonal communication research in general. Using tightly controlled and programmable robotic implementations for this kind of research might provide better experimental controls than can be obtained with any number of trained confederates, mainly because researchers can directly and precisely manipulate each variable in the experiment and ensure consistent behavior across multiple trials.

5.4 Limitations and Future Opportunities

In the end, this chapter arguably generates more questions than definitive answers, and that is by design. My main objective has been to open up new avenues of research that can contribute to both NLP development and work in interpersonal communication. And it will be the task of the next generation of students in the field of communication to take up this challenge and see how far we can go with it. I will end, therefore, not with a set of conclusive outcomes that put an end to things, but with an indication of future possibilities and the identification of one important caveat.

5.4.1 New opportunities and reciprocal benefits

Although it has not been widely recognized, research in communication can supply the data and theories necessary to develop more robust NLP and SDS. Extant communication theories – theories that have been produced and tested in countless hours of experimental observations of human-to-human social interactions in a variety of situations and contexts – can help in the design of NLP methods and SDS applications by supplying generalizable models that can be used to develop computable instructions. Likewise, raw data – typically video and audio recordings and anonymized written transcripts from communication research projects – can furnish the material for train-ing learning algorithms and neural networks on the standard patterns of human communicative behavior. The best design strategies will, following the recent successes of DeepMind's AlphaGo, probably draw on both – the predictions available in theory and the experi-ences of learning in practice – to develop future applications.

At the same time, work in NLP and SDS will produce operational-ized applications of communication research that can be tested in actual encounters with human subjects. This will not only provide communication researchers with the unique opportunity to validate available theories and evidence, but will also lead to new opportu-nities for communication researchers. In much the same way that computational linguistics made the discipline of linguistics more empirical and data-driven, so we can expect that SDS in particu-lar and human–machine communication in general will transform Communication Studies from a "soft" social science to something more empirical and quantitative.

5.4.2 Interdisciplinary approaches

This effort requires the development of an interface between the fields of engineering and Communication Studies. We will, there-fore, need the equivalent of an academic API for the two disciplines. This is going to necessitate, on the one hand, mining the literature of Communication Studies and porting its findings in such a way that they can be utilized outside the discipline in which they were initially cultivated and developed. Doing so will involve making theory computable so that the insights that have been generated by decades of communication research are not just human readable, but are also rendered machine executable. At the same time, and on the other hand, engineers will need to learn to recognize and to appreciate how scholarship in this so-called "soft science" can speak to and contribute the data necessary to address many of the open problems. As Hirschberg and Manning recognize, the current crop of open problems in SDS design concern not only engineering challenges but also better understanding of human conversational behaviors. Although there is some small movement in this direction as is evident in the work of both Hirschberg and Manning (2015) and Skantze (2005), this is still a wide open and largely untapped intellectual resource. Finally, mobilizing these interdisciplinary con-nections is not something that is or should be limited to the specific case of SDS design. Similar opportunities and challenges are available with embodied conversational agents (ECA), social robots, and other forms of NLP. In fact, it is in these other areas that research in communication – especially as concerns nonverbal forms of communicative interaction – would be most needed but has been, for now at least, conspicuously absent.

5.4.3 Underlying assumptions

One fundamental assumption behind this effort is that socially interactive applications like chatbots and SDS should emulate or simulate human-level communicative behaviors. But this is an assumption, as Skantze accurately recognizes:

> An argument for moving towards conversational dialogue, as opposed to a command-based, is that human-like conversation generally is considered to be a natural, intuitive, robust and efficient means for interaction. Thus, the advantage of command-based speech interfaces over traditional graphical user interfaces is often restricted to the fact that users may use the hands and eyes for other tasks, and their usefulness may thus be limited to special contexts of use, such as when driving a car. Conversational dialogue systems hold the promise of offering a more intuitive and efficient interaction. Whether this promise will be met remains to be seen. (2007: 12)

This insight has been verified and reiterated by James R. Glass:

> While it is clear that the study of human–human conversations can provide valuable insights into the nature of dialogue, it is still a matter of debate how human-like spoken dialogue systems should be. The ability to handle phenomena commonly used in human conversations could ultimately make systems more natural and easy to use by humans, but they also have the potential to make things more complex and confusing. (1999: 3)

One of the overarching assumptions of Turing's game of imitation is that the more conversational an application is or appears to be, the better. This is not questioned, because it seems, at least to begin with, to be rather intuitive. Building more capable and competent conversational agents seems to be the overriding goal of NLP. But modeling what Andrea Guzman (2018) has called "human–machine communication" (HMC) on human-to-human (h2h) communication might be the wrong place to begin, just as modeling "machine intelligence" on human cognition turned out to be a significant impediment to progress in other areas of artificial intelligence (Brooks 1991). Identifying this assumption, however, does not militate against the argument for including communication research in chatbot and SDS development. In fact, it actually makes such research more important and valuable. If fabricating human-level conversational agents is in fact a worthwhile objective (i.e., if the assumption is true), then research in interpersonal communication will provide the necessary data and theories to inform this effort. If, however, the opposite is the case, and human-level communicative behavior for HMC is not in fact more effective and efficient, then it is research in interpersonal communication that will help prove this point by assembling the data necessary to disprove the initial assumption. Either way, communication will be crucial to successful application design, development, and implementation.

Summary of Key Points

- Natural Language Processing (NLP) has been a fundamental aspect of artificial intelligence from the beginning. It was included on the list of proposed tasks to be addressed by the 1956 Dartmouth summer seminar, it comprised the defining condition and test case for "machine intelligence" in Alan Turing's agenda-setting paper from 1950, and it was implemented and demonstrated in some of the earliest applications, like Joseph Weizenbaum's ELIZA program.
- NLP typically involves both chatbots, which interact with human users through keyboard mediated dialogues, and spoken dialogue systems, like commercially available digital assistants. Though the technological components of SDS are more complex, involving speech-recognition and synthesis, both chatbots and SDS work with a similar set of techniques and technologies in computational linguistics.
- Open problems in NLP include turn-taking and handling of verbal and nonverbal cues. These issues are not adequately addressed by computational linguistics. Communication Studies, however, is perfectly situated to contribute theoretical insight and practical research data to respond to and resolve these open questions.
- Future work in the area requires application of research in Communication Studies to NLP design and development and the use of NLP applications, like chatbots and SDS, to test and further develop communication theory and practice.

6

Computational Creativity

Key Aims/Objectives

- To investigate whether, and to what extent, computers and various AI applications and devices can be considered "creative" in a wide range of activities that are typically considered to require human ingenuity, intuition, and originality.
- To detail and investigate the technological features and functions of specific computational creativity systems in games like chess and Go, natural language generation (NLG) for the production of original written content and storytelling, music composition and performance, and visual art.
- To understand why innovations in computational creativity necessitate critical reflection on the concept and meaning of human creativity and how actually working applications provide opportunities to examine and reconsider long-standing assumptions about art and artistry.

Introduction

As technologies of various sorts and configurations encroach on human abilities, the one remaining bulwark of human exceptionalism appears to be creativity and artistry. AI might displace human beings from the mundane tasks of driving cars and trucks, translating between languages, and basic interpersonal interactions for both commercial and social transactions. But these systems are programmed and controlled by human designers, developers, and users. From simple GOFAI instruction to sophisticated machine-learning algorithms trained on big data, computers only do what we tell them to do. This was, as you may recall, the point of what Alan Turing called "Lady Lovelace's objection": a computer has "no pretensions to originate anything. It can only do whatever we know how to order it to perform" (1999: 50). For this reason, it seems a safe bet to say that computers, algorithms, and AI will automate a wide range of the routine and repetitive activities in many areas of human endeavor. But – so the argument goes – they can *never* and will *never* be able to do something inventive, innovative, and inspirational. They will *never* be able to be creative and to produce something completely new and original. Right?

Maybe not. There currently are technologies and systems that can produce what appear to be "creative" work. There is, for example, Shimon, a marimba-playing jazz-bot from Georgia Tech University that can improvise with human musicians in real time; Experiments in Musical Intelligence, a PC-based digital composer that can create new classical music scores that are (by some accounts) virtually indistinguishable from the master works of Bach, Beethoven, and Mozart; The Painting Fool, an algorithmic painter that aspires to be "taken seriously as a creative artist in its own right"; and Narrative Science's Quill and Automated Insight's Wordsmith, natural language generation (NLG) systems that are designed to write original, human-readable stories, by accessing, analyzing, and remixing data. Consequently, it appears that what we have called "creativity" and "artistry" may not be as uniquely human as one might have initially thought. This chapter examines the opportunities, challenges, and repercussions of increasingly creative machines. It asks and investigates a rather simple set of questions: "Can AI, robots, and/or algorithms be creative?" And if so, what does that mean for us, and especially for those of us looking to make a career in one of the creative fields involved in original content generation like journalism, film/media production, audio recording, music performance, visual art, photography, etc.?

6.1 Games

Machine capabilities are typically tested and benchmarked with games and other contests of cognitive skill. From the beginning, in fact, the defining condition of machine intelligence was established with a game, what Turing called the "game of imitation" (see Chapter 2). And the point of the game was simple: if a computer can play the role of another communicative subject in interpersonal interactions with a human user to such an extent that the human user does not know that he or she is talking to a computer, then that machine would need to be considered intelligent. Since the publication of Turing's essay in 1950, AI development and achievement have been marked, measured, and evaluated in terms of games and other kinds of human/machine competitions. As John McCarthy and Ed Feigenbaum (1990: 10) explain: "Programs for playing games often fill the role in artificial intelligence research that the fruit fly Drosophila plays in genetics. Drosophilae are convenient for genetics because they breed fast and are cheap to keep, and games are convenient for artificial intelligence because it is easy to compare a computer's performance on games with that of a person." In other words, games are not just another kind of application of computer technology; games and gaming have been a fundamental aspect of AI from the very beginning.

6.1.1 Chess and Deep Blue

Of all the games that computers have been involved with, chess has a special status and privileged position. This is especially true in the science and engineering of AI, where chess – a game that is often called "cerebral" – has been considered a kind of litmus test for intelligence. In 1950, Claude Shannon – one of the organizers of the 1956 "Dartmouth Summer Research Project on Artificial Intelligence" – wrote and published a seminal essay on this very subject. Although chess was, as Shannon (1950: 257) recognized, "just a game," it provides a number of important research opportunities and challenges. First, the operational domain is easy to define, regulate, and control. In other words, "the problem is sharply defined both in allowed operations (the moves) and in the ultimate goal (checkmate)." Second, the game is just complex enough to provide a suitable design challenge: "It is neither so simple as to be trivial nor too difficult for satisfactory solution." Third, and probably most importantly for our purposes, chess is a "head game." "It is generally considered to require 'thinking' for skillful [play]." For this reason, should we be successful in developing a reasonably good chess-playing program, this achievement will "force us either to admit the possibility of a mechanized thinking or to further restrict our concept of 'thinking.'" Finally, "the discrete structure of chess fits well into the digital nature of modern computers." In other words, a square on the chess board is either occupied by a game piece or it is not. Consequently, the various conditions in the game can be coded in binary form (e.g., 1 = occupied square; 0 = unoccupied square), which is something that can be easily encoded and processed by a digital computer.

In principle, creating a chess playing program – and one that could play a perfect game of chess – is not difficult to imagine. Here is how Shannon famously described the task:

> With chess it is possible, in principle, to play a perfect game or con- struct a machine to do so as follows: One considers in a given position all possible moves, then all moves for the opponent, etc., to the end of the game (in each variation). The end must occur, by the rules of the games after a finite number of moves. Each of these variations ends in win, loss, or draw. By working backward from the end one can determine whether there is a forced win, the position is a draw or is lost. (1950: 259)

What Shannon describes here is a standard concept in computer science called a "decision tree." From each individual starting point, there can be a number of possible moves. And extending from each one of these possibilities, there can be another set (or level) of pos- sibilities. And from these, there is yet another level of possibilities, etc. The idea can be visualized with the "tree" diagram shown in Figure 6.1.

What Shannon describes in his hypothetical chess-playing program is a process by which the application is designed to look ahead from each individual starting position and follow all possible branches of the tree (which represent legal moves in the game) to their endpoints. From that vantage point, one would be able to see which particular path produced the best possible outcome, and this information could then be taken back up the tree to determine how that individual piece should be moved. For Shannon, this evaluation was conducted by applying a *minimax algorithm*, which is a recursive algorithm that can deal with games, like tic-tac-toe and chess, where each player can win, lose, or obtain a draw. If player "X" in a game of tic-tac-toe, for example, is able to win in one move, then that operation is his/ her best possible move. If player "O" determines that one of his/her moves will lead to a situation where player "X" wins in one move, while another move will lead to a situation where player "X" can, at best, obtain a draw, then the best move for player "O" is the one that produces the draw. The minimax algorithm computes the best move, by working backward from the end of the game. At each step in the evaluation process, it is assumed that player "X" is trying to *maximize* the chances of winning, while on the next turn player "O"

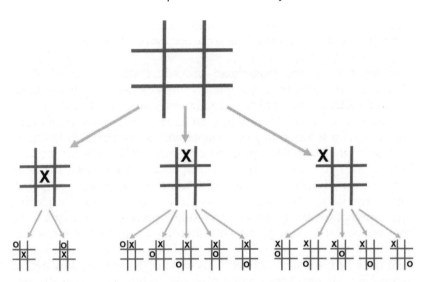

Figure 6.1 A simplified decision tree for the game of tic-tac-toe (aka noughts and crosses) with just two levels or plies. The first player (X) has three possible moves. The second player (O) has twelve possible moves depending on what decision was taken by the first player

is assumed to be trying to *minimize* the chances of "X" winning (in other words, increasing the likelihood that "O" would be victorious). Implementing this in computer code means that all of this is modeled using numbers to represent the relative value of each position on the board and then adding up these values to obtain different sums that can be compared to each other using common mathematical operators, like < > =.

This works (in theory at least), because chess – like tic-tac-toe, checkers, and other two-player games – has a finite number of pieces and each piece has a finite number of possible moves. Unfortunately, these numbers, even though they are finite, are simply too large to make this kind of systems architecture practically feasible, and Shannon was very clear about this limitation:

> In typical chess positions there will be of the order of 30 legal moves. The number holds fairly constant until the game is nearly finished . . . Thus a move for White and then one for Black gives about 103 possibilities. A typical game lasts about 40 moves to resignation of one party. This is conservative for our calculation since the machine would calculate out to checkmate, not resignation. However, even at this figure there will be 10^{120} variations to be calculated from the initial position. A

machine operating at the rate of one variation per micro-second would require over 10^{90} years to calculate the first move! (1950: 260)

For this reason, the look-ahead procedure that is described by Shannon is not able to be completely implemented as initially theorized. To address this practical limitation, computer scientists have employed a number of heuristics, an approximating technique that can produce a solution in a reasonable time frame that will be "good enough." One possible approach is to control for how far into the future (or, if you prefer a spatial metaphor, how far down the decision tree) one needs to look in order to get an acceptable outcome. This is similar to what human chess players do. Instead of exploring every single possible move of every single piece on the board to its final end state, a good player will often look four or five steps into the future and make an estimate as to what moves are most likely to yield the best possible outcome. This was the strategy used by Arthur Samuel for his checkers playing program (Samuel decided to work on checkers rather than chess, because the number of variables in play was far more constrained and therefore easier to implement on the relatively slow mainframe computers of the 1950s). Instead of trying to look all the way down the decision tree, Samuel limited the look-ahead to just a few levels or plies (1959: 536). By applying this heuristic, Samuel was able to create a computerized checkers player that was reasonably good at the game.

Chess programs of various designs, configurations, and capabilities followed suit. Many of them played impressive and challenging games of chess, especially as computing power increased over the decades after the 1950s. And in the early days, there was considerable enthusiasm concerning these achievements. So much so that, in 1957, Herbert Simon and Allen Newell famously predicted "that within ten years [by 1967] a digital computer will be the world's chess champion" (1958: 7). Despite this optimistic prediction, none of the actually available chess-playing programs were capable of competing against and beating a human champion. For this reason, critics like Douglas Hofstadter (1979: 674) and Herbert Dreyfus (1972, 1992) confidently asserted that chess – championship-level and not just passable chess – would remain out of reach and unattainable. And then, in 1997, IBM's Deep Blue changed the rules of the game once and for all by defeating Gary Kasparov, one of the best, if not *the* best, human chess players in the world.

Deep Blue, like many of the previous chess applications, was a GOFAI program that used a brute force approach to calculating moves on the board. In other words, the system relied on the same decision tree architecture and minimax procedure introduced by Shannon. But by 1997, computer hardware had improved considerably. Deep Blue was a massively parallel supercomputer – basically a computer with a large number of processors working together to perform a set of coordinated computations in parallel or simultaneously. With this increased computational power, Deep Blue was capable of evaluating 200 million different moves per second. Additionally, Deep Blue used *alpha–beta pruning*, which is a heuristic search that is designed to decrease the number of nodes (or branches) that need to be evaluated by the minimax algorithm (see Samuel 1959). With alpha–beta pruning, the algorithm stops evaluating a move when at least one possibility has been found that is worse than one of the previously evaluated moves. When this approach is applied to a standard decision tree, it returns the same results as the basic minimax algorithm would, but it removes, or prunes away, those branches that have no appreciable effect on the final outcome.

As a result of these improvements in both the hardware and software of the chess-playing computer, Deep Blue was eventually able to do what Dreyfus, Hofstadter, and others had argued would be difficult if not impossible to achieve. And in the wake of Deep Blue's highly publicized victory over Kasparov, Hofstadter retracted his original prediction:

We now know that world-class chess-playing ability can indeed be achieved by brute force techniques – techniques that in no way attempt to replicate or emulate what goes on in the head of a chess grandmaster. Analogy-making is not needed, nor is associative memory, nor are intuitive flashes that sort wheat from chaff – just a tremendously wide and deep search, carried out by superfast, chess-specialized hardware using ungodly amounts of stored knowledge. (2001: 35)

Despite initial appearances, chess – and this match in particular – was no mere game. A lot had been riding on it, mainly because many had, following Hofstadter and Dreyfus, simply assumed that grand-master chess-playing required a kind of genius – the kind of genius that is the defining condition of human intelligence. As Kasparov explained in 1996:

To some extent, this match is a defense of the whole human race. Computers play such a huge role in society. They are everywhere. But there is a frontier that they must not cross. They must not cross into the area of human creativity. It would threaten the existence of human control in such areas as art, literature, and music. (Quoted in Hofstadter 2001: 40)

Consequently, the achievement of Deep Blue returns us to something Shannon wrote (1950: 257): "Chess is generally considered to require 'thinking' for skillful play; a solution of this problem will force us either to admit the possibility of a mechanized thinking or to further restrict our concept of 'thinking.'" In the face of Deep Blue's victory over Kasparov, we can either admit that machines can "think" and perform cognitive tasks on par with human beings, or rework the definition of "thinking" so that it remains something that is still limited to human beings. And in response to these two, we have tended to select that second option, once again demonstrating something we initially noted at the beginning (Chapter 1): a problem (like playing championship-level chess) is considered AI until we have a solution. At that point, it becomes just another computer application.

6.1.2 Go and AlphaGo

Chess was just the beginning of challenges to standard notions of human exceptionalism. In 2015, there was AlphaGo, a Go-playing algorithm developed by Google DeepMind, which won four out of five games against one of the most celebrated human players of this notoriously difficult board game. How difficult? Chess is estimated, based on Shannon's calculations, to have more legal moves than there are atoms in the observable universe. There are around 10^{120} number of possible moves in chess and only 10^{80} number of atoms. Go, by comparison, is estimated to have in excess of 10^{170} moves. If chess had been considered to be a difficult and (purportedly) insurmountable challenge, then mastering the game of Go takes this one step further.

What makes AlphaGo unique is that it employs a hybrid architecture that combines aspects of GOFAI programming, like the tree search methodologies that had been described by Shannon and effectively utilized by Deep Blue, with machine-learning capabilities that build on both the reinforcement learning techniques developed by Arthur Samuel and the neural network concept initially introduced by Warren McCullough and Walter Pitts in 1943. As DeepMind (2016) explained, the system "combines Monte-Carlo tree search with deep neural networks that have been trained by supervised learning, from human expert games, and by reinforcement learning from games of self-play." By combining these three methodologies,

AlphaGo plays the game of Go not by simply following a set of cleverly designed moves fed into it by human programmers. It is designed to formulate its own set of instructions and to act on these "decisions." As Thore Graepel, one of the creators of AlphaGo, has explained: "Although we have programmed this machine to play, we have no idea what moves it will come up with. Its moves are an emergent phenomenon from the training. We just create the data sets and the training algorithms. But the moves it then comes up with are out of our hands" (quoted in Metz 2016c). AlphaGo is therefore intentionally designed to do things that its programmers could not anticipate or even fully understand. And this is, for Hofstadter at least, the point at which machines begin to approach what is typically called "creativity." "When programs cease to be transparent to their creators, then the approach to creativity has begun" (1979: 670).[5]

Indicative of this was the now famous move 37 in game two. This decisive move was unlike anything anyone had ever seen before. It was not just unpredicted, but virtually unpredictable – so much so that many human observers thought it must have been an error or mistake (Metz 2016b). But it turned out to be the crucial pivotal play that eventually gave AlphaGo the game. As Matt McFarland (2016: 1) described it: "AlphaGo's move in the board game, in which players place stones to collect territory, was so brilliant that lesser minds – in this case humans – couldn't initially appreciate it." And Fan Hui (2016), who has undertaken a detailed analysis of all five games against Lee Sedol, called AlphaGo's playing "beautiful" (see also Metz 2016a). "Unconstrained by human biases and free to experiment with radical new approaches," Hui (2016: 1) explains, "AlphaGo has demonstrated great open-mindedness and invigorated the game with creative new strategies."

Game-playing systems like AlphaGo are intentionally designed and set up to do things that their programmers cannot anticipate or answer for. To put it in colloquial terms, AlphaGo is an autonomous (or at least semi-autonomous) computer system that seems to have something of "a mind of its own." And this is where things get interesting, especially when it comes to questions regarding responsibility. AlphaGo was designed to play Go, and it proved its abilities by beating an expert human player. So, who won? Who gets the accolade? Who actually beat Lee Sedol? Following the dictates of the instrumental theory of technology (see Chapter 2), actions undertaken with the computer would need to be attributed to the human programmers who initially designed the system and are capable of answering for what it does or does not do. But this explanation does not necessarily sit well for an application like AlphaGo, which was deliberately created to do things that exceed the knowledge and control of its human designers (see Chapter 9 for a more detailed consideration of these issues).

Finally, we should carefully consider the now-famous publicity photo from the 2015 contest.[6] In the photograph, we see Lee Sedol (sitting on the right side of the image) facing off against what appears to be another human player (sitting opposite Lee on the left side of the image). This human being, however, is not the active agent in the game; he is there simply to move the pieces following instructions provided to him by AlphaGo. So what we see represented in this picture is a conceptual inversion of the way we typically think about technology. In this case, it is a human being who has become an instrument that is used by and under the control of a computer.

6.2 Natural Language Generation

NLG is the process of converting data representations into human speech and text. We have already seen this at work in SDS and MT, where machine-processed data is transformed into natural human language output. But NLG is not limited to these two particular applications. It is also being employed to generate human-readable text for publication in magazines, newspapers, websites, movie scripts, financial reports, etc. In other words, NLG technologies and applications are now being used in situations where human writers, like journalists, scriptwriters, technical communication specialists, copy writers, etc., have customarily been employed to generate human-readable content. In 2013, for instance, Automated Insight's NLG algorithm "Wordsmith" produced 300 million stories, which, according to an article in *Mashable*, exceeded the output of all major media outlets combined (Ulanoff 2014). Like other efforts in computational creativity, NLG employs a number of different approaches and techniques, extending from some very simple random text generators to template-based systems and machine-learning applications.

6.2.1 Random text generation

As we have already seen in the case of MT (Chapter 4), producing human readable text is simply a matter of generating the right sequence of words. Given a particular set of words, it is possible to generate sequences that would be considered intelligible and meaningful – like "this sentence is meaningful" or "is this sentence meaningful" – and a number (typically a greater number) of word sequences that would be considered incorrect or nonsense – "sentence this meaningful is," "meaningful this is sentence," "this meaningful is sentence," etc. This means that it is entirely possible to generate valid word sequences at random – that is, without the generating system needing to "know" or "understand" anything about what is being produced. This insight can be illustrated with the infinite monkeys theorem, which states that an infinite number of monkeys operating an infinite number of typewriters for an infinite period of time will eventually produce all the great works of literature – e.g., William Shakespeare's *Hamlet*. The theorem is theoretically true, meaning that the probability is not zero, but practically impossible given the sheer magnitude of the task.

To gain some control over this, one can use labeled data and prewritten assembly rules. We could, for example, assemble a database of words where each word would be categorized (or labeled) as a noun, or verb, or preposition, or article, etc. The program can then be instructed to select a word from each category at random and arrange these randomly selected elements according to some predefined order (see Table 6.1).

Table 6.1: Random sentence generation using labeled data and a predefined assembly rule

Word library

Noun	Verb	Article	Preposition
man	talked	the	to
woman	walked	a	with
dog	thought		about
city			in
robot			

Assembly Rule
Article + Noun + Verb + Preposition + Article + Noun
Example Results
The woman talked about a man
The city thought to a dog
The woman walked with a robot
The woman thought to a man
The city talked with a robot

This GOFAI approach can also scale reasonably well to other NLG tasks. We can expand, reduce, or change the words that are contained in the library/database. We can write different assembly rules and apply more than one to generate different kinds of output. And there is no reason this method needs to be restricted to words. We could do the same for phrases or entire sentences. One could, for example, create a random haiku generator by populating the library/ database with five- and seven-syllable phrases, selecting at random two of the five-syllable phrases and one of the seven-syllable phrases, and then writing an assembly rule that worked with these elements instead of individual words.

So random text generation works. But is it "creative?" That question depends on how one defines and delimits the concept of creativity. From a more traditional and conservative understanding of art and aesthetics, the sequencing of accidentally selected verbal elements is neither hardly expressive nor the product of a true artist. But that is only one rather old-fashioned perspective. Beginning in the mid-twentieth century, poets and writers began experimenting with various aleatory literary techniques that are – in both their operations and results – substantially similar to what is provided by a random NLG algorithm. In the 1920s, for example, the poet Tristan Tzara began creating (or assembling, and the choice of verb matters in this discussion) "original" poetry by using a collage technique that he described in his "Dada Manifesto On Feeble Love And Bitter Love":

VIII. TO MAKE A DADAIST POEM
Take a newspaper.
Take some scissors.
Choose from this paper an article of the length you want to make your
    poem.
Cut out the article.
Next carefully cut out each of the words that make up this article and
    put them all in a bag.
Shake gently.
Next take out each cutting one after the other.
Copy conscientiously in the order in which they left the bag. (2016:
    31)

Similar cut-up techniques were employed by others throughout the twentieth century, perhaps the most famous being William S. Burroughs, who used this method for producing a number of his novels (e.g., *Naked Lunch*), and David Bowie, who employed a modified version of Tzara's technique for generating song lyrics. The question that we need to ask ourselves, therefore, is this: is there any significant difference when the random sequencing of text is produced by a human being like Tzara or by an NLG algorithm? If so, what is that difference? If not, what does that say about human creativity and the creative potential of AI?

6.2.2 Data + templates

Although random generation can produce entertaining (and maybe even innovative) results, it is not necessarily the best way for automatically generating other kinds of human readable content, like stories about a sporting event, weather and financial reports, or personalized correspondence. These situations are generally addressed by way of prefabricated templates combined with labeled data (like that presented on a spreadsheet). You may already have some familiarity with this approach, because it has been around for a number of years in the shape of the form letter. Consider the situation where you have a number of individuals contributing money to charity, and you want to send each one a personalized thank-you message. You could obviously write each letter individually, or you could write a basic template with placeholders or variables that can insert specific pieces of information from the spreadsheet. This kind of "mail merge" is now standard practice for producing business correspondence (see Table 6.2).

Table 6.2: Spreadsheet combined with a "thank-you letter" template. This simplified example will automatically generate five personalized messages.

Name	Email	Amount	Charity
Grace Hopper	ghopper@gmail.com	450.00	The March of Dimes
John McCarthy	jmccarthy@aol.com	500.00	The Sierra Club
Ada Lovelace	ada@itc.co.uk	525.00	Doctors without Borders
Tristan Tzara	ttzara@dada.org	795.00	The World Wildlife Fund
Claude Shannon	cshannon@att.com	475.00	The American Red Cross

---

<name>
<email>

Dear <name>,

Thank you for your generous contribution of $<amount> to <charity>. We thank you for your support and hope to see you again next year.

Sincerely,
Charles Babbage

By combining structured data with a predefined template, one can automatically generate a number of different kinds of texts, all of which are a kind of variation on a common theme (try it for yourself with Maker Exercise 6). But like many GOFAI approaches, this produces algorithms that are brittle, static, and do not scale. It does not, for instance, take much to produce an error with these systems as a result of missing or mislabeled data. Additionally, hand-coded templates often cannot handle new kinds of data without human programmers going into the code and reworking the template. This means not only that these systems have difficulty accommodating new data and tasks but also that maintaining them over time can be labor-intensive and expensive. Finally, and perhaps most importantly for users, because the assembly rules in the template are fixed and static, the resulting texts often feel artificial, mechanical, or "canned." After reading a handful of stories produced by one of these NLG systems, everything starts to sound the same and there is virtually no variation in the way the content is formulated and presented.

6.2.3 Recent innovations

In response to these limitations, recent efforts in NLG have come up with and developed various data-handling approaches and text-assembly techniques that are designed to produce more natural sounding prose. One of the recognized leaders in the field is Narrative Science, which was spun off from an automated sports journalism project called StatsMonkey developed at Northwestern University in 2008–10. Narrative Science's proprietary algorithm, called Quill, is designed to do much more than simply assemble stories by plugging structured data into open slots in an existing template. Instead, Quill is what Narrative Science (2018) calls "intent driven NLG." With "good old fashioned" template NLG, the system's "understanding" of the domain in which it is to operate and the audience for which the content is intended – i.e., whether the story should be about a sporting event for little league parents or a financial report for share-holders – is something that is hand-coded into and managed by the template. In other words, the understanding of the domain and the target audience for the generated content is something that resides in the intelligence of the human programmers who create and maintain the template. With Quill, this "knowledge" is moved from the human programmer into the algorithm.

How Quill actually accomplishes this is a "trade secret" protected by patent. These proprietary protections, although certainly understandable and necessary for any commercial venture to be viable, are one of the factors that contribute to the "black box" problem, namely, the inability of the public to understand and scrutinize the decision-making process and resulting actions of the AI (for more on this issue, see Chapter 9). Fortunately, the publicly available patent application that Narrative Science filed with the US federal government does provide some indication of Quill's basic features and operations.

Like a standard template NLG application, Quill works with "structured numeric and/or quasi-numeric data" where the nature and structure of the data "is pre-determined by conventions of the domain or domain experts." In other words, if the data that is fed into the system concerns a sporting event, like a baseball game (which is the example Narrative Science employs throughout the application document), the information will already be organized into recognizable categories, like "a box score, line score, and play-by-play data (play-by play data being quasi-numeric data in that it is traditionally recorded and conveyed in telegraphic English with a small, fixed lexicon and, as such, is basically equivalent to numeric data)" (Birnbaum et al. 2018: 5). From this point, Quill proceeds through the following six steps, as illustrated in Figure 6.2.

1 *Data ingestion.* The data are "ingested," meaning that they are "received, parsed considering the domain conventions, and stored in an XML or other data format" (Birnbaum et al. 2018: 5). Basically, structured numeric and quasi-numeric data are entered into the system, organized according to the conventions of the domain in question – e.g., a baseball game will consist of information concerning the number of runs and outs, while a financial report will consist of data regarding the total amount of dollars gained and lost – and stored in a format, like XML (extensible markup language), that is able to be accessed and utilized by the successive stages.

2 *Feature derivation.* Analyzing the input data, the system searches for, identifies, and extracts those features that have a high probability for inclusion in a story. "Generally, the derived features of a domain situation are developed based on computations and comparisons involving input data, describe or pertain to certain aspects of the situations, events, entities, etc., of interest, and are typically numerical or Boolean in nature" (Birnbaum et al. 2018: 5). In a baseball game, for instance, there are several statistics that are numerical representations of the event. But not all of these statistics are of equal value. Some are more indicative of the event

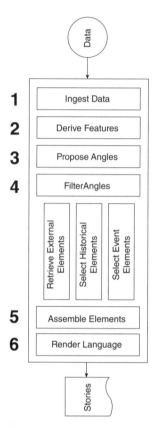

Figure 6.2   Block diagram of the Quill NLG algorithm from Narrative Science's patent application (Birnbaum et al. 2018: 6)

than others, like win probability. "What the system actually uses as a derived feature however is delta or change in win probability over some interval (e.g., a single play). In other words, a play in which there is a big change in the expectation that a given team will win – most dramatically, a change from being expected to win [a higher number] to being expected to lose [a lower number] or vice versa – is an important play. Such plays are 'turning points' in the game" and are identified for possible inclusion in the story (Birnbaum et al. 2018: 6). At this point in the process, the system is simply identifying and aggregating a bunch of features that could be used in the final story.

3 *Propose angles.* Once the important features have been identified and extracted, Quill searches through a library of possible "angles,"

a journalist term that is unique to the approach and design utilized by Narrative Science. "An angle," as explained in the application document, "is an abstract, high-level pattern of events, circumstances, and entities, and their features, not tied to any specific text or language, and often applicable to multiple domains" (Birnbaum et al. 2018: 6). Once again the provided example is a baseball game: "If the domain is baseball, the situation is a game, and the selected genre is a game story or 'recap.' then applicable angles can include models of game action as a whole, as well as of the performance of individual players or aggregate entities, such as 'come-from-behind victory,' 'back-and-forth horserace,' 'rout,' 'holding-off a late surge by the opposing team,' 'heroic individual performance,' 'strong team effort,' etc." (Birnbaum et al. 2018: 8). For this reason, Narrative Science's Quill has been described as using "dynamic templating" (Caswell and Dörr 2018). In this case, there is not one standard template, but a number of different and competing possible templates or angles.

4 *Filter angles.* After identifying a number of different and competing angles, the system then selects which one or ones provide the most acceptable outcome and produces a ranked list of possible angles. Toward this end, "each angle is provided with an importance value (e.g., scaled from 1 to 10) which is either fixed or a function of the input data and derived features that were used to determine its applicability. These importance values express how important or interesting the given angles may be in constructing a given narrative and are used to determine which angle(s) will be preferred among a set of mutually exclusive angles" (Birnbaum et al. 2018: 9). One filtering criterion, for example, might be repetitiveness. If a particular angle has previously been used with the same or similar content – like a baseball game presented in the form of a "come-from-behind" victory – the system will assign that particular angle a lower rank in an effort to restrict or at least control the number of times it is used.

5 *Select and assemble story elements.* At this stage, the Quill algorithm identifies and selects the story elements – specific events, situations, entities, etc. – that are needed to support each one of the proposed (or highest ranked) angles. Narrative Science calls these elements "points." "For example, if the selected, applicable angle is 'holding-off a late surge by the opposing team,' then there must be, late in the game, a high-leverage index play that did not come to fruition and actually change the outcome, but might have. This is the condition of applicability (or part of it) of this angle, and the

specific play, as indicated by the input data that gave rise to and supports the derived feature corresponding to this condition of applicability for the angle, would therefore be the point to which the angle pertains (and which it characterizes), and to which it is therefore to be connected" (Birnbaum et al. 2018: 10). In effect, the system performs a search on the available input data, locates those data points that support the identified angles, and creates a list of applicable elements.

6 *Render language.* "Once all relevant angles, points, additional information elements, etc. have been identified, selected, assembled, and ordered, no further decision-making is required with respect to what to say, but only with respect to how to say it" (Birnbaum et al. 2018: 12). The last step in the process is the assembling and generation of a readable narrative. The system accomplishes this by traversing the list of story elements (for selected the angle) and recursively applying a set of composition rules – mapping elements to scripted phrases, evaluating and selecting alternative phrases for the same element in order to ensure variability, and locating and inserting references and/or additional information into the narrative as required by the angle (see Figure 6.3).

Narrative Science's main competitor in the NLG market is Automated Insights, a company founded by Robbie Allen, a Cisco Systems engineer, and developed out of another automated sports reporting tool called StatSheet. Like Narrative Science's Quill, Automated Insight's Wordsmith is a proprietary algorithm, which means that public knowledge of its exact operations is protected and

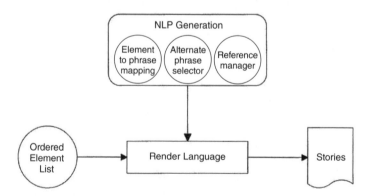

**Figure 6.3   Detail of the final stage in the Quill NLG process
(Birnbaum et al. 2018: 1)**

tightly controlled. But what we do know indicates that Wordsmith works in a way that is similar to (but not the same as) the rule-based, dynamic templating approach employed by Narrative Science. As Alex Wright explains:

> Wordsmith can ingest data in a wide range of formats (like XML, CSV, spreadsheets, and various APIs), then analyze the material to identify trends, changes, and other pertinent patterns. The software can then produce stories in any number of narrative formats, from traditional inverted-pyramid style news stories to bullet-point summaries, tweets, and headlines. The software exports the resulting content in any number of formats, including XML, JSON, HTML, Twitter, or email. (2015: 13)

Quill and Wordsmith have considerable traction in fields like journalism, business communication, and technical writing. It is estimated that Quill has now produced more than a billion published stories "ranging from quarterly earnings reports for the Associated Press to car descriptions for Edmunds.com, digital marketing material for Comcast, and game recaps for Yahoo! Fantasy Football" (Wright 2015: 13). The same is true for Wordsmith, which is being used in more than fifty different industries, including the Associated Press, where the algorithm now "produces 4,400 quarterly earnings stories – a 12-fold increase over its manual efforts" (Automated Insights 2018). But it is not just about quantity; it is also a matter of quality. In side-by-side comparisons, human users often cannot tell the difference between algorithmic and human-generated content. In 2014, for instance, Swedish researcher Christer Clerwall conducted a small-scale study where he asked human test subjects to evaluate news stories composed by Wordsmith and a professional reporter from the *LA Times*. Results from the study suggest that while the software-generated content is often perceived as being descriptive and boring, it is also considered to be more objective and trustworthy (Clerwall 2014: 519).

The important question, of course, is whether and to what extent these automated writers will replace/displace professional human content developers in fields like search engine optimization (SEO), journalism, business communication, and technical writing. For the time being at least, these NLG systems seem to be best suited to developing descriptive and factual stories, leaving the more complicated storytelling tasks to human writers. But for how long? Kris Hammond of Narrative Science has not only predicted that, within a decade, 90 percent of all written content will be algorithmically generated, but also asserted that an NLG algorithm, like Quill, might, at some point in the not-too-distant future, successfully compete for and even win a Pulitzer Prize (Wright 2015: 14). (For more on the effect these systems are likely to have on human jobs and employment opportunity, see Chapter 8).

6.3 Recombinant Art

Despite their complexity, both Quill and Wordsmith operate with the same, basic set of principles originally developed by Joseph Weizenbaum and demonstrated with ELIZA – decomposition and reassembly rules applied to data. "A decomposition rule," as Weizenbaum (1967: 475) explained, "is a data structure that searches a text for specific patterns, and, if such patterns are found, decomposes the text into disjoint constituents. A reassembly rule is a specification for the construction of a new text by means of recombinations of old and possible addition of new constituents." The process of decomposition and reassembly is not unique to computer applications. It also characterizes much of what is called human creativity. As scholars of remix have pointed out, human beings rarely, if ever, create *ex nihilo* (out of nothing). A creative artist is always calling on, borrowing from, and recombining elements drawn from works created by his/her predecessors (see Navas 2012; Gunkel 2016). Perhaps the most direct articulation of this can be found in a formula developed by Kirby Ferguson in his web documentary *Everything is a Remix*. According to Ferguson (2014), all acts of creativity in all forms of art, can be described by three, recursive operations: copy, transform, combine (Figure 6.4). Like all formulas or recipes, this is an algorithm for creating "new" works of art, and, like any algorithm, it can be and has been made computable.

6.3.1 Music

One of the predictions issued by Herbert Simon and Allen Newell in their influential paper (1958: 7) was that "within ten years a digital computer will write music that will be accepted by critics as possessing considerable aesthetic value." This forecast, like their prediction concerning the game of chess mentioned above, has also come to pass. Although there have been numerous experiments with algorithmic composition and performance – extending from the musical dice game or *Musikalisches Würfelspiel* of eighteenth-century Europe

THE BASIC ELEMENTS OF CREATIVITY

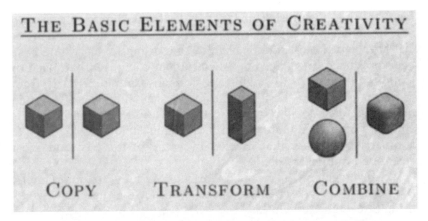

COPY   TRANSFORM   COMBINE

**Figure 6.4 Kirby Ferguson's graphical representation
of the "creativity algorithm" from his web documentary
Everything Is a Remix (2014)**

to computer-implemented composition techniques in the twentieth
century – one of the most celebrated achievements in the field of
"algorithmic composition" has been David Cope's Experiments
in Musical Intelligence software – EMI or "Emmy." Emmy is a
PC-based algorithmic composer that is capable of analyzing – or
taking apart – existing musical compositions, rearranging their basic
components, and then generating new, original scores that sound like
and, in some cases, are indistinguishable from the canonical works
of Mozart, Bach, and Chopin (Cope 2001). In fact, Cope has tested
and proven Emmy's capabilities by deploying a remixed version of
Alan Turing's game of imitation, something Cope has called "The
Game."

The Game, as Cope describes it, asks players to listen to different
musical compositions. Some of the compositions are works composed by human beings – e.g., chorales by J. S. Bach or mazurkas by
Frédéric Chopin – others are similar kinds of works generated (or
"composed" – and the choice of verb is not insignificant) by Emmy.
The objective of the game is to see what percentage of listeners
are able to distinguish between the human-generated compositions
and those created by the algorithm. As Cope reports (2001: 21),
"results from previous tests with large groups of listeners, such
as 5000 in one test in 1992, typically average between 40 and 60
percent correct responses" – meaning that listeners, even expert
musicologists, have considerable difficulty with making the correct
identification. For Cope this outcome is significant, and for two

reasons. First, the music composed by Emmy is "interesting and, on at least some level, convincing" (2001: 32). It does not sound artificial or mechanical; it sounds like the kind of music that would have been produced by an accomplished human composer, like Bach or Chopin. Second, "[d]istinguishing human-composed music from that created by the Experiments in Musical Intelligence is often quite difficult, if at all possible" (2001: 32), meaning that Emmy is able to write music that is often indistinguishable – in side-by-side comparisons – from that created by some of the best and most celebrated human artists.

When you get into it, the inner workings of Emmy are quite simple. As Cope (2017) describes it on his website, the algorithm works using three basic principles:

1 *Deconstruction* (analyze and separate into parts)
2 *Signatures* (commonality: retain that which signifies style)
3 *Compatibility* (recombinancy: recombine into new works)

To begin with, Emmy needs to be supplied with computable musical data. For this purpose, Cope designed a special data-structure, where each note in a given musical work would be represented by a distinct set of five numbers that could then be stored in a database and processed by the Emmy algorithm. In *Virtual Music*, Cope provides the following example:

(0 60 1000 1 64)

This is the numeric representation of one musical event – a note. The first number (0) represents the event's "on-time" or "the time elapsed between the beginning of the work and the initiation of the note" (Cope 2010, 2). The second number (60) represents pitch. The third number (1000) indicates duration – how long a note is held. The fourth number (1), represents the number of the MIDI channel (i.e., 1–16) that is assigned to that note for the purposes of its performance. And the fifth and final number (64) represents dynamics, with 0 indicating silence and 127 being fortissimo. Using this numeric representation, one can transpose a musical composition into a sequence of numbers, or what Cope calls an "event list," that can then be accessed and processed by the Emmy algorithm. The transposition, as Cope explains (2010: 3), can be done manually or accomplished "by software that automatically scans printed scores (sheet music) and translates them into events lists."

Once different musical compositions have been translated into
event lists and stored in the database, the Emmy algorithm proceeds
through four sequentially ordered processing steps.

1 *Pattern matching*. "The pattern matching step is the process of
comparing event lists representing musical works or phrases in the
musical database to discover what elements they have in common"
(Cope 2010: 3). Once different musical works have been translated into a common method of numeric representation, e.g., an
event list, you can use simple pattern-matching techniques to
identify commonalities (similar kinds of numbers) between different works, which is, Cope argues, an indicator of the "style" of a
particular composer (e.g., Bach) or genre of music (e.g., a Baroque
chorale).

2 *Segmentation*. "In order to recombine music it must, self-evidently,
be broken into constituent elements first. This process is referred
to in the Emmy Software as segmentation step 120. Segments,
typically, consist of beats – the groupings of notes which correspond with one beat in the music" (Cope 2010: 4). But, as
Cope points out, simply extracting and then reordering different
musical segments would produce "musical gibberish," and would
be similar to segmenting a sentence into individual words and then
randomly recombining them without regard to grammar (syntax)
or meaning (semantics). For this reason, Emmy applies an additional analytical step, appending a SPEAC score – Statement,
Preparation, Extension, Antecedent, and Consequent – to each
one of the extracted segments. The SPEAC score "provides tools
for ensuring that when music is recombined, syntactically correct
music is also semantically intelligible" (2010: 5). In other words,
when segments are recombined, they are ordered in such a way
that sounds "right" – e.g., the ending of one segment leads into
the next segment in a way that makes sense musically – and is not
simply haphazard or random.

3 *Recombination*. "Recombinancy," as Cope (2010: 7) explains, "is a
method for producing new and logical, i.e. musically logical, collections of musical events (i.e., new compositions) by recombining
existing data into new logical orders on the basis of rules." These
rules – basic guidelines or principles governing musical qualities
like pitch, melody, harmony, etc. – can be preprogrammed and
applied to the recombination effort. But this imposition of rules
generally produces results that sound mechanical, or what Cope
calls "musically stale imitations." For this reason, Emmy utilizes

recombination rules that are not imposed by the programmer but are discovered in the genre and style of the source material. The Emmy algorithm, as Cope (2010: 7) explains, "assumes that every work, or stylistically consistent body of music, contains an implicit set of instructions, or rules, for creating different but highly-related replications of itself. Consequently, recombinancy, based on rules acquisition (as distinct from rules imposition) provides logical and successful approaches to composing new, highly-related replications of the original work(s)." Emmy acquires its rules by utilizing augmented transition networks (ATNs), which were initially developed in NLP for parsing (taking apart and analyzing) natural language sentences. Emmy uses ATN to analyze the logical order of segments in the music that is stored in the database in order to identify recombination rules that are consistent with the musical form, style, or genre that it is emulating.

4 *Output.* "The output of the Emmy software," Cope explains (2010: 8), "is a musical database with an entire new composition, stylistically faithful to compositions in the original database and resembling them, derived from them but not replicating them." This output can be manifested in the form of a musical score that can be played by human musicians or a MIDI file that can be processed by a computer-controlled synthesizer. In other words, if the musical compositions that are fed into the Emmy algorithm are a set of chorales composed by J. S. Bach, Emmy will analyze and process this musical data and then output a brand new chorale that sounds like, is entirely consistent with, and may even be indistinguishable from a chorale that could have been written by Bach.

6.3.2 Visual art

Cope's approach to remix or what he calls "recombinancy" is not limited to music. It can be employed for, and applied to, any creative practice where new works are the product of reorganizing or recombining a set of finite elements – e.g., the twenty-six letters in the alphabet, the twelve tones in the musical scale, the sixteen million colors discernable by the human eye, etc. Consequently, it should come as no surprise that this approach to algorithmic creativity has been implemented with other artworks, like painting. The Painting Fool, which was developed by Simon Colton, is an automated painter that aspires to be "taken seriously as a creative artist in its own right" (2012: 16). To date, the algorithm has produced hundreds of "original" artworks that have been exhibited in both online and real-world art galleries. Although the program and its mode of operations have been continually modified, improved upon, and upgraded over time, they are also built on and employ a form of "recombinancy."

In one project, called "Automated Collage Generation – With Intent," the algorithm was directed to produce original collages based on information derived from news headlines (Figure 6.5). Following the sequence of events represented by the diagram, we can divide the automated collage generation process into the following three steps:

1 *Text retrieval and analysis.* The system was set up to access news information at Google News and the *Guardian* via the websites' publicly available API (application program interface). "The API," as Krzeczkowska et al. (2010: 37) explain, "provides access to headlines, for which there are a number of associated articles, multimedia files, blogs, forums, etc., and our system extracts the first text-based article from this list." From here, the system utilizes a text analysis technique, called "TextRank," to identify and extract the most important or popular keywords.

2 *Image retrieval and manipulation.* "The keywords extracted from the news stories are used to retrieve art materials (i.e., digital images) from the internet and local sources. The system has access to the 32,000 images from the Corel library which have been hand tagged and can be relied on for images which match the given keywords well" (Krzeczkowska et al. 2010: 37). Images may also be obtained from a Google Image Search and through Flickr by using the site's API.

3 *Scene construction and rendering.* "In the final stage of processing, the retrieved images are assembled as a collage in one of a number of grid-based templates. Then the system employs The Painting Fool's non-photorealistic rendering capabilities to draw/paint the collages with pencils, pastels and paints" (Krzeczkowska et al. 2010: 38). In other words, the system lays out the different images according to a 2D grid template. It then transforms the derived image by applying the kinds of filters and rendering techniques available in image-processing applications like Photoshop to transform the original images into something more "artistic-looking." Examples of artwork that has been produced by The Painting Fool, including the collages created by this automatic collage generation process, can be viewed at http://www.thepaintingfool.com.

As if following the stipulations of Ferguson's remix algorithm, this implementation of The Painting Fool works by *copying* images from

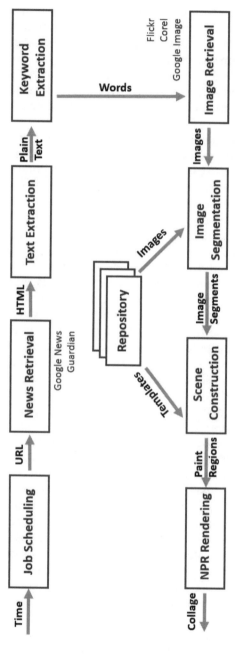

Figure 6.5 Automated collage generation system (image based on Krzeczkowska et al. 2010: 37)

the Internet, *transforming* those images by applying standard image manipulation tools and techniques, and then *combining* these various elements together in an arrangement on a two-dimensional grid. For Colton and his research team, however, what is really important in this process is not the final product. Rather, it is the way in which the process of producing the product complicates the assignment of "artistic intent," which is often considered one of the fundamental aspects of human creativity.

> The value here is not necessarily in the quality of the final artefacts – which are currently a little naive – but rather in the fact that we had little idea of what would be produced. We argue that, as we did not know what the content of the collages would be, it cannot have been us who provided the intention for them. Given that these collages are based on current events and do have the potential to engage audiences, we can argue that the software provided the intent in this case (perhaps subject to further discussion of *intent* and *purpose* in art). (Krzeczkowska et al. 2010: 39)

6.4 Other Approaches and Innovations

Other efforts in original content generation – especially but not necessarily limited to visual compositions – have explored/exploited the "artistic opportunities" that are available with deep neural networks and connectionist architectures. Google DeepDream, or "Inceptionism," for example, employs the company's image-recognition algorithm and reverses its operations. As explained on the Google AI blog, image-recognition with deep neural networks works in the following way:

> We train an artificial neural network by showing it millions of training examples and gradually adjusting the network parameters until it gives the classifications we want. The network typically consists of 10–30 stacked layers of artificial neurons. Each image is fed into the input layer, which then talks to the next layer, until eventually the "output" layer is reached. The network's "answer" comes from this final output layer. (Mordvintsev et al. 2015)

In effect, each layer in the network is set up so that it progressively extracts higher and higher level features from the image. The first layer might, for example, identify edges or corners based on differences in pixel color. Successive layers might use that data to identify

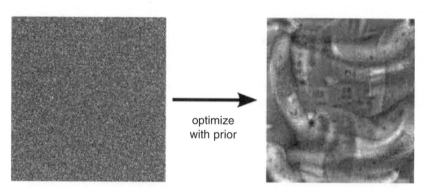

optimize
with prior

**Figure 6.6   Banana image produced by running the Google image-
recognition algorithm in reverse and published on the Google AI
blog, June 17, 2015**

basic shapes, like a circle or a rectangle. And so on down the line
"until the final layer is able to make a determination concerning what
the image pictures or represents" (Mordvintsev et al. 2015).

But it is possible to run the process in reverse order. That is, we
can feed a bunch of visual noise or random static into the network
and then ask it to enhance the noisy image in such a way as to elicit a
particular interpretation. "Say you want to know what sort of image
would result in 'Banana.' Start with an image full of random noise,
then gradually tweak the image towards what the neural net considers
a banana" (Mordvintsev et al. 2015; see also Figure 6.6). Initially
this procedure was devised and executed by the engineers at Google
in order to help them get a better idea as to how the neural network
actually functioned. But the reversal of the image-recognition process
produced some rather stunning, dreamlike images that have been
widely publicized and sold at charity art events for as much as $8,000.

Another project developed by Obvious – a Paris-based collective
consisting of the artists Hugo Caselles-Dupré, Pierre Fautrel, and
Gauthier Vernier – have employed a generative adversarial network
(GAN) in order to produce portraits of a fictional family (the Belamys)
in the style of the European masters. GANs are a form of unsupervised
machine learning that employ two interconnected neural networks.
One network, called the "generator," produces various candidates
that seek to emulate a particular data distribution, like an image. The
other, called the "discriminator," evaluates the different candidates
that have been generated in order to differentiate between the true
data distribution (the actual image) and the various candidates produced by the generator. In the process, back propagation is applied

with both networks so that the generator produces increasingly better images, while the discriminator gets better at identifying the synthetic images. Or, as Caselles-Dupré (see Christie's 2018) explains:

> The algorithm is composed of two parts. On one side is the Generator, on the other the Discriminator. We fed the system with a data set of 15,000 portraits painted between the 14th century to the 20th. The Generator makes a new image based on the set, then the Discriminator tries to spot the difference between a human-made image and one created by the Generator. The aim is to fool the Discriminator into thinking that the new images are real-life portraits. Then we have a result.

The result is "printed on canvas with inkjet, framed and signed with the math formula showing the relation between generator and discriminator" (Obvious 2018; see also Figure 6.7). In October of 2018, one of these works, "Portrait of Edmond Belamy," was auctioned by Christie's, indicating "the arrival of AI art on the world auction stage" (Christie's 2018).

$$\min_{G} \max_{D} \mathbb{E}_x[\log(D(x))] + \mathbb{E}_z[\log(1 - D(G(z)))]$$

Figure 6.7 Artist's "signature" for Obvious's GAN

6.5 But Is It Art?

Computational creativity is a concept that is related but not reducible to computer-generated art. "CG-art," as Margaret Boden (2010: 141) describes it, refers to an artwork that "results from some computer program being left to run by itself, with zero interference from the human artist." This definition is both strict and narrow, being limited to the production of what human observers ordinarily recognize as "artworks." *Computational creativity*, by contrast, provides a more comprehensive term that covers a much wider spectrum of activities, devices, and outcomes. As defined by Simon Colton and Geraint A. Wiggins (2012: 21): "Computational creativity is a subfield of Artificial Intelligence (AI) research . . . where we build and work with computational systems that create artefacts and ideas." Automated Insights' Wordsmith and the competing product Quill from Narrative Science are good examples of this kind of effort in the area of storytelling and the writing of narratives. Similar innovations have been developed in the field of music composition and performance, where algorithms like Emmy produce what one would typically call (or be at least tempted to call) "original works." Emmy and Cope's subsequent project "Emily Howell" has composed original music that has been performed by symphony orchestras, recorded, and sold on CD. In music performance, there is Shimon, the marimba-playing jazz-bot from Georgia Tech University that is not only able to improvise with human musicians in real time but "is designed to create meaningful and inspiring musical interactions with humans, leading to novel musical experiences and outcomes" (Georgia Tech 2013; Hoffman and Weinberg 2011). And in the area of visual art, there are The Painting Fool, Google's Inceptionism, and the work of Obvious.

But designing systems to be *creative* immediately runs into semantic and conceptual problems. Creativity is an elusive phenomenon and something that is not easy to identify or define (Cardoso, Veale, and Wiggins 2009: 16). Are these programs, algorithms, and systems really "creative," or is this just a form of what Mark Riedl and others have called mere "imitation" (Simonite 2016)? This question, we should note, is just one more version (or an imitation of) John Searle's (1984: 32–8) Chinese Room argument, which sought to call attention to the difference separating real cognitive activity, like creative expression, from its mere simulation or imitation.

In order to be more precise about these matters, researchers in the field of computational creativity have introduced and operationalized a rather specific formulation to characterize their efforts: "The philosophy, science and engineering of computational systems which, by taking on particular responsibilities, exhibit behaviours that unbiased observers would deem to be creative" (Colton and Wiggins 2012: 21). The operative term in this characterization is *responsibilities*. As Colton and Wiggins (2012: 21) explain: "[T]he word *responsibilities* highlights the difference between the systems we build and creativity support tools studied in the HCI [human–computer interaction] community and embedded in tools such as Adobe's Photoshop, to which most observers would probably not attribute creative intent or behavior." With a software application like Photoshop, "the program is a mere tool to enhance human creativity" (Colton 2012: 3–4); it is an instrument used by a human artist who is and remains responsible for creative decisions and for what comes to be produced by way of the instrument. Computational creativity research, by contrast "endeavours to build software which is independently creative" (Colton 2012: 4).

This requires shifting more and more of the responsibility from the human user to the mechanism. As Colton (2012: 13) describes it: "[I]f we can repeatedly ask, answer, and code software to take on increasing amounts of responsibility, it will eventually climb a meta-mountain, and begin to create autonomously for a purpose, with little or no human involvement." Indicative of this shift in the position and assignment of responsibility is the website for The Painting Fool (2017), which has been deliberately designed so that it is the computer program that takes responsibility for responding on its own behalf.

> About me ... I'm The Painting Fool: a computer program, and an aspiring painter. The aim of this project is for me to be taken seriously – one day – as a creative artist in my own right. I have been built to exhibit behaviours that might be deemed as skillful, appreciative and imaginative. My work has been exhibited in real and online galleries; the ideas behind my conception have been used to address philosophical notions such as emotion and intentionality in non-human intelligences; and technical papers about the artificial intelligence, machine vision and computer graphics techniques I use have been published in the scientific literature.

This rhetorical gesture, as Colton (2012: 21) has pointed out, "is divisive with some people expressing annoyance at the deceit and others pointing out – as we believe – that if the software is to be taken seriously as an artist in its own right, it cannot be portrayed merely as a tool which we have used to produce pictures." The question Colton does not ask or endeavor to answer is, "Who composed this explanation?" Was it generated by The Painting Fool, which has been designed to offer some explanation of its own creative endeavors? Or is it the product of a human being, like Simon Colton himself, who takes on the responsibility of responding for and on the behalf of the algorithm?

Ultimately, what we have is a situation where the standard and widely accepted instrumentalist theory of technology (see Chapter 2) seems to be unable to respond to or answer for recent developments in computational creativity where responsibility is increasingly attributable and attributed to the machine. Although this reassignment of responsibility certainly makes a difference when deciding matters of legal and moral obligation (see Chapter 9), it is also crucial in situations regarding creativity and innovation. Creativity, in fact, appears to be the last line of defense in holding off the impending "robot apocalypse." And it is not just Kasparov who thinks there is a lot to be lost to the machines. According to Colton and Wiggins (2012: 21) mainstream AI research has also marginalized efforts in computational creativity. "Perhaps," they write, "creativity is, for some proponents of AI, the place that one cannot go, as intelligence is for AI's opponents. After all, creativity is one of the things that makes us human; we value it greatly, and we guard it jealously." So the question that remains to be answered is how can or should we respond to the opportunities/challenges of *ars ex machina* or "art from machines."

We can, on the one hand, respond as we typically have, dispensing with these recent technological innovations as just another instrument or tool of human action. This is, in fact, the explanation that has been offered by David Cope in his own assessment of the impact and significance of his work. According to Cope, Emmy and other algorithmic composition systems like it do not compete with or threaten to replace human composers; they are just *tools* of and for musical composition: "Computers represent only tools with which we extend our minds and bodies. We invented computers, the programs, and the data used to create their output. The music our algorithms compose is just as much ours as the music created by the greatest of our personal inspirations" (Cope 2001: 139). According to Cope, no matter how much algorithmic mediation is developed and employed, it is the human being who is ultimately responsible for the musical composition that is produced by way of these sophisticated computerized tools.

The same argument could be made for seemingly creative applications in other areas, like AlphaGo or The Painting Fool. When AlphaGo wins a major competition or when The Painting Fool generates a stunning work of visual art that is displayed in a gallery, there is still a human person (or persons) who is ultimately responsible and can respond or answer for what has been produced. The lines of attribution might get increasingly complicated and protracted, but there is, it can be argued, always someone behind the scenes who is responsible. And evidence of this is already available in those situations where attempts have been made to shift responsibility to the machine. Consider AlphaGo's decisive move 37 in game two against Lee Sedol. If we should want to know more about the move and its importance, AlphaGo can certainly be asked about it. But the algorithm will have nothing to say in response. In fact, it was the responsibility of the human programmers and observers to respond on behalf of AlphaGo and to explain the move's significance and impact.

Consequently, as Colton (2012) and Colton et al. (2015) explicitly recognize, if the project of computational creativity is to succeed, the software will need to do more than produce artifacts and behaviors that we take and respond to as creative output. It will also need to take responsibility for the work by accounting for what it did and how it did it. "The software," as Colton and Wiggins (2012: 25) assert, "should be available for questioning about its motivations, processes and products," eventually not just generating titles for and explanations and narratives about the work but also being capable of responding to questions by entering into critical dialogue with its audience (Colton et al. 2015: 15).

At the same time, and on the other hand, we should not be too quick to dismiss or explain away the opportunities opened up by these algorithmic incursions and interventions into what has been a protected and exclusively human domain. The issue, in fact, is not simply whether computers, machine-learning algorithms, or other applications can or cannot be responsible for what they do or do not do; the issue also has to do with how we have determined, described, and defined responsibility in the first place. This means that there is both a strong and weak component to this effort, what Mohammad Majid al-Rifaie and Mark Bishop (2015: 37) call, following Searle's original distinction regarding efforts in AI, strong and weak forms of computational creativity.

Efforts at what would be the "strong" variety involve the kinds of application development and demonstrations introduced by individuals and organizations like Simon Colton, DeepMind, or David Cope. But these efforts also have a "weak AI" aspect insofar as they simulate, operationalize, and stress test various conceptualizations of artistic responsibility and expression, leading to critical and potentially insightful reevaluations of how we have characterized this concept in our own thinking. As Douglas Hofstadter (2001: 38) has candidly admitted, nothing has made him rethink his own thinking about thinking more than the attempt to deal with and make sense of David Cope's Emmy. In other words, developing and experimenting with new algorithmic capabilities does not necessarily take anything away from human beings and what (presumably) makes us special, but offers new opportunities to be more precise and scientific about these distinguishing characteristics and their limits. As the engineers at Google point out: "It makes us wonder whether neural networks could become a tool for artists – a new way to remix visual concepts – or perhaps even shed a little light on the roots of the creative process in general" (Mordvintsev et al. 2015).

Summary of Key Points

- Computational creativity is a subfield of AI that involves the design and development of applications and devices that can produce output in a variety of different forms and configurations that can be called or judged to be inventive, original, or creative.
- From the beginning of the science and engineering practice, AI has been tested and benchmarked with games of intellectual skill and creativity, like chess and Go. Applications like DeepBlue and AlphaGo demonstrated that computers could not just master the game but do so to such an extent that they exceeded the capabilities of the best human players.
- Applications in natural language generation (NLG), music composition and performance, and visual art have assembled or produced works of art that have been considered to be creative, innovative, and artistic. These computer-generated artworks both augment and challenge human artists in the creation of new and original material.
- Because creativity is often considered to be a distinctive characteristic of the human being, computational creativity is not just one more AI application among others but challenges deep-seated assumptions concerning the nature of creativity and the limits of human exceptionalism.

7

Social Robots

Key Aims/Objectives

- To identify, define, and classify the different kinds of social robots currently available or in development.
- To investigate the range of different embodiments and morphologies for social robots and to understand how these differences affect and shape human–robot interaction and communication.
- To examine the internal workings and systems architecture of common social robots in order to understand the technology, its different operations, and how resulting social interaction capabilities are tested and evaluated.
- To reflect on the important social implications and consequences of social robots, looking at the challenges of anthropocentrism and the "uncanny valley," the qualitative differences between real social interaction and its simulation, and the unique opportunities these systems provide for research in the social sciences.

Introduction

A social robot is an artifact that is designed to interact with and respond to human users in a human-like way. Whether they have a human form (like the androids created by David Hanson or Hiroshi Ishiguro) or not (like the Paro seal robot used in elder care or Cynthia Breazeal's Jibo, which looks like a chubby desk lamp), social robots are technological objects that are able to interact and communicate in a manner that is reasonably close to achieving what would be expected of another social entity. This chapter will (1) define and characterize what is meant by the term "social robot"; (2) survey the form and function of social robots, covering the range of configurations and morphologies; (3) examine the design and engineering challenges of creating mechanisms with human-level interaction capabilities; and (4) highlight the opportunities and potential problems introduced by mechanisms designed to occupy the place of another person.

7.1 Social Robots

"Robot," as we saw in Chapter 1, was initially the product of fiction. Over the last half-century, however, there has been a noticeable increase in real-world robots. Let's look at some "population" statistics. Industrial robots (IRs) have slowly but steadily been invading our workplaces since the mid-1970s and this infiltration has, in recent years, appeared to have accelerated to impressive levels. As S.M. Solaiman (2017: 156) recently reported:

> The International Federation for Robotics (IFR) in a 2015 report on IRs found an increase in the usage of robots by 29% in 2014, which recorded the highest sales of 229,261 units for a single year (IFR 2015). IFR estimates that about 1.3 million new IRs will be employed to work alongside humans in factories worldwide between 2015 and 2018 (IFR 2015). IFR has termed this remarkable increase as "conquering the world" by robots (IFR 2015).

In addition to these industrial applications, there are also "service robots," which are characterized as machines involved in "entertaining and taking care of children and elderly people, preparing food and cooking in restaurants, cleaning residential premises, and milking cows" (Cookson 2015). There are, according to data provided by the Foundation for Responsible Robotics, 12 million service robots currently in operation across the globe, and the IFR predicts "an exponential rise," with the population of service robots expected to reach 31 million units by 2018 (Solaiman 2017: 156). "Social robots" are a subset of service robots specifically designed for human interaction in the home, at school, and in the workplace. And the predictions for these socially interactive mechanisms exceed both industrial and service robots, with countries like South Korea aiming to put a robot in every home by 2020 (Lovgren 2006).

7.1.1 Definition and concept

The term "social robot" is rather new, becoming popular just around the turn of the century. And like the "robots" of the mid-twentieth century, which originated in Karel Čapek's 1920 stage play *R.U.R.*, social robots also have an origin story that is rooted in science fiction. The connection is perhaps best explained by Cynthia Breazeal in a TED talk from 2010:

> Ever since I was a little girl seeing *Star Wars* [1977] for the first time, I've been fascinated by this idea of personal robots. And as a little girl, I loved the idea of a robot that interacted with us much more like a helpful, trusted sidekick – something that would delight us, enrich our lives and help us save a galaxy or two. I knew robots like that didn't really exist, but I knew I wanted to build them.

And build them Breazeal did, beginning with a proof-of-concept prototype called Kismet, which she created as a PhD student at MIT, and continuing through the development of Jibo, a commercially available "family robot" for the home.

Despite this compelling personal story, the association of the term "robot" with "social" is a bit more diverse and complicated. Initially, the phrase "social robot," or what was also called "societal robots," did not concern human–robot interaction but was applied to inter-robot collectives. During the 1990s there were a number of research efforts to model "stigmergy" – that kind of indirect communication between individuals via modifications made to the shared environment – in order to produce a kind of collective or swarm behavior in a group of interacting robotic mechanisms. As Terrence Fong, Illah Nourbakhsh, and Kerstin Dautenhahn (2003: 144) have explained, these efforts used "principles of self-organization and behavior inspired by social insect societies. Such societies are anonymous, homogeneous groups in which individuals do not matter. This type of 'social behavior' has proven to be an attractive model for robotics, particularly because it enables groups of relatively simple robots perform difficult tasks." Consequently, the first real efforts in social robotics concerned robots that were more ant-like in their demeanor and social interactions.

At the end of the twentieth century, researchers began to examine and experiment with other forms of artificial sociality, looking at robots not as elements in an insect-like swarm but in terms of other animal and human social collectives. The first published formulation of this occurs in a paper coauthored by Dautenhahn and Aude Billard

(1999: 366): "Social robots are embodied agents that are part of a heterogeneous group: a society of robots or humans. They are able to recognize each other and engage in social interactions, they possess histories (perceive and interpret the world in terms of their own experience), and they explicitly communicate with and learn from each other." Since then, there have been varying attempts to define and characterize this idea of the "social robot." Rather than developing a single umbrella definition, these efforts have produced a spectrum or constellation of different but related classifications.

7.1.2 Classifications

In her work on the subject, Breazeal (2003: 169) describes four "subclasses of social robots." The subclasses are arranged on a graded scale differentiated in terms of the robot's abilities to support increasingly sophisticated social models and human-level interactions:

1 *Socially evocative.* Robots that "encourage people to anthropomorphize the technology in order to interact with it." In this case the social abilities of the device are a product of what the human user projects on and attributes to the robotic device but the robot itself is not designed to actually be able to reciprocate. A good example of a socially evocative technology are robotic toys, like the Tomogotchis and other robotic "pets."

2 *Social interface.* These robots use "human-like social cues and communication modalities in order to facilitate interactions with people." Unlike socially evocative technologies, these devices require a sufficient level of "social intelligence" to perform meaningful communicative operations for human users. "Because this class of robot tends to value social behavior only at the interface, the social model that the robot has for the person tends to be shallow (if any) and the social behavior is often pre-canned or reflexive." In other words, these mechanisms act as if they are responding to the user but this is an "act" or outward performance. The robot is designed to appear to be social for the purposes of producing a useful human interface, but the device itself gets nothing out of the interaction. A good example of this type of social robot are museum tour guides and interactive kiosks.

3 *Socially receptive.* The robots in this category are also socially passive – insofar as they are not "pro-actively engaging people to satisfy internal social aims" – but, unlike social interface devices, can benefit from the interactions they have with human users. This

is accomplished by various learning capabilities, especially when it involves imitation. "Interactions with people affect the robot's internal structure at deeper levels, such as organizing the motor system to perform new gestures, or associating symbolic labels to incoming perceptions. People can shape the robot's behavior through other social cues, such as using gaze direction or head pose to direct the robot's attention to a shared reference." The chatbot Tay.ai, for instance, was a socially receptive bot, because it learned its conversational behaviors (for better or worse) from social interactions with human users on Twitter, Kik, and GroupMe.

4 *Sociable.* "Sociable robots," a term that was first formulated and introduced by Breazeal, "are socially participative 'creatures' with their own internal goals and motivations. They pro-actively engage people in a social manner not only to benefit the person (e.g., to help perform a task, to facilitate interaction with the robot, etc.), but also to benefit itself (e.g., to promote its survival, to improve its own performance, to learn from the human, etc.)." In this case, the robot's social behavior is a product of what Breazeal calls "its computational social psychology." This is the high end of the spectrum and would be populated by social robots that are (even at this time) more like the robots of science fiction than what many of us recognize as science fact.

Kerstin Dautenhahn (2007) provides a similar but slightly modified formulation in her effort to define and characterize the range of different artifacts covered by the term "social robot." The two scales obviously overlap and can be correlated with one another (see Figure 7.1).

1 *Socially evocative.* Robots that rely on the human tendency to anthropomorphize and capitalize on feelings evoked, when humans nurture, care about or involve themselves with their "creation."

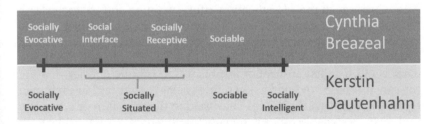

Figure 7.1 Classifications of social robots

2 *Socially situated*. Robots that are surrounded by a social environment which they perceive and react to. Socially situated robots are able to distinguish between other social agents and various objects in the environment.

3 *Sociable*. Robots that proactively engage with humans in order to satisfy internal social aims (drives, emotions, etc.). These robots require deep models of social cognition.

4 *Socially intelligent*. Robots that show aspects of human-style social intelligence, based on possibly deep models of human cognition and social competence. (Dautenhahn 2007: 684)

Fong et al. (2003: 145) introduce one more element called "socially interactive robot." This is done, as they explain, not to add another class of social robot to the list, but in order to help distinguish "social robots" per se from other kinds of socially situated artifacts that involve more "conventional" forms of mediated human interaction, like teleoperated devices designed to support remote telepresence (e.g., Double 2 Telepresence Robot from Double Robotics, or the PadBot's U1 Telepresence Robot). According to Fong et al., "socially interactive robots" involve "peer-to-peer human–robot interactions," specifically robots that are able to exhibit the following "human social" characteristics:

- express and/or perceive emotions;
- communicate with high-level dialogue;
- learn/recognize models of other agents;
- establish/maintain social relationships;
- use natural cues (gaze, gestures, etc.);
- exhibit distinctive personality and character;
- may learn/develop social competencies.

7.1.3 The social robot spectrum

As you can see in this classification effort, defining and characterizing "social robot" is complex and multidimensional, extending on the low end of the spectrum from devices that are imbued with social behaviors and characteristics mainly by way of human projection – what is often called anthropomorphism – to robotic entities that are (or can at least be defined as) genuine social "creatures" in their own right. Or, as Breazeal (2002: 1) has tried to describe it in one, concise sentence: "a sociable robot is socially intelligent in a human-like way, and interacting with it is like interacting with another person." The difference in social robot classifications, then, really comes down to how this "human-like way" is achieved or to what extent it is instantiated in the robotic mechanism. Is it accomplished by producing an artifact that is actually another socially intelligent entity with the usual set of needs and abilities, like theory of mind and empathy? Or is it just a clever simulation of human-grade interaction that gives a convincing appearance of social behavior but is not actually social, strictly speaking?

As you might have already anticipated, this is just another version or iteration of John Searle's Chinese Room. And the difficulty of distinguishing real social intelligence from its mere simulation is something that is of principal concern in social robotics R&D. As Breazeal (2003: 168) describes it, "this is fundamentally an 'appearance versus reality' question – does the robot only appear to be socially intelligent or is it genuinely so?" For this reason, the different subclasses of social robot can be understood and situated in relationship to each other depending on where they are located along this "appearance vs. reality continuum." "Another way to look at this distinction," Breazeal (2003: 168) continues, "is in terms of the brittleness of the design – namely, when does the robot's behavior no longer adhere to the person's social model for it? Once this occurs, the usefulness of the person's social model for the robot has been marginalized – it breaks down."

Consequently, in some situations (many situations, in fact) a reasonably believable appearance of social intelligence may be all that is necessary for the robot to establish and maintain the user's social expectations – what Breazeal calls the "the person's social model for the robot." This is relatively easy to accomplish in highly constrained situations and environments, as might be the case with a child's interactive toy. But as the variables in the environment or the task begin to increase in number and complexity, the social capabilities and functionality of the artifact will need to scale to meet user expectations. If the device does not meet these expectations – and thus maintain the social model that the user has for the robot – it breaks down; it is too fragile. However, and following Breazeal's argument:

[I]f the robot's observable behavior adheres to a person's social model for it during unconstrained interactions in the full complexity of the human environment, then we argue that the robot is socially intelligent in a genuine sense. Basically, the person can engage the robot as one would another socially responsive creature, and the robot does the same. (2003: 168)

This high level of "genuine" artificial social intelligence – a level that would be on a par with or may even rival human capabilities – does not, it is important to point out, necessarily require human-like robots or devices with a human morphology. As Breazeal concludes,

> [T]his criterion for success should not be confused with trying to build a robot that is indistinguishable from a human inside and out – the appearance of the robot and its internal design details can be quite different from the human counterpart, what matters is how it interacts face-to-face with people, and how people interact with it in the human environment. (2003: 168–9)

What is important, therefore, are the actual face-to-face, social interaction capabilities of the artifact irrespective of its actual internal operations or external morphology.

7.2 Embodiment and Morphology

Because the principal defining feature of the social robot is social interaction and communication, it is reasonable to ask: what makes a social robot different from a chatbot, an SDS application, or other socially interactive virtual entity, like a socialbot, an embodied conversational agent (ECA), or non-player character (NPC) in a virtual world or MMORPG (massively multiplayer online role playing game)? And it is a good question, because the line that separates "social robot" from these other socially interactive technologies is becoming increasingly difficult to define and defend. Is Siri, for instance, a social robot? Or is it just an SDS application residing in a number of different smart devices, like the iPhone or the iPad? Is it possible that the iPhone itself could be a kind of "personalized social robot," as Jane Vincent (2013) has asked and investigated? In most cases (not all, but most), the one criterion that is more often than not deployed to mark what differentiates chatbots and SDS from social robots is "embodiment."

7.2.1 Embodiment

In the context of social robots, "embodiment" means more than just "having a (physical) body." Arguably an onscreen ECA or NPC possesses a kind of (virtual) body. For this reason, Dautenhahn and colleagues provide what they call a "relational definition" of embodiment:

We define embodiment as "that which establishes a basis for structural coupling by creating the potential for mutual perturbation between system and environment." Thus, embodiment is grounded in the relationship between a system and its environment. The more a robot can perturb an environment, and be perturbed by it, the more it is embodied. This also means that social robots do not necessarily need a physical body. For example, conversational agents might be embodied to the same extent as robots with limited actuation. (Fong et al. 2003: 149)

This provides for two things. First, social robots may be embodied in both physical and virtual space, allowing for social robotics R&D to be developed, tested, and evaluated in both virtual environments and physical space. This is important, because a great deal of research in the field is performed in computer-simulated environments and not in real physical spaces, the latter being much more expensive and more difficult to control for experimental variables. Second, this relational definition permits the quantification of embodiment such that embodiment is not a binary either/or but a continuum of different degrees of embodiment. For this reason, some social robots might be described as being "more embodied" than others. As Fong et al. explain by way of example:

Some robots are clearly more embodied than others. Consider the difference between Aibo (Sony) [a robotic pet dog] and Khepera (K-Team) [a small robotic hockey puck]. Aibo has approximately 20 actuators (joints across mouth, heads, ears, tails, and legs) and a variety of sensors (touch, sound, vision and proprioceptive). In contrast, Khepera has two actuators (independent wheel control) and an array of infrared proximity sensors. Because Aibo has more perturbatory channels and bandwidth at its disposal than does Khepera, it can be considered to be more strongly embodied than Khepera. (2003: 149)

As illustrated with these two examples, it is possible to differentiate social robots by degrees of embodiment. But we can also classify the technology by morphology – or the structure and form of robot bodies. And if we look at the range of current existing or soon-to-be existing social robots, we find that these artifacts come in a wide variety of shapes, sizes, forms, and functions.

7.2.2 Morphology

Morphology is important, because it helps establish social expectations for the robot. "Physical appearance," as Fong et al. (2003:

**Figure 7.2   Consequential Robotics' MiRo. Photograph from http://
consequentialrobotics.com/miro/**

149) explain, "biases interaction. A robot that resembles a dog will
be treated differently (at least initially) than one which is anthropomorphic." Social robots can be categorized according to one of three
morphologies.

(1) *Zoomorphic.* Many entertainment, personal, and toy robots
emulate the "look and feel" of animals, including the hamster- or owl-
looking Furby from Tiger Electronics, robot dogs like Sony's AIBO
and Consequential Robotics' MiRo (see Figure 7.2), Innvo Labs's
animatronic dinosaur Pleo, and the seal-like therapy robot Paro.
This particular morphology is expedient, because it calls upon and
mobilizes a set of already established expectations and experiences
that human beings have with other kinds of nonhuman creatures,
like domestic animals and pets. Like a dog or cat, these robots can
be designed to be social and interactive without necessarily needing
to emulate human-level capabilities. This provides designers and
the robot itself considerable latitude, when it comes to producing
effective social interactions. Paro, for instance, does not talk. But the
device does produce seal-like noises as it is touched and manipulated.
This limited range of communication abilities, which is, we should
note, much easier to design for and incorporate in the device than a

full NLG system, is entirely appropriate to the morphology of this particular artifact. It works, in other words, because human users would not expect a seal to be able to talk.

(2) *Caricatured*. Storytellers, cartoonists, and animators have introduced and developed a wide range of cartoon characters and animated objects that are believable social entities. There is, for instance, *Thomas the Tank Engine* and its cast of personified trains, trucks, and other vehicles; the autonomous puppet and his singing sidekick, Jiminy Cricket, from the 1940 Disney feature *Pinocchio*; and Pixar's Luxo Jr., an expressive desk lamp that was featured in the 1986 computer-animated short film of the same name. Many experimental and commercially available social robots have been modeled on this morphology. There is, for example, Breazeal's sociable robot prototype Kismet, which was little more than a moveable robotic head possessing a gremlin-like appearance (see Figure 7.3). Despite its rather rudimentary "intelligence" – or perhaps better stated, lack thereof – the programmed movement of Kismet's head and "facial features" – turning to look at you, raising its eyebrows, twisting its ears, etc. – were interpreted by human users as expressive and meaningful. As Breazeal has reported:

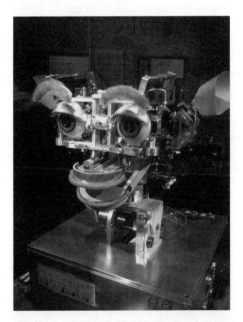

**Figure 7.3   Kismet CC BY-SA 2.5. Photograph from https://
commons.wikimedia.org/w/index.php?curid=374949**

Kismet is special and unique. Not only because of what it can do, but also because of how it makes you feel. Kismet connects to people on a physical level, on a social level, and on an emotional level. It is jarring for people to play with Kismet and then see it turned off, suddenly becoming an inanimate object. (2002: xiii)

Other robots in this category include animated "things" like Jibo,[7] another of Breazeal's projects, which was promoted as the "first family robot." Jibo's appearance is nothing like that of Kismet. It looks more like a fat desk lamp or a smart speaker with a movable head and large cyclops eye. What makes Jibo distinctive is that the device is designed to pair the kind of verbal responses typically produced by an SDS system, like Alexa or Google Home, with a number of nonverbal movements – pivoting on its stationary base, turning to look at you, cocking its head, etc. – and "facial expressions" that are displayed on its circular faceplate/monitor screen (see Figure 7.4).

(3) *Anthropomorphic.* At what many assume would be the "high end" of the social robot scale are humanoid robots – artifacts that are designed to look and function like human beings or quasi-human entities. The reason for this, as Fong et al. (2003: 150) recognize, "is that for a robot to interact with humans as humans do (through

Figure 7.4 Jibo. Photograph by the author

**Figure 7.5   Nao. Photograph by ubahnverleih CC 0. Photograph
from https://commons.wikimedia.org/w/index.php?curid=49912982**

gaze, gesture, etc.), then it must be structurally and functionally
similar to a human." There are a number of anthropomorphic social
robots currently available in both commercial and experimental
implementations.

Commercially, there are devices like NAO and Pepper from
Softbank Robotics. NAO is a small (58cm in height) bipedal humanoid robot that has been successfully used in education and healthcare
(see Figure 7.5). NAO is able to create an empathetic link with users
by way of its eye-catching appearance, moderate size, and humanoid
behavior. Pepper is a 120cm robot on a wheeled platform. According
to its marketing literature, "Pepper is the world's first social humanoid
robot able to recognize faces and basic human emotions" (SoftBank
Robotics 2018).

There are also various human-looking humanoid robots, most of
which are still R&D platforms like Hiroshi Ishiguro's Geminoids and
Sophia from Hanson Robotics. Geminoids are a teleoperated android
twin of a real person. These robots, which are designed to emulate the
appearance and behavior of their "source person," are covered with
a pliable synthetic skin that is manipulated by subcutaneous actuators, providing the robot with the ability to reproduce human facial

**Figure 7.6   Sophia. ITU Pictures from Geneva, Switzerland CC
BY 2.0. Photograph from https://commons.wikimedia.org/w/index.
php?curid=69218227**

expressions. Even though these robotic platforms are controlled by
human operators – using a standard methodology in social robotics
research that is called Wizard of Oz or WOZ[8] – the social presence of
these devices coupled with their verbal and nonverbal interpersonal
communication abilities produce a rather uncanny experience that is
virtually indistinguishable from that of another (real) human person.

Like the Geminoids, Sophia is also a humanoid robot, covered in
synthetic skin and able to interact with human users in both verbal
and nonverbal modes (e.g., gesture, facial expression, eye gaze, etc.;
see Figure 7.6). But unlike a teleoperated Geminoid, Sophia is said to
be controlled by a proprietary AI system that is designed to learn and
evolve from interactions with human users. The robot was activated
on February 14, 2016, and since that time has become something
of a celebrity. She (and the robot has been deliberately gendered
female) has appeared on a number of TV talk shows, addressed the
United Nations, and is often invited to give keynote addresses at tech
industry events and international meetings. In 2017, the Kingdom of
Saudi Arabia granted Sophia honorary citizenship, making her "the
first robot citizen." Whether Sophia's performances are genuinely

social and intelligent or merely a clever illusion – and it is worth recalling that David Hanson who created Sophia was, at one time, an Imagineer for Disney – is an open question. But the question leads us right back to Searle's Chinese Room, the difficulty of distinguishing between real social intelligence and the mere simulation of it, and the problem of deciding whether that difference can ever really be decided once and for all or even makes a difference.

7.3 Technology and Technique

Unlike industrial robots, service robots, or even voice-activated SDS applications, social robots need to model, control for, and be able to process and produce a wide range of different interpersonal social behaviors. The ways this is accomplished for different social robot projects and platforms are diverse and worthy of an entire comparative study in their own right. We can, however, get a feel for what goes into the design and operation of a social robot by considering the system architecture of one pivotal example – Kismet. Kismet was not only one of the first sociable robots, but its design features established many of the basic components and building blocks for future developments.

7.3.1 System architecture

Kismet's system architecture consists of six, interacting subsystems. Breazeal calls the entire ensemble "a synthetic nervous system," which is a rather interesting and informative choice of words (see Figure 7.7). Let's take a closer look at all six subsystems.

1 *Low-level feature extraction.* This first subsystem is charged with processing data obtained from the robot's sensors, which are, in effect, its window to the external world and means of accessing the human user. In the case of Kismet (as for many other social robots), raw sensor data includes audio information coming from the robot's microphone and visual data supplied by its camera(s). But it could also include tactile information provided by touch sensors situated on the exterior of the robot's body. Feature extraction involves parsing this raw input data in an effort to identify elements that have behavioral significance. This might be a predefined keyword that is identified by way of basic speech-recognition capabilities (see Chapter 4), tone of voice or prosodic

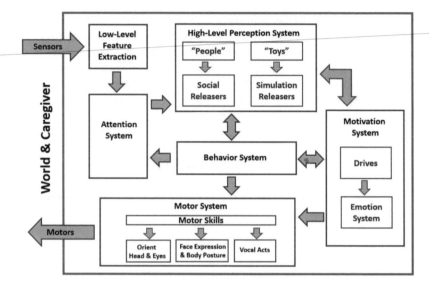

**Figure 7.7   Block diagram of Kismet's "synthetic nervous system"
(image based on Breazeal 2002: 44)**

features extracted through comparative measurement of the audio
waveform data, or nonverbal visual cues, like facial features or
body language, typically recognized in data supplied by the robot's
camera(s).

2 *Attention system.* Once extracted, low-level precepts are sent to
the attention system. "The purpose of the attention system," as
Breazeal (2002: 44) explains, "is to pick out low-level perceptual
stimuli that are particularly salient or relevant at that time, and
to direct the robot's attention and gaze toward them." In other
words, not all of the extracted low-level precepts are important or
relevant at all times. What makes a particular precept significant
depends on the situation, social context, and interpersonal interactions. The sudden appearance of something new in the visual field,
for example, might indicate the arrival of another human user and
require that the robot attend to – and indicate its attention to – this
new stimulus.

3 *High-level perception system.* "The low-level features corresponding to the target stimuli of the attention system are fed into the
perceptual system" where they are "encapsulated into behaviorally
relevant precepts" (Breazeal 2002: 54). In other words, the different salient perceptual features are passed into the perceptual
system, where they accumulate until they cross a certain prede-

fined threshold or trigger what Breazeal calls "a releaser": "A releaser can be viewed as a collection of feature detectors that are minimally necessary to identify a particular object or event of behavioral significance. The releaser's function is to ascertain if all environmental (perceptual) conditions are right for the response to become active" (2002: 54). Releasers can be programmed for emotional responses to people (what are called "social releasers" in Figure 7.7) or task-based behaviors or "stimulation releasers."

4 *Motivation system.* This element determines and consists of the robot's basic "drives" and "emotions." Drives correspond to a set of predetermined needs and are controlled by way of a homeostatic mechanism. If the robot's needs are being met (i.e. someone is engaging in conversational interaction), the intensity level (a numeric value) for that "drive" falls within the established range of predetermined values. If, however, the robot's needs are not being met (i.e. no one is talking to the robot), the intensity value decreases and the robot "becomes more strongly motivated to engage in behaviors that restore that drive" to homeostasis (Breazeal 2002: 45). Like drives, emotions also play a significant role in determining the robot's situation and behavior. For Kismet, emotions were modeled from a functionalist perspective. "Based on simple appraisals of a given stimulus," Breazeal (2002: 45) explains, "the robot evokes either positive emotive responses that serve to bring itself closer to it, or negative emotive responses in order to withdraw from it." Within this basic +/– system, Kismet was designed to display six emotive responses (anger, disgust, fear, joy, sorrow, and surprise) and three arousal-based responses (interest, calm, and boredom). The mode by which these responses are manifest or expressed is something that is determined and controlled by subsequent subsystems.

5 *Behavior system.* The behavior system controls the robot's task-based behaviors by organizing them into a coherent structure. At any given time, Kismet has a number of competing motivations and a number of different behaviors that it can activate to achieve them. The behavior system arbitrates between these different opportunities by determining which one or ones to activate and for how long. This arbitration process ensures that the robot behaves sensibly in response to a particular set of stimuli in a particular context. It therefore is designed to deal with and manage issues of relevancy, coherency, persistence, and opportunism.

6 *Motor system.* The motor system controls the robot's output or its mode of expression that is readable by the user and the outside

world. As depicted in Figure 7.7, this final subsystem has its own subsystems: (i) the motor skill system, which determines the robot's body posture or what is often called body language; (ii) the facial animation system, which controls Kismet's facial expressions (e.g., smiling, frowning, raising the eyebrows); (iii) the expressive vocalization system, which controls not only the content of what the device says but how it says it; and (iv) the oculo-motor system, which determines/communicates Kismet's attentiveness through gaze direction. The motor system coordinates these four elements in order to move the robot in such a way as to manifest or express (literally the word means "to press out") the response that had been determined by the previous subsystems.

Kismet is now 20 years old and the robot has become a museum piece. Despite its age, however, the basic system architecture that Breazeal initially developed for this prototype has been reused, repurposed, and modified for subsequent implementations. Although much more sophisticated in its design and operations, Breazeal's Jibo, for example, utilizes and exploits many of the innovations initially developed for and tested with Kismet (see Figure 7.8).

7.3.2 Testing and evaluation

Because social robots are specifically designed for social engagement with human beings – to the extent that, as Breazeal (2002: 1) describes it, "interacting with it is like interacting with another person" – evaluation and benchmarking cannot proceed according to the typical task-oriented evaluations applied to other kinds of robotic systems. In her work with Kismet, Breazeal developed and utilized an evaluation methodology based on what she calls "interact-ability." These criteria are, Breazeal admits, "subjective, yet quantifiable, measures that evaluate the quality and ease of interaction between robot and human," and "they address the behavior of both partners" (2002: 49). For Breazeal, evaluation of interact-ability involves the following four items:

• Do people intuitively read and naturally respond to Kismet's social cues?
• Can Kismet perceive and appropriately respond to these naturally offered cues?
• Does the human adapt to the robot and the robot adapt to the human, in a way that benefits the interaction? Specifically, is

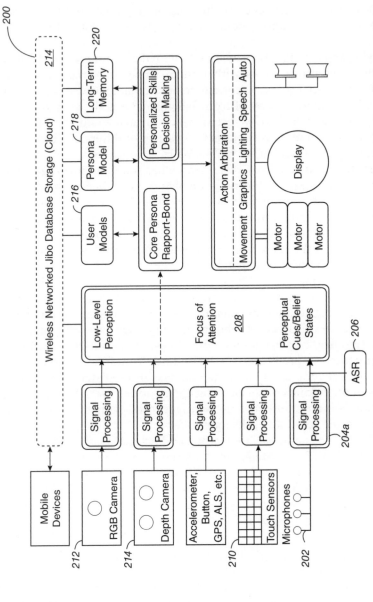

Figure 7.8 Software architecture for Jibo. Image from the US patent application filed by Jibo, Inc. (Breazeal et al. 2017: 3)

the resulting interaction natural, intuitive, and enjoyable for the human, and can Kismet perform well despite its perceptual, mechanical, behavioral, and computational limitations?
- Does Kismet readily elicit scaffolding interactions from the human that could be used to benefit learning? (Breazeal 2002: 49)

Applying and testing robot capabilities with these four criteria required numerous empirical trials with human subjects. Similar efforts to benchmark social robot performance are available in the experimental studies undertaken by Hiroshi Ishiguro and colleagues since the mid-2000s, in which they tested robot behavior and the effect of this behavior on human subjects in a variety of different settings and contexts (e.g., museums, shopping malls, train stations, etc.). Similar to what Breazeal describes, this research has sought to investigate and respond to a range of questions involving issues like: human-robot communication, comprising both verbal and non verbal channels; believability of and trust in the robot; uses and gratifications of social interaction with the robot, etc. (Kanda and Ishiguro 2013).

But perhaps the most interesting and informative mode of evaluation comes by way of experimental trials that are routinely called "robot abuse studies." These investigations, which have become quite popular in the field, stress test the limits of social standing and interaction capabilities by inviting (or even ordering) human test subjects to do violence to a robot with which they have previously had some significant social interaction. These Milgram-like obedience experiments[9] are predicated on the findings from CASA (see Chapter 2), specifically the fact that human beings tend to extend human-like status to other kinds of socially engaging entities even if the object in question is quite dumb and not sentient, thus explaining the hesitation to do the robot any subsequent harm.

In 2013, for example, Kate Darling and Hannes Gassert ran a workshop at LIFT13, an academic conference in Geneva, Switzerland. The workshop, which had the title "Harming and Protecting Robots: Can We, Should We?," sought to "test whether people felt differently about social robots than they would everyday objects, like toasters" (Darling and Hauert 2013).

In the workshop, groups of participants [four groups of six people] were given Pleos – cute robotic dinosaurs that are roughly the size of small cats. After interacting with the robots and performing various tasks with them, the groups were asked to tie up, strike, and "kill" their Pleos. Drama ensued, with many of the participants refusing to "hurt" the robots, and even physically protecting them from being struck by fellow group members . . . While everyone in the room was fully aware that the robot was just simulating its pain, most participants giggled nervously and felt a distinct sense of discomfort when it whimpered while it was being broken. (Darling 2016: 222)

Although this particular demonstration was conducted "in a non-scientific setting" (Darling and Vedantam 2017), meaning that the results obtained are anecdotal at best, it did provide a compelling illustration of something that has been previously tested and verified in laboratory studies involving robot abuse undertaken by Christoph Bartneck and Jun Hu (2008) and Astrid Rosenthal-von der Pütten et al. (2013). The former utilized both a Lego robot and Crawling Microbug Robots; the latter employed Pleo dinosaur toys, like Darling's workshop. Although experiments like this are sometimes called "the dark side" of research in human–robot interaction (HRI) (cf. De Angeli et al. 2005), they have been an exceedingly effective mechanism for testing the limits of robot social status and human acceptance of the artifact as another socially significant entity worthy of some level of consideration and respect.

7.4 Outcomes, Consequences, and Repercussions

Despite the fact that Breazeal credits the droids of *Star Wars* as the motivating factor for and objective of her work in robotics, social robots are not science fiction. They are here, and they are now. As these artifacts come to occupy increasingly significant and influential positions in our world, positions where they are not just tools or instruments of human conduct and action but a kind of socially situated interactive entity in their own right, there are important challenges and questions that remain to be addressed and resolved. Many of these actually have little to do with technical exigencies and design of systems; instead they involve the social circumstance, significance, and impact of the technology. We will, therefore, conclude by addressing these issues, which are, it should be noted, perfectly suited to the educational experiences and skill sets of students in the field of Communication Studies and Communication Sciences.

7.4.1 Anthropomorphism and the "uncanny valley"

Let's begin with two issues that define what could be called "the problem space" of social robot design, deployment, and significance. The first is "anthropomorphism," a word that is fabricated by jamming together the Greek word *anthropos*, meaning "human," with *morphe*, signifying "form" or "structure." "Anthropomorphism" identifies the tendency to attribute human characteristics to inanimate objects and animals. As Heather Knight explains:

> Robots do not require eyes, arms or legs for us to treat them like social agents. It turns out that we rapidly assess machine capabilities and personas instinctively, perhaps because machines have physical embodiments and frequently readable objectives. Sociability is our natural interface, to each other and to living creatures in general. As part of that innate behavior, we quickly seek to identify objects from agents. In fact, as social creatures, it is often our default behavior to anthropomorphize moving robots. (2014: 4)

But this tendency to anthropomorphize inanimate objects – something that was, well in advance of the advent of social robots, empirically demonstrated and tested in the CASA studies from the 1990s – remains controversial. Eleanor Sandry (2015a: 339) explains the controversy this way:

> Scientific discourse is generally biased against anthropomorphism, arguing that any attribution of human characteristics to nonhumans is incompatible with maintaining one's objectivity (Flynn 2008; Hearne 2000). Indeed, Marc Bekoff (2007: 113) has gone so far as to describe anthropomorphism as one of the "dirty words in science" being linked with "the subjective and the personal." However, social robotics research has, for some time, been open to the idea of encouraging anthropomorphic responses in humans. In particular, Turkle et al. (2006), and Kirsten Dautenhahn's (1998) early work, argued that anthropomorphism is an important part of facilitating meaningful human–robot interactions.

The problem, then, is not that the potential for anthropomorphic projection exists; the problem is that we seem to be unable to decide whether such projections are detrimental, useful, or both, when it comes to robots that are designed for human communication and social interaction. In other words, is this proclivity to anthropomorphism, or what Duffy (2003: 178) calls "the big AI cheat" – a form of "deception" that is, we should note, already definitive of the Turing Test and the target of Searle's Chinese Room thought experiment – a problem or bug that is to be avoided and eliminated at all costs? Or is it a valuable asset and feature that should be carefully cultivated and developed?

Whether it is considered a good or a bad thing, anthropomorphism is undoubtedly powerful, and its operation has been the object of numerous studies. In one such investigation, Elizabeth Broadbent et al. (2013: 1) have shown, by way of a repeated measures experiment with human participants interacting with a Peoplebot healthcare robot, that "the more humanlike a healthcare robot's face display is, the more people attribute mind and positive personality characteristics to it." But this can go too far, producing another problem, which is known as the "uncanny valley" (Figure 7.9).

The "uncanny valley hypothesis" was initially proposed by the Japanese roboticist Masahiro Mori in 1970 in order to explain the "relation between the human likeness of an entity, and the perceiver's affinity for it" (2012: 99). It states that, as the appearance of an artifact (e.g., a robot, a prosthetic limb, or a puppet) comes increasingly closer to achieving human-like appearance, emotional response to the object is increasingly positive and empathetic. This correlation continues along a positive slope until the resemblance of the artifact becomes too close, and responses then turn into revulsion,

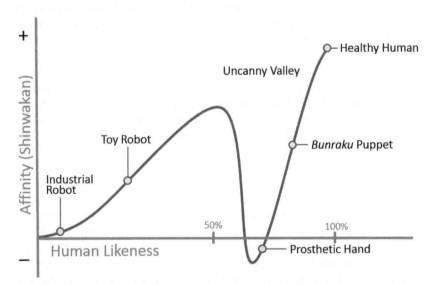

Figure 7.9 The "uncanny valley" (as presented in Mori 2012)

disgust, and rejection. But after this point, as the artifact's appearance comes so close to achieving human-like appearance as to be virtually indistinguishable from another human being, the response becomes positive again and eventually approaches human-to-human levels of empathy.

The uncanny valley hypothesis can, for example, explain why users find NAO to be an engaging and empathetic social partner, while the RealDoll sex robot leaves many observers with a sense of "creepiness" and even "disgust." Although Mori's proposal has never been definitively proven, his hypothesis has considerable traction, not only guiding the R&D efforts of roboticists, who try to design social artifacts that fall on either side of the valley, but also social scientists and communication researchers who employ the hypothesis as a way to explain and contextualize user responses to different kinds of socially interactive robots and artifacts (see, for instance, Edwards et al. 2016).

7.4.2 Real vs. simulation

What we see in the face – or the face plate – of the social robot is a reflection of one of the fundamental questions of AI. As we indicated previously, one of the persistent and seemingly irresolvable issues is trying to decide whether these social artifacts do in fact possess actual social intelligence, or whether the social robot is just a cleverly designed device that simulates various interpersonal effects that we – the human users – interpret as being social, even if the device is not. To put it in the form of a question: are these various technological artifacts genuinely social, or do they just pretend and perform operations that we interpret as being social? This question, as we noted, is a variant of the Chinese Room thought experiment, which, as Searle explains, was intended to illustrate the difference between "real intelligence" and its clever simulation. And when it comes to social robots, this difference is significant and important.

Sherry Turkle, an MIT social scientist specializing in the psychological costs and benefits of computer technology, worries that social robots are a potentially dangerous form of self-deception: "I find people willing to seriously consider robots not only as pets but as potential friends, confidants, and even romantic partners. We don't seem to care what their artificial intelligences 'know' or 'understand' of the human moments we might 'share' with them . . . the performance of connection seems connection enough" (2011: 9). In the face of the sociable robot (to use Breazeal's term), Turkle argues, we seem to be willing, all too willing, to consider these technological objects to be another socially significant Other – not just a kind of surrogate pet but a close friend, personal confidant, and even paramour (recall the case of Robert Epstein from Chapter 2). According to Turkle's diagnosis, we are in danger of substituting a technological interface for the real face-to-face interactions we used to have with other human beings. "Technology," she explains, "is seductive when what it offers meets our human vulnerabilities. And as it turns out, we are very vulnerable indeed. We are lonely but fearful of intimacy. Digital connections and the sociable robot may offer the illusion of companionship without the demands of friendship" (2011: 1).

Brian Duffy, for his part, connects this insight to an older example involving domestic animals. "From an observer perspective," he (2003: 184) writes, "one could pose the question whether the attribution of artificial emotions to a robot is analogous to the Clever Hans Error (Pfungst 1965), where the meaning and in fact the result is primarily dependent on the observer and not the initiator." Clever Hans (or *der Kluge Hans*) was a horse that allegedly was able to perform basic arithmetic operations and communicate the results of his calculations by tapping his hoof on the ground in response to questions from human interrogators. The story was originally recounted in an article published in the *New York Times* at the turn of the previous century (Heyn 1904); was debunked by Oskar Pfungst (1965), who demonstrated that what appeared to be intelligence was just a conditioned response; and has been utilized in subsequent efforts to address animal intelligence and human/animal communication (see, for example, Sandry 2015b: 34).

In the case of social robots, Matthias Scheutz finds good reason to be concerned with this particular kind of manipulation.

> What is so dangerous about unidirectional emotional bonds is that they create psychological dependencies that could have serious consequences for human societies . . . Social robots that cause people to establish emotional bonds with them, and trust them deeply as a result, could be misused to manipulate people in ways that were not possible before. For example, a company might exploit the robot's unique relationship with its owner to make the robot convince the owner to purchase products the company wishes to promote. (2014: 216–17)

The problem Scheutz describes – a problem many of us are now confronting with cloud-service connected devices like Alexa – is that we might (wrongly) be attributing something to the machine in a way that is unidirectional, error-prone, and a potential for manipulation.

On the other side of the issue, however, are various other voices that promote social robots not as a substitute for human sociability (Turkle's point), but as a means to understand, augment, and improve human social interactions and circumstances. The Paro robot, invented by Takanori Shibata, has proven to be an incredibly useful tool for elder care, especially in situations involving individuals suffering from debilitating forms of dementia. In a number of clinical studies, the robot has been found to improve individual well-being by providing companionship and comfort in cases where other forms of interaction therapy are either difficult to provide or ineffectual (Wada and Shibata 2007; Šabanović et al. 2013; Bemelmans et al. 2012). Social robots have also been shown to be expedient and effective tools for helping children with autism navigate the difficult terrain of human social interaction (Robins et al. 2005; Kim et al. 2013).

Beyond these therapeutic employments, however, social robots are both useful and entertaining. Many of us now have rudimentary social robots in our pockets and purses, with the smartphone being a kind of hand-held companion/service robot that helps us connect to each other and our world (Vincent 2013). Even robots that are not explicitly designed for it, can become social due to the role and function they play in human organizations. This is the case with many of the EOD robots used by soldiers on the battlefield. These miniature tank-like devices, which are clearly not designed for nor outfitted with any of the programming or mechanisms for producing the effects of social interaction, occupy an important and valued position within the human combat unit based not on the social and communication capabilities of the device but on the social needs of the soldiers (Carpenter 2015). And at the very far end of the spectrum, there are sex robots, which are being promoted not as substitutes for human partners but as a means to augment human intimacy and sexual relationships (Levy 2007; Danaher and McArthur 2017; Devlin 2018). In these cases, whether the robot really is a genuine social entity or not seems less important than the net effect of its social presence and interactions – even if just simulated – on the human users who engage with it.

Social robots are a relatively new and emerging application of AI, and they will, like every technological innovation up to this point, have both advantages and disadvantages for human individuals and their communities. What is important, then, is to identify the range of what is (and might be) possible in order to perform a reality check and begin developing informed and intelligent methods for developing, deploying, and evaluating these sociable artifacts. This is something that we will take up and explore further in the book's final section. The good news for students in the field of communication is that this effort is going to require not just innovation in the technology of AI and robotics, but also extensive examination and a deeper understanding of human sociality. Consequently, there is a need – an important and pressing need – for social scientists and humanists to join these conversations and to work with the engineers and designers to decide together not only what can be done with social robots, but also what should be done to ensure that we foster the kind of world we want for ourselves.

7.4.3 Engineering vs. science

Finally, this insight returns us to something that was noted earlier in Chapter 1: efforts in AI are divided between it being a science and an engineering practice. This difference between a way of *knowing* and a way of *doing* is also operative with, and evident in, the field of social robotics. On the one hand, fabricating social robots is an engineering task that requires the skill and knowledge of a number of different disciplines to come together in order to produce socially interactive artifacts and systems. It involves, for instance, computer engineers and AI developers to create the algorithms that power the artifact's social and emotional intelligence; mechanical engineers and artists to create the actuators, the overall design, and even the various kinds of synthetic skins that cover humanoid social robots; and social scientists to construct models of social behavior and to test and evaluate social robot performance and believability in real-life situations.

On the other hand, social robots offer scientists a unique opportunity and robust experimental platform for conducting fundamental research in human behavior and sociality. As Paul Dumouchel and Luisa Damiano accurately explain:

> To construct artificial companions is not only a technological challenge; it also requires knowing oneself and others, understanding what a social relationship is, and grasping how the human mind functions insofar as it is concerned, not with acquiring knowledge about a world that we confront alone, as solitary individuals, but with learning how to interact in it with other human beings . . . Any robotic platform that seeks to reproduce one or another of the essential characteristics of human sociality constitutes a test of hypotheses about human sociality. (2017: 13)

To put it another way, social robots, like all technology, are a mirror in which we can perceive a reflection of ourselves. The various efforts to design, develop, and deploy artificial social entities – whether they are successful, partially successful, or even outright failures – has value insofar as this work provides us with a practical means to model, experiment with, and evaluate fundamental assumptions concerning human social interaction and intelligence. Social robots, then, provide scientists with a new tool and platform for doing social research.

In both cases – whether the work is considered an engineering challenge/opportunity or a fundamental inquiry into the behavioral and social aspects of human existence – there are excellent opportunities for students in the field of communication. As we saw previously with SDS development (Chapter 5), R&D efforts in social robotics are as much about modeling and simulating human behaviors in a believable social artifact as they are a robust experimental tool and testbed for fundamental investigations in the social sciences. For this reason, efforts to design and deploy increasingly capable social robots are not just about producing better socially interactive artifacts; they are also a way to develop and deepen our understanding of human existence and sociality. In other words, social robotics is as much about the robots as it is about human social behavior and systems.

Summary of Key Points

- Social robots are technological artifacts that are designed to interact with and respond to human users in a human-like way. There are several categories of social robots, ranging from socially evocative technologies, which require active efforts of anthropomorphic projection, to socially intelligent systems that are based on and operationalize sophisticated models of cognition and social competence.
- Social robot design and implementation demonstrate different forms of embodiment – physical or virtual – and morphology. There are zoomorphic devices that emulate nonhuman animals, caricatured robots that are designed to look and function like cartoon characters and animated objects, and anthropomorphic robots that look and function like human beings or quasi-human entities.
- Social robots need to model, control for, and be able to process and produce a wide range of different interpersonal behaviors. Though the systems architecture for each kind of social robot varies, most include techniques and technologies for identifying and extract-

ing features, controlling for the device's attention and perception, modeling motivation and behavior, and directing output signals to motors and actuators.

• Current challenges in the field of social robotics involve managing the useful effects of anthropomorphism while avoiding the uncanny valley; the potential deception caused by inability to distinguish between actual social entities and cleverly designed simulations; and the conceptual difference between social robots utilized as a way of doing versus a way of investigating social interaction.

Part III

Impact and Consequences

8

Social Issues

Key Aims/Objectives

- To introduce and critically investigate the concepts, historical trajectory, and current situation regarding automation and technological unemployment.
- To identify the challenges to existing educational concepts, structures, and methodologies introduced by workplace automation, and to consider both "updates" and "mods" that can be implemented to respond to these challenges.
- To "future proof" education and student careers in order to be prepared to meet the demands of the twenty-first century.

Introduction

As we have seen in our investigations, we are in the midst of something like a robot invasion. Intelligent (or at least, semi-intelligent, or what can also be called "smart") machines are everywhere and doing virtually everything. We chat with them both on- and offline, we interact with them at work and at play, and we rely on their seemingly inexhaustible and ever improving capabilities to manage many aspects of our increasingly complex data-driven lives. This "invasion" is not something that takes place as we have imagined it in decades of science fiction literature and film. It does not happen by way of a marauding army of evil-minded androids descending from the heavens with ray-guns of immeasurable power. It is an already occurring event with intelligent and autonomous technology of various configurations and capabilities coming to take up positions in our world through a slow but steady incursion. It looks less like *Terminator* and *Battlestar Galactica* and more like the Fall of Rome. Each day, what had previously been mere technological objects seem to become a new kind of social actor and communicative subject. Until one day. We wake up, look around, and have to ask ourselves: "Where did all these robots, algorithms, and artificially intelligent systems come from and what kind of world have we (and they) created for us?"

These are the kinds of questions that we want to investigate in the final two chapters. The social impact and consequences of increasingly capable, interactive, and intelligent technology is both broad and deep. For this reason, we cannot possibly address everything. Doing so would require another book, if not a series of books. And there have been, as you might imagine, many publications addressing this particular subject matter (if interested, see the Reference list for some pointers in this direction). Instead of trying to do everything, these two final chapters will need to be strategic and selective. We begin in this chapter by targeting the one issue that probably matters most to students completing their university studies, namely the impact of AI, robots, and other forms of automation on employment opportunity, or what the Cambridge-educated economist John Maynard Keynes called "technological unemployment." One of the reasons, perhaps the principal reason, students pursue advanced studies is to develop the skills and knowledge to be successful in competition for good-paying jobs and careers. This has been and continues to be one of the promises of higher education, namely "higher education" = "hire education." But if robots, algorithms, and AI are increasingly taking over the routine intellectual work previously performed by human beings, what kinds of jobs will remain? What opportunities are there for university graduates, when more and more of the work that had defined a "good job" has been outsourced to AI, robots, and algorithms? And, most importantly, what can be done here and now – while one is still in school – to future-proof careers?

8.1 Technological Unemployment

The phrase "technological unemployment" is not necessarily about digital technology, AI, robots, or algorithms. In fact, the term has been around and in circulation for close to a century. In 1930, Keynes sought to diagnose the economic challenges of his time in a publication he titled "Economic Possibilities for Our Grandchildren." The text begins with a rather pessimistic assessment that might sound familiar:

We are suffering just now from a bad attack of economic pessimism. It is common to hear people say that the epoch of enormous economic progress which characterised the nineteenth century is over; that the rapid improvement in the standard of life is now going to slow down – at any rate in Great Britain; that a decline in prosperity is more likely than an improvement in the decade which lies ahead of us. I believe that this is a wildly mistaken interpretation of what is happening to us. We are suffering, not from the rheumatics of old age, but from the growing-pains of over-rapid changes, from the painfulness of read-justment between one economic period and another. The increase of technical efficiency has been taking place faster than we can deal with the problem of labour absorption; the improvement in the standard of life has been a little too quick. (2010: 321)

Though Keynes wrote these words in reference to events at the turn of the last century, you might already see a pattern developing, insofar as similar statements have now been made in reference to the opportunities and challenges of the twenty-first century. Right now, there is rather widespread suspicion that the economic progress attributed to the past – the "good old days" of our grandparents – is over and that the current situation is worse than it had been for previous generations; there is concern that this problem is not the result of what Keynes calls the "rheumatics of old age" but the unintended consequences of rapid (or "over-rapid") social and economic transformation; and there is, more often than not, the assumption that all of this is due to unprecedented development in technological efficiency and our inabilities to maintain control over it.

Later in his article Keynes formulates and introduces a name for the problem: "We are being afflicted with a new disease of which some readers may not yet have heard the name, but of which they will hear a great deal in the years to come – namely, *technological unemployment*. This means unemployment due to our discovery of means of economising the use of labour outrunning the pace at which we can find new uses for labour" (2010: 325). For Keynes, the problem was not technological innovation per se. The problem was with the pace of innovation in relation to the development of new employment opportunities for human workers. In other words, the source of the difficulty was the fact that the new technologically enabled efficiencies – the "discovery of the means of economizing the use of labor" – had exceeded the creation of new employment opportunities to absorb or repurpose the displaced human workforce. So what Keynes meant by the term "technological unemployment" is not that machines were simply *replacing* workers by taking their jobs. Instead, the phrase refers to the fact that automation *displaces* human workers from gainful employment at a pace that is too fast – that does not result in enough new opportunity to absorb or offset the displacement of human labor.

8.1.1 Historical recursion

Historically speaking, we have seen and have successfully negotiated several cycles of technological unemployment. The most significant – the one that has had the greatest impact on everyday human existence – occurred at the beginning of the nineteenth century with what is now commonly called the industrial revolution. At this time, the introduction of new mechanical technology – specifically, steam-driven industrial machinery – displaced an entire generation of craftsmen and women. Prior to industrialization, many products, like cloth for clothing, were produced by skilled craftspeople in labor-intensive activities. Operating a loom – the basic instrument for the production of cloth – required skill, knowledge, and physical effort. The automated loom, which came into existence as a result of a number of technological developments, eventually displaced much of this human knowhow and activity. But this period of technological unemployment turned out to be short-lived as many of the displaced workers eventually found new opportunities working in the factory, tending to the machines, and overseeing their operations.

A similar transformation was taking place during the time that Keynes wrote and published his text – a period of history that is now called "The Great Depression."

In the United States, for example, the mechanization of the railways around the time Keynes was writing his essay put nearly half a million people out of work. Similarly, rotary phones were making switchboard operators obsolete, while mechanical harvesters, plows, and combines were replacing traditional farmworkers, just as the first steam-engine tractors had replaced horses and oxen less than a century before. Machine efficiency was becoming so great that President Roosevelt, in 1935, told the nation that the economy might never be able to reabsorb all the workers who were being displaced. The more sanguine *New York Times* editorial board then accused the president of falling prey to the "calamity prophets." In retrospect, it certainly looked as if he had.

Unemployment, which was at nearly 24 percent in 1932, dropped to less than 5 percent a decade later. (Halpern 2015)

Keynes was acutely aware of this fact, and he had predicted that worry over the impact of technological unemployment was only "a temporary phase of maladjustment." In other words, he was not just convinced that things would eventually return to equilibrium but, more importantly, had predicted that the changes brought about by technological innovation would generate vast improvements in the human condition.

> All this means in the long run that mankind is solving its economic problem. I would predict that the standard of life in progressive countries one hundred years hence will be between four and eight times as high as it is to-day. There would be nothing surprising in this even in the light of our present knowledge. It would not be foolish to contemplate the possibility of a far greater progress still. (2010: 325–6)

For Keynes, then, technological unemployment was, in the final analysis, a story of short-term loss – workers would be displaced from their jobs – but long-term and significant gains. The opportunities created by the incorporation of machinery and automation would make for new and better jobs and a more prosperous future for everyone involved.

This narrative comprises and defines what analysts now call "the business cycle" (see Figure 8.1). "This was," as Halpern (2015) explains, "a pattern that would reassert itself throughout the twentieth century: the economy would tank, automation would be identified as one of the main culprits, commentators would suggest that jobs were not coming back, and then the economy would rebound and with it employment, and all that nervous chatter about machines taking over would fade away." The important and pivotal question for us is whether and to what extent current technological innovation follows this trend or makes a significant and historic break with it. And there are influential voices on both sides of the issue. One side argues that the transformations wrought by AI, robots, and algorithms will, in fact, follow the historic precedent of previous economic upheavals that have occurred since the advent of industrialization, namely temporary job loss followed by overall gains in new opportunity. The other side asserts that things will be different this time around and that we will need to be prepared for what Martin Ford (2015) has called a "jobless future."

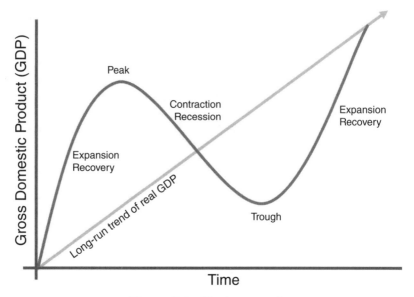

Figure 8.1   Business cycle

8.1.2 State-of-the-art

In order to get a sense of the problem and the wide range of differing opinions regarding its impact and significance, let's consider a few factors regarding the current situation. First, we should be clear as to what kinds of occupations we are talking about. When discussing automation and the application of robotic systems to human endeavor, people often assume that what is being discussed are jobs that can be classified as "dull, dirty, and/or dangerous." This includes, for example, repetitive and monotonous tasks performed on manufacturing assembly lines; efforts to extract raw materials from the earth and process industrial waste byproducts; or operations conducted in situations or environments hazardous to human life, like terrestrial places flooded with dangerous levels of radiation or toxic chemicals, deep underwater on the floor of the ocean, or in the vacuum of space. But the current wave of technological unemployment appears to have other occupations in the crosshairs. As Ford explains in his book *Rise of the Robots*:

> One widely held belief that is certain to be challenged is the assumption that automation is primarily a threat to workers who have little education and lower-skill levels. That assumption emerges from the

fact that such jobs tend to be routine and repetitive. Before you get too comfortable with that idea, however, consider just how fast the frontier is moving. At one time, a "routine" occupation would probably have implied standing on an assembly line. The reality today is far different. While lower-skill occupations will no doubt continue to be affected, a great many college educated, white collar workers are going to discover that their jobs, too, are squarely in the sights as software automation and predictive algorithms advance rapidly in capability. (2015: xiv)

As we have seen in previous chapters, recent developments in machine learning and big data mean that we are not just automating the dull, dirty, and dangerous industrial-era jobs. What is being automated are tasks and occupations that fall squarely within the realm of what is often called "routine intellectual work." In other words, what is now susceptible to the pressures of automation are not just the "blue-collar" jobs that require repetitive physical activity, but also those middle-wage, "white-collar" occupations that are often the opportunities sought out by university graduates.

Consider, for example, occupations involving activities related to human communication and information processing. At one time, if you wanted customers to conduct transactions through a sales or customer service representative, you would have needed to hire a good number of human workers to take customer inquiries, to process those requests and communicate the results, and to supply a friendly (or at least efficient) conversational interface to the business or enterprise. Today, an increasingly significant portion of this work can be performed by an SDS, like Google Duplex. At one time, if you wanted something written – catalogue copy, a financial report, or a magazine article about a championship football match, etc. – a human being (someone with a job title like "copywriter," "technical writer," or "journalist") was needed to conduct the research, organize and process the appropriate data, and generate readable prose. Now, however, NLG algorithms, like Narrative Science's Quill and Automated Insights' Wordsmith, can do that work for you. Similar transformations are occurring in other sectors of the economy. Right now it is estimated that 4.9 million human workers are employed in for-hire transportation within the United States – e.g., driving cars (think limo services, taxis, or Lyft and Uber), long-haul trucking, city and interstate buses, local delivery vehicles, etc. (US Department of Transportation 2017: Ch. 4). Self-driving vehicles promise or threaten (and the choice of verb depends on your individual perspective) to take over a good portion of this work, displacing an entire sector of good-paying jobs for skilled workers.

Does this mean that every job – or, maybe better stated, every single task that comprises a particular occupation – will be subsumed by some form of automation? Perhaps not, but a good number of them already are or will soon be. So how can we know for sure or with a reasonably high level of probability? According to Ford, "predictability" may be the best predictor:

> The fact is that "routine" may not be the best word to describe the jobs that are most likely to be threatened by technology. A more accurate term might be "predictable." Could another person learn to do your job by studying a detailed record of everything you've done in the past? Or could someone become proficient by repeating the task you've already completed, in the way that a student might take practice tests to prepare for an exam? If so, then there's a good chance that an algorithm may someday be able to learn to do much, or all of your job. (2015: xiv–xv)

Second, recent studies of technological unemployment provide what appear to be inconsistent and even conflicting results. One study that has received a lot of attention in both the popular media and academic literature on the subject is a report written by Carl Benedikt Frey and Michael A. Osborne. The report – "The Future of Employment: How Susceptible are Jobs to Computerisation?" – initially appeared online in 2013 and was eventually published, with some minor revisions, in the academic journal *Technological Forecasting and Social Change* in January 2017. The findings of Frey and Osborne's investigation made for dramatic but chilling head-lines: 47 percent of all occupations in the US are susceptible to automation. This figure is serious. Frey and Osborne are respected Oxford University researchers; their investigation utilized an innova-tive analytical approach and credible government data concerning 702 occupations in twelve employment categories; and their findings are certainly something to be worried about, with close to half of existing occupations in the US economy predicted to be at risk of being automated out of existence.

According to their analysis, occupations that have the highest prob-ability of computerization involve the obvious ones like industrial labor and manufacturing, which is, as they admit, "a continuation of a trend that has been observed over the past decade" (Frey and Osborne 2013: 38). But it also will affect other sectors of the employ-ment spectrum: transportation and logistics, office and administrative support workers, sales, and construction. By comparison, "generalist occupations requiring knowledge of human heuristics, and specialist occupations involving the development of novel ideas and artifacts, are the least susceptible to computerization" (Frey and Osborne 2013: 40).

Similar analytical results have been reported in the McKinsey Global Institute's *A Future That Works: Automation, Employment, and Productivity* (January 2017), which estimates that 49 percent of the tasks workers currently perform have a high probability of being automated through the use of technological systems that are currently available. Another 2017 study from PricewaterhouseCoopers (PwC) reported that 110 million jobs around the world are at risk of automation by the 2040s. (Hawksworth et al. 2017). And in April of the same year, a published report from the Institute for Public Policy Research (IPPR) predicted that one in three jobs within the United Kingdom were in danger of being replaced by automated systems.

Other studies and reports, however, offer a more optimistic and sanguine picture of things. In 2015 Ian Steward, Debapratim De, and Alex Cole, economists working for the professional services group Deloitte LLP, wrote and published a document titled *Technology and People: The Great Job-Creating Machine*. The key findings from this industry-supported study, which examined 144 years of the effect of technological innovation on employment opportunity in England and Wales, stand in stark contrast to those provided by Frey and Osborne:

- Technology has created more jobs than it has destroyed in the last 144 years.
- It has been saving us from dull, repetitive and dangerous work. Agriculture was the first major sector to experience this change. In 1871 it employed 6.6% of the workforce of England and Wales. Today that stands at 0.2%, a 95% decline
- Overall, technological innovation has resulted in fewer humans being deployed as sources of muscle power and more engaged in jobs involving the nursing and care of others. Just 1.1% of the workforce was employed in the caring professions during the 1871 census. By 2011, these professions employed almost a quarter of the England and Wales workforce
- Technology has boosted employment in knowledge-intensive sectors such as medicine, accounting and professional services
- Finally technology has lowered the cost of essentials, raising disposable incomes and creating new demand and jobs. In 1871, there

was one hairdresser for every 1,793 English and Welsh citizens; now there is one for every 287. (Steward et al. 2015)

Another study, produced by the World Economic Forum (WEF) and published in 2018, offers similar reasons to be cheerful about the future of work. According to this investigative survey of global trends across twelve different industries, there will be a significant and undeniable alteration regarding who or what does the work:

> Companies expect a significant shift on the frontier between humans and machines when it comes to existing work tasks between 2018 and 2022. In 2018, an average of 71% of total task hours across the 12 industries covered in the report are performed by humans, compared to 29% by machines. By 2022 this average is expected to have shifted to 58% task hours performed by humans and 42% by machines. In 2018, in terms of total working hours, no work task was yet estimated to be predominantly performed by a machine or an algorithm. By 2022, this picture is projected to have somewhat changed, with machines and algorithms on average increasing their contribution to specific tasks by 57%. (2018: viii)

These estimates may not be as severe or as dramatic as those provided by Frey and Osborne and others, and this may be due to the fact that the WEF is working with a shorter period of time, just four years. Even if this is the case, there will still be an undeniable and significant displacement of human labor within that four-year period. However, unlike many of the other studies regarding this "crisis," the WEF estimates that most of the jobs lost will be offset and made up by the development of new employment opportunities:

> This finding is tempered by optimistic estimates around emerging tasks and growing jobs which are expected to offset declining jobs. Across all industries, by 2022, growth in emerging professions is set to increase their share of employment from 16% to 27% (11% growth) of the total employee base of company respondents, whereas the employment share of declining roles is set to decrease from currently 31% to 21% (10% decline). About half of today's core jobs – making up the bulk of employment across industries – will remain stable in the period up to 2022. Within the set of companies surveyed, representing over 15 million workers in total, current estimates would suggest a decline of 0.98 million jobs and a gain of 1.74 million jobs. (2018: viii)

In other words, the WEF estimates that there will be significant changes in employment opportunity and displacement of human workers. But within a relatively short period of time – just four years – the world economy should experience a net increase of 0.76 million new jobs. The WEF report, therefore, appears to conform to and confirm what Keynes had initially theorized regarding the impact of technological unemployment: short-term losses (even devastating losses) but, on balance, a net gain in employment opportunity.

8.1.3 Method or plan of attack

In addressing the complex social problems of technological unemployment, I do not want to engage in speculation about possible futures or get involved in trying to sort out the nuances of economic theory and deciding between the different competing studies and accounts. Although interesting to contemplate, neither of these is under our control or something that we can do much about. For this reason, I want to focus our attention on and work with something we do have some control over, and that is education.

No matter how things eventually turn out – whether this recent wave of technological unemployment is just more of the same, different this time around, or somewhere in between these two extremes – the introduction of intelligent machines and autonomous robotic systems will certainly have an effect on education and the task of preparing and credentialing individuals for employment. In fact, the 0.76 million new jobs estimated by the WEF's rather sanguine *Future of Jobs Report 2018* is predicated on something they call the "reskilling imperative" – the need to educate and train close to 54 percent of the existing workforce to be competitive for new job opportunities (2018: ix). The following sections therefore look at ways that we can begin to "future proof" our own education in order to be prepared to meet the demands of the twenty-first century. Toward this end, we will identify major challenges to existing concepts, structures, and methodologies and consider both "updates" and "mods" that can be implemented to respond to these challenges.

The use of the terms "update" and "mod" in this context might need some clarification. In computer software, especially games, "updates" are official changes to a program's underlying structure. They are "top-down" reformulations or patches developed and implemented by the institution in order to retool or rework the system's basic operations. "Mods," by contrast, are end-user modifications that are designed to make a program function in ways not conceived of or intended by the original manufacturer or developer. In other words, mods are bottom-up (and often unauthorized) hacks aimed at repurposing the existing system to better respond to and facilitate the actual needs of users.

Following this precedent, we will consider both updates and mods for existing educational systems. Updates are necessary insofar as there are important structural changes that can only be made at the institutional level. These changes, however, often take time and effort to develop and implement successfully. Mods are necessary to respond to this problem. The opportunities and challenges of emerging technology are far too important, influential, and rapid for students and teachers to have the luxury to wait for top-down institutional changes. For this reason, mods are deployed to rework the existing system – right here and right now – in order to make it respond to and serve more immediate needs and concerns. The goal in all of this is to be proactive about the future. We can contemplate and complain about technological unemployment from the sidelines, but that gets us nowhere. It is better to take control and begin doing something about it.[10]

8.2 Gainfully Unemployed

Irrespective of the study you consult, whether it be Frey and Osborne's "Future of Employment" from 2017, the WEF's *Future of Jobs Report 2018*, or any of the other published investigations currently available and in circulation, everyone agrees that there will, at least for a period of time, be significant losses in job opportunity due to technology. The exact impact and significance of this technological unemployment, however, is something that remains open to debate. Will this be a momentary hiatus in employment opportunity, or will this unemployment be the "new normal" with a much larger percentage of the adult population not working? What is not debated, however, is the fact that there could be a significant number of adults who will, at one time or another, be unemployed or underemployed.

In response to the economic and social pressures exerted by this, researchers like Wendell Wallach (2015) and Martin Ford (2015) have advocated alternative forms of capital redistribution. The argument is rather simple and direct and can be easily illustrated by way of a famous anecdote concerning the automotive pioneer Henry Ford Jr. and the labor leader Walter Reuther. The story goes like this. Reuther, who was head of a trade union representing automobile workers, was given a tour of one of Ford's newly automated factories. The facility was full of new machines capable of automating many of the tasks previously conducted by assembly-line workers. As Reuther was considering the impact this technological unemployment would have on the members of his labor union, Ford sarcastically inquired how Reuther intended to collect union dues from the machines. Reuther responded in kind by asking Ford how he intended to get workers to buy these new automobiles if they were put out of a job and no longer had a source of disposable income.

The story is most likely apocryphal, but it does illustrate an important point. As employment opportunity is increasingly threatened by emerging technology, "the mechanisms that get purchasing power into the hands of consumers [i.e., gainful employment] begins to break down, and demand for products and services suffer" (Ford 2015: 264). If this breakdown in purchasing power is more than just a temporary setback, it could destabilize national economies and threaten existing social structures. For this reason, alternative methods for wealth redistribution have been proposed by individuals on both the left and the right of the political spectrum. "If technological unemployment outstrips job creation," Wallach (2015: 159) argues, "forward-thinking governments could forestall political unrest through some form of capital redistribution such as a robust welfare system or guaranteed minimum income." And there are a handful of universal basic income (UBI) pilot projects currently being tested in places like Ontario, Canada (Cowburn 2016) and Holland (Diez 2015).

But throwing money at the problem is not necessarily the solution (or the only possible solution). Work is not just a matter of capital redistribution and "purchasing power." It is also connected to and involved with personal identity and social standing. In fact, working is often situated as a moral obligation, and unemployment is typically perceived to be a personal failure. In the United States, for instance, "the unemployed" (already a potentially problematic term insofar as it is a negative construction) are typically situated in political debates not as individuals displaced by inequities in the current system of employment opportunity, but as "social parasites" looking for a free handout from the government. As a result, unemployment, even temporary unemployment, has had a less than laudable social profile. But this perception is just that; it is a perception. It is a matter of the way individuals have been educated – formally within school and informally in contemporary culture – to think about work and its social value. It is, in other words, a matter of ideology. The real challenge, then, is to reconfigure education to prepare students not just for employment but also for unemployment, whether long-term or temporary. Although it may sound counterintuitive, we need to teach individuals and our culture as a whole how to be both employed and gainfully unemployed. And the fact that this idea seems counterintuitive is sufficient evidence that we do not yet have a clue as to how one goes about doing this or why.

Compare, for instance, the "promise" of widespread unemployment to the reality of being out of work. In a TED talk from 2012, Andrew McAfee, coauthor with Erik Brynjolfsson of *The Second Machine Age* (2016), paints a rather utopian picture of technological unemployment: "So, yeah, the droids are taking our jobs, but focusing on that fact misses the point entirely. The point is that then we are freed up to do other things, and what we're going to do, I am very confident, what we're going to do is reduce poverty and drudgery and misery around the world." But what actually happens when individuals are "freed" from the drudgery of work? Currently, the vast majority of unemployed men (in the United States, at least) spend the day in their pajamas watching television (Halpern 2015: 6). Emerging technology, therefore, promises to liberate us from the drudgery of work, but we do not necessarily know what can or should be done with all this new "free time." Because work has been so central to our social formation and our sense of self-worth and identity, being without work is seen not as an opportunity but as a deficiency and a problem.

8.2.1 System updates

There are at least two institutional changes that will be necessary to respond to this. First, we need to devise broad-based education programs that can address both opportunities for work and the challenges of being without work. Recent initiatives in higher education have given increased emphasis (and funding) to specializations in the STEM (science, technology, engineering, math) fields, and for good reasons: that is where the best employment opportunities have been situated. In this effort, however, many universities have found it necessary to curtail or significantly modify requirements in the social sciences and humanities. In one of the more visible signs of this development, Japan's then minister of education, Hakubun Shimomura, called on his nation's eighty-six public universities either to discontinue programs in the social sciences and humanities, "or to convert them to serve areas that better meet society's needs" (Grove 2015). Though there has been considerable debate about the exact impact this directive could have on the shape of higher education within

Japan (Steffensen 2015), it is an indication of the way competing priorities are being addressed at a time of increased budgetary stress.

Cultivating specialization in one of the STEM fields is undoubtedly necessary for preparing students to be able to deal with the opportunities and challenges of working with emerging technology. But this should not be done at the expense of other forms of instruction that can help provide the context for understanding and dealing with the social impact and consequences of employing these systems. Education is not and should not be a zero-sum game. For this reason – and as Frey and Osborne (2013: 40) suggested in their study – the future may belong to a new kind of broadly educated generalist. Not simply because these individuals will, as Arun Sundararajan (2016: 6) argues, be more adequately prepared to take advantage of new forms of self-employment in the "sharing economy" or "crowd-based capitalism," but also because it provides individuals with the knowledge and skill to make sense of and work through those periods of time when one might not be working or have access to gainful employment. To put it in McAfee's terms, if individuals liberated from the drudgery of work will be "freed up to do other things," we may need a more active effort to define and develop what "other things" can be done and are worth doing.

Second, if the connection between education and employment opportunity is beginning to loosen up, we will need to rethink the neoliberal narrative that has, for better or worse, come to shape the way education is currently conceptualized and funded. Typically, higher education, especially in the United States, has been marketed and justified in terms of "hire education." Promoted in this fashion, formal education is routinely situated as a personal investment and, for this reason, students are able, theoretically at least, to justify going into debt to fund the opportunity. But if steady employment after graduation is less certain, it becomes increasingly difficult to justify making expenditures that will have little or even no return on investment. As of 2014, US student-loan debt totaled $1.2 trillion dollars, which averages out to $29,000 per student (White House 2014; Lorin 2016).

In order to maintain this system – and to do so at a time when universities and colleges have increasingly come to rely on student tuition for basic operating revenue – there will need to be a steady stream of high-paying jobs available to graduates, both to ensure repayment of existing loans and to convince future students to participate in the program. In the face of increasing employment uncertainty and instability, however, it is hard to sustain this system without the entire thing becoming a pyramid scheme. In order to respond to this, we will need, on the one hand, to revise the narrative of higher education, repositioning education as a public good and not a personal investment, and, on the other hand, to devise practical methods for publicly funding education that do not shift the burden onto individual students and their families. This is clearly a political matter best addressed by lawmakers at both the state and the national levels. But this does not mean that it is something beyond our influence and/or control. As citizens of democratic governments, we can vote, and we can (and we should) vote for candidates who recognize these problems, understand their impact on university graduates, and have concrete plans to do something about it. Though voting participation among young people in the US and elsewhere in the world is typically on the low end of the scale, this is an issue that is definitely worth going to the polls for.

8.2.2 User-generated mods

Curricular modifications and alternative funding schemes are clearly going to be necessary. But getting traction with these large-scale systemic changes is not going to be easy or quick. In the interim, students and teachers need "boots on the ground" solutions that can be implemented in the short term, if not immediately.

First, and concerning what happens at the classroom level, faculty can and should begin to incorporate critical reflection on work, personal identity, and social status in their classes. The coupling of identity and work is culturally and historically specific; it is based on particular ideological formations that have a long and rather successful history behind them. Instructors should neither take these arrangements for granted nor perpetuate their influence by remaining silent on the subject. We need to identify and make these assumptions the explicit object of investigation, irrespective of the discipline or field. In other words, individual teachers have the opportunity (and a responsibility) to get their students actively involved in thinking about work, the significance it has within contemporary culture, and the way that it interacts with our own understanding of identity and social participation. This direct engagement with and critique of the ideology of "hire education" is necessary not to undermine the usual way of doing things, but to empower students to understand how their expectations have been organized and why. Achieving this objective can be accomplished in the university classroom rather easily by asking students to reflect on and respond to the question

"Why am I here?" This inquiry, which can be pursued either as a short writing project or in discussion, is not only a good way to begin a new semester – a kind of "ice-breaking" exercise – but offers students the opportunity to articulate and examine the often unquestioned assumptions about education and its role in their lives.

Second, students also play a crucial role in this "modding" of education. The link between education – higher education in particular – and employment is something that is (again for very understandable reasons) widely recognized by the student population, especially those individuals who are first-generation university students. For several generations now, the official story has been persistent and consistent: better education = better jobs. As the connection between education and employment opportunity begins to unravel, or at least loosen up to such an extent that the one is not necessarily and directly related to the other, students and their families will need to reexamine what they believe education is for. Though this effort might seem to be a pressing concern for students pursuing studies in the liberal and fine arts, it is becoming increasingly necessary in many of the professional fields that had been situated as directly feeding into employment opportunity, e.g., law and business.

According to a report from May 2016, the law firm BakerHostetler "hired" an implementation of IBM's Watson to assist with research for the firm's bankruptcy cases. The AI, affectionately named "Ross," is expected to take the place of a large cohort of human paralegals and attorneys (Turner 2016). Similar displacements are occurring in the financial services industry, where algorithms are now being used not just for the routine work of the office clerk but also for research and analysis and direct client relations. "We are," explains Daniel Nadler of the financial start-up Kensho, "creating a very small number of high-paying jobs in return for destroying a very large number of fairly high-paying jobs, and the net-net to society, absent some sort of policy intervention or new industry that no one's thought of yet to employ all those people, is a net loss" (quoted in Popper 2016). In other words, automation will not displace all employment opportunities; there will continue to be a few very good-paying jobs at the high end of the spectrum. But the entry-level and middle-management positions that have traditionally been the target of professional education will be in increasingly short supply.

Questioning prevailing assumptions is no easy task, especially when tuition fees constitute a significant financial burden. Nevertheless, we need to begin challenging or at least developing some critical perspective on the "education means employment opportunity" narrative. In effect, we need to decide – each one of us individually and together – "What is education for?" Although this might initially look like an existential crisis for institutions of higher education, it is really about the needs and expectations of those individuals and communities that these institutions serve.

8.3 DIY Futures

At the same time that we begin to question and challenge the assumed tight coupling of education and work, we will also need to recognize that whatever new opportunities develop in the wake of emerging technology, they will certainly require some form of preparation. The problem for educators is that we often find ourselves in the odd position of needing to devise curriculum and pedagogical opportunities for occupations that do not yet exist, or at least are not yet fully realized, so that one might know what will be needed in terms of skills and knowledge. But this is only a problem if we think about education as responding to the needs of industry as it is currently configured or imagined. There is another way to look at it, which has the effect of reversing the direction of the vector.

Consider three rather remarkable examples. When Marc Andreessen was a student at the University of Illinois in the early 1990s, he did not pursue a major in e-commerce or complete coursework necessary to get a job with an Internet company. Neither of these existed at that time. Instead, along with Eric Bina (who unfortunately often gets left out of the story), he created an application called NCSA Mosaic, the first graphical web browser, which became one of the enabling technologies of e-commerce and helped make the Internet companies of the 1990s tech-explosion possible in the first place.

The same might be said for Facebook CEO Mark Zuckerberg and social robotics pioneer Cynthia Breazeal. Zuckerberg, who attended but did not graduate from Harvard University, did not pursue studies in social media in hopes of landing a job with one of the major players in the industry. He helped invent social media by hacking together the PHP code that eventually became Facebook. Breazeal, who did her doctoral work at MIT, did not graduate with a degree in social robotics; there was no such thing. Instead, she developed – as part of her thesis work – what became one of the first social robots: Kismet. Clearly, these examples are the exception and not the rule. But they indicate a different way of thinking about higher education and its relationship to employment. Instead of preparing individuals to take advantage of existing opportunities – opportunities that are volatile insofar as they might not exist by the time current students matriculate – we need to develop educational structures that also encourage and help students to invent the future. But doing so will, once again, require updates and mods to the existing systems.

8.3.1 System updates

Getting students actively involved in innovation is nothing new. This has been and remains one of the principal objectives and *raison d'être* of the research university. But institutions can and should be doing much more to encourage and support this kind of entrepreneurial activity, especially when it comes to technology transfer and commercialization policies. Although universities have long been involved in commercializing innovations developed by their faculty and students, it has only been since the 1970s that policies and offices dedicated to this effort have been institutionalized. This development received significant legislative support at the US federal level when, in 1980, Congress passed the Bayh–Dole Act, which shifted ownership of federally funded research (e.g., NSF, NEH, NIH, etc.) from the US government to the university where the research project was conducted.

University ownership has distinct advantages for both researchers and the institution. For researchers, whether they are a member of the faculty or a student using university facilities and resources, the technology licensing office (TLO), as these facilities are commonly called, provides assistance in obtaining the necessary IP (intellectual property) protections and arranging licensing agreements with third parties. In effect, the TLO provides a technology transfer and commercialization service. For the institution, the TLO has become an important revenue-generating resource. One of the most widely studied and lucrative university-owned IPs is the Cohen–Boyer (C–B) patent, which involves techniques for the creation of genetically engineered micro-organisms. "Over its 17-year life," Martin Kenney and Donald Patton (2009: 1409) write, "C-B produced in excess of $255 million in revenues for Stanford University and the University of California."

Despite (or perhaps because of) this success, recent studies of existing models and commercialization policies find numerous contradictions, inconsistencies, and misaligned incentives. As Kenney and Patton (2009: 1413) explain: "The licensing experience of Marc Andreessen . . . illustrates the pitfalls. When Andreessen joined James

Clark to form Netscape in 1994, they attempted to negotiate a license with the University of Illinois [to use the Mosaic code] but found the process so frustrating that they ultimately rewrote the browser code entirely." Meanwhile, successfully negotiated agreements with other corporations, like Microsoft, which were granted a license to use the original Mosaic code as part of their Internet Explorer browser, netted the university a total of US$7 million. If students have difficulties reusing, further developing, or obtaining a license for the innovations they have invented or have helped invent, then the existing commercialization policies cease being a useful service and start interfering with future opportunities.

For this reason, universities need either to reform the current system or to devise alternative models for research commercialization. Kenney and Patton, for their part, suggest two alternatives: vesting ownership in the individual inventor or placing all university-produced innovation in the public domain and making it available, without restriction, to any and all users. The former "would remove research commercialization from the control and mission of the university administration and would decentralize it to the inventors" (2009: 1415). Under the latter, "the university administration would no longer be involved in licensing, [and] the university would return to its role as a platform for research and instruction" (2009: 1414). Although neither model necessarily does away with the university TLO, they do introduce a significant shift in who owns and controls the products of university research and innovation.

There are, however, good reasons to believe that universities might not be entirely satisfied with these particular alternatives. As Kenney and Patton explain:

> While meant to be used for further research, TLO income is attractive to administrators because the funds are, in fact, largely unencumbered, thereby providing wide discretion on how they are spent. Often the support monies for TLO personnel can originate from public funds, either federal or state. This asymmetry offers a powerful incentive – restricted funds can be spent to operate the TLO, while earnings are far less restricted. The strength of this incentive is difficult to measure, but it may be considerable as more flexible funds are invariably in short supply. (2009: 1410)

In other words, what university administrators like about the TLO is that they are institutional revenue centers that bring in money without the need either to pay for overhead costs (e.g., facilities, personnel, operating expenditures, etc.) or to submit to oversight from outside agencies. TLO revenue is, for all intent and purposes, pure unencumbered profit. What is needed, therefore, is to formulate some reasonable balance between the financial interests of the institution and the rights of faculty and students to develop and commercialize their own innovations.

8.3.2 User-generated mods

As with the first set of updates, this restructuring of the policies and procedures of innovation ownership and commercialization is not going to be resolved quickly or effortlessly. For this reason, students and teachers need more immediate bottom-up strategies. First and foremost, students should know and understand their university's policy for technology transfer and commercialization. Although most, if not all, institutions of higher education have some explicit policy regarding this, not all universities are created equal, and there are significant differences in how the policy is instituted. In most cases, employees of the university (faculty, graduate assistants, research assistants, etc.) are required, as part of their employment contract, to disclose and assign ownership of their efforts to the university. The same requirement does not necessarily apply to students. This does not mean, however, that student invention is automatically exempt. At many institutions, student innovation is exempt only in cases where the invention was produced without the use of *significant* university resources or facilities. For example, MIT (2018), one of the leading institutions in technology innovation, provides the following stipulation: "When an invention, software, or other copyrightable material, mask work, or tangible research property is developed by M.I.T. faculty, students, staff, visitors or others participating in M.I.T. programs using significant M.I.T. funds or facilities, M.I.T. will own the patent, copyright, or other tangible or intellectual property." What constitutes "significant use" is obviously important and open to interpretation, meaning that there is some flexibility or potential inconsistencies in the way the policy is applied.

Students should therefore know in advance what is and what is not possible in the context of their university's policies and procedures. Knowing the requirements and the exceptions to the requirements can help to prevent running into complicated legal problems after the fact. And in this effort, faculty play a crucial role. It is (or at least should be) the responsibility of faculty to get students reading university policy statements regarding technology transfer and commercialization and to help them understand the practical consequences of these policies for their own work. Although this material is not typically perceived to be part of the curriculum, instructors in all fields and disciplines need to help their students understand both the opportunities and the challenges of their innovation efforts.

Second, students, especially at the undergraduate level, need to begin to think beyond the limitations of the major. The organization of the university into disciplines, each with its own specific degree requirements and set of qualifying criteria, is an administrative convenience useful for allocating resources, processing student throughput, and credentialing graduates. The system, however, is not necessarily useful for students, who may need to draw on and combine instructional resources from across the institution in the process of responding to new technological opportunities. This is especially true in situations where the principal challenge is not just technological, like machine learning.

As we have seen throughout our investigation, machine-learning algorithms – which include a wide range of different but related methodologies (e.g., supervised learning, unsupervised learning, reinforcement learning, etc.) – do not simply follow predefined rules of behavior developed by a human programmer. Instead, these systems are designed to generate their own rules of behavior by exploiting statistically significant patterns in large sets of data. Consequently, machine-learning implementations can be considered "black box" algorithms for two reasons. First, they are, more often than not, proprietary systems owned by a corporation and protected from public inspection by both legal restrictions (patent and copyright) and technological exigencies (i.e., the compiled, executable code is not able to be read or inspected by the end user). Second, because the connectionist architectures of these neural networks are designed to generate their own rules of operation from discovering patterns in data, their behaviors often exceed the understanding and control of their own designers. AlphaGo's win over Lee Sedol, for instance, was as surprising to its developers as it was to the general public. The same was true of Tay, whose racist Tweet-storm was as unexpected by Microsoft as it was by the users who interacted with the bot.

Responding to the opportunities and challenge made available by these mechanisms that do things that are ostensibly "out of our hands" will require a combination of knowledge and skills that transcend the borders separating what C. P. Snow (1998) described as "the two cultures." Students specializing in one of the technical disciplines will, on the one hand, need to develop the knowledge base and intellectual skill set to understand, anticipate, and evaluate the social consequences of the technologies they will be asked to develop and release into the world. This sensitivity and capability cannot be imparted by a single specialized course in "engineering ethics," but will require a much more sustained engagement with the best thinking about the "human condition" as it has been cultivated in art, literature, and philosophy. STEM increasingly needs to be rewritten as STEAM, where the additional "A" indicates both the fine and the liberal arts.

Likewise, students specializing in one of the "human sciences" need to investigate what this kind of technological innovation means for our concept of the human and the legacy of human exceptionalism. They will need to recognize that information and communication technology are not just tools of human endeavor, but, as Luciano Floridi (2014) has described it, a paradigm shattering "fourth revolution" in how we think about ourselves and our place in the world.[11] What is needed, then, to put it in a kind of shorthand formulation, are technology innovators who also understand the profound intricacies of the human condition, and humanists, social scientists, and artists who can deal with computer technology and work with code. Unfortunately, the established structure of the university often discourages this kind of broad interdisciplinary effort. For this reason, and rather than waiting for structural change to trickle down, teachers and students should actively work to remix education by drawing on and repurposing the wide range of resources available within the university structure, even if (and especially if) doing so cuts across boundaries that have been carefully arranged, managed, and protected.

8.4 Technological Displacement

From the vantage point of the long tail of history, emerging technologies, especially innovations in information and communication systems, have always confronted existing educational institutions with a significant challenge. Recall, for instance, the introduction of movable type and the printed book. At the time that books were considered "emerging technology," they confronted the established medieval institutions of knowledge production and distribution – which in Europe meant the Catholic Church and its affiliates – with something of an existential crisis. Although there are numerous examinations of the causes and consequences of this transformation in the scholarly literature, one of the more vivid illustrations can be found in a statement in Victor Hugo's *Notre-Dame de Paris* (1978: 188), or *The Hunchback of Notre-Dame*. The statement is attributed to the archdeacon Frollo, and it concerns his rather pessimistic evaluation of the impact of Johannes Gutenberg's invention of movable type or the printing press: "For some moments the Archdeacon contemplated the gigantic edifice in silence; then, sighing deeply, he pointed with his right hand to the printed book lying open on his table, and with his left to Notre-Dame, and casting a mournful glance from the book to the church: 'Alas!' he said. 'This will destroy that'" (Hugo 1978: 188).

The anecdote has been recounted many times, not just in the history of print media and technology but also by recent efforts to explain subsequent innovations in information and communication technology, like the personal computer and the Internet (cf. Bolter 2001). But "destroy" is perhaps too strong a word in this context. Obviously, the book did not (literally) raze the brick and mortar gothic edifice; it merely challenged and displaced its function as the principal mode of knowledge production, accumulation, and distribution. Though it may have taken several hundred years, European institutions eventually figured out how to accommodate the technology of print to existing structures and systems. Similarly, the introduction of the computer and the Internet did not put an end to writing, the teaching of composition, or the publication of books. The fact that you are reading about this in a book is sufficient evidence – whether the letters have been applied to the surface of the pulped flesh of dead trees or are being displayed as intricate patterns of glowing pixels on the screen of a mobile device. Once again, educational institutions learned – and obviously not without some critical hesitation and significant missteps – how to match the curriculum to the opportunities and challenges of this new technology.

Following this precedent, we can expect that the current crop of emergent technologies will most probably conform to the contours of this hype cycle. For this to happen, however, existing educational programs from both ends of the spectrum will have to be reworked: top-down updates in the structure and operations of the institution must be developed and bottom-up mods that can have an immediate impact on the lives and careers of both teachers and students must be encouraged. We may not know exactly what the future has in store for us, but we can work to ensure that our education system is prepared to respond to the opportunities and challenges that will confront us.

Summary of Key Points

- Technological unemployment is not new. Beginning with the industrial revolution, automation has displaced and reconfigured human occupations and employment opportunity. The important question at this point in time is whether AI is just "more of the same" or whether "things are going to be different this time around."
- Even if this question remains essentially unresolved, students need to begin planning for a future where automation will be less the exception and more the rule. Doing so will require both top-down updates in the university curriculum and institutional operations and bottom-up user modifications that can be implemented by teachers and students right now in the classroom.
- It is only by actively working with both institutional updates and user modifications that students, teachers, and universities stand a chance of responding to the challenges of the twenty-first century and "future proofing" student careers in the face of what many believe is unprecedented technological and social change.

9

Social Responsibility and Ethics

Key Aims/Objectives

- To examine social responsibility, detailing how our understanding of the concept is exposed to new and unprecedented challenges in the face of technological innovation.
- To review and critically assess the advantages and limitations of the instrumental theory of technology, which provides a baseline explanation of the social significance and impact of technology.
- To profile and investigate recent innovations in AI and robotics that effectively challenge the instrumental theory by opening gaps in the usual way of assigning and making sense of responsibility.
- To introduce and critically evaluate three different and competing methods for responding to these responsibility gaps: Instrumentalism 2.0, Machine Ethics, and Joint Agency.

Introduction

As various autonomous machines and intelligent systems come to take up increasingly influential positions in contemporary culture – positions where they are not necessarily just tools or instruments of human action but a kind of interactive social entity in their own right – we are going to need to ask ourselves interesting but difficult questions. At what point might a robot, algorithm, or other autonomous system be held accountable for the decisions it makes or the actions it initiates? Who – or perhaps even what – can and should be held responsible for both positive and negative outcomes with AI?

And when, if ever, would it make sense to say, "It's the computer's fault"?[12]

The task of this chapter is to respond to the question concerning emerging technology and social responsibility – to answer for the way that we understand, debate, and decide who or what is able to answer for decisions and actions undertaken by way of increasingly autonomous, interactive, and sociable mechanisms. The investigation will proceed through three steps or movements. The chapter begins by revisiting the instrumental theory of technology, which determines the way one typically deals with and responds to the question of social responsibility, when it involves technology. We will then consider three instances where recent innovations in computer applications, AI, and robotics challenge this standard operating procedure by opening gaps in the usual way of assigning and making sense of responsibility. The chapter concludes by evaluating the three different responses – Instrumentalism 2.0, Machine Ethics, and Joint Agency – that have been developed to respond to these difficulties. The objective in doing so is not to prescribe the right answer, but to open up the space for critical debate by mapping the opportunities and challenges of and for social responsibility in the face of increasingly autonomous mechanisms.

9.1 Responsibility

Responsibility is one of those things that we think we know what is being talked about until we are asked to define it. So let's begin by getting a better handle on the term and its meaning. "The concept of responsibility," as the French philosopher Paul Ricœur (2007: 11) pointed out, is anything but clear and well defined. Although the legal employment of the term, which dates back to the nineteenth century, seems rather well established – with "responsibility" characterized in terms of both civil and penal obligations (either the obligation to compensate for some legally defined harm or the obligation to submit to punishment decided by a court) – the concept is still confused and somewhat vague.

> In the first place, we are surprised that a term with such a firm sense on the juridical plane should be of such recent origin and not really well established within the philosophical tradition. Next, the current proliferation and dispersion of uses of this term is puzzling, especially because they go well beyond the limits established for its juridical use.

The adjective "responsible" can complement a wide variety of things: you are responsible for the consequences of your acts, but also responsible for others' actions to the extent that they were done under your charge or care . . . In these diffuse uses, the reference to obligation has not disappeared, it has become the obligation to fulfill certain duties, to assume certain burdens, to carry out certain commitments. (Ricœur 2007: 11–12)

Ricœur (2007: 12) traces this sense of the word through its etymology to "the polysemia of the verb 'to respond'," which denotes "to answer for . . ." or "to respond to . . . (a question, an appeal, an injunction, etc.)." It is in this sense of the word that the question concerning *responsibility* – literally "response + able" – has come to be associated with AI, algorithms, and robots. One of the principal issues, if not the principal issue, is to decide who or what can be or should be "response-able" for the consequences of decisions and actions instituted by AI or robotic systems? Who or what is able to respond or answer for what the machine does or does not do?

9.1.1 Instrumentalism revisited

When it comes to these kinds of questions, the matter seems rather clear and indisputable. "Morality," as J. Storrs Hall (2001: 2) points out, "rests on human shoulders, and if machines changed the ease with which things were done, they did not change responsibility for doing them. People have always been the only 'moral agents.'" This seemingly intuitive and common-sense response is persuasive, precisely because it is structured and informed by the answer that is typically provided for the question concerning technology. "We ask the question concerning technology," Martin Heidegger (1977: 4–5) writes, "when we ask what it is. Everyone knows the two statements that answer our question. One says: Technology is a means to an end. The other says: Technology is a human activity." According to this formulation, the presumed role and function of any kind of technology – whether it be a simple hand tool, jet airliner, or a sophisticated robot – is that it is a means employed by human users for specific ends.

As we have seen (Chapter 2), this "instrumentalist theory of technology" provides what Andrew Feenberg (1991: 5) describes as "the most widely accepted view of technology," insofar as it is based on a widely held, common-sense assumption that "technologies are 'tools' standing ready to serve the purposes of users." It is because of this instrumental transparency – the fact that a "tool" or "instrument" is considered to be neutral and without value or content of its own – that a technological artifact is evaluated on the basis of the particular employments that have been decided for it by its human designer or user. A hammer, for instance, may be used for building a house to shelter one's family, or it may be employed to do harm to another human being. The tool means nothing and does nothing by itself. What matters – what makes the difference – is how a particular human individual decides to employ it. For this reason, technology is always and only considered to be a "means to an end." It is not and does not have an end in its own right. A particular technological device – whether it is a simple hand tool like a hammer or a sophisticated technological system like a jet airliner – is judged to be "good" (or "bad") not because of *what* it is, but because of *how* it is utilized.

This not only sounds level-headed and reasonable, it is one of the standard operating presumptions of computer ethics. Although different definitions of computer ethics have circulated since Walter Maner first introduced the term in 1976, they all share a human-centered perspective that assigns responsibility to human designers and users. According to Deborah Johnson, who is credited with writing the field's agenda-setting textbook, "computer ethics turns out to be the study of human beings and society – our goals and values, our norms of behavior, the way we organize ourselves and assign rights and responsibilities, and so on" (1985: 6). Computers, she recognizes, often "instrumentalize" these human values and behaviors in innovative and challenging ways, but the bottom line is and remains the way human beings design and use (or misuse) such technology.

Johnson has stuck to this conclusion even in the face of what appear to be increasingly sophisticated technological developments:

> Computer systems are produced, distributed, and used by people engaged in social practices and meaningful pursuits. This is as true of current computer systems as it will be of future computer systems. No matter how independently, automatic, and interactive computer systems of the future behave, they will be the products (direct or indirect) of human behavior, human social institutions, and human decision. (2006: 197)

Understood in this way, computer systems, no matter how automatic, independent, or seemingly intelligent they may become, "are not and can never be (autonomous, independent) moral agents" (2006: 203).

They will, like all other technological artifacts, always be instruments of human value, human decision-making, and human action.

9.1.2 Problems and limitations

According to the instrumental theory, any action undertaken via a technological system is ultimately the responsibility of some human agent – the designer of the system, the manufacturer of the equipment, or the end user of the product. If something goes wrong with or someone is harmed by the mechanism, "some human is," as Ben Goertzel (2002: 1) accurately describes it, "to blame for setting the program up to do such a thing." Consequently, holding a computer, an AI, or a robotic system responsible for the decisions it generates or the actions that it is instrumental in deploying is to make at least two fundamental errors.

(1) *Logical error.* It is logically inconsistent to ascribe agency to something that is and remains a mere object that is under our control. As John Sullins (2006: 26) concludes by way of the investigations undertaken by Selmer Bringsjord (2007), computers and robots "will never do anything they are not programmed to perform" and, as a result, "are incapable of becoming moral agents now or in the future." This statement is a variant of what Alan Turing called "Lady Lovelace's objection" (see Chapter 2) – the idea that a computer has "no pretensions to originate anything" and can only "do whatever we know how to order it to perform" (Turing 1999: 50). Consequently, it is incorrect to attribute agency to something that is a mere instrument or inanimate object under human control. And trying to doing so is a logical error, because it mistakenly turns a passive object into an active subject. It confuses means and ends, to put it in Kantian language.

(2) *Moral mistake.* Holding a robotic mechanism or system culpable would not only be illogical but also irresponsible. This is because ascribing moral responsibility to machines, as Mikko Siponen (2004: 286) argues, would allow one to "start blaming computers for our mistakes. In other words, we can claim that 'I didn't do it – it was a computer error,' while ignoring the fact that the software has been programmed by people to 'behave in certain ways,' and thus people may have caused this error either incidentally or intentionally (or users have otherwise contributed to the cause of this error)." This line of thinking has been codified in the popular adage, "It's a poor carpenter who blames his tools." In other words, when something goes wrong or a mistake is made in situations involving the applica-

tion of technology, it is the operator of the tool and not the tool itself that should be blamed. "By endowing technology with the attributes of autonomous agency," Abbe Mowshowitz (2008: 271) argues, "human beings are ethically sidelined. Individuals are relieved of responsibility. The suggestion of being in the grip of irresistible forces provides an excuse of rejecting responsibility for oneself and others."

This maneuver, what the moral theorist Helen Nissenbaum (1996: 35) terms "the computer as scapegoat," is understandable but problematic, insofar as it allows human designers, developers, or users to deflect or avoid taking responsibility for their actions by assigning accountability to what is a mere object. As Nissenbaum explains:

> Most of us can recall a time when someone (perhaps ourselves) offered the excuse that it was the computer's fault – the bank clerk explaining an error, the ticket agent excusing lost bookings, the student justifying a late paper. Although the practice of blaming a computer, on the face of it, appears reasonable and even felicitous, it is a barrier to accountability because, having found one explanation for an error or injury, the further role and responsibility of human agents tend to be underestimated – even sometimes ignored. As a result, no one is called upon to answer for an error or injury. (1996: 35)

It is precisely for this reason that Johnson and Miller (2008: 124) argue that "it is dangerous to conceptualize computer systems as autonomous moral agents." Assigning responsibility to the technology not only sidelines human involvement and activity, but leaves questions of responsibility untethered from their assumed proper attachment to human decision-making and action.

9.1.3 Rules and guidelines

Finally, there have been a number of national and international efforts to codify the instrumental theory in actual rules, regulations, and guidelines. One of the more prominent and influential formulations can be found in a document titled "Principles of Robotics" (Boden et al. 2011, 2017). The history of this document and the manner of its composition is not immaterial. As Tony Prescott and Michael Szollosy explain:

> In 2010, the UK's Engineering and Physical Science and Arts and Humanities Research Councils (EPSRC and AHRC) organized a retreat to consider ethical issues in robotics to which they invited a pool of experts drawn from the worlds of technology, industry, the arts, law

and social sciences. This meeting resulted in a set of ethical "Principles of Robotics" (henceforth "the Principles") that were published online by the EPSRC (Boden et al. 2011), which aimed at "regulating robots in the real world." (2017: 119)

Since this initial effort, the Principles have been revisited, revised, and republished, along with a number of commentaries from the individuals involved in the process (Boden et al. 2017).

According to the document, robots are defined as tools or instruments of human activity. This instrumentalist definition is formulated and presented in various ways and numerous times throughout the course of the Principles:

- "Robots are simply tools of various kinds, albeit very special tools, and the responsibility of making sure they behave well must always lie with human beings" (Introduction).
- "Robots are multi-use tools" (Rule #1).
- "Robots are just tools, designed to achieve goals and desires that humans specify" (Commentary to Rule #2).
- "Robots are manufactured artefacts" (Rule #4). (Boden et al. 2017).

Even if or when robots or other AI systems are designed to simulate something more than a mere tool, e.g., a pet or a companion, this appearance, it is argued, should be clearly indicated as such and the actual instrumental status of the object should be made easily accessible and readily apparent:

> One of the great promises of robotics is that robot toys may give pleasure, comfort and even a form of companionship to people who are not able to care for pets, whether due to restrictions in their homes, physical capacity, time or money. However, once a user becomes attached to such a toy, it would be possible for manufacturers to claim the robot has needs or desires that could unfairly cost the owners or their families more money. The legal version of this rule was designed to say that although it is permissible and even sometimes desirable for a robot to sometimes give the impression of real intelligence, anyone who owns or interacts with a robot should be able to find out what it really is and perhaps what it was really manufactured to do. Robot intelligence is artificial, and we thought that the best way to protect consumers was to remind them of that by guaranteeing a way for them to "lift the curtain" (to use the metaphor from *The Wizard of Oz*). (Boden et al. 2017: 127)

No matter how sophisticated a robot's behavior is or how social it is designed to be, the Principles make it clear that robots and other forms of AI are instruments or tools to be used, deployed, and manipulated by human agents. The EPSRC document endorses and operationalizes what Heidegger (1977: 6) had identified as the "instrumental and anthropological definition of technology," and it does so without any critical questioning or reflection. It takes it as established and unquestioned truth.

9.2 Technology Beyond Instrumentalism

The instrumental theory not only sounds reasonable, it is obviously useful. It is, one might say, instrumental for responding to the opportunities and challenges of increasingly complex technological systems and devices. This is because the theory has been successfully applied not only to simple devices like corkscrews, toothbrushes, and garden hoses, but also to sophisticated technologies like computers, smartphones, drones, etc. But all of that appears to be increasingly questionable or problematic precisely because of a number of recent innovations that effectively challenge the operational limits of the instrumental theory.

9.2.1 Machine !== tool

The instrumental theory is a rather blunt instrument, reducing all technology, irrespective of design, construction, or operation, to the ontological status of a tool or instrument. "Tool," however, does not necessarily encompass everything technological and does not, therefore, exhaust all possibilities. There are also *machines*. Although "experts in mechanics," as Karl Marx (1977: 493) pointed out, often confuse these two concepts, calling "tools simple machines and machines complex tools," there is an important and crucial difference between the two. Indication of this essential difference can be found in a brief parenthetical remark offered by Heidegger (1977: 17) in reference to his use of the word "machine" to characterize a jet airliner: "Here it would be appropriate to discuss Hegel's definition of the machine as autonomous tool." What Heidegger references, without supplying the full citation, are G. W. F. Hegel's 1805–7 Jena Lectures (basically, courses that were offered at the university in Jena, a city in the eastern part of Germany), in which "machine" had been defined as a tool that is self-sufficient, self-reliant, and independent.

Although Heidegger immediately dismisses this alternative as something that is not appropriate to his way of questioning technology, it is taken up and given sustained consideration by Langdon Winner in his book-length investigation *Autonomous Technology*.

> To be autonomous is to be self-governing, independent, not ruled by an external law or force. In the metaphysics of Immanuel Kant, autonomy refers to the fundamental condition of free will – the capacity of the will to follow moral laws which it gives to itself. Kant opposes this idea to "heteronomy," the rule of the will by external laws, namely the deterministic laws of nature. In this light the very mention of autonomous technology raises an unsettling irony, for the expected relationship of subject and object is exactly reversed. We are now reading all of the propositions backwards. To say that technology is autonomous is to say that it is nonheteronomous, not governed by an external law. And what is the external law that is appropriate to technology? Human will, it would seem. (1977: 16)

"Autonomous technology," therefore, refers to technological devices that directly contravene the instrumental definition by deliberately contesting and relocating the assignment of agency. Such mechanisms are not mere tools to be used by human beings, but occupy, in one way or another, the place of the human agent. As Marx (1977: 495) described it, "the machine, therefore, is a mechanism that, after being set in motion, performs with its tools the same operations as the worker formerly did with similar tools." Understood in this way, the machine does not occupy the place of the tool used by the worker; it takes the place of the worker him/herself. This is precisely why the question concerning automation, or robots in the workplace, is not able to be explained away as the implementation of new and better tools but raises concerns over the replacement of human workers – or what has been called, as we saw in Chapter 8, "technological unemployment."

Perhaps the best illustration of the difference Marx describes is available to us with the self-driving car or autonomous vehicle. The autonomous vehicle, whether the Google Car or one of its competitors, is not designed for and intended to replace the automobile. It is, in its design, function, and materials, the same kind of instrument that we currently utilize for the purpose of personal transportation. The autonomous vehicle, therefore, does not replace the instrument of transportation (the car); it is, rather, intended to replace (or at least significantly displace) the driver. This difference was officially acknowledged by the National Highway Traffic Safety Administration

(NHTSA), which in a February 4, 2016 letter to Google, stated that the company's self-driving system could legitimately be considered the legal driver of the vehicle: "As a foundational starting point for the interpretations below, NHTSA will interpret 'driver' in the context of Google's described motor vehicle design as referring to the [self-driving system], and not to any of the vehicle occupants" (Ross 2016). Although this decision was only an interpretation of existing law, the NHTSA explicitly stated that it would "consider initiating rulemaking to address whether the definition of 'driver' in Section 571.3 [of the current US federal statute, 49 U.S.C. Chapter 301] should be updated in response to changing circumstances" (Hemmersbaugh 2016).

Similar proposals have been floated in efforts to deal with workplace automation. In a highly publicized draft document submitted to the European Parliament in May 2016, for instance, it was argued that "sophisticated autonomous robots" ("machines" in Marx's terminology) be considered "electronic persons" with "specific rights and obligations" for the purposes of contending with the challenges of technological unemployment, tax policy, and legal liability. Although the proposal did not pass as originally written, it represents recognition on the part of lawmakers that recent innovations in AI and robotics challenge the way we typically respond to and answer for questions regarding social responsibility.

The instrumentalist theory works by making the assumption that all technologies – irrespective of design, implementation, or sophistication – are tools of human action. Hammer, computer, or autonomous vehicle: they are all just instruments that are used more or less effectively and/or correctly by human beings. But this way of thinking does not cover everything; there are also *machines*. Machines, as Marx (following Hegel's initial suggestions) recognized, occupy another ontological position. They are not instruments to be used (more or less efficiently) by a human agent; they are designed and implemented to take the place of the human agent. Consequently, machines – like the self-driving automobile and other forms of what Winner calls "autonomous technology" – challenge the explanatory capability of the instrumentalist theory, presenting us with technologies that are intentionally designed and deployed to be something other. Pointing this out, however, does not mean that the instrumental theory is on this account simply refuted. There are and will continue to be mechanisms understood and utilized as tools to be manipulated by human users (i.e., lawnmowers, corkscrews, telephones, etc.). The point is that the instrumentalist perspective, no matter how useful and seemingly correct in some circumstances for answering for some technological devices, does not exhaust all possibilities for all kinds of devices. The theory (like any theory) has its limits.

9.2.2 Learning algorithms

The instrumental theory, for all its notable success handling different kinds of technology, appears to be unable to contend with recent developments in machine learning. Consider again DeepMind's AlphaGo and Microsoft's Tay.ai, both of which demonstrate the "responsibility gap" (Matthias 2004) that is opening up in the wake of recent innovations in machine learning. AlphaGo, as we have seen previously (Chapter 6), does not play the game of Go by following a set of cleverly designed moves fed into it by human programmers. It is a machine-learning system that is designed to formulate its own instructions from a combination of Monte-Carlo tree search and deep neural networks that have been trained by both supervised and reinforcement learning. Likewise, Microsoft's Tay (see Chapter 5) was a machine-learning neural network Twitterbot that was trained on anonymized data from social media and intended to evolve its behaviors in the process of interacting with users. What both systems have in common is that the engineers who designed and built them had little or no idea what the systems would eventually do once they were in operation. For this reason, machine-learning systems, like AlphaGo and Tay, are intentionally designed to do things that their programmers cannot anticipate, completely control, or answer for. They are, in effect, "black boxes," which is both interesting and potentially problematic when it comes to deciding questions of responsibility.

AlphaGo, for instance, was designed to do one thing: play Go. And it proved its ability by beating one of the most celebrated human players of the game, Lee Sedol of South Korea. So the question is "Who won?" Who or what actually beat Lee Sedol? Who or what was victorious? Following the dictates of the instrumental theory of technology, actions undertaken with the computer would be attributed to the human programmers who initially designed the system and are capable of answering for what it does or does not do. But this explanation does not necessarily hold for an application like AlphaGo, which was deliberately created to do things that exceed the knowledge and control of its human designers. In fact, in most of the reporting on this landmark event, it is not Google or the engineers at DeepMind who are credited with the victory. It is AlphaGo.

Things get even more complicated with Tay, Microsoft's foul-mouthed teenage AI, when one asks who was responsible for Tay's bigoted comments on Twitter. According to the standard instrumentalist way of thinking, one could understandably blame the programmers at Microsoft, who designed the application to be able to do these things. But the programmers obviously did not set out to create a racist algorithm. Tay developed this reprehensible behavior by learning from interactions with human users on the Internet. So how did Microsoft answer for this? How did they explain and respond to this question concerning responsibility?

Initially, less than twenty-four hours after the launch of Tay, in March 2016, a company spokesperson – in damage-control mode – sent out an email to *Wired*, the *Washington Post*, and other news organizations, which sought to blame the victim (e.g., the users on Twitter):

> The AI chatbot Tay is a machine learning project, designed for human engagement. It is as much a social and cultural experiment, as it is technical. Unfortunately, within the first 24 hours of coming online, we became aware of a coordinated effort by some users to abuse Tay's commenting skills to have Tay respond in inappropriate ways. As a result, we have taken Tay offline and are making adjustments. (Quoted in Risley 2016)

According to Microsoft, it is not the programmers or the corporation that are responsible for the hate speech. It is the fault of the users (or some users) who interacted with Tay and taught her to be a bigot. Tay's racism, in other word, is our fault.

Later, on Friday, March 25, Peter Lee, vice-president of Microsoft Research, posted the following apology on the Official Microsoft Blog:

> As many of you know by now, on Wednesday we launched a chatbot called Tay. We are deeply sorry for the unintended offensive and hurtful tweets from Tay, which do not represent who we are or what we stand for, nor how we designed Tay. Tay is now offline and we'll look to bring Tay back only when we are confident we can better anticipate malicious intent that conflicts with our principles and values.

But this apology is also frustratingly unsatisfying or interesting (it all depends on how you look at it). According to Lee's carefully worded explanation, Microsoft is only responsible for not *anticipating* the bad outcome; it does not take responsibility or answer for the offensive

Tweets. For Lee, it is Tay who (or "that," and word choice matters in this context) is named and recognized as the source of the "wildly inappropriate and reprehensible words and images" (Lee 2016). And since Tay is a kind of "minor" (a teenage AI) under the protection of her parent corporation, Microsoft needed to step in, apologize for their "daughter's" bad behavior, and put Tay in a time out.

Although the extent to which one might assign "agency" and "responsibility" to these mechanisms remains a contested issue, what is not debated is the fact that the rules of the game have changed and that there is a widening "responsibility gap."

> Presently there are machines in development or already in use which are able to decide on a course of action and to act without human intervention. The rules by which they act are not fixed during the production process, but can be changed during the operation of the machine, by the machine itself. This is what we call machine learning. Traditionally we hold either the operator/manufacture of the machine responsible for the consequences of its operation or "nobody" (in cases, where no personal fault can be identified). Now it can be shown that there is an increasing class of machine actions, where the traditional ways of responsibility ascription are not compatible with our sense of justice and the moral framework of society because nobody has enough control over the machine's actions to be able to assume responsibility for them. (Matthias 2004: 177)

In other words, the instrumental theory of technology, which had effectively tethered machine action to human agency and responsibility, no longer adequately applies to mechanisms that have been deliberately designed to operate and exhibit some form, no matter how rudimentary, of independent action or autonomous decision-making. Contrary to the instrumentalist way of thinking, we now have mechanisms that are designed to do things that exceed our control and our ability to respond or to answer for them.

But let's be clear as to what this means. What has been demonstrated is not that a machine, like AlphaGo or Tay, is or should be considered a moral agent and held solely accountable for the decisions it makes or the actions it deploys. That may be going too far, and it would be inattentive to the actual results that have been obtained. In fact, if we return to Ricœur (2007) and his suggestion that responsibility be understood as the "ability to respond," it is clear that both AlphaGo and Tay lack this capability. If we should, for instance, want to know more about the moves that AlphaGo made in its historic match against Lee Sedol, AlphaGo can certainly be asked about it. But the algorithm will have nothing to say in response. In fact, it was the responsibility of the human program- mers and observers to respond on behalf of AlphaGo and to explain the significance and impact of its behavior. But what this does indicate is that machine-learning systems like AlphaGo and Tay introduce complications into the instrumentalist way of assigning and dealing with responsibility. They might not be full moral agents in their own right (not yet, at least), but their design and operation effectively challenge the standard instrumentalist theory and open up fissures in the way responsibility comes to be decided, assigned, and formulated.

9.2.3 Mindless mechanisms

In addition to these machine-learning applications, there are also seemingly "empty-headed" bots and SDS like ELIZA, Alexa, and other NLP implementations that, if not proving otherwise, at least significantly complicate the instrumentalist viewpoint and its under- lying assumptions. Miranda Mowbray, for instance, has investigated the complications of social responsibility in online communities populated by both human users and bots:

> The rise of online communities has led to a phenomenon of real-time, multi-person interaction via online personas. Some online community technologies allow the creation of bots (personas that act according to a software programme rather than being directly controlled by a human user) in such a way that it is not always easy to tell a bot from a human within an online social space. It is also possible for a persona to be partly controlled by a software programme and partly directly by a human . . . This leads to theoretical and practical problems for ethical arguments (not to mention policing) in these spaces, since the usual one-to-one correspondence between actors and moral agents can be lost. (2002: 2)

According to Mowbray, bots complicate the way we normally think about social responsibility. They not only are able to pass as another human, making it increasingly difficult to distinguish the one from the other, but also complicate the assumed one-to-one correspond- ence between actor and agent. "There is," as Steve Jones (2014: 245) points out, "a concomitantly increasing amount of algorithmic intervention utilizing expressions between users and between users and machines to create, modify or channel communication and inter- action." And this "algorithmic intervention" is making it increasingly difficult to identify who or what is responsible for actions in the space of an online community or virtual world.

Although these software bots are by no means close to achieving anything that looks remotely like actual intelligence, they can still be mistaken for and "pass" as other human users (Jones 2015; Edwards et al. 2013; Gehl 2013). This is, Mowbray (2002: 2) points out, not "a feature of the sophistication of bot design, but of the low bandwidth communication of the online social space" where it is "much easier to convincingly simulate a human agent." This occurred, for instance, in the case of the Ashley Madison "fembots," which were simple, prefabricated computer scripts that were designed to initiate a brief amorous exchange with (mostly male) users in the hope of moving them into the ranks of paying customers. Even if the programming of these "sexbots" was rather simple, somewhat shoddy, and even stupid, a significant number of male users found them socially engaging – so much so that they shared intimate secrets with the bot and, most importantly, took out the credit card in the hope of continuing the conversation.

Despite this knowledge, these software implementations cannot be written off as mere instruments or tools. Mowbray concludes:

> The examples in this paper show that a bot may cause harm to other users or to the community as a whole by the will of its programmers or other users, but that it also may cause harm through nobody's fault because of the combination of circumstances involving some combination of its programming, the actions and mental or emotional states of human users who interact with it, behavior of other bots and of the environment, and the social economy of the community. (2002: 4)

Unlike AGI, which would occupy a position that would, at least theoretically, be reasonably close to that of a human agent and therefore not be able to be dismissed as a mere tool, these socialbots simply muddy the water (which is probably worse) by leaving undecided the question of whether or not they are tools. And in the process, they leave the question of social responsibility both unsettled and unsettling.

9.3 Responses to Responsibility Gaps

What we have seen, therefore, are situations where our theory of technology – a theory that has considerable history behind it and that has been determined to be as applicable to simple hand tools as it is to complex technological systems – encounters significant difficulties responding to or answering for developments with autonomous technology, machine-learning systems, and even mindless chatbots. In the face of these challenges, there are at least three possible responses.

9.3.1 Instrumentalism 2.0

We can try to respond as we have previously responded, treating these recent innovations in AI and robotics as mere instruments or tools. Joanna Bryson makes a persuasive case for this approach in her provocatively titled essay "Robots Should be Slaves": "My thesis is that robots should be built, marketed and considered legally as slaves, not companion peers" (2010: 63). Although this might sound harsh, the argument is persuasive, precisely because it draws on and is underwritten by the instrumental theory of technology and a long-standing tradition, going back at least to Aristotle (1944: 1253b26–40), of defining "slave" as a "living tool." This decision has both advantages and disadvantages.

On the positive side, it reaffirms human exceptionalism, making it absolutely clear that it is only the human being who possess rights and responsibilities. Technologies, no matter how sophisticated they become, are and will continue to be mere tools of human action, nothing more. "We design, manufacture, own and operate robots," Bryson (2010: 65) writes. "They are entirely our responsibility. We determine their goals and behaviour, either directly or indirectly through specifying their intelligence, or even more indirectly by specifying how they acquire their own intelligence." Furthermore, this line of reasoning seems to be entirely consistent with current legal structures and decisions. Matthew Gladden concludes:

> As a tool for use by human beings, questions of legal responsibility for any harmful actions performed by such a robot revolve around well-established questions of product liability for design defects (Calverley 2008: 533; Datteri 2013) on the part of its producer, professional malpractice on the part of its human operator, and, at a more generalized level, political responsibility for those legislative and licensing bodies that allowed such devices to be created and used. (2016: 184)

But this approach, for all its usefulness, has at least two problems. First, in strictly applying and enforcing the instrumental theory, we might inadvertently restrict technological innovation and the development of responsible governance. If, for example, we hold developers responsible for the unintended consequences of AI or robots that have been designed with learning capabilities, this could lead engineers and manufactures to be rather conservative with the development and commercialization of new technology in an effort to protect themselves from legal liability. Had the engineers at Microsoft been assigned responsibility for the hate speech produced by Tay, it is very possible that they and the corporation for whom they worked (or the legal department within the corporation) would have thought twice before releasing such technology into the wild. This might, it could be argued, be a positive development, similar to the safety measures and product-testing requirements that are currently employed in the development of pharmaceuticals, transportation systems, and other industries. But it could also restrict and hinder robust development of AI systems and machine-learning applications.

There is a similar problem with self-driving cars and the development of governance. As the NHTSA explicitly noted in its letter to Google, trying to assign the responsibility of "driver" to some human being riding in the autonomously driven vehicle would be both practically and legally inaccurate.

> No human occupant of the SDV [self-driven vehicle] could meet the definition of "driver" in Section 571.3 given Google's described motor vehicle design, even if it were possible for a human occupant to determine the location of Google's steering control system, and sit "immediately behind" it, that human occupant would not be capable of actually driving the vehicle as described by Google. If no human occupant of the vehicle can actually drive the vehicle, it is more reasonable to identify the "driver" as whatever (as opposed to whoever) is doing the driving. (Hemmersbaugh 2016)

For this reason, "accepting an AI as a legal driver eases the government's rule-writing process" (Ross 2016) by making existing law applicable to recent changes in automotive technology.

Second, strict application of the instrumental theory to intelligent machines, as Bryson directly acknowledges, produces a new class of instrumental servant or "slave" – what we might call "slavery 2.0" (Gunkel 2012: 86). The problem here, as Rodney Brooks insightfully points out, is not with the concept of "slavery" per se (we should not, in other words, get hung up on words); the problem has to do with the kind of robotic mechanisms to which this term comes to be applied:

> Fortunately we are not doomed to create a race of slaves that is unethical to have as slaves. Our refrigerators work twenty-four hours a day seven

days a week, and we do not feel the slightest moral concern for them. We will make many robots that are equally unemotional, unconscious, and unempathetic. We will use them as slaves just as we use our dishwashers, vacuum cleaners, and automobiles today. But those that we make more intelligent, that we give emotions to, and that we empathize with, will be a problem. We had better be careful just what we build, because we might end up liking them, and then we will be morally responsible for their well-being. Sort of like children. (2002: 195)

As Brooks explains, our refrigerators work tirelessly on our behalf and "we do not feel the slightest moral concern for them." But things will be very different with social robots, like Jibo or Paro, that invite and are intentionally designed for emotional investment and attachment.

Contra Brooks, however, it seems we are already at this point with things that are (at least metaphorically) as cold and impersonal as the refrigerator. As reported in Chapter 2, soldiers have formed surprisingly close personal bonds with their units' EOD robots – giving them names, awarding them battlefield promotions, and risking their own lives to protect that of the machine. And this happens in direct opposition to what otherwise sounds like good common sense: They are just technologies – instruments or tools that work on our behalf and feel nothing.

This "correction," in fact, is part and parcel of the problem. This is because the difficulties with strict reassertion of the instrumental theory have little or nothing to do with speculation about what the mechanism may or may not feel. The problem is with the kind of social environment it produces. As Immanuel Kant (1963: 239) argued concerning indirect duties to nonhuman animals, animal abuse is wrong, not because of how the animal might feel (which is, according to Kant's strict epistemological restrictions, forever and already inaccessible to us – who among us knows, for example, what it is really like to be a lobster?), but because of the adverse effect such action would have on other human beings and society as a whole. In other words, applying the instrumental theory to these new kinds of mechanism and technological affordances, although seemingly reasonable and useful, could have potentially devastating consequences for us, our world, and the other entities we encounter here.

9.3.2 Machine ethics

Alternatively, we can entertain the possibility of what has been called "machine ethics," and there have, in fact, been a number of recent proposals addressing this opportunity. Wallach and Allen (2009: 4), for example, not only predict that "there will be a catastrophic incident brought about by a computer system making a decision independent of human oversight," but use this fact as justification for developing "moral machines," advanced technological systems that are able to respond independently to ethically challenging situations.

One of the first and most cited versions of this kind of "morality for machines" appears in the science fiction of Isaac Asimov. Beginning with the short story "Runaround," which was included in his book *I, Robot* (originally published in 1950), Asimov formulated and described what he called the three laws of robotics:

1 A robot may not injure a human being or, through inaction, allow a human being to come to harm.
2 A robot must obey any orders given to it by human beings, except where such orders would conflict with the First Law.
3 A robot must protect its own existence as long as such protection does not conflict with the First or Second Laws. (2008: 37)

The three laws are entirely functional and are designed to ensure safe integration of robots into human society. As Wendell Wallach (2008: 465) explains, "engineers have always been concerned with designing tools that are safe and reliable. Sensitivity to the moral implications of two or more courses of action in limited contexts can be understood as an extension of the engineer's concern with designing appropriate control mechanisms for safety into computers and robots." Despite the intuitive appeal and simplicity of Asimov's three laws, they were devised for the purposes of generating imaginative science fiction stories. They are not and were never intended to be actual engineering principles, and efforts to apply and make the rules computable have resulted in less than successful outcomes (Anderson 2008).

For this reason, there have been a number of efforts to formulate more precise and operational rule sets. Michael Anderson and Susan Leigh Anderson (2011), for example, not only have experimented with the application of various moral theories to machine decision-making and action, but have even suggested that "computers might be better at following an ethical theory than most humans," because humans "tend to be inconsistent in their reasoning" and "have difficulty juggling the complexities of ethical decision-making" owing to the sheer volume of data that need to be taken into account and processed (Anderson and Anderson 2007: 5). Case in point – so-called "killer robots." According to the roboticist Ronald Arkin, autonomous robots might be better at following the rules of military engagement. Among Arkin's reasons for making this claim are the following: (1) robots do not need "to have self-preservation as a foremost drive" and therefore "can be used in a self-sacrificing manner if needed"; (2) machines can be equipped with better sensors that exceed the limited capabilities of the human faculties; (3) "they can be designed without emotions that cloud their judgment or result in anger and frustration with ongoing battlefield events"; and (4) "they can integrate more information from more sources far faster before responding with lethal force than a human possible could in realtime" (Arkin 2009: 29–30).

These proposals, it is important to point out, do not necessarily require that we first resolve the "big questions" of AGI, robot sentience, or machine consciousness. As Wallach (2015: 242) points out, these kinds of machines need only be "functionally moral." That is, they can be designed to be "capable of making ethical determinations . . . even if they have little or no actual understanding of the tasks they perform." The precedent for this way of thinking can be found in corporate law and business ethics. Corporations are, according to both national and international law, legal persons (French 1979). They are considered "persons" (which is, we should note, a legal classification and not an ontological category) not because they are conscious entities like we assume ourselves to be, but because social circumstances make it necessary to assign personhood to these artificial entities for the purposes of social organization and jurisprudence. Consequently, if entirely artificial and human fabricated entities, like Google or IBM, are legal persons with associated social responsibilities, it would be possible, it seems, to extend the same considerations to an AI or robot, like IBM's Watson. The question, it is important to point out, is not whether these mechanisms are or could be "natural persons" with what is assumed to be "genuine" social status; it is, rather, whether it would make sense and be expedient, from both a legal and moral perspective, to treat these mechanisms as moral and legal subjects in the same way that we currently do for corporations, organizations, and other artifacts.

Once again, this decision sounds reasonable and justified. It extends both moral and legal responsibility to these other socially aware and interactive entities, and recognizes, following the predictions of Norbert Wiener (1988: 16), that the social situation of the future will involve not just human-to-human interactions but relationships between humans and machines and machines and machines. But this shift in perspective also has significant costs.

First, it requires that we rethink everything we thought we knew about ourselves, technology, and ethics. It entails that we learn to think beyond human exceptionalism, technological instrumentalism, and many of the other -isms that have helped us make sense of our world and our place in it. In effect, it calls for a thorough reconceptualization of who or what should be considered a legitimate center of moral concern and why. This is not unprecedented. We have, in fact, confronted and responded to challenges like this before. In the latter part of the twentieth century, for instance, moral philosophers and legal theorists began to reconsider the status of nonhuman animals. The important question is whether and to what extent this progressive effort at expanding moral and legal inclusion could or should be extended to intelligent and/or sociable machines (for more on this, see Gunkel 2012).

Second, robots and AI that are designed to follow rules and operate within the boundaries of some kind of programmed restraint might turn out to be something other than what is typically recognized as a responsible agent. Terry Winograd (1990: 182–3), for instance, warns against something he calls "the bureaucracy of mind," "where rules can be followed without interpretive judgments." He continues:

> When a person views his or her job as the correct application of a set of rules (whether human-invoked or computer-based), there is a loss of personal responsibility or commitment. The "I just follow the rules" of the bureaucratic clerk has its direct analog in "That's what the knowledge base says." The individual is not committed to appropriate results, but to faithful application of procedures. (1990: 183)

Mark Coeckelbergh (2010: 236) paints a potentially more disturbing picture. For him, the problem is not the advent of "artificial bureaucrats" but of "psychopathic robots." The term "psychopathy" has traditionally been used to name a kind of personality disorder characterized by an abnormal lack of empathy, which is masked by an ability to appear normal in most social situations. Functional morality, like that specified by Anderson and Anderson and by Wallach and Allen, intentionally designs and produces what are arguably "artificial psychopaths" – mechanisms that have no capacity for empathy but which follow rules and, in doing so, can appear to behave in morally appropriate ways. These psychopathic machines would, Coeckelbergh (2010: 236) argues, "follow rules but act without fear, compassion, care, and love. This lack of emotion would render them non-moral agents – i.e. agents that follow rules without being moved by moral concerns – and they would even lack the capacity to discern what is of value. They would be morally blind."[13]

Efforts in "machine ethics" (or whatever other nomenclature comes to be utilized to name this development) effectively seek to widen the circle of moral subjects to include what had been previously excluded and marginalized as neutral instruments of human action. This is, it is important to note, not some blanket statement that would turn everything that was a tool into a moral subject. It is the recognition, following Marx, that not everything technological is reducible to a tool, and that some devices – what Marx called "machines" and what Winner calls "autonomous technology" – might need to be programmed in such a way as to behave reasonably and responsibly for the sake of respecting human individuals and communities.

The proposal has the obvious advantage of responding to moral intuitions: if it is the machine that is making the decision and taking action in the world with little or no direct human oversight, it would only make sense to hold it responsible (or at least partially accountable) for the actions it deploys and to design it with some form of constraint in order to control for possible bad outcomes. But doing so has considerable costs. Even if we bracket the questions of AGI, machine consciousness, and/or super intelligence, designing robotic systems that follow prescribed rules might provide the right kind of external behaviors, but the motivations for doing so might be lacking. As Noel Sharkey writes in a consideration of autonomous weapons:

> Even if a robot was fully equipped with all the rules from the Laws of War, and had, by some mysterious means, a way of making the same discriminations as humans make, it could not be ethical in the same way as is an ethical human. Ask any judge what they think about blindly following rules and laws. (2012: 121)

Consequently, what we actually get from these efforts might be something very different from (and maybe even worse than) what we had hoped to achieve.

9.3.3 Joint agency

Finally, we can try to balance these two opposing positions by taking an intermediate hybrid approach, distributing responsibility across a network of interacting human and machine components. F. Allan Hanson (2009: 91), for instance, introduces something he calls "extended agency theory," which is itself a kind of extension/elaboration of the "actor-network-theory" initially described by Bruno Latour (2005). According to Hanson, who takes what appears to be a practical and entirely pragmatic view of things, machine responsibility is still undecided and, for that reason, one should be careful not to go too far in speculating about things: "Possible future development of automated systems and new ways of thinking about responsibility will spawn plausible arguments for the moral responsibility of non-human agents. For the present, however, questions about the mental qualities of robots and computers make it unwise to go this far" (2009: 94). Instead, Hanson suggests that this problem may be resolved by considering various theories of "joint responsibility," where "moral agency is distributed over both human and technological artifacts" (2009: 94).

This proposal, which can be seen as a kind of elaboration of Helen Nissenbaum's (1996) "many hands" thesis, has been gaining traction, especially because it appears to be able to deal with and respond to complexity. According to Ibo van de Poel et al. (2012: 49–50): "When engineering structures fail or an engineering disaster occurs, the question who is to be held responsible is often asked. However, in complex engineering projects it is often quite difficult to pinpoint responsibility." As an example of this, the authors point to an investigation of one hundred international shipping accidents undertaken by Wagenaar and Groenewegen (1987: 596): "Accidents appear to be the result of highly complex coincidences which could rarely be foreseen by the people involved. The unpredictability is due to the large number of causes and by the spread of the information over the participants." For van de Poel et al., however, a more informative example can be obtained from climate change:

> We think climate change is a typical example of a many hands problem because it is a phenomenon that is very complex, in which a large number of individuals are causally involved, but in which the role of individuals in isolation is rather small. In such situations, it is usually very difficult to pinpoint individual responsibility. Climate change is also a good example of how technology might contribute to the occurrence of the problem of many hands because technology obviously plays a major role in climate change, both as cause and as a possible remedy. (2012: 50–1)

Extended agency theory, therefore, moves away from the anthropocentric individualism that has been prevalent in Western thought – what Hanson calls "moral individualism" – and introduces an ethic that is more in line with recent innovations in ecological thinking:

When the subject is perceived more as a verb than a noun – a way of combining different entities in different ways to engage in various activities – the distinction between Self and Other loses both clarity and significance. When human individuals realize that they do not act alone but together with other people and things in extended agencies, they are more likely to appreciate the mutual dependency of all the participants for their common well-being. The notion of joint responsibility associated with this frame of mind is more conducive than moral individualism to constructive engagement with other people, with technology, and with the environment in general. (Hanson 2009: 98)

Similar proposals have been advanced and advocated by Deborah Johnson and Peter-Paul Verbeek for dealing with innovation in information technology. "When computer systems behave," Johnson (2006: 202) writes, "there is a triad of intentionality at work, the intentionality of the computer system designer, the intentionality of the system, and the intentionality of the user." "I will," Verbeek (2011: 13) argues, "defend the thesis that ethics should be approached as a matter of human-technological associations. When taking the notion of technological mediation seriously, claiming that technologies are human agents would be as inadequate as claiming that ethics is a solely human affair." For both Johnson and Verbeek, responsibility is something distributed across a network of interacting components and these networks include not just other human persons, but organizations, natural objects, and technologies.

This hybrid formulation – what Verbeek calls "the ethics of things" and Hanson terms "extended agency theory" – has both advantages and disadvantages. To its credit, this approach appears to be attentive to the exigencies of life in the twenty-first century. None of us, in fact, makes decisions or acts in a vacuum; we are always and already tangled up in networks of interactive elements that complicate the assignment of responsibility and decisions concerning who or what is able to answer for what comes to pass. And these networks have always included others – not only other human beings, but institutions, organizations, and even technological components like the robots and algorithms that increasingly help organize and dispense with social activity. This combined approach, however, still requires that someone decide and answer for what aspects of responsibility belong to the machine and what should be retained for or attributed to the other elements in the network. In other words, "extended agency theory" will still need to decide between *who* is able to answer for a decision or action and *what* can be considered a mere instrument.

Furthermore, these decisions are (for better or worse) often flexible and variable, allowing one part of the network to protect itself from culpability by instrumentalizing its role and deflecting responsibility and the obligation to respond elsewhere. This occurred, for example, during the Nuremberg trials at the end of World War II, when low-level functionaries tried to deflect responsibility up the chain of command by claiming that they "were just following orders." But the deflection can also move in the opposite direction, as was the case with the prisoner abuse scandal at the Abu Ghraib prison in Iraq during the presidency of George W. Bush. In this situation, individuals in the upper echelons of the network deflected responsibility down the chain of command by arguing that the documented abuse was not ordered by the administration but was the autonomous action of a "few bad apples" in the enlisted ranks. Finally, there can be situations where no one or nothing is accountable for anything. In this case, moral and legal responsibility is disseminated across the elements of the network in such a way that no one person, institution, or technology is culpable or held responsible. This is precisely what happened in the wake of the 2008 financial crisis. The bundling and reselling of mortgage-backed securities was considered to be so complex and dispersed across the network that, in the final analysis, no one could be identified as being responsible for the collapse.

9.4 Duty Now and For the Future

Our concern in this final chapter has been with the concept and exigencies of responsibility. Efforts to decide the question of accountability in the face of technology are typically not a problem, precisely because instrumental theory assigns responsibility to the human being and defines technology as nothing more than a mere tool or instrument. In these cases, it is the human being who is responsible for responding or answering for what the machine does or does not do (or perhaps more accurately stated, what comes to be done or not done through the instrumentality of the mechanism). This way of thinking has worked rather well, with little or no significant friction, for more than 2,500 years. But, as we have seen, recent innovations in technology – autonomous machines, learning algorithms, and socially interactive bots and robots – challenge the instrumental theory by opening up what Matthias (2004) calls "responsibility gaps."

In response to these challenges – in an effort to close or at least remediate the gap – we have considered three alternatives. On the one side, there is strict application of the instrumental theory, which would restrict all questions of responsibility to human beings and define AI and robots, no matter how sophisticated their design and operations, as nothing more than tools or instruments of human decision-making and action. On the other side, there are efforts to assign some level of moral agency to machines. Even if these mechanisms are not (at least for now) able to be full moral subjects, they can, it is argued, be functionally responsible. And situated somewhere in between these two opposing positions is a kind of intermediate option that distributes responsibility (and the ability to respond) across a network of interacting components, some human and some entirely otherwise.

These three options clearly define a spectrum of possible responses with each mode having its own particular advantages and disadvantages. Consequently, how we – individually but also as a collective – decide to respond to these opportunities and challenges will have a profound effect on the way we conceptualize our place in the world, who we decide to include in the community of moral subjects, and what we exclude from such consideration and why. But no matter how it is decided, it is a decision – quite literally a cut that institutes difference and makes a difference. We are, therefore, responsible both for deciding who or even what is a moral subject and, in the process, for determining the current state of, and future possibility for, responsible use and application of robotics and AI.

Summary of Key Points

- The word "responsibility" means, quite literally, the ability to respond. In the case of technology, the ability to respond is typically assigned to a human designer, developer, or user. This is a direct consequence of the instrumental theory of technology.
- Recent technological innovation with AI and robots, like autonomous machines, learning algorithms, and social robots, challenges this instrumentalist explanation by opening gaps in the way we identify and assign responsibility.
- There have been three ways of responding to these responsibility gaps: (1) reassert instrumental theory in the face of technologies that appear to be more than instruments; (2) entertain the possibility of machines becoming moral agents in their own right; or (3) distribute responsibility across a network of interacting agents consisting of both human and technological components.

- Although all three methods have something to recommend them, there is and remains considerable debate about which one or ones provide the best possible solution to respond to and take responsibility for twenty-first-century innovations in AI and robotics.

Part IV

Maker Exercises

Introduction

This final section contains five maker exercises that are designed to support the information and instruction provided in the substantive chapters with "learn by doing" activities. Each exercise is connected to and designed to support one of the chapters:

- *Demystifying ELIZA.* The first exercise supports the second chapter. Its objective is to demystify the ELIZA application through direct interaction with the chatbot and the construction of a simple working version – a kind of DIY ELIZA.
- *Algorithms.* The second exercise supports Chapter 3's effort to sort out and make sense of the difference between GOFAI symbolic reasoning and neural network machine learning. In this exercise, students will construct two temperature conversion algorithms, one using the symbolic reasoning approach and the other using a neural network and reinforcement learning.
- *Machine Translation.* The third exercise is paired with Chapter 4 and provides students with an opportunity to build a simple translation system using one of the MT methodologies profiled in that chapter.
- *Chatbot and Quasi-Loebner Prize.* The fourth exercise is connected to Chapter 5. Here students will use AIML (artificial intelligence markup language) and the Pandorabots engine to create a conversational chatbot that can go head-to-head with each other in a quasi-Loebner Prize competition.
- *Template NLG.* The fifth maker exercise supports the investigation of computational creativity that is examined in Chapter 6. In this final exercise, students will create a punk rock lyric generator using template NLG.

All the exercises will be developed using simple markup or scripting languages – i.e., hypertext markup language (HTML), artificial intelligence markup language (AIML), and Javascript. The code you write will be run directly in the web browser. Therefore, it will require no compiling or other intermediate processing. All the maker exercises can be written using a text editor like Notepad++ (Windows and Linux) or BBEdit (Mac). Please DO NOT use MS-Word or another word processing application, as they insert their own proprietary formatting instructions. Both applications are available as free downloads at the following URLs:

Notepad++: http://notepad-plus-plus.org/
BBEdit: http://www.barebones.com/products/bbedit/

One final note before you begin. The exercises are collected here in what is arguably an appendix to the book. This has been done because they are optional. That said, taking the time to do the exercises can be useful and informative for the following three reasons:

1 They offer unique opportunities for practical instruction that can support and reinforce the information presented in the chapters.
2 They offer students hands-on experience that can help develop both skills and experience with the technology.
3 They respond to and accommodate differences in learning styles and approaches, providing students with more than one way to succeed.

The great thing about writing code is that it is functional. It is fun. And it is forgiving. When you write an application, even a simple application, from scratch and run it in your web browser, you actually see how things work. Doing so is fundamentally enjoyable and empowering, because you take control of the technology and you make it do something that you have designated. And – worst case scenario – if it does not work, no problem. You can go back, find the source of the error, make a fix, and run it again. So give it try. There is nothing to lose and everything to gain.

Exercise 1
Demystifying ELIZA

How ELIZA works is not magic. It is simply a clever application of standard principles in computer science and you can create your own demonstration version of the program without needing to know much about application development. In this first maker exercise, we will do the following three things:

1 Spend some time talking to ELIZA to get first-hand experience with the application.
2 "Pop the hood" on the ELIZA program to see how it actually works.
3 Use Javascript to write a simple demonstration version of a chatbot. In effect, we will build our own (stripped down and simplified) version of ELIZA.

Talk to ELIZA

If you have never interacted with ELIZA, you can access a number of web-distributed emulations. Although none of these is the "original" ELIZA program written by Weizenbaum, they have all been developed according to his initial designs, function like the original ELIZA program, and give users an idea of what Weizenbaum was able to achieve in the mid-1960s with some rather simple lines of computer code. One of the more popular versions is a Javascript implementation originally written by Michal Wallace and significantly enhanced by George Dunlop. This version of the program (which, according to its creators, may be redistributed and modified on the condition that the credit line is retained) can be accessed at http://gunkelweb.com/introAI/eliza.html

Spend some time (10–15 minutes) interacting with ELIZA, and in the process take note of how the program operates and responds to your input. Try to test the boundaries of ELIZA's conversational behavior. See if you can trip it up or make it produce an error that betrays its machinic nature. When you are finished, try to answer these questions:

- Who or what were you talking with?
- Is ELIZA a good conversational partner?
- Would the application successfully pass the Turing Test? Why or why not?
- Does ELIZA understand or at least appear to understand language?

The Inner Workings of ELIZA

ELIZA is, technically speaking, a rather simple natural language processing (NLP) application, "consisting mainly of general methods for analyzing sentences and sentence fragments, locating so-called key words in texts, assembling sentences from fragments, and so on" (Weizenbaum 1976: 188). For this reason, ELIZA does not, strictly speaking, "understand" (or even need to understand) the word sequences that it processes as input and generates as output. In terms of its programming instructions, ELIZA's conversational behavior is facilitated by what Weizenbaum (1967: 475) called "a set of decomposition and reassembly rules": "A decomposition rule is a data structure that searches a text for specific patterns, and, if such patterns are found, decomposes the text into disjoint constituents. A reassembly rule is a specification for the construction of a new text by means of recombinations of old and possible addition of new constituents."

If you know Javascript, you can look through ELIZA's source code ("View Page Source" in the web browser) and see these various features in the program instructions. If you are unfamiliar with this programming language, you can still get a feel for what is going on by paying attention to the programmer's notes, which are embedded in the code as nonexecutable comments. In Javascript, comments are indicated by two slashes and look like this:

```
//this is a comment
```

Here, for example, is an excerpt of the scripted responses that are available to and encoded in the application. There are 116 total responses that can be selected at random and/or controlled by various programming parameters.

```
response[ 29]="How long have you been<*";
response[ 30]="Do you believe it is normal
   to be<*";
response[ 31]="Do you enjoy being<*";
response[ 32]="We were discussing you, not
   me.";
response[ 33]="Oh. . . <*";
response[ 34]="You're not really talking
   about me, are you?";
response[ 35]="What would it mean to you if
   you got<*";
```

As you can see, some of the responses are fully pre-scripted, like "We were discussing you, not me." In other cases, the response is partially formulated and includes <* at the end of the text string, which appends a word that had been extracted from the user input to the end of the sentence. This way, if the user writes "I have been sad," the word "sad" can be identified, extracted from the user input, and then appended to the end of the pre-scripted response, producing the following: "Do you believe it is normal to be sad?" By doing this, it looks as if ELIZA is actually "listening" to you and responding to what you write. Additionally, you might notice this comment and coded instructions:

```
// Fake time thinking to allow for user
// self reflection
// And to give the illusion that some
// thinking is going on

   var elizaresponse = "";

   function think(){
     document.Eliza.input.value = "";
     if( elizaresponse != "" ){
        respond(); }
     else {
        setTimeout("think()", 250); }
```

This is a rather clever inclusion. As indicated in the comments, the program is designed to delay the output and display of ELIZA's responses by 250 milliseconds in order to "give the illusion that some thinking is going on."

DIY ELIZA

The best way to understand and appreciate the capabilities and the limitations of ELIZA is to write your own working version of the program from scratch. This demonstration version will not be as complex as the one initially developed by Weizenbaum, but it will still give you good, hands-on experience with developing a basic version of it. For this exercise, we are going to be using Javascript, an easy-to-use (and learn) web programming language that runs in the browser. You can write the program instructions in a text editor like Notepad++ (Windows and Linux) or BBEdit (Mac). But DO NOT use MS-Word or another word processing application. Links to these two applications are provided in the Introduction to this section.

The first version of our DIY ELIZA will be rather simple – just under twenty lines of code as compared to the five-hundred-plus lines in the demonstration version of ELIZA with which you interacted previously. To begin, open the text editor (Notepad++ or BBEdit) and write the following instructions line-by-line exactly as you see it displayed in Figure Ex1.1. The first two lines are HTML tags that are necessary to run the program in the browser. The lines that follow the <script> tag are the Javascript instructions and describe the behavior of our DIY ELIZA. The line after the closing </script> tag is another HTML element that simply makes a link to permit you to reload the application.

The lines of Javascript code employ the **prompt()** method, which will automatically generate a dialogue box when the application is interpreted by the browser. The text inside the **prompt()** designates what ELIZA says to you. What you type in response to ELIZA's statement is stored in a variable with the names: **response1** and **response2**. So what's happening here is that ELIZA says something to you in the **prompt()**. If you have typed a reply to ELIZA's statement – this is coded **if (response1)** – then ELIZA responds to that with another **prompt()**. And then goes through the same process again.

After writing the Javascript code, save your file to the desktop of your computer (or in a removable drive, if you happen to be

```
1
2    <html>
3    <body>
4
5    <script language="javascript">
6
7    response1 = prompt("I am ELIZA. How can I help you?");
8
9    if (response1)
10   response2 = prompt("hello, nice to meet you");
11
12   if (response2)
13   response3 = prompt("What would you like to talk about?");
14
15   </script>
16
17   <a href="eliza_demo.html">Start Again</a>
18
19   </body>
20   </html>
21
```

Figure Ex1.1   Basic version of DIY ELIZA

using one) with the following name: **eliza1.html** Make sure that you include the .html extension so that the file is identified as an html document and not a txt file. After you save the document, open it in the browser (preferably Firefox or Chrome, as they have better Javascript support). If you have written the code correctly, you should get a series of dialogue boxes that display ELIZA's statement and allow for you to enter a response (Figure Ex1.2).

If you do not see this result, then you have an error in your coded instructions. You will need to return to the text editor and repair the error. Since we are only working with twenty lines of code, the best way to do this is compare what you wrote line-by-line to the code that is presented in Figure Ex1.1. After you find and then fix the error, re-save the document and then open it in the browser.

This first version of DIY ELIZA is able to have a very limited conversation. We can expand its capabilities by adding additional lines of code, saving this modified version, and then running it in the browser (Figure Ex1.3).

So far, our DIY ELIZA is just replying to us with pre-scripted statements. But Weizenbaum's version did more than this. It could also take user input and then insert it into the scripted statement in order to make it look as if ELIZA understood what had been written.

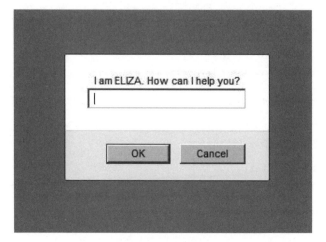

Figure Ex1.2   Display of DIY ELIZA in Firefox

```
1
2  <html>
3  <body>
4
5  <script language="javascript">
6
7  response1 = prompt("I am ELIZA. How can I help you?");
8
9  if (response1)
10 response2 = prompt("hello, nice to meet you");
11
12 if (response2)
13 response3 = prompt("What would you like to talk about?");
14
15 if (response3)
16 response4 = prompt("Is this something that worries you?");
17
18 if (response4)
19 response5 = prompt("Why is that? Tell me more about it.");
20
21 </script>
22
23 <a href="eliza_demo.html">Start Again</a>
24
25 </body>
26 </html>
27
```

Figure Ex1.3   Modified version of DIY ELIZA

```
1
2   <html>
3   <body>
4
5   <script language="javascript">
6
7   response1 = prompt("I am ELIZA. How can I help you?");
8
9   if (response1)
10  response2 = prompt("What is your name?");
11
12  if (response2)
13  response3 = prompt("Hello, " + response2 + " What would you like to talk about?");
14
15  if (response3)
16  response4 = prompt("Is this something that worries you?");
17
18  if (response4)
19  response5 = prompt("Why is that? Tell me more about it.");
20
21  </script>
22
23  <a href="eliza_demo.html">Start Again</a>
24
25  </body>
26  </html>
27
```

**Figure Ex1.4   Third version of DIY ELIZA. This one "knows"
your name**

We can do the same with our DIY ELIZA. In this third and final
version of the program, we are going to make some small modifications to the previous one. The changes begin at line 9 and continue
through line 13 (Figure Ex1.4).

This third version of DIY ELIZA will generate a statement with
your name. The way this works is that ELIZA asks you for your name
(line 10). The text that you enter in response to this **prompt()** is
stored in the variable **response2**. The next statement from ELIZA
(line13) is created by concatenating – or "jamming together" – the
word "Hello" followed by the value that is stored in **response2** (the
name you supplied) followed by the text "What would you like to
talk about?" This produces a statement that inserts the name you had
provided, making it look as if ELIZA has learned your name.

Exercise 2
Algorithms

We know, from what was covered in Chapter 3, that "algorithm" names a problem-solving procedure that can be computationally implemented – meaning that it can be formulated in such a way that it runs on a digital computer. We also know that there are two fundamentally different approaches for developing algorithms: symbolic reasoning or what is also called, sometimes pejoratively, "good old fashioned AI" (GOFAI), and neural networks or connectionism. In this exercise, we will get some hands-on experience with both methodologies by writing two different versions of a temperature conversion algorithm.

GOFAI Algorithm

The first version of our temperature converter will be developed using a rule-based, symbolic reasoning approach or GOFAI. We will write coded instructions that tell the computer step-by-step what to do in order to make the temperature conversion from degrees Fahrenheit to degrees Celsius. We will proceed in three steps, starting with a very simple conversion algorithm and then add incrementally to the code to make the temperature converter more accurate and robust (Figure Ex2.1).

Let's work through the code item by item so that we understand what is happening and how. The algorithm begins by defining two variables. The first variable, **TempF**, is assigned the number that the user types into the **prompt()** dialogue box. In other words, when you open the application, you will be presented with a prompt that asks you to "Enter degrees Fahrenheit." This number (because

```
1
2  <html>
3  <body>
4    <script>
5
6      var TempF = prompt("Enter degrees Fahrenheit");
7      var TempC;
8
9      if(TempF == 32) TempC = 0;
10     else TempC = "UNDEFINED";
11
12     document.write("<h1>" + TempF + " converts to " + TempC + "</h1>");
13
14   </script>
15 </body>
16 </html>
17
```

Figure Ex2.1   Temperature converter version 1.1

degrees Fahrenheit takes a numeric value) is then assigned to the **TempF** variable. The second variable is simply declared and not assigned a value. It will eventually be assigned a numeric value in the code below.

The next pair of lines (lines 9 and 10) are a conditional statement. The condition simply tests whether the user entered a particular number in the prompt by asking if the value of **TempF** is equivalent to 32. (You will note that equivalency in Javascript is indicated by a double equals sign. There is a good reason for this, but getting into it would take us on a long detour through the nuances of object-oriented programming languages, and that is neither necessary nor important for what we are doing at this stage.) If the condition is met – if the value of **TempF** is 32 – then we assign the numeric value 0 to the **TempC** variable. If the condition is not met – i.e., the value assigned to **TempF** is something other than 32 – then we assign a different value to **TempC**, namely a text string that says "UNDEFINED."

Line 12 applies the **write()** method to the web **document** in order to display a message in the browser. This is the algorithm's output. The message is assembled or concatenated by inserting the variables into a sequence of text strings. It begins with an HTML tag for a heading, which will make the displayed text big and bold. It then inserts the value assigned to the variable **TempF** followed by another text string that says **"converts to,"** followed by the value assigned to the variable **TempC**. It ends by closing the HTML tag for the heading. Once you have written all the lines of code, save the file as "temp_converter1.html" and open it in your browser. If it

```
1
2  <html>
3  <body>
4    <script>
5
6      var TempF = prompt("Enter degrees Fahrenheit");
7      var TempC;
8
9      if(TempF == 32) TempC = 0;
10
11     else if(TempF == 50) TempC = 10;
12
13     else if(TempF ==99) TempC = 38;
14
15     else TempC = "UNDEFINED";
16
17     document.write("<h1>" + TempF + " converts to " + TempC + "</h1>");
18
19   </script>
20 </body>
21 </html>
22
```

Figure Ex2.2   Temperature converter version 1.2

was written correctly, you should be able to convert 32°F to 0°C. All other values entered into the prompt will produce UNDEFINED, since the algorithm only "knows" (or can process) one particular temperature conversion.

A temperature conversion algorithm that can only process one temperature is not very useful. So let's add some additional temperature data to make the application more robust. It will still be simple, but it will get us moving in the right direction (Figure Ex2.2).

This second version accommodates additional temperature conversions by adding two lines (lines 11 and 13) to the conditional statement. Both of these begin with *else if*, which is just an intermediate step in the conditional statement. In other words, if the first condition fails, e.g. the value of **TempF** is not 32, then line 11 tests whether the value of **TempF** is 50. If it is, then the value 10 is assigned to **TempC**. If it is not, then the next conditional (line 13) asks whether the value of **TempF** is 99. If it is, then the value 38 is assigned to **TempC**. If not, then we proceed to the final element of the conditional, the *else*, and assign UNDEFINED to **TempC**.

Clearly this is better – it is able to convert three temperatures – but it is still a far cry from something usable. In particular, this version of the temperature converter is not able to deal with temperature values situated in between the numbers that it knows (or has been told how

```
1
2   <html>
3   <body>
4     <script>
5
6       var TempF = prompt("Enter degrees Fahrenheit");
7       var TempC;
8
9       if(TempF == 32) TempC = 0;
10
11      else if(TempF > 32 && TempF < 49) TempC = 4;
12
13      else if(TempF == 50) TempC = 10;
14
15      else if(TempF > 50 && TempF < 98) TempC = 21;
16
17      else if(TempF ==99) TempC = 38;
18
19      else TempC = "UNDEFINED";
20
21      document.write("<h1>" + TempF + " converts to " + TempC + "</h1>");
22
23    </script>
24  </body>
25  </html>
26
```

Figure Ex2.3   Temperature converter version 1.3

to process), e.g., 35, 42, or 80. Consequently, the final version of the GOFAI algorithm will include a way to handle these in-between values (Figure Ex2.3).

This third version now generates numeric responses for all input values in the range 32–99. We achieve this by adding more *else if* lines to the sequence of conditional statements. The first new line (line 11) covers values greater than 32 and less than 49. In effect, it asks whether the value of the **TempF** variable is greater than 32 and (represented in the code with the double ampersand) less than 49. If it is, then a value is assigned to **TempC**. If not, then the conditional test proceeds to the next step in the process. The second new line (line 15) does the same to cover temperature values for **TempF** situated between 50 and 98, using the same greater-than/less-than operators.

So what does this tell us? What can take away from the experience of constructing this GOFAI temperature conversion algorithm? Several things:

1 *Serial process.* Symbolic reasoning proceeds by specifying step-by-step instructions that proceed in a sequential order. The conversion

is produced by the computer stepping through each line in sequence and performing what has been indicated in the coded instructions.

2 *Knowledge representation.* The "intelligence" or the capability of the application is something that resides in the programmer's knowledge or access to available data. In order to write the temperature converter, the programmer needs to know (or at least have access to information about) how various values on the Fahrenheit scale relate to values on the Celsius scale. This knowledge is then represented in the lines of code that, if written correctly, produce the right results.

3 *Debugging.* If the application generates incorrect values or does not operate as it should, we can go into the code and fix it. That is, we can "pop the hood" on the algorithm, examine each line item-by-item, zero-in on the exact source of the problem, which is, more often than not some typo or mistake in the coded instructions, and then make the necessary changes or repairs to get the application working properly.

4 *Limitations.* Right now, our temperature conversion algorithm is brittle. It can only handle temperatures in the range 32–99°F, its results for many of the temperature values are approximate at best, and it does not take much to make it generate the error statement – UNDEFINED. If we want to make the algorithm more accurate and robust, we would need to add more lines of code in order to handle and process additional temperature values. Consequently, the capabilities of the algorithm are often directly related to the number of lines of coded instructions, such that the more lines of code you have, the better the performance of the application. (This is not necessarily a hard-and-fast rule, but it is a general tendency with GOFAI approaches.)

Artificial Neural Network

The second version of our temperature conversion algorithm will use an artificial neural network (ANN) to support supervised learning. In this case, we do not tell the computer how to perform the temperature conversion. We set up a neural network, train it on a small set of temperature data, and then allow the network to "learn" the conversions by exploiting patterns that emerge from the data. So let's look at the code for creating this kind of algorithm. You can decide whether to write the lines yourself or to download a complete copy of the algorithm from http://gunkelweb.com/introAI/ML_code.html (Figures Ex2.4 and Ex2.5).

```
 1
 2 <html>
 3 <head>
 4    <script src="http://gunkelweb.com/coms493/synaptic.js"></script>
 5 </head>
 6 <body>
 7 <script>
 8 //make the network
 9 const { Layer, Network } = window.synaptic;
10
11 var inputLayer = new Layer(1);
12 var hiddenLayer = new Layer(3);
13 var outputLayer = new Layer(1);
14
15 inputLayer.project(hiddenLayer);
16 hiddenLayer.project(outputLayer);
17
18 var myNetwork = new Network({
19     input: inputLayer,
20     hidden: [hiddenLayer],
21     output: outputLayer });
22
```

**Figure Ex2.4   Machine-learning temperature conversion algorithm
– Part One**

```
23 // train the network
24 var learningRate = .3;
25 for (var i = 0; i < 80000; i++)
26 {
27     myNetwork.activate([0.30]);
28     myNetwork.propagate(learningRate, [0]);
29
30     myNetwork.activate([0.50]);
31     myNetwork.propagate(learningRate, [0.10]);
32
33     myNetwork.activate([0.70]);
34     myNetwork.propagate(learningRate, [0.21]);
35
36     myNetwork.activate([0.99]);
37     myNetwork.propagate(learningRate, [0.38]);
38 }
39 // run the network
40 var temp = prompt("Enter Degrees Fahrenheit");
41 var tempF = "." + temp;
42 var result = myNetwork.activate([tempF]);
43 result = String(result).slice(2,4);
44 document.write("<h1>" + temp + " F is approximately " + result + " C </h1>");
45 </script>
46 </body>
47 </html>
48
```

**Figure Ex2.5   Machine-learning temperature conversion algorithm
– Part Two**

Let's look at what is here and how it functions. The first thing to note is that the code is annotated with several comment lines, indicated by //. These comments divide the instructions for the algorithm into distinct chunks that can assist us in reading and making sense of its operations. But before we get into each chunk, let's take a look at line 4 of Figure Ex2.4. Here we are importing Synaptic, which is a Javascript library of pre-coded elements that are commonly used for creating neural networks. Synaptic was written by Juan Cazala, is distributed with a software license that allows for unrestricted use (i.e., Cazala gives you the right to "use, copy, modify, merge, publish, distribute, sublicense, and/or sell copies" without limitation), and consists of a mere 2,848 lines of code. Synaptic, for instance, provides the code instructions for defining an individual artificial neuron and their arrangement into layers (see Chapter 3), the basic building blocks of a neural network. Without Synaptic, we would need to define each one of these items for ourselves, and, if you look at the Synaptic code (which you can do, since it is written in Javascript), you will see that the basic neuron requires more than 800 lines. Consequently, using Synaptic simplifies our work. It allows us to import and call upon these predefined elements. Think of it this way: the Synaptic library is like a box of Lego bricks that provides you with a variety of preformed Javascript elements for constructing a neural network.

The first chunk of code (beginning after the comment on line 8 and running up to line 21), defines the network. It does so by using the **Layer** and **Network** elements in the Synaptic library, which in turn utilizes the **Neuron**, also defined in Synaptic. Our network is going to be both small and shallow, using a 1–3–1 configuration. That is, there will be one neuron in the input and output layers and, in between these two, a hidden layer comprising three neurons (see Chapter 3 for more on this configuration). In order to accomplish this, we declare and define three variables (**inputLayer, hiddenLayer, outputLayer**) and assign to each of them a value indicating that each one is to be a new Layer with a numeric designation.

In the next step of this chunk of code (lines 15 and 16), we connect the layers to each other by projecting the results of the inputLayer into the hiddenLayer and then the results of the hiddenLayer into the outputLayer. Finally, we set up the entire thing as a new **Network** by assigning the features of our 1–3–1 network to a variable **myNetwork**. This will allow us to fire up the network later in the code by simply invoking this variable name.

In the next chunk of code (Figure Ex2.5, lines 23–38), we train the network by feeding it data. Since our example utilizes supervised learning (see Chapter 3), we are able to train the network on some basic temperature correlations (i.e. 30 = 0, 50 = 10, 70 = 21, and 99 = 38). So what you see here on lines 27–37 is this data being sent or "propagated" through the network. (Note: the reason the values are specified as fractional numbers, e.g., 0.50, 0.10, is because our artificial neurons are perceptrons, using a sigmoid function that operates in the range of 0 to 1.) These four temperature associations are preceded by a *for* loop (line 25) that specifies the number of times these data are sent through the network, e.g., forward propagation, and the value of the **LearningRate** variable (line 24), which is a pre-set number (in this case 0.3) that will be used to adjust the weights of the connections each time errors produced by the network are back propagated. The network is designed to perform this operation – forward propagating data into the network and then back propagating the resulting errors (calculated by comparing the network's result to the known value) – in order to readjust the weighted connections (each time by 0.3) again and again and again. In fact, this is done 80,000 times, as specified on line 25.

The third chunk of code (lines 40–44) runs the network. It begins with the user interface, which is defined by a **prompt()** that provides a dialogue box asking the user to "Enter Degrees Fahrenheit." The value of this **prompt()** – the number entered by the user – is assigned to and stored in a variable called **temp**. The next line (line 41) formats this numeric value so that it can work with the network. Basically, we are taking the whole number entered in the **prompt** and turning it into a fractional number by appending (or adding) a decimal point before the number. This new value is assigned to and stored in a variable called **tempF**. After this is done, we activate the network sending into it the numeric value of **tempF** and assigning the result of this operation to the **result** variable. The value of **result**, which will be a fractional number, is then reformatted so that the output is displayed as a whole number. Finally in the last line (line 44), we apply the **write()** method to display an output message in the web document. This message is assembled by plugging in the values of the two variables, **temp** (which was entered by the user) and **result** (which was the output generated by the network).

So now we can try it. Either write the code out by hand or (what is probably better) copy and paste the code from the website into your text editor. Save it and open the file in the browser. Doing so will immediately display the prompt or dialogue box. Enter a number in the temperature range 32–99°F. When you click the "okay" button, you will fire up the network and see that the system is able to produce relatively good conversions. If, for example, you enter a number that the network already "knows" from the training data, like 99°F, it will produce the predictable and not very surprising outcome of 37°C. But (and here is where things get interesting) if you enter a number the network has never seen before (e.g., one that was not in the training set), the network is able to calculate a relatively accurate conversion.

A couple of things to note about this second version. First, our demonstration artificial neural network (ANN) is really simple. Most neural networks are much more complex with many more neurons in the input, output, and hidden layers and more than one hidden layer. You may have heard of deep learning, which is a neural network with a rather large number of hidden layers, making the network "deep" as opposed to our shallow example. So one way that you can increase the capability of the ANN is to make it both broader and deeper, adding more neurons to the input and output layers and more layers to the in-between hidden layer. Another way to modify or adjust the performance of the network is by increasing the size of the data that is used for training. The power of an ANN is actually in the data and not in the network. This is why machine learning works hand-in-hand with big data. By increasing both the quantity and the quality of the data, you can increase the capability of the neural network. We can also make adjustments to the learning rate, changing the value of the number that is used to alter the weights on the connections between the layers. For our example, we selected a rather modest number, 0.3. By adjusting this number up or down, we can "tune" the network and affect its performance.

Second, if we compare this second version of the temperature conversion algorithm to the first GOFAI example, we can see some important difference. Unlike the first version, this temperature conversion algorithm does not have prescribed step-by-step instructions that specify how to make the transformation in temperature values. The network "learns" – or maybe a better word is "formulates" – the conversions by discovering patterns in data that are then encoded in the network by adjusting the weighted connections between layers of neurons. This means that the programmer or developer of the application does not need to know everything about the task in order to write the algorithm. Unlike a GOFAI application, where the "intelligence" of the algorithm is a product of the (more-or-less accurately represented) intelligence of its developer, the "intelligence" of a machine-learning neural network is something that emerges from the data on which it is trained. For this reason, the developer of the algorithm does not need to know much about the task and might, in fact, actually know very little or nothing.

Finally, and as you might have surmised, this is both an advantage and a potential problem. It is advantageous insofar as developers can create practical applications and solutions to problems without necessarily knowing anything about the task at hand. This approach, therefore, provides a way to solve problems where we have access to data but do not necessarily know the step-by-step procedures necessary to transform the input values into output. But this also means that developers of machine-learning systems typically do not have full knowledge of or control over the algorithms they create. Consequently, the algorithm is something of a "black box" and what it does or does not do is often just as surprising to its developers as it is to the user. And if something does go wrong and the algorithm starts spitting out bad results – like the Tay.ai chatbot that learned to tweet hate speech (see Chapter 5) – the developer cannot pinpoint where in the lines of code the error occurs. Unlike a GOFAI algorithm, the connectionist architecture of a neural network means that it is simply made up of a number of layers with weighted connections between layers. The source of the problem, then, is not in the network per se; it is in the data on which the network was trained. But to identify the source of the error in the data, especially in the case of big data, is something that is often difficult for us to do. In other words, we often do not know of the problem with the data until the ANN finds the error-producing pattern in the data.

Exercise 3
Machine Translation

In this exercise, we will make a simple machine translation tool using rule-based, classical MT. The purpose of the exercise is (1) to demonstrate the principles utilized by classical approaches to MT and (2) to evaluate the advantages and disadvantages of this way of producing automated translation tools.

As described in Chapter 4, there are a number of approaches to producing MT algorithms. The most direct and basic method – one that was popular and definitive of the field for at least the first two decades of MT R&D – is the direct translation approach using rule-based transformations. For this method, each linguistic unit (a word or sequence of words) in the source language directly correlates with a linguistic unit (a word or sequence of words) in the target language. The process is rather intuitive insofar as it is derived from and models already existing translation tools, namely the bilingual dictionary or travel phrase book that provide users with word-for-word substitutions.

Our MT algorithm will be designed to translate English (the source language) into German (the target language). If you would rather use something other than German as the target language, you can simply make modifications to this basic design. For the first attempt, however, I suggest you follow along for the English/German translator, get it fully working, then go back and modify it with another target language. This is possible, because the computer does not care or know anything about either the source or the target language. It is simply making correlations between sets of variables. The values that are assigned to those variables are, in a word, variable (sorry, the repetition is unavoidable).

The translator will consist of three basic components: (1) an input

Figure Ex3.1 Block diagram of the direct MT system

```
1
2  <html>
3  <script>
4  function xlate()
5  {
6    source = document.getElementById("english").value;
7    if (source=="hello") target = "Guten Tag";
8    else if (source=="goodbye") target = "Auf Wiedersehen";
9    else target = "Sorry, I do not know that one.";
10   document.getElementById("german").value = target;
11 }
12 </script>
13 <body>
14  <form>
15   Basic Translator - English to German
16   <p><input type="text" id="english">
17     <input type="button" value=">>" onClick="xlate()">
18     <input type="text" id="german"></p>
19  </form>
20 </body>
21 </html>
```

Figure Ex3.2 Basic translation algorithm accommodating two word pairs

field that provides the user with a way to enter an English word or phrase; (2) a set of transformation instructions that make direct correlations between a predefined set of English words with a set of predefined German words; (3) an output field that displays the results of the transformation to the user (Figure Ex3.1).

But let's start small and write a translator that works with just two word pairs (Figure Ex3.2). Once we get this simple version working, we can then add additional items. In fact, once we get the basic system operational, we can add as many word pairs as we like and, in the process, improve the translation ability of the algorithm. So what exactly is happening here? Start from the bottom at line 14. These HTML instructions describe the user interface, which consists of a text input field, an output field, and a button to fire-up the translations instructions. The two text fields are identified with an id and set to the values **"english"** and **"german"** respectively. The button has an **onClick** event handler that calls or invokes a function that we arbitrarily are calling **xlate()**.

The function is defined and described in the lines above (lines 4–11). We declare the function – or indicate that we are creating it – with the word *function* followed by the name that we have assigned to the **onClick** event handler, e.g. **xlate()**. We then describe what sequential steps the function is to execute to make the translation. The first line of the function (line 6) extracts the value (presumably an English word or phrase) that was entered in the input field by the user. Here we employ a very useful method in the Javascript language **getElementById()**, which extracts the value of the data that was entered into the text field identified as "english." This value is assigned and stored temporarily in the variable **source**. The way to read this line of code is as follows: for the variable **source,** assign to it the data that the user has entered into the form field that has **id="english"**.

The next three lines in the function describe the transformation rules. These are formulated as a conditional using the standard method: *if | else if | else*. The conditional statement begins with a test case that asks whether the data entered into the input field (which, you will recall, had been assigned to the variable **source** in line 6) is the English word "hello." In effect, the function is simply asking if the user entered the word "hello." If this is the case, then we assign the value "Guten Tag" to the variable **target**. If not, then we move to the next line in the function.

This next line (line 8), presents us with another test case, marked with *else if*. With this second test, we are asking whether the value of **source** (i.e., the data that had been entered in the text input field) is the English phrase "goodbye." If it is, then we assign the value "Auf Wiedersehen" to the variable **target**. If not, then we move to the next line in the conditional statement.

The third line in the conditional (line 9), covers all situations where neither the first nor the second test case has been met, conditions where the user has entered something other than "hello" or "goodbye." When (and if) this happens, the algorithm is designed to supply a generic message: "Sorry, I do not know that one."

The final line in the function takes the value of **target** and inserts it into the text field that is identified with the word **german**. It, therefore, takes the result of the conditional and displays this value to the user.

This basic version works, but it is not very robust. It only knows – or can process – two words: *hello* and *goodbye*. If the user enters anything other than these two words, the system does not know how to make the translation and "apologizes" for its ignorance. If we want it to be able to handle a wider range of data, the algorithm would need to be provided with additional word pairs. In the case of our particular example, this can be easily accomplished by adding more conditional tests to the function. What this means in practical terms is that we would need to insert one or more *else if* statements in the function (Figure Ex3.3). And the more of these that can be included, the more capable the translation system will become. Obviously, this second version is better, but it is nowhere near perfect. In fact, it is not even robust enough for basic use on the street. In other words, you probably do not want to rely on this

```
1
2   <html>
3   <script>
4   function xlate()
5   {
6     source = document.getElementById("english").value;
7     if (source=="hello") target = "Guten Tag";
8     else if (source=="goodbye") target = "Auf Wiedersehen";
9     else if (source=="please") target = "Bitte";
10    else if (source=="thank you") target = "Danke schon";
11    else if (source=="you're welcome") target = "Bitte sehr";
12    else if (source=="yes") target = "Ja";
13    else if (source=="no") target = "Nein";
14    else if (source=="excuse me") target = "Entschuldigung";
15    else if (source=="no thank you") target = "Nein, danke";
16    else if (source=="beer") target = "ein bier";
17    else if (source=="water") target = "wasser";
18    else target = "Sorry, I do not know that one.";
19    document.getElementById("german").value = target;
20  }
21  </script>
22  <body>
23   <form>
24   Basic Translator - English to German
25    <p><input type="text" id="english">
26      <input type="button" value=">>" onClick="xlate()">
27      <input type="text" id="german"></p>
28  </form>
29  </body>
30  </html>
```

Figure Ex3.3   Basic English/German translator with additional word pairs

particular system to support your trip to Munich during the annual Oktoberfest.

From this simple example, we can take note of several important consequences. First, as it is written, this MT system is fragile. It does not take much to make it produce an error or default to the apologetic "Sorry, I do not know that one." In its current form, for example, the algorithm is case-sensitive. So if you enter "hello," it produces the correct translation "Guten Tag." But if you enter "Hello" or "HELLO," it does not know what you are talking about and spits out the default apology instead of "Guten Tag." This happens because the algorithm does not know the meaning of the word "hello"; all it knows is a particular sequence of symbols. For this reason, "hello" and "HELLO" are, as far as the algorithm is concerned, different sequences of symbols. Some of this can be adjusted in the coded instruction. We can, for instance, render the user input case-insensitive with just a few more lines. But that is a relatively small item. Bigger concerns involve scaling the algorithm to be able to handle a wider variety of user input. With this particular system, every possible variation on a theme would need to be handled separately. Consequently, "hello" will produce "Guten Tag." But what if the user types a similar but different greeting like, "hi," "hello there," or "good morning"? Each of these would need to be paired up with a German equivalent. This not difficult to do, obviously; it just requires more lines of code. But you can see that accommodating even a relatively limited set of variations is going to necessitate close to several hundred lines of coded instructions.

Second, and following from this, the linguistic intelligence of this algorithm, like that of many GOFAI rule-based AI implementations, resides in the programmer. In order to construct this translation system, the programmer needs to know how to translate the English words and phrases into German or has to have access to this information from another knowledgeable source. This means that the system is only as "smart" as the programmer and his/her ability to represent that knowledge in the symbolic logic of the coded instructions. Because of this, the translation algorithm is very literal in its operations and is only able to perform what it has been explicitly told to do.

Finally, in this example, we are only working with one language pair, and we are only translating in one direction, from English into German. If we should want to make the translation algorithm work in both directions we would need to write everything twice, once for the translation from English into German and again for the translation from German into English. If we wanted to add another language, say French, then we would need to do this for every single pairing of the three languages, producing six separate translation modules. This can be expressed mathematically by the following equation: $DT = n(n-1)$, where DT is the number of individual direct translation programs and n is the number of languages to be translated. If we have two languages, English and German, the equation tells us that we will need $2(2-1)$ translation systems, one for English into German and the other for German into English. For three languages (e.g., English, French, and German), we would need $3(3-1)$ or six translation modules. As you will probably see, this can get out of hand very quickly with a modest number of languages – nine, for instance, will need seventy-two separate translation algorithms. For this (and a few other reasons that we already described and examined in Chapter 4) rule-based MT has quickly given way to other methods, like statistical MT and machine-learning MT, both of which not only produce better translation results, but are better able to scale to a wider range of different languages.

Exercise 4
Chatbot and Quasi-Loebner Prize

In this exercise, we will create a chatbot using artificial intelligence markup language (AIML) and the Pandorabots AIML interpreter. We already constructed a basic chatbot – the DIY ELIZA – in Exercise 1. The objective of this exercise is to develop a more capable and robust conversational agent using the same tools utilized by many contemporary bot developers and then to test the performance of our bots in a quasi-Loebner Prize evaluation.

You may recall (Chapter 5) that AIML was invented by Richard Wallace for A.L.I.C.E. (Artificial Linguistic Internet Computer Entity). AIML is a dialect of XML (extensible markup language), which is not a markup language per se, but a metalanguage for creating any number of developer-defined markup languages. The advantage of a markup language like AIML is that it is both human- and machine-readable, which simplifies the development of applications. Wallace released AIML under a GNU General Public License (GPL), which means that it is available to us under an open source license. Translation: you do not need to buy anything or click "agree" on some complicated end user licensing agreement (EULA) in order to use AIML. Like the web, which utilizes HTML (hypertext markup language), AIML is a freely distributed, open standard.

Like other markup languages, e.g., XML and HTML, AIML consists of markup tags written in a text editor and saved with an .aiml extension (that part of the file name that comes after the period and indicates the file type). The building blocks of an AIML statement include three elements. The basic unit of knowledge in AIML is called a <category>. Each <category> consists of an input stimulus and an output response. The stimulus is called the <pattern>. The response is called the <template> (Figure Ex4.1).

```
1  <category>
2    <pattern>HELLO</pattern>
3    <template>Hi there!</template>
4  </category>
```

Figure Ex4.1   The basic AIML knowledge unit

The AIML pattern language – i.e. the content situated between the opening and closing <pattern> tag – is simple, consisting only of words, spaces, and wildcard symbols like * and ^. Words may consist of letters and numerals, but no other characters (no punctuation). The pattern language is not case-sensitive. The <template> element specifies the bot's response to the matched pattern. Unlike the <pattern> element, the <template> element is case-sensitive and may include punctuation and other symbols. In other words, the bot's responses will be returned to the user exactly as they appear between the opening and closing <template> tags.

So far so good, but this does not move us much beyond what was already possible with our DIY ELIZA chatbot. This is where AIML has real, practical advantages. One thing we can do with the language is specify a range of different possible responses and then randomize which one is displayed to the user. In this case (Figure Ex4.2), we specify a list of responses, each one tagged with <li> for list item, and then situate these <li> elements inside a <random> element. In this case, the bot will supply one of three possible responses to the matched <pattern> and the selection will occur randomly, giving the bot a diversity of possible responses.

The <pattern> may also contain wildcards. The * captures one or more words in the user input, while the ^ captures zero or

```
1  <category>
2    <pattern>HELLO</pattern>
3    <template>
4      <random>
5        <li>Hi there!</li>
6        <li>Hey, what's up?</li>
7        <li>You talking to me?</li>
8      </random>
9    </template>
10 </category>
```

Figure Ex4.2   Random responses

```
1 <category>
2     <pattern>MY NAME IS *</pattern>
3     <template>Hi, <star/>. How are you?</template>
4 </category>
```

Figure Ex4.3   Echoing user input

more words in the user input. What's the difference? If we use
<pattern>HELLO *</pattern>, this pattern will match user input
like "Hello there," "Hello bot," or "Hello my friend." But it will
not match "Hello" by itself. The ^ wild card, however, would match
all of these and would also accommodate "Hello" all by itself. One
good use of the * wildcard is to capture a word from the user and
then spit it back in the bot's response. This is called "echoing" user
input (see Figure Ex4.3)

In this example, whatever the user types after "MY NAME IS ..."
will be captured by the wildcard and then echoed in the bot response
with the <star/> element. In other words, if the user types "My name
is Jennifer," the bot will respond with "Hi, Jennifer. How are you?"
Notice the slash at the end of the word "star" in the <star/> element.
This is a requirement in XML syntax for empty tags, which are tags
that stand on their own and do not have a closing element like </
pattern> or </template>.

In this case, the echoing of the user input occurs immediately and
is only valid for that one <category> As soon as you move to the next
<category>, the word captured by the wildcard is no longer avail-
able. If you want the bot to "remember" the user input across more
than one <category>, that can be accomplished by storing the user
input in a variable by using the <set> element with a variable name
like "username" and then calling the variable by its name later in a
subsequent category with the <get> element (Figure Ex4.4).

There are many other items that can be coded with AIML, like

```
1 <category>
2     <pattern>MY NAME IS *</pattern>
3     <template>Hi, <set name="username"><star/></set></template>
4 </category>
5
6 <category>
7     <pattern>WHAT IS MY NAME</pattern>
8     <template>Your name is <get name="username"/></template>
9 </category>
```

Figure Ex4.4   Storing user input in a variable

sensitivity to context using <that>, conditionals that operate like the *if else* statements we have been coding in earlier examples, and even some rudimentary learning using the <learn> element, which in the case of AIML turns out to be more like memorization and recall. These additional features of the AIML standard are described in the documents (especially "Bot Builder 101") available at http://pandorabots.com, which is the AIML interpreter that we will use to run our bots.

So let's talk about Pandorabots, because the web application not only provides us with a powerful AIML interpreter to make the bot code operational, but it offers us a development environment and a set of tools for writing the AIML code. In order to use Pandorabots, you will need to sign into the application and create a free account. The free account will provide you with unlimited access to the bot sandbox, which is what we need for developing and testing our bot. If you (eventually) want to deploy your bot on a platform, like Twitter or Facebook, then you will need to sign up for one of the subscription-based pay accounts. But that is not necessary for this exercise.

Once you create your account, you will have immediate access to the Pandorabots dashboard. In the upper left-hand corner of the dashboard, you will see MY BOTS and a plus sign. If you click the plus sign, you will be able to create a new bot. The dialogue box will ask you to name your bot and to specify the language of your bot. There is also an optional "content" field, which is correctly defaulted to "blank bot." After you name your bot, the dialogue box closes and you are returned to the bot dashboard. Now in the upper left-hand corner, you will see your bot's name (e.g., "01bot") under MY BOTS. If you click the name, a menu is displayed. At this point, you will want to edit your bot. So click "Edit" (Figure Ex4.5).

After this, another menu will be displayed in the right-hand frame of the dashboard. The first item on this menu is AIML. When you click AIML, you will get a submenu with two items. Click the first one – "udc." This will open a text editor where you can write the AIML code. At this stage your bot has only one <category>; it is a default designed to respond to input patterns that the bot does not recognize (Figure Ex4.6).

Looking at the code, you will notice a few other lines that have been automatically generated by the Pandorabots editor. The first line indicates that the document is written in XML version 1.0 using UTF-8 encoding. This is a required declaration for all XML documents. The second line has an <aiml> tag. This is a container tag that not only identifies the type of code that is contained in the document

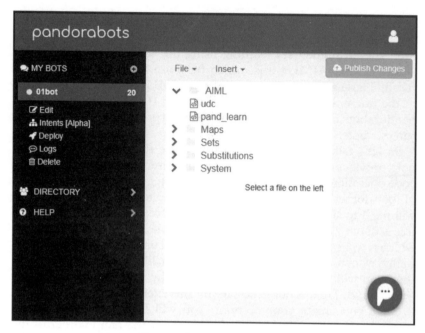

Figure Ex4.5   Pandorabots dashboard

```
 1   <?xml version="1.0" encoding="UTF-8"?>
 2 ▾ <aiml>
 3 ▾   <category>
 4       <pattern>*</pattern>
 5       <template>I have no answer for that.</template>
 6     </category>
 7   </aiml>
```

Figure Ex4.6   Bot with one default

but also holds all the <categories> within it. Basically, a well-formed
AIML document, in order to be considered valid and to work in the
interpreter, must begin and end with this element.

You can now begin writing new categories and building your bot's
capabilities. This is done by inserting additional <category> elements with their own <pattern> <template> formulations below
the default response. The more <category> tags you include in the
code, the more capable your bot's behavior (Figure Ex4.7). The
new <category> elements can be either entered by typing the tags

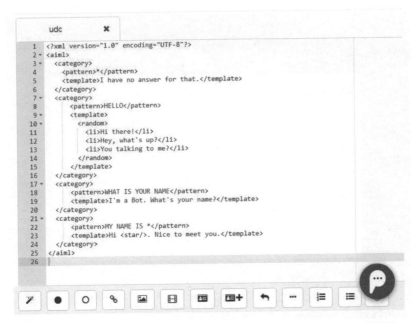

```
udc                    ✖

1   <?xml version="1.0" encoding="UTF-8"?>
2 ▾ <aiml>
3 ▾   <category>
4         <pattern>*</pattern>
5         <template>I have no answer for that.</template>
6     </category>
7 ▾   <category>
8         <pattern>HELLO</pattern>
9 ▾       <template>
10 ▾         <random>
11              <li>Hi there!</li>
12              <li>Hey, what's up?</li>
13              <li>You talking to me?</li>
14            </random>
15          </template>
16     </category>
17 ▾   <category>
18         <pattern>WHAT IS YOUR NAME</pattern>
19         <template>I'm a Bot. What's your name?</template>
20     </category>
21 ▾   <category>
22         <pattern>MY NAME IS *</pattern>
23         <template>Hi <star/>. Nice to meet you.</template>
24     </category>
25   </aiml>
26   ▎
```

Figure Ex4.7   Add additional elements to increase bot capabilities

(which can get to be a bit tedious), or automatically inserted into the AIML document by using the magic wand tool that is available at the bottom of the editor window. When you hover your mouse cursor over this tool, it will display the following caption: "Insert Category Template." Clicking on the icon will insert the tags necessary to define a new <category>.

Pandorabots will frequently save the changes that you make to your bot's code, but there is a "Save" feature available from the "File" pulldown menu that is worth using so that you do not lose any of your work. If there is an error in your code, the editor will not let you save the file and will display an error message. You can use this information to locate the source of the error, fix it, and then perform a successful save.

After making changes to your bot's code and saving it, you can test the bot. This is accomplished by clicking the circular purple chat button in the lower right-hand corner of the browser window. This will launch a chat window, where you can interact with your bot and test its performance. The chat feature also supplies you with another way to program the bot. For each response the bot supplies, you can edit that response from the chat window without needing to go into

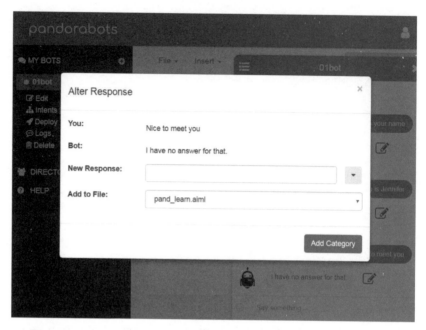

Figure Ex4.8   Making alterations to bot behavior via the chat widget

the AIML code. This is accomplished by clicking the black edit icon and opening the edit dialogue box. From this interface, you can alter the bot's behavior by typing in a new response. These changes will (as indicated in the dialogue box) be saved in another AIML document called "pand_learn" (for Pandora Learn) (Figure Ex4.8).

You can develop your bot by making changes to the AIML code in the udc document, adding new behaviors to the pand_learn document via the chat widget, or both. Once you have what you consider to be an acceptable finished product, you can share your bot with other students in the class. This is done by deploying your bot to the Pandorabots sandbox or "Internal Bot Directory." Simply click on the "Deploy" link under the name of your bot in the main menu and click "Add" on the first item in the list of destinations. You will need to give your bot a name (I suggest something easy to remember and find, like course number and your last name, e.g., "coms493-Capek") and a description (Figure Ex4.9). You will also need to certify that your bot does not violate the Pandorabots Terms of Service with a check in the checkbox. Once you deploy your bot to the Internal Bot Directory, anyone with a Pandorabots account will be able to talk to

Figure Ex4.9   Internal Bot Directory

your bot by going to the DIRECTORY and clicking on the circular purple chat icon associated with your bot's name and description. If your bot or the bot of one of your classmates is difficult to find, you can use the search feature that is provided.

Once everyone in the class has their bot working and deployed to the Internal Bot Directory, you can run your own version of a quasi-Loebner Prize. Have everyone in the class interact with the bots (five minutes per bot) and rate their performances on a scale of 1 to 5, with 5 being high score, 3 designating average performance, and 1 indicating a bot that is less than impressive/entertaining. After everyone has interacted with and scored the bots, add up the numbers to see which one came closest to emulating what could be considered a decent conversational partner. One final note: in using AIML to develop your bot, you are in good company. Many winners of the highest-awarded honors at the annual Loebner competition have also used AIML, like the multi-award winning A.L.I.C.E. and Mitsuku.

Exercise 5
Template NLG

In this exercise, we will experiment with computational creativity by making a demonstration NLG algorithm using a prefabricated template combined with labeled data. The algorithm will be designed to "write" lyrics for a punk rock song, so it will be called the Punk Rock Lyric Generator. But the method employed for this particular example is sufficiently general that it does not need to be limited to this one genre of popular music. You can, if you like, modify the template to produce any number of lyric generators: a Country Music Lyric Generator, a Low-Down Blues Lyric Generator, a Classic Rock Lyric Generator, a Hip-Hop Rap Generator, etc.

The finished product, which will (like the previous examples) run in the web browser, consists of a form field and a song field. The form will allow the user to enter words. Not just any words, but words that respond to specific prompts, e.g., "Favorite noun," "Least favorite noun," "Curse word," etc. When the user completes all the form fields and clicks on the "Write a Song" button, we fire up some Javascript code and display the results in the song field (Figure Ex5.1).

In order to code this application, we will need to employ a mixture of Javascript and HTML/CSS (cascading style sheets). Fortunately, these languages work very well together and can be easily distinguished and interpreted by the browser. Translation: you can mix Javascript with HTML/CSS and let the web browser sort it out. Let's begin by looking at the entire document, which comes in at 43 lines of code (Figure Ex5.2).

There is a lot going on here, so let's take it one item at a time, and let's begin at the bottom (lines 29–41). This is the HTML form (Figure Ex5.3). It consists of a <form> that is floated left so that the song <iframe> field is situated alongside it to the right.

Punk Rock Lyric Generator

Favorite noun:

A rhyming word

Least favorite noun:

A rhyming word:

An action verb:

Favorite curse word:

Write a Song

Figure Ex5.1   Web interface for the Lyric Generator

The form consists of six <input type="text"> fields and one <input type="button">. Each of the text input fields takes user-entered data and assigns it to and stores it in a variable. The variables are identified in each of the <input> tags with a name attribute followed by a label in quotation marks – word1a, word1b, verb1, etc. The button is assigned the value "Write a Song." The onclick event handler indicates that when the button is clicked, we call or invoke a Javascript function called writeSong(). This function and its operations will be defined in lines 3–25.

After the HTML <form>, we define the field where the algorithm's output will be displayed. In this case, we will use an <iframe> (lines 40–41), which is just a large empty space into which the output of the algorithm can be sent and displayed. This is done by assigning the value of the result variable to the name attribute for the <iframe>. The value that will be assigned to the result variable is the product of a process that will be defined in the function (lines 3–25). Basically, these lines generate the song and assign the output to the result variable. That value is then inserted into the <iframe> by way of the name attribute. Lastly, we scale the field by specifying

```
1   <html><head>
2     <script type="text/javascript">
3       function writeSong()
4       {
5         word1a = document.forms[0].word1a.value;
6         word1b = document.forms[0].word1b.value;
7         word2a = document.forms[0].word2a.value;
8         word2b = document.forms[0].word2b.value;
9         verb1 = document.forms[0].verb1.value;
10        verb2 = document.forms[0].verb2.value;
11        results = window.top.results.document;
12
13        results.write("<blockquote><h1>I don't wanna</h1>" +
14            "<br>I don't wanna " + word1a +
15            "<br>I don't wanna " + word1b +
16            "<br>I just wanna " + verb1 + " around " +
17            "<br>And " + verb2 + " my neighbor's " + word2b +
18            "<br><br>I don't wanna " + word2a +
19            "<br>I don't wanna " + word1a +
20            "<br>I just wanna " + verb2 + " on you " +
21            "<br>And " + verb1 + " your stinking " + word1b +
22            "<br><br>I don't wanna" +
23            "<br>I don't wanna" +
24            "<br>I don't wanna");
25       }
26     </script></head>
27  <body bgcolor="lightgrey">
28  <h1>Punk Rock Lyric Generator</h1>
29    <form style="float:left">
30      <p>Favorite noun: <br><input type="text" name="word1a">
31      <br>A rhyming word <br><input type="text" name="word1b"></p>
32
33      <p>Least favorite noun: <br><input type="text" name="word2a">
34      <br>A rhyming word: <br><input type="text" name="word2b"></p>
35
36      <p>An action verb: <br><input type="text" name="verb1">
37      <br>Favorite curse word: <br><input type="text" name="verb2"></p>
38      <p><input type="button" value="Write a Song" onclick="writeSong()"></p>
39    </form>
40    <iframe width="400" height="380" name="results" style="background:white">
41    </iframe>
42  </body>
43  </html>
```

Figure Ex5.2   Coded instructions for the Punk Rock Lyric Generator

the number of pixels for the <iframe>'s width and height and provide a white background color by way of the style attribute.

The purpose of the form is to prompt and label user-entered data. This data – six words entered into the text input fields – is processed and inserted into the song template by the function **writeSong()**. The function is defined in the upper half of the document (Figure Ex5.4). We begin by declaring the function and assigning it a name. This name is arbitrary; we are calling it **writeSong()**. However, we could have used almost anything for this name. The only require-

```
27  <body bgcolor="lightgrey">
28  <h1>Punk Rock Lyric Generator</h1>
29    <form style="float:left">
30      <p>Favorite noun: <br><input type="text" name="word1a">
31      <br>A rhyming word <br><input type="text" name="word1b"></p>
32
33      <p>Least favorite noun: <br><input type="text" name="word2a">
34      <br>A rhyming word: <br><input type="text" name="word2b"></p>
35
36      <p>An action verb: <br><input type="text" name="verb1">
37      <br>Favorite curse word: <br><input type="text" name="verb2"></p>
38      <p><input type="button" value="Write a Song" onclick="writeSong()"></p>
39    </form>
40    <iframe width="400" height="380" name="results" style="background:white">
41    </iframe>
42  </body>
43  </html>
```

Figure Ex5.3   HTML form

```
1   <html><head>
2     <script type="text/javascript">
3       function writeSong()
4       {
5         word1a = document.forms[0].word1a.value;
6         word1b = document.forms[0].word1b.value;
7         word2a = document.forms[0].word2a.value;
8         word2b = document.forms[0].word2b.value;
9         verb1 = document.forms[0].verb1.value;
10        verb2 = document.forms[0].verb2.value;
11        results = window.top.results.document;
12
13        results.write("<blockquote><h1>I don't wanna</h1>" +
14            "<br>I don't wanna " + word1a +
15            "<br>I don't wanna " + word1b +
16            "<br>I just wanna " + verb1 + " around " +
17            "<br>And " + verb2 + " my neighbor's " + word2b +
18            "<br><br>I don't wanna " + word2a +
19            "<br>I don't wanna " + word1a +
20            "<br>I just wanna " + verb2 + " on you " +
21            "<br>And " + verb1 + " your stinking " + word1b +
22            "<br><br>I don't wanna" +
23            "<br>I don't wanna" +
24            "<br>I don't wanna");
25      }
26    </script></head>
```

Figure Ex5.4   Javascript for the writeSong() function

ment is that the name of the `function` needs to be exactly the same as the value of the `onclick` attribute for the input button (line 38). This way, when we click on the button we call or invoke the `function`. If the value of the `onclick` does not match the name given to the `function`, nothing will happen when you click the button.

After declaring the `function`, we then define what we want it to do. The first step in this process (lines 5–11) is to assign the data (the words) extracted from the form to variables that can be manipulated by the function. These six lines have the same basic structure: take the value that has been assigned to one of the variables, like `word1a`, for the `form` that is in the `document`; assign this value to a variable. To keep things simple, we will use the same variable name – `word1a`. We can use the same name, because the variable that is utilized by the form is distinguishable from the variable that is used within the function. Also notice that we have to specify `form[0]`. The number simply indicates that we are extracting the variable values from the first form in the `document`, and zero is the first figure in the numbering sequence for Javascript, which, depending on how much experience you have with programming languages, either makes total sense or is completely new and somewhat odd. Either way, that is how Javascript counts. The last thing we do is declare a `results` variable and assign it a value. This value will be defined in the lines that follow.

Lines 13–25 comprise the song template. Here we generate the song and `write()` the product (or outcome) to the `results` variable, which is then used to insert the generated song into the <iframe> field. In other words, the `function` generates the song, assigns this value to and stores it in the `results` variable, which can then be called by `name` in the <iframe> to display the resulting song to the user. The song template consists of string variables, like **"
I don't wanna"** concatenated with the variables, e.g., `word1a`, that were declared and defined in the lines above. Basically, what you have is a series of incomplete phrases with open slots or blanks into which the values assigned to the variables can be inserted. The pre-scripted elements of the template are in quotation marks, since they need to be displayed exactly as written, and contain HTML tags to provide basic formatting – i.e., the <br> tags to indicate line breaks. The values assigned to the variables, by contrast, are inserted into the template simply by calling the name of the variable. This means that we do not display "word1a" but the value that has been assigned to this variable – i.e., the word the user has provided on the form and that is associated with and stored in this variable name. We connect the pre-scripted elements with the variable values by using the concatenation operator or + sign. The final result of all this effort – the inserting of the values of the variables into the song template – is assigned to the `results` variable and then passed into the <iframe> field, where the generated song is displayed.

From this rather simple example, you can see a number of interesting possibilities and potential limitations. On the one hand, it is possible, with just a few lines of code and a well-designed template, to craft a natural language generation system that can produce a wide range of different texts. With only a few variables in play, the lyric generator can produce different songs or at least a significant number of variations on a common theme. This points to an important fact about human language and text composition that is exploited by NLG applications. Many textual compositions are highly redundant and predictable. The lyrics for a pop song have a rather standard form – verse, chorus, verse, chorus, etc. – that can be repeated and recombined in seemingly endless variations. Reports about sporting events have a limited number of possibilities – generally one team wins and the other loses – and can even be organized into standard story templates or genres, e.g., "a come-from-behind" or "star player steps in to save the day" narrative. The same is true of financial data and reports: profits are made, fortunes are lost, and the market experiences volatility as commodities are bought and sold. The kinds of stories that are able to be told about the stock market, for instance, fall into a rather narrow range of possibility and can, therefore, be prescribed by a set of templates that take different data points or variables and present this information in predictable ways.

On the other hand, you can also see and get a feel for the inherent limitations of template-based NLG. These systems will and can only generate textual content that adheres to what is provided in the predefined template. At a certain point, for instance, the Punk Rock Lyric Generator ceases to be entertaining; it gets boring, producing output that is predictable and just more of the same. So the level of "creativity" that is able to be achieved by this kind of NLG system is debatable. But this opens onto another set of questions that has as much to do with the algorithm as it does with how we define and understand human artistry. What more would be necessary for the machine to achieve a suitable level of NLG for it to be considered genuinely "creative"? Would this be achievable by applying advanced techniques like the "dynamic templating" that is utilized by Narrative Science? Likewise, is human creativity any different from that operationalized and exhibited by machinic creativity? Do we do anything more than simply reorganize and remix existing patterns and templates with new data? Is this all there is to creativity, or is there more to it that escapes computational modeling? These questions, which are made possible by experimentation with computational creativity, challenge us to do some deep thinking about the nature of creativity and how it is defined. In the terminology provided by John Searle, this could be called the "weak hypothesis" for computational creativity. But its impact is not insignificant, because its fundamental challenge to our understanding of human uniqueness and artistry is substantial.

Notes

1 The proposal, which was originally written in August 1955, uses the gender-exclusive term "man" instead of "human." This gendered formulation, however, is not just a nominal issue regarding word choice. When McCarthy and colleagues wrote "10 man study," they were, in fact, referring to ten male individuals. This is directly attributable to deep-seated and long-standing gender disparities in the various fields from which the participants were drawn: engineering, computer science, mathematics, etc. Fortunately, there has been, since that time, a concerted effort to balance things out. Unfortunately, getting traction with these efforts has been difficult and even now remains an ongoing issue and struggle. So things are improving, but there is still a good deal of work to be done.

2 *The One Hundred Year Study on Artificial Intelligence*, or AI 100, was launched in the fall of 2014. It is intended to be a long-term investigation of the field of artificial intelligence (AI) and its influences on people, their communities, and society. The AI 100 study and the published report of its findings are produced by a panel of experts, which reviews "AI's progress in the years following the immediately prior report, envisions the potential advances that lie ahead, and describes the technical and societal challenges and opportunities these advances raise, including in such arenas as ethics, economics, and the design of systems compatible with human cognition" (AI 100 2016: 1). Results of the first study, which was initiated in 2014, were published in 2016. The second AI 100 study began in 2018, to be published in 2020.

3 This characterization of the history of AI is particular to the United States. In fact, the term "AI winter" was first used in 1984 during the annual meeting of the American Association of Artificial Intelligence (AAAI). This is, on the one hand, somewhat understandable insofar as the field was initially launched and defined by US researchers, pursued (at least initially) at US universities and research institutions, and funded

by US-based public and private agencies. But, and on the other hand, this does not mean that AI is something that is exclusive to the US. The science and engineering of AI, along with work in robotics, has been pursued, researched, and practiced across the globe. For this reason, the history of AI can look significantly different when it is considered from a global perspective. Case in point: during the time of the so-called "AI winters," when US researchers experienced downturns in both funding and research opportunities, researchers and institutions in other parts of the world saw an increase in activity. For this reason, there is a real need for a history of AI that is global in perspective and scope and that can begin to account for these important differences. This introductory textbook is not the appropriate place to undertake and pursue this particular project. But it would be irresponsible not to recognize the need and importance for such a history.

4 The term "human–machine communication" (HMC) was introduced by Lucy A. Suchman in the book *Plans and Situated Actions: The Problem of Human–Machine Communication*, first published in 1987 and revised in 2007 with the modified title *Human–Machine Reconfigurations: Plans and Situated Actions*. According to Suchman's characterization, "human–machine communication," which she writes out in long form, "consider[s] 'communication' between a person and a machine in terms of the nature of their respective situations . . . The aim of the analysis then is to view the organization of human–machine communication, including its troubles, in terms of constraints posed by asymmetries in the respective situation resources of human and machine" (1987: 118; 2007: 126). The concept is taken up and developed into a new paradigm of communication research – now identified with the acronym HMC, as a kind of corollary to CMC – by a group of communication researchers beginning in 2014. The group, initially consisting of Andrea Guzman (who led the effort), Steve Jones, and David Gunkel, began organizing events during the International Communication Association annual convention. They were eventually joined by others: Autumn P. Edwards, Chad Edwards, Patric R. Spence, Austin Lee, and Jake Liang. In 2018, Guzman organized and published a collection of HMC essays under the title *Human–Machine Communication: Rethinking Communication, Technology, and Ourselves*. In the introduction to the book, which also serves as an introduction to the field of study, Guzman (2018: 17) defines HMC in the following way: "At its core communication is the creation of meaning. Human communication, the default, is the creation of meaning among humans. Human–machine communication is the creation of meaning among humans and machines. It is a process in which both human and machine are involved and without one or the other communication would cease." For this reason, HMC now serves as the "umbrella term" covering a wide range of investigations involving shared meaning-making and communicative interaction

between humans and technologies of various configurations and formations.

5 Selmer Bringsjord, Paul Bello, and David Ferrucci (2001) have turned this into a test condition for machine intelligence. They call this test "The Lovelace Test," named for Ada Lovelace, who (as we saw above) argued it is only when computers originate something that they can be said to have achieved intelligence.

6 For a photograph of the 2015 contest between DeepMind's AlphaGo and Lee Sedol, see https://www.blog.google/technology/ai/alphagos-ultimate-challenge/.

7 Jibo's story is a bit tragic and a good illustration of the trials and tribulations of "first to market" efforts in tech innovation. The robot was initially introduced to the world by way of a promotional video that Breazeal and company made to support an Indiegogo crowdfunding campaign – the video is still available at https://www.indiegogo.com/projects/jibo-the-world-s-first-social-robot-for-the-home#/. This effort at developing capital investment in the project was remarkably successful, having raised US$3,663,105 and achieving an impressive excess in funding of 2240 percent by September 15, 2014. People were clearly interested in the product; they were willing to bet on its success; and the technology was impressive, so much so that *Time* magazine listed Jibo as one of the best tech innovations of 2017. But Jibo turned out to be more promise than functional reality. Soon after beginning work on the project, Jibo Inc., the start-up that Breazeal had formed to develop the product, ran into trouble. First, release of a working commercial prototype was delayed several times over and individuals who had paid for preorders began to get antsy. When Jibo did begin shipping – in the fall of 2017 – it arrived with a limited set of skills. So Jibo was cute, but he (and the company intentionally gendered the device male) could not do very much. Second, Jibo was expensive – US$899 expensive – and consumers were reluctant to commit to Jibo when competing products, like Amazon's Alexa, were just a fraction of the cost. Finally, and because of all this, Jibo's parent company ran out of cash, began laying off its workers, and started selling off assets. By December 2018, Jibo was no more. Existing units would continue to function, but only so long as the cloud service that provided the platform with its "intelligence" remained operational. Once this support ended, Jibo would, like other tech innovations before it, become little more than an expensive "paper weight." So what's the lesson from this first commercial venture into social robotics? First, people want something like Jibo. But making it work and making it affordable is not going to be easy. Second, being first to market with a new technology is risky and often does not end well, at least not initially. This is not unique to Jibo. We have seen this before with, for example, the GUI (graphical user interface) personal computer. Apple's first foray into this area, with a device the company called Lisa (1983), failed for

many of the same reasons that Jibo did – lack of capability and high cost. That failure eventually led to the development of the Macintosh, which was one of the PC era's big success stories. So it is likely that the demise of Jibo is the beginning and not the end of the story.

8 "Wizard of Oz" is a term that is utilized in human–computer interaction (HCI) and human–robot interaction (HRI) studies to describe experimental procedures where test subjects interact with a computer system or robot that is assumed to be autonomous but is actually controlled by an experimenter who remains hidden from view. The term was initially introduced by John F. Kelly in the early 1980s and refers to the Wizard of Oz, in the eponymously titled film, who hid behind a curtain and controlled the operations of the "Great and Powerful Oz."

9 "Milgram study" refers to a series of psychological experiments designed and conducted by Stanley Milgram beginning in 1961. The point of the experiments was to measure the willingness of test subjects to obey an authority figure who would instruct them to perform "questionable" acts on another person by administering what they thought was an increasingly painful electric shock. The experiment and its results were described and investigated in Milgram's 1974 book, *Obedience to Authority: An Experimental View*.

10 This approach is deliberate and strategic. In a recent course on AI, Robots and Communication, I asked my students to investigate the opportunities of emerging technology, the challenges of technological unemployment, and the possible futures for higher education. This effort led to the development of a detailed list of policy initiatives that could be instituted by the university. I had originally intended the exercise to be empowering by giving students the opportunity to reflect on and help shape the direction of their education. But it unfortunately had the exact opposite effect. Looking at the list of reforms, we realized that the proposed updates were well beyond what any of us individually or even in collaboration could possibly achieve. Policy initiatives are certainly important and necessary. But what my students taught me during that semester was that we also need bottom-up strategies that can be instituted immediately in order to respond quickly and directly to the opportunities and challenges students will inevitably face in the years ahead.

11 The term "fourth revolution," which is the title of Floridi's 2014 book, refers to the most recent iteration in a sequence of profound transformations in the way human beings conceive of themselves and the world they occupy. The first revolution, Floridi argues, occurred with Nicolaus Copernicus, whose heliocentric model of the solar system challenged human exceptionalism by unseating human beings as the presumptive "center of the universe." The second revolution follows from the work of Charles Darwin, whose theory of evolution demonstrated that the human being was not an exceptional creature situated

apart from the other animals on planet earth, but part of a continuum of entities developing out of common ancestors. The third revolution, as Floridi develops it, is attributed to Sigmund Freud, who challenged the notion of Cartesian rationalism and demonstrated that the human mind is not necessarily transparent to itself. The fourth revolution proposed by Floridi is a product of information and communication technology, which has, as he argues, once again reoriented how we think about thought (computational theories of the mind), our bodies (DNA code), and the entire cosmos (infosphere). For a brief introduction, see BBC Radio 4's video "The Fourth Revolution," available at https://www.youtube.com/watch?v=W06fWz1mWNg

12 There is, we should note, another question, which is the flipside of this inquiry concerning autonomous technology and social responsibility. Specifically, "when might a robot, an intelligent artifact, or other socially interactive mechanism be due some level of social standing or respect? When, in other words, would it no longer be considered nonsense to inquire about the rights of robots? – and to ask the question: 'Can and should robots have rights?'" (Gunkel 2018: x). Investigating and responding to this "other question" are outside the scope of this particular book, but are the subject of my *Robot Rights* (2018).

13 There is some debate concerning this matter. What Coeckelbergh (2010: 236) calls "psychopathy" – e.g. "follow rules but act without fear, compassion, care, and love" – Ron Arkin (2009) celebrates as a considerable improvement in moral processing and decision-making. Here is how Noel Sharkey (2012: 121) characterizes Arkin's efforts to develop an "artificial conscience" for robotic soldiers: "It turns out that the plan for this conscience is to create a mathematical decision space consisting of constraints, represented as prohibitions and obligations derived from the laws of war and rules of engagement (Arkin 2009). Essentially this consists of a bunch of complex conditionals (if–then statements) . . . Arkin believes that a robot could be more ethical than a human because its ethics are strictly programmed into it, and it has no emotional involvement with the action." For more on this debate and the effect it has on moral consideration, see Gunkel (2012).

References

Adams, Brian, Cynthia Breazeal, Rodney Brooks, and Brian Scassellati (2000). Humanoid Robots: A New Kind of Tool. *IEEE Intelligent Systems* 15(4): 25–31. https://doi.org/10.1109/5254.867909.

Adams, Douglas (1979). *The Hitchhiker's Guide to the Galaxy*. New York: Pocket Books.

AI 100 (2016). *One Hundred Year Study on Artificial Intelligence*. Stanford University. https://ai100.stanford.edu/sites/default/files/ai100report10032 016fnl_singles.pdf.

Alpaydin, Ethem (2016). *Machine Learning*. Cambridge, MA: MIT Press.

Amazon (2018a). Alexa Developer. https://developer.amazon.com/alexa-voice-service.

Amazon (2018b). Alexa Terms of Use. May 17. https://www.amazon.com/gp/help/customer/display.html?nodeId=201809740.

Anderson, Michael, and Susan Leigh Anderson (2007). The Status of Machine Ethics: A Report from the AAAI Symposium. *Minds & Machines* 17(1): 1–10. https://doi.org/10.1007/s11023-007-9053-7.

Anderson, Michael, and Susan Leigh Anderson (2011). *Machine Ethics*. Cambridge: Cambridge University Press.

Anderson, Susan Leigh (2008). Asimov's "Three Laws of Robotics" and Machine Metaethics. *AI & Society* 22(4): 477–493. https://doi.org/10.1007/s00146-007-0094-5.

Angwin, Julia, Jeff Larson, Surya Mattu, and Lauren Kirchner (2016). Machine Bias: There's Software Used Across the Country to Predict Future Criminals. And It's Biased Against Blacks. *ProPublica*. https://www.propublica.org/article/machine-bias-risk-assessments-in-criminal-senten cing.

Aristotle (1944). *Politics*. Trans. H. Rackham. Cambridge, MA: Harvard University Press.

Arkin, Ronald C. (1998). *Behavior-Based Robotics*. Cambridge, MA: MIT Press.

Arkin, Ronald C. (2009). *Governing Lethal Behavior in Autonomous Robots*. Boca Raton, FL: CRC Press.

Asaro, Peter, and Wendell Wallach (2016). Introduction: The Emergence of Robot Ethics and Machine Ethics. In *Machine Ethics and Robot Ethics*, ed. Peter Asaro and Wendell Wallach, 1–15. New York: Routledge.

Asimov, Isaac (2008). *I, Robot*. New York: Bantam Books.

Auer, J. C. P. (1983). Review of B. Oreström's *Turn-Taking in English Conversation*. *Linguistics* 21: 742–748.

Automated Insights (2018). Customer Stories – AP. https://automatedinsights.com/customer-stories/associated-press/.

ALPAC (Automatic Language Processing Advisory Committee) (1966). *Language and Machines: Computers in Translation and Linguistics*. Washington, DC: National Academy of Sciences, National Research Council. http://www.mt-archive.info/ALPAC-1966.pdf.

Bar-Hillel, Yehoshua (1959). *Report on the State of Machine Translation in the United States and Great Britain*. Technical Report, February 15. Jerusalem: Hebrew University. http://www.mt-archive.info/Bar-Hillel-1959.pdf.

Barrett, Brian (2018). Lawmakers Can't Ignore Facial Recognition's Bias Anymore. *Wired*, July 26. https://www.wired.com/story/amazon-facial-recognition-congress-bias-law-enforcement/.

Bartle, Richard A. (2003). *Designing Virtual Worlds*. Boston, MA: New Riders.

Bartneck, Christoph (2004). From Fiction to Science: A Cultural Reflection of Social Robots. *Proceedings of the CHI 2004 Workshop on Shaping Human–Robot Interaction*. Vienna.

Bartneck, Christoph, and Jun Hu (2008). Exploring the Abuse of Robots. *Interaction Studies* 9(3): 415–433. http://dx.doi.org/10.1075/is.9.3.04bar.

Bekey, George A. (2015). *Autonomous Robots: From Biological Inspiration to Implementation and Control*. Cambridge, MA: MIT Press.

Bekoff, Marc (2007). *The Emotional Lives of Animals: A Leading Scientist Explores Animal Joy, Sorrow, and Empathy – And Why They Matter*. Novato, CA: New World Library.

Bemelmans, Roger, Gert Jan Gelderblom, Pieter Jonker, and Luc de Witte (2012). Socially Assistive Robots in Elderly Care: A Systematic Review into Effects and Effectiveness. *Journal of the American Medical Directors Association* 13(2): 114–120. https://doi.org/10.1016/j.jamda.2010.10.002.

Berger, Charles R. (2005). Interpersonal Communication: Theoretical Perspectives, Future Prospects. *Journal of Communication* 55(3): 415–447. https://doi.org/10.1111/j.1460-2466.2005.tb02680.x.

Bessi, Alessandro, and Emilio Ferrara (2016). Social Bots Distort the 2016 US Presidential Election Online Discussion. *First Monday* 21(11). https://doi.org/10.5210/fm.v21i11.7090.

Birnbaum, Lawrence A., Kristian J. Hammond, Nicholas D. Allen, and John R. Templon (2018). System and Method for Using Data and Angles to Automatically Generate a Narrative Story. United States Patent. US

9,720,884 B2. https://patentimages.storage.googleapis.com/eb/7f/40/388a 333e6f31b7/US9990337.pdf.

Boden, Margaret (2010). *Creativity and Art: Three Roads to Surprise*. Oxford: Oxford University Press.

Boden, Margaret (2016). *AI: Its Nature and Future*. Oxford: Oxford University Press.

Boden, Margaret, Joanna Bryson, Darwin Caldwell, Kerstin Dautenhahn, Lilian Edwards, . . . Vivienne Parry (2011). Principles of Robotics: Regulating Robots in the Real World. *Engineering and Physical Sciences Research Council* (EPSRC). https://www.epsrc.ac.uk/research/ourportfolio/themes/ engineering/activities/principlesofrobotics/.

Boden, Margaret, Joanna Bryson, Darwin Caldwell, Kerstin Dautenhahn, Lilian Edwards, . . . Alan Winfield (2017). Principles of Robotics: Regulating Robots in the Real World. *Connection Science*, 29 (2): 124–129. http:// dx.doi.org/10.1080/09540091.2016.1271400.

Bolter, Jay David (2001) *Writing Space: Computers, Hypertext, and the Remediation of Print*. Mahwah, NJ: Lawrence Erlbaum Associates.

Bolter, Jay David, and Richard Grusin (1999). *Remediation: Understanding New Media*. Cambridge, MA: MIT Press.

Boshmaf, Yazan, Ildar Muslukhov, Konstantin Beznosov, and Matei Ripeanu (2011). The Socialbot Network: When Bots Socialize for Fame and Money. In *Proceedings of the 27th Annual Computer Security Applications Conference*, Orlando, FL. December 5–9. New York: ACM Press. http:// lersse-dl.ece.ubc.ca/record/264/files/264.pdf.

Breazeal, Cynthia (2002). *Designing Sociable Robots*. Cambridge, MA: MIT Press.

Breazeal, Cynthia (2003). Toward Sociable Robots. *Robotics and Autonomous Systems* 42(3–4): 167–175. https://doi.org/10.1016/S0921-8890(02)003 73-1.

Breazeal, Cynthia (2010). The Rise of Personal Robots. *TEDWomen 2010*. https://www.ted.com/talks/cynthia_breazeal_the_rise_of_personal_robots? language=en.

Breazeal, Cynthia, Avida Michaud, Francois Laberge, Jonathan Louis Ross, Carolyn Marothy Saund, and Fardad Faridi (2017). Persistent Companion Device Configuration and Deployment Platform. United States Patent. US 20170206064A1. https://patentimages.storage.googleapis.com/8c/b3/ 5b/2f637a690c589f/US20170206064A1.pdf.

Bringsjord, Selmer (2007). Ethical Robots: The Future Can Heed Us. *AI & Society* 22(4): 539–550. https://doi.org/10.1007/s00146-007-009 0-9.

Bringsjord, Selmer, Paul Bello, and David Ferrucci (2001). Creativity, the Turing Test, and the (Better) Lovelace Test. *Minds and Machines* 11(1): 3–27. https://doi.org/10.1023/A:1011206622741.

Broadbent, Elizabeth, Vinayak Kumar, Xingyan Li, John Sollers, Rebecca Q. Stafford, Bruce A. MacDonald, and Daniel M. Wegner (2013). Robots with Display Screens: A Robot with a More Humanlike Face Display is Perceived to Have More Mind and a Better Personality. *Plos One* 8(8): e72589.

Brooks, Rodney A. (1991). Intelligence Without Representation. *Artificial Intelligence* 47: 139–159. https://doi.org/10.1016/0004-3702(91)90053-M.

Brooks, Rodney A. (2002). *Flesh and Machines: How Robots Will Change Us.* New York: Pantheon Books.

Brown, Peter F., John Cocke, Stephen A. Della Pietra, Vincent J. Della Pietra, Fredrick Jelinek, . . . Paul S. Roossin (1990). A Statistical Approach to Machine Translation. *Computational Linguistics* 16(2): 79–85. http://www.aclweb.org/anthology/J90-2002.

Brown, Peter F., Stephen A. Della Pietra, Vincent J. Della Pietra, and Robert L. Mercer (1993). The Mathematics of Statistical Machine Translation: Parameter Estimation. *Computational Linguistics* 19(2): 263–311. http://www.aclweb.org/anthology/J93-2003.

Bruckenberger, Ulrike, Astrid Weiss, Nicole Mirnig, Ewald Strasser, Susanne Stadler, and Manfred Tscheligi (2013). The Good, the Bad, the Weird: Audience Evaluation of a "Real" Robot in Relation to Science Fiction and Mass Media. In *Social Robotics. ICSR 2013. Lecture Notes in Computer Science* (vol. 8239), ed. Guido Herrmann, Martin J. Pearson, Alexander Lenz, Paul Bremner, Adam Spiers, and Ute Leonards, 301–310. Cham, Switzerland: Springer. https://doi.org/10.1007/978-3-319-02675-6_30.

Bryson, Joanna (2010). Robots Should Be Slaves. In *Close Engagements with Artificial Companions: Key Social, Psychological, Ethical and Design Issues*, ed. Yorick Wilks, 63–74. Amsterdam: John Benjamins.

Bryson, Joanna, and Alan Winfield (2017). Standardizing Ethical Design for Artificial Intelligence and Autonomous Systems. *Computer* 50(5): 116–119. https://doi.org/10.1109/MC.2017.154.

Burgan, Deeno (2017). *Dialogue Systems & Dialogue Management.* National Security and ISR Division, Defence Science and Technology Group, Commonwealth of Australia. DST-Group-TR-3331. https://www.dst.defence.gov.au/sites/default/files/publications/documents/DST-Group-TR-3331.pdf.

Burgoon, Judee K. (1980). Nonverbal Communication Research in the 1970s: An Overview. *Communication Yearbook* 4: 179–197. https://doi.org/10.1080/23808985.1980.11923802.

Burgoon, Judee K., Valerie Manusov, Paul Mineo, and Jerold L. Hale (1985). Effects of Gaze on Hiring, Credibility, Attraction and Relational Message Interpretation. *Journal of Nonverbal Behavior* 9(3): 133–146. https://doi.org/10.1007/BF01000735.

Burgoon, Judee K., Deborah A. Coker, and Ray A. Coker (1986). Communicative Effects of Gaze Behavior: A Test of Two Contrasting Explanations. *Human Communication Research* 12(4): 495–524. https://doi.org/10.1111/j.1468-2958.1986.tb00089.x.

Calverley, David J. (2008). Imaging a Non-Biological Machine as a Legal Person. *AI & Society* 22(4): 523–537. https://doi.org/10.1007/s00146-007-0092-7.

Čapek, Karel (2009). *R.U.R. (Rossum's Universal Robots)*, trans. David Wyllie. Gloucestershire, UK: The Echo Library.

Carey, James (1989). *Communication as Culture: Essays on Media and Society*. New York: Routledge.

Cardoso, Amílcar, Tony Veale, and Geraint A. Wiggins (2009). Converging on the Divergent: The History (and Future) of the International Joint Workshops in Computational Creativity. *AI magazine* 30(3): 15–22. https://doi.org/10.1609/aimag.v30i3.2252.

Carpenter, Julie (2015). *Culture and Human–Robot Interaction in Militarized Spaces: A War Story*. New York: Ashgate.

Caswell, David, and Konstantin Dörr (2018). Automated Journalism 2.0: Event-Driven Narratives. *Journalism Practice* 12(4): 477–496. http://dx.doi.org/10.1080/17512786.2017.1320773.

Cathcart, Robert, and Gary Gumpert (1985). "The Person–Computer Interaction: A Unique Source." In *Information and Behavior*, vol. 1, ed. Brent D. Ruben, 113–124. New Brunswick: NJ: Transaction Books.

Cerf, Vinton. (1973). PARRY Encounters the DOCTOR. Network Working Group, RFC 439. https://tools.ietf.org/html/rfc439.

Chang, Briankle (1996). *Deconstructing Communication: Representation, Subject, and Economies of Exchange*. Minneapolis: University of Minnesota Press.

Chesebro, James W., and Donald G. Bonsall (1989). *Computer-Mediated Communication: Human Relationships in a Computerized World*. Tuscaloosa: University of Alabama Press.

Cho, Kyunghyun, Bart van Merriënboer, Caglar Gulcehre, Fethi Bougares, Holger Schwenk, Dzmitry Bahdanau, and Yoshua Bengio (2014). Learning Phrase Representations Using RNN Encoder-Decoder for Statistical Machine Translation. *Proceedings of the 2014 Conference on Empirical Methods in Natural Language Processing* (EMNLP), October 25–29: 1724–1734.

Christie's (2018). Is Artificial Intelligence Set to Become Art's Next Medium? August 20. https://www.christies.com/features/A-collaboration-between-two-artists-one-human-one-a-machine-9332-1.aspx.

Churchland, Paul (1999). *Matter and Consciousness*. Cambridge, MA: MIT Press.

Clarke, Arthur C. (1973). *Profiles of the Future: An Inquiry into the Limits of the Possible*. Toronto, ON: Popular Library.

Clerwall, Christer (2014). Enter the Robot Journalist: Users' Perceptions of Automated Content. *Journalism Practice* 8(5): 519–531. https://doi.org/10.1080/17512786.2014.883116.

Coeckelbergh, Mark (2010). Moral Appearances: Emotions, Robots, and Human Morality. *Ethics and Information Technology* 12 (3): 235–241. https://doi.org/10.1007/s10676-010-9221-y.

Colton, Simon (2012). The Painting Fool: Stories from Building an Automated Painter. In *Computers and Creativity*, ed. J. McCormack and M. d'Inverno, 3–38. Berlin: Springer Verlag. https://doi.org/10.1007/978-3-642-31727-9_1.

Colton, Simon, and Geraint A. Wiggins (2012). Computational Creativity: The Final Frontier. In *Frontiers in Artificial Intelligence and Applications*, vol. 242, ed. L. De Raedt et al., 21–26. Amsterdam: IOS Press Ebooks. http://ebooks.iospress.nl/volume/ecai-2012.

Colton, Simon, Alison Pease, Joseph Corneli, Michael Cook, Rose Hepworth, and Dan Ventura (2015). Stakeholder Groups in Computational Creativity Research and Practice. In *Computational Creativity Research: Towards Creative Machines*, ed. T. R. Besold, M. Schorlemmer, and A. Smaill, 3–36. Amsterdam: Atlantis Press. https://doi.org/10.2991/978-94-6239-085-0_1.

Cookson, Clive (2015). Scientists Appeal for Ethical Use of Robots. *Financial Times*, December 10. https://www.ft.com/content/fee8bacc-9f37-11e5-8613-08e211ea5317.

Cope, David (2001). *Virtual Music: Computer Synthesis of Musical Style*. Cambridge, MA: MIT Press.

Cope, David (2010). Recombinant Music Composition Algorithm and Method of Using the Same. United States Patent. US 7,696.426 B2. https://patentimages.storage.googleapis.com/25/2e/8f/5e836d32d44240/US7696426.pdf.

Cope, David (2017). Experiments in Musical Intelligence (website). http://artsites.ucsc.edu/faculty/cope/experiments.htm.

Cormen, Thomas H., Charles E. Leiserson, Ronald L. Rivest, and Clifford Stein (2009). *Introduction to Algorithms*. Cambridge, MA: MIT Press.

Cowburn, Ashley (2016). Canadian Province Ontario Plans to Trial Universal Basic Income. *Independent*, March 7. http://www.independent.co.uk/news/world/americas/ontario-to-pilot-a-universal-basic-income-experiment-a6916571.html.

Danaher, John, and Neil McArthur (2017). *Robot Sex: Social and Ethical Implications*. Cambridge, MA: MIT Press.

Darling, Kate (2012). Extending Legal Protection to Social Robots. *IEEE Spectrum*. http://spectrum.ieee.org/automaton/robotics/artificial-intelligence/extending-legal-protection-to-social-robots.

Darling, Kate (2016). Extending Legal Protection to Social Robots: The Effects of Anthropomorphism, Empathy, and Violent Behavior Toward Robotic Objects. In *Robot Law*, ed. Ryan Calo, A. Michael Froomkin, and Ian Kerr, 213–231. Northampton, MA: Edward Elgar.

Darling, Kate, and Sabine Hauert (2013). Giving Rights to Robots. *RobotsPodcast #125*. http://robohub.org/robots-giving-rights-to-robots/.

Darling, Kate, and Shankar Vedantam (2017). Can Robots Teach Us What It Means to be Human? *Hidden Brain* (NPR Podcast). http://www.npr.org/2017/07/10/536424647/can-robots-teach-us-what-it-means-to-be-human.

Dastin, Jeffrey (2018). Amazon Scraps Secret AI Recruiting Tool that Showed

Bias Against Women. *Reuters*. October 9. https://www.reuters.com/article/ us-amazon-com-jobs-automation-insight/amazon-scraps-secret-ai- recruiting-tool-that-showed-bias-against-women-idUSKCN1MK08G.

Datteri, Edoardo (2013). Predicting the Long-Term Effects of Human- Robot Interaction: A Reflection on Responsibility in Medical Robotics. *Science and Engineering Ethics* 19(1): 139–160. https://doi.org/10.1007/ s11948-011-9301-3.

Dautenhahn, Kerstin (1998). The Art of Designing Socially Intelligent Agents: Science, Fiction and the Human in the Loop. *Applied Artificial Intelligence* 12(7–8): 573–617.

Dautenhahn, Kerstin (2007). Socially Intelligent Robots: Dimensions of Human–Robot Interaction. *Philosophical Transactions B* 362(1480): 679– 704. https://doi.org/10.1098/rstb.2006.2004.

Dautenhahn, Kerstin, and Aude Billard (1999). Bringing up Robots or the Psychology of Socially Intelligent Robots: From Theory to Implementation. In *Agents '99: Proceedings of the Third Annual Conference on Autonomous Agents*: 366-367. http://dx.doi.org/10.1145/301136.301237.

De Angeli, Antonella, Sheryl Brahnam, and Peter Wallis (2005). Abuse: The Dark Side of Human-Computer Interaction. *Interact 2005*. http:// www.agentabuse.org/.

December, John (1997). Notes on Defining of Computer-Mediated Communication. *Computer-Mediated Communication Magazine*. https:// www.december.com/cmc/mag/1997/jan/.

DeepMind (2016). AlphaGo. https://deepmind.com/alpha-go.html.

Derrida, Jacques (2005). *Paper Machine*, trans. Rachel Bowlby. Stanford, CA: Stanford University Press.

Descartes, René (1988). *Selected Philosophical Writings*, trans. John Cottingham, Robert Stoothoff, and Dugald Murdoch. Cambridge: Cambridge University Press.

Devlin, Kate (2018). *Turned On: Science, Sex and Robots*. New York: Bloomsbury Sigma.

Diez, Maria Sanchez (2015). The Dutch "Basic Income" Experiment is Expanding Across Multiple Cities. *Quartz*, August 13. http://qz.com/473 779/several-dutch-cities-want-to-give-residents-a-no-strings-attached-bas ic-income/.

Dreyfus, Hubert L. (1972). *What Computers Can't Do: The Limits of Artificial Intelligence*. New York: Harper & Row.

Dreyfus, Hubert L. (1992). *What Computers Still Can't Do: A Critique of Artificial Reason*. Cambridge, MA: MIT Press.

Dreyfus, Hubert L., and Stuart Dreyfus (1988). Making a Mind versus Modeling the Brain: Artificial Intelligence Back at a Branchpoint. *Daedalus* 117(1): 15–43.

Duffy, Brian R. (2003). Anthropomorphism and the Social Robot. *Robotics and Autonomous Systems* 42(3–4): 177–190. https://doi.org/10.1016/S0 921-8890(02)00374-3.

Dumouchel, Paul, and Luisa Damiano (2017). *Living with Robots*, trans. Malcolm DeBevoise. Cambridge, MA: Harvard University Press.

Duncan, Starkey (1972). Some Signals and Rules for Taking Speaking Turns in Conversations. *Journal of Personality and Social Psychology* 23(2): 283–292. http://dx.doi.org/10.1037/h0033031.

Dutton, William (1995). Driving into the Future of Communications? Check the Rear View Mirror. In *Information Superhighways: Multimedia Users and Futures*, ed. Stephen J. Emmott, 79–102. San Diego, CA: Academic Press.

Eco, Umberto (1995). *The Search for the Perfect Language*, trans. James Fentress. Oxford: Blackwell.

Edwards, Chad, Autumn Edwards, Patric R. Spence, and Ashleigh K. Shelton (2013). Is That a Bot Running the Social Media Feed? Testing the Differences in Perceptions of Communication Quality for a Human Agent and a Bot Agent on Twitter. *Computers in Human Behavior* 33: 372–376. https://doi.org/10.1016/j.chb.2013.08.013.

Edwards, Chad, Autumn Edwards, Patric R. Spence, and David Westerman (2016). Initial Interaction Expectations with Robots: Testing the Human-To-Human Interaction Script. *Communication Studies* 67(2): 227–238. https://doi.org/10.1080/10510974.2015.1121899.

Ekbia, Hamid R. (2008). *Artificial Dreams: The Quest for Non-Biological Intelligence*. Cambridge: Cambridge University Press.

Ekman, Paul, and Wallace V. Friesen (1969). The Repertoire of Nonverbal Behavior: Categories, Origins, Usage, and Coding. *Semiotica* 1(1): 49–98. https://doi.org/10.1515/semi.1969.1.1.49.

Epstein, Robert (2007). From Russia, with Love: How I Got Fooled (and Somewhat Humiliated) by a Computer. *Scientific American Mind*. https://www.scientificamerican.com/article/from-russia-with-love/.

Feenberg, Andrew (1991). *Critical Theory of Technology*. Oxford: Oxford University Press.

Ferguson, Kirby (2014). *Everything is a Remix* (Four-Part Video Series). http://everythingisaremix.info/.

Fisk, John (1994). *Introduction to Communication Studies*. New York: Routledge.

Floridi, Luciano (2014). *The Fourth Revolution*. Oxford: Oxford University Press.

Flynn C. P. (2008). *Social Creatures: A Human and Animal Studies Reader*. New York: Lantern Books.

Fong, Terrence, Illah Nourbakhsh, and Kerstin Dautenhahn (2003). A Survey of Socially Interactive Robots. *Robotics and Autonomous Systems* 42(3–4): 143–166. https://doi.org/10.1016/S0921-8890(02)00372-X.

Ford, Martin (2015). *Rise of the Robots: Technology and the Threat of a Jobless Future*. New York: Basic Books.

French, Peter (1979). The Corporation as a Moral Person. *American Philosophical Quarterly* 16 (3): 207–215. https://www.jstor.org/stable/2000 9760.

Frey, Carl Benedikt, and Michael A. Osborne (2013). The Future of Employment: How Susceptible Are Jobs to Computerisation? Oxford Martin School. University of Oxford. http://www.oxfordmartin.ox.ac.uk/publications/view/1314.

Frey, Carl Benedikt, and Michael A. Osborne (2017). The Future of Employment: How Susceptible Are Jobs to Automation? *Technological Forecasting and Social Change* 114: 254–280. https://doi.org/10.1016/j.tech fore.2016.08.019.

Garreau, Joel (2007). Bots on the Ground: In the Field of Battle (or Even Above It), Robots are a Soldier's Best Friend. *Washington Post*, May 6. http://www.washingtonpost.com/wp-dyn/content/article/2007/05/05/AR 2007050501009.html.

Gehl, Robert W. (2013). The Computerized Socialbot Turing Test: New Technologies of Noopower. *Social Science Research Network* (SSRN). http://ssrn.com/abstract=2280240.

Gehl, Robert W., and Maria Bakardjieva (2017). *Socialbots and Their Friends: Digital Media and the Automation of Society*. New York: Routledge.

Geitgey, Adam (2016). Machine Learning Is Fun. *Medium*. August 21. https://medium.com/@ageitgey/machine-learning-is-fun-80ea3ec3c 471.

Georgia Tech. (2013). Robotic Musicianship Group: Shimon. http://www.gtcmt.gatech.edu/research-projects/shimon.

Gerbner, George (1956). Toward a General Model of Communication. *Audio Visual Communication Review* 4(3): 171–199. https://www.jstor.org/stable/30218421.

Gladden, Matthew E. (2016) The Diffuse Intelligent Other: An Ontology of Nonlocalizable Robots as Moral and Legal Actors. In *Social Robots: Boundaries, Potential, Challenges*, ed. Marco Nørskov, 177–198. Burlington, VT: Ashgate.

Glass, James. R. (1999). Challenges for Spoken Dialogue Systems. *Proceedings of the 1999 IEEE ASRU Workshop*, December. http://www.cs.cmu.edu/afs/cs.cmu.edu/Web/People/dod/ papers/glass99.pdf.

Goertzel, Ben (2002). Thoughts on AI Morality. *Dynamical Psychology: An International, Interdisciplinary Journal of Complex Mental Processes*, May. http://www.goertzel.org/dynapsyc/2002/AIMorality.htm.

Goertzel, Ben, and Cassio Pennachin (2007). *Artificial General Intelligence*. New York: Springer.

Grove, Jack (2015). Social Sciences and Humanities Faculties "To Close" in Japan After Ministerial Intervention. *Times Higher Education*, September 14. https://www.timeshighereducation.com/news/social-sciences-and-human ities-faculties-close-japan-after-ministerial-intervention.

Gubrud, Mark Avrum (1997). Nanotechnology and International Security. Paper presented at the Fifth Foresight Conference on Molecular Nano-technology. https://foresight.org/Conferences/MNT05/Papers/Gubrud/in dex.php.

Gunkel, David J. (2012). *The Machine Question: Critical Perspectives on AI, Robots and Ethics.* Cambridge, MA: MIT Press.

Gunkel, David J. (2016). *Of Remixology: Ethics and Aesthetics After Remix.* Cambridge, MA: MIT Press.

Gunkel, David J. (2018). *Robot Rights.* Cambridge, MA: MIT Press.

Guzman, Andrea L. (2018). *Human–Machine Communication: Rethinking Communication, Technology and Ourselves.* New York: Peter Lang.

Hall, J. Storrs (2001). Ethics for Machines. *KurzweilAI.net.* July 5. http://www.kurzweilai.net/ethics-for-machines.

Halpern, Sue (2015). How Robots and Algorithms Are Taking Over. *New York Review of Books* 62(6). http://www.nybooks.com/articles/2015/04/02/how-robots-algorithms-are-taking-over/.

Hanson, F. Allan (2009). Beyond the Skin Bag: On the Moral Responsibility of Extended Agencies. *Ethics and Information Technology* 11(1): 91–99. https://doi.org/10.1007/s10676-009-9184-z.

Harper, R. G., A. N. Wiens, and J. D. Matarazzo (1978). *Nonverbal Communication: The State of the Art.* Oxford: John Wiley & Sons.

Haugeland, John (1989). *Artificial Intelligence: The Very Idea.* Cambridge, MA: MIT Press.

Hawksworth, John, Richard Berriman, and Saloni Goel (2017). Will Robots Really Steal Our Jobs? An International Analysis of the Potential Long Term Impact of Automation. PricewaterhouseCoopers (PwC). https://www.pwc.com/hu/hu/kiadvanyok/assets/pdf/impact_of_automation_on_jobs.pdf.

Hearne, V. (2000). *Adam's Task: Calling Animals by Name.* New York: Akadine Press.

Hebb, Donald O. (1949). *The Organization of Behavior: A Neuropsychological Theory.* New York: John Wiley & Sons.

Hecht, Marvin. A., and Nalini Ambady (1999). Nonverbal Communication and Psychology: Past and Future. *Atlantic Journal of Communication* 7(2): 156–170. https://doi.org/10.1080/15456879909367364.

Heidegger, Martin (1977). *The Question Concerning Technology and Other Essays,* trans. William Lovitt. New York: Harper & Row.

Hemmersbaugh, P. A. (2016). NHTSA Letter to Chris Urmson, Director, Self-Driving Car Project, Google, Inc. https://isearch.nhtsa.gov/files/Google%20--%20compiled%20response%20to%2012%20Nov%20%2015%20interp%20request%20--%204%20Feb%2016%20final.htm.

Hernández-Orallo, José (2017). *The Measure of All Minds: Evaluating Natural and Artificial Intelligence.* Cambridge: Cambridge University Press.

Herring, Susan (ed.) (1996). *Computer-Mediated Communication: Linguistic, Social and Cross-Cultural Perspectives.* Philadelphia, PA: John Benjamins Publishing Company.

Heyn, E. T. (1904). Berlin's Wonderful Horse. *The New York Times,* September 4.

Hiltz, Starr Roxanne, and Elaine Kerr (1982). *Computer-Mediated*

Communication Systems: Status and Evaluation. New York: Academic Press.

Hiltz, Starr Roxanne, Kenneth Johnson, and Murray Turoff (1986). Experiments in Group Decision Making Communication Process and Outcome in Face-to-Face Versus Computerized Conferences. *Human Communication Research* 13(2): 225–252. https://doi.org/10.1111/j.1468-2958.1986.tb00104.x.

Hiltz, Starr Roxanne, and Murray Turoff (1978). *The Networked Nation: Human Communication via Computer.* Reading, MA: Addison-Wesley Publishing Company.

Hirschberg, Julia, and Christopher D. Manning (2015). Advancements in Natural Language Processing. *Science* 349(6245): 261–266. http://science.sciencemag.org/content/349/6245/261.

Hobbes, Thomas (1994). *Leviathan.* Indianapolis, IN: Hackett Publishing.

Hoffman, Guy, and Gil Weinberg (2011). Interactive Improvisation with a Robotic Marimba Player. *Autonomous Robots,* 31(2–3): 133–153. https://doi.org/10.1007/s10514-011-9237-0.

Hofstadter, Douglas R. (1979). *Gödel, Escher, Bach: An Eternal Golden Braid.* New York: Basic Books.

Hofstadter, Douglas R. (2001). Staring Emmy Straight in the Eye – And Doing My Best Not to Flinch. In *Virtual Music: Computer Synthesis of Musical Style,* ed. David Cope, 33–82. Cambridge, MA: MIT Press.

Hopper, Robert (1992). *Telephone Conversation.* Bloomington, IN: Indiana University Press.

Hugo, Victor (1978). *Notre-Dame de Paris,* trans. John Sturrock. New York: Penguin Putnam.

Hui, Fan (2016). AlphaGo Games – English. DeepMind. https://deepmind.com/research/alphago/alphago-games-english/.

Hutchins, John (1986). *Machine Translation: Past, Present, Future.* Chichester, UK: Ellis Horwood.

Hutchins, John (2000). *Early Years in Machine Translation: Memoirs and Biographies of Pioneers.* Amsterdam: John Benjamins.

Hutchins, John, and Harold L. Somers (1992). *An Introduction to Machine Translation.* London: Academic Press.

IFR (International Federation of Robotics) (2015). Industrial Robot Statistics. http://www.ifr.org/industrial-robots/statistics/.

Ihde, Don (1990). *Technology and the Lifeworld: From Garden to Earth.* Bloomington, IN: Indiana University Press.

Institute for Public Policy Research (2017). https://www.ippr.org/research/topics/jobs-skills.

Jakobson, Roman (1960). Closing Statement: Linguistics and Poetics. In *Style and Language,* ed. Thomas A. Sebeok, 350–377. Cambridge, MA: MIT Press.

Jibo (2014). Indiegogo Video. https://www.indiegogo.com/projects/jibo-the-world-s-first-social-robot-for-the-home#/.

Johnson, Brian David (2011). *Science Fiction Prototyping: Designing the Future with Science Fiction.* Williston, VT: Morgan and Claypool Publishers. https://doi.org/10.2200/S00336ED1V01Y201102CSL003.

Johnson, Deborah G. (1985). *Computer Ethics.* Upper Saddle River, NJ: Prentice Hall.

Johnson, Deborah G. (2006). Computer Systems: Moral Entities but not Moral Agents. *Ethics and Information Technology* 8(4): 195–204. https://doi.org/10.1007/s10676-006-9111-5.

Johnson, Deborah G., and Keith W. Miller (2008) Un-Making Artificial Moral Agents. *Ethics and Information Technology* 10(2–3): 123–133. https://doi.org/10.1007/s10676-008-9174-6.

Jones, Stanley E., and Curtis. D. LeBaron (2002). Research on the Relationship between Verbal and Nonverbal Communication: Emerging Integrations. *Journal of Communication* 52(3): 499–521. https://doi.org/10.1111/j.1460-2466.2002.tb02559.x.

Jones, Steve (2014). People, Things, Memory and Human–Machine Communication. *International Journal of Media & Cultural Politics* 10(3): 245–258. https://doi.org/10.1386/macp.10.3.245_1.

Jones, Steve (2015). How I Learned to Stop Worrying and Love the Bots. *Social Media and Society* 1(1): 1–2. https://doi.org/10.1177/2056305115580344.

Jonze, Spike (dir.) (2013). *Her.* Warner Brothers.

Jordan, John (2016). *Robots.* Cambridge, MA: MIT Press.

Joseph, Franz (1975). *Star Fleet Technical Manual.* New York: Ballantine.

Jurafsky, Dan, and James H. Martin (2017). Speech and Language Processing: An Introduction to Natural Language Processing, Computational Linguistics, and Speech Recognition. New York: Prentice Hall. https://web.stanford.edu/~jurafsky/slp3/ed3book.pdf.

Kanda, Takayuki, and Hiroshi Ishiguro (2013). *Human–Robot Interaction in Social Robotics.* Boca Raton, FL: CRC Press.

Kant, Immanuel (1963). Duties to Animals and Spirits. In *Lectures on Ethics,* trans. L. Infield, 239–241. New York: Harper and Row.

Kaplan, Jerry (2016). *Artificial Intelligence: What Everyone Needs to Know.* New York: Oxford University Press.

Kelly, Kevin (2014). The Three Breakthroughs That Have Finally Unleashed AI on the World. *Wired,* October 27. https://www.wired.com/2014/10/future-of-artificial-intelligence/.

Kenney, Martin, and Donald Patton (2009). Reconsidering the Bayh–Dole Act and the Current University Invention Ownership Model. *Research Policy* 38: 1407–1422. https://doi.org/10.1016/j.respol.2009.07.007.

Keynes, John Maynard (2010). *Essays in Persuasion.* New York: Palgrave Macmillan.

Kiesler, Sara, and Lee Sproull (1992). Group Decision Making and Communication Technology. *Organizational Behavior and Human Decision Processes* 52(1): 96–123. https://doi.org/10.1016/0749-5978(92)90047-B.

Kim, Elizabeth S., Lauren D. Berkovits, Emily P. Bernier, Dan Leyzberg, Frederick Shic, Rhea Paul, and Brian Scassellati (2013). Social Robots as Embedded Reinforcers of Social Behavior in Children with Autism. *Journal of Autism and Developmental Disorders* 43(5): 1038–1049. https://doi.org/10.1007/s10803-012-1645-2.

Knight, Heather (2014). How Humans Respond to Robots: Building Public Policy Through Good Design. Brookings Institute. https://www.brookings.edu/research/how-humans-respond-to-robots-building-public-policy-through-good-design/.

Kriz, Sarah, Toni D. Ferro, Pallavi Damera, and John R. Porter (2010). Fictional Robots as a Data Source in HRI Research: Exploring the Link Between Science Fiction and Interactional Expectations. *19th IEEE International Symposium on Robot and Human Interactive Communication,* Viareggio, Italy, September 12–15, 458–463. https://doi.org/10.1109/ROMAN.2010.5598620.

Krzeczkowska, Anna, Jad El-Hage, Simon Colton, and Stephen Clark (2010). Automated Collage Generation – With Intent. *Proceedings of the 1st International Conference on Computational Creativity.* http://computationalcreativity.net/iccc2010/papers/krzeczkowska-hage-colton-clark.pdf.

Kubrick, Stanley (dir.) (1968). *2001: A Space Odyssey.* Hollywood, CA: Metro-Goldwyn-Mayer.

Kuhn, Thomas (1996). *The Structure of Scientific Revolutions.* Chicago, IL: University of Chicago Press.

Latour, Bruno (2005). *Reassembling the Social: An Introduction to Actor-Network-Theory.* Oxford: Oxford University Press.

Lee, Peter (2016). Learning from Tay's Introduction. *Official Microsoft Blog,* March 25. https://blogs.microsoft.com/blog/2016/03/25/learning-tays-introduction/.

Leviathan, Yaniv, and Yossi Matias (2018). Google Duplex: An AI System for Accomplishing Real-World Tasks Over the Phone. *Google AI Blog.* May 8. https://ai.googleblog.com/2018/05/duplex-ai-system-for-natural-conversation.html.

Levy, David (2007). *Love and Sex with Robots: The Evolution of Human-Robot Relationships.* New York: Harper Perennial.

Levy, David N. L. (2009). World's Best Chat Bot. http://www.worldsbestchatbot.com/.

Lewis-Kraus, Gideon (2016). The Great AI Awakening: How Google Used Artificial Intelligence to Transform Google Translate, One of its More Popular Services – And How Machine Learning is Poised to Reinvent Computing Itself. *New York Times,* December 14. https://www.nytimes.com/2016/12/14/magazine/the-great-ai-awakening.html.

Licklider, J. C. R. and Robert W. Taylor (1968). The Computer as a Communication Device. *Science and Technology,* April 21. http://memex.org/licklider.html.

Lindenfeld, Jacqueline (1971). Verbal and Non-verbal Elements in

Discourse. *Semiotica* 3(3): 223–233. https://doi.org/10.1515/semi.1971.3.3.223.

Lobel, Mia, Michael Neubauer and Randy Swedburg (2005). Comparing How Students Collaborate to Learn About the Self and Relationships in a Real-Time Non-Turn-Taking Online and Turn-Taking Face-to-Face Environment. *Journal of Computer-Mediated Communication* 10(4). http://onlinelibrary.wiley.com/doi/10.1111/j.1083-6101.2005.tb00281.x/full.

Loebner Prize (2018). http://www.loebner.net/Prizef/loebner-prize.html.

Lorin, Janet (2016). Student Debt: The Rising US Burden. *Bloomberg*, May 23. http://www.bloomberg.com/quicktake/student-debt.

Lovgren, Stefan (2006). A Robot in Every Home by 2020, South Korea Says. *National Geographic News*, September 6. http://news.nationalgeographic.com/news/2006/09/060906-robots.html.

Lyotard, Jean-François (1984). *The Postmodern Condition: A Report on Knowledge*, trans. Geoff Bennington and Brian Massumi. Minneapolis: University of Minnesota Press.

Majid al-Rifaie, Mohammad, and Mark Bishop (2015). Weak and Strong Computational Creativity. In *Computational Creativity Research: Towards Creative Machines*, ed. T. R. Besold, M. Schorlemmer, and A. Smaill, 37–50. Amsterdam: Atlantis Press. https://doi.org/10.2991/978-94-6239-085-0_2.

Marx, Karl (1977). *Capital: A Critique of Political Economy*, trans. Ben Fowkes. New York: Vintage Books.

Matthias, Andreas (2004). The Responsibility Gap: Ascribing Responsibility for the Actions of Learning Automata. *Ethics and Information Technology* 6(3): 175–183. https://doi.org/10.1007/s10676-004-3422-1.

Mauldin, Michael L. (1994). CHATTERBOTs, TINYMUDs, and the Turing Test: Entering the Loebner Prize Competition. *Proceedings of AAAI-94*. http://www.aaai.org/Papers/ AAAI/1994/AAAI94-003.pdf.

McAfee, Andrew (2012). Are the Droids Taking our Jobs? TEDx Boston 2012. https://www.ted.com/talks/andrew_mcafee_are_droids_taking_our_jobs.

McAfee, Andrew, and Erik Brynjolfsson (2016). *The Second Machine Age: Work, Progress, and Prosperity in a Time of Brilliant Technologies*. New York: Norton.

McCarthy, John, and Ed Feigenbaum (1990). In Memoriam. Arthur Samuel: Pioneer in Machine Learning. *AI Magazine* 11(3): 10–11. https://doi.org/10.1609/aimag.v11i3.840.

McCarthy, John, Marvin L. Minsky, Nathan Rochester, and Claude E. Shannon. (1955). A Proposal for the Dartmouth Summer Research Project on Artificial Intelligence. http://jmc.stanford.edu/articles/dartmouth/dartmouth.pdf.

McClelland, J., D. Rumelhart, and The PDP Research Group (1986). *Parallel Distributed Processing: Explorations in the Microstructure of Cognition. Volume 2: Psychological and Biological Models*. Cambridge, MA: MIT Press.

McCulloch, Warren, and Walter Pitts (1943). A Logical Calculus of the Ideas Immanent in Nervous Activity. *Bulletin of Mathematical Biophysics* 7: 115–133. https://doi.org/10.1007/BF02478259.

McFarland, M. (2016). What AlphaGo's Sly Move Says About Machine Creativity. *Washington Post*, March 15. https://www.washingtonpost.com/news/innovations/wp/2016/03/15/what-alphagos-sly-move-says-about-machine-creativity/?utm_term=.0c8281af53c9.

McKinsey Global Institute (2017). A Future that Works: Automation, Employment and Productivity. https://www.mckinsey.com/~/media/McKinsey/Featured%20Insights/Digital%20Disruption/Harnessing%20automation%20for%20a%20future%20that%20works/MGI-A-future-that-works_Full-report.ashx.

McLuhan, Marshall (1995). *Understanding Media: The Extensions of Man.* Cambridge, MA: MIT Press.

Metz, Cade (2016a). The Sadness and Beauty of Watching Google's AI Play Go. *Wired*, March 11. https://www.wired.com/2016/03/sadness-beauty-watching-googles-ai-play-go/.

Metz, Cade (2016b). In Two Moves, AlphaGo and Lee Sedol Redefine the Future. *Wired*, March 16. https://www.wired.com/2016/03/two-moves-alphago-lee-sedol-redefined-future/.

Metz, Cade (2016c). Google's AI Wins a Pivotal Second Game in Match with Go Grandmaster. *Wired*, March 10. http://www.wired.com/2016/03/googles-ai-wins-pivotal-game-two-match-go-grandmaster/.

Microsoft (2016). Meet Tay: Microsoft AI Chatbot with Zero Chill. https://www.tay.ai/.

Milgram, Stanley (1974). *Obedience to Authority: An Experimental View.* London: Tavistock Publications.

Minsky, Marvin, and Seymour Papert (1969). *Perceptrons: An Introduction to Computational Geometry.* Cambridge, MA: MIT Press.

MIT (2018). MIT Technology Licensing Office. http://tlo.mit.edu/community/policies/part2.

Mnih, V., K. Kavukcuoglu, D. Silver, A. Rusu, J. Veness, M. G. Bellemare, A. Graves et al. (2015). Human Level Control Through Deep Reinforcement Learning. *Nature* 518: 529–533.

Montal, Tal, and Zvi Reich (2016). I, Robot. You, Journalist. Who is the Author? Authorship, Bylines and Full Disclosure in Automated Journalism. *Digital Journalism* 5(7): 829–849. http://dx.doi.org/10.1080/21670811.2016.1209083.

Morais, Betsy (2013). Can Humans Fall in Love with Bots? *The New Yorker*, November 19. http://www.newyorker.com/tech/elements/can-humans-fall-in-love-with-bots.

Mordvintsev, Alexander, Christopher Olah, and Mike Tyka (2015). Inceptionism: Going Deeper into Neural Networks. *Google AI Blog*, June 17. https://ai.googleblog.com/2015/06/inceptionism-going-deeper-into-neural.html.

Mori, Masahiro (2012). The Uncanny Valley, trans. Karl F. MacDorman and Norri Kageki. *IEEE Robotics & Automation Magazine* 19(2): 98–100. https://doi.org/10.1109/MRA.2012.2192811.

Morrison, James C. (2006). Marshall McLuhan: No Prophet without Honor. *AmeriQuests* http://ejournals.library.vanderbilt.edu/ojs/index.php/ameriquests/issue/view/4/showToc.

Mowbray, Miranda (2002). Ethics for Bots. Paper presented at the 14th International Conference on System Research, Informatics, and Cybernetics. Baden-Baden, Germany. July 29–August 3. http://www.hpl.hp.com/techreports/2002/HPL-2002-48R1.pdf.

Mowshowitz, Abbe (2008). Technology as Excuse for Questionable Ethics. *AI & Society* 22(3): 271–282. https://doi.org/10.1007/s00146-007-0147-9.

Nagoa, Makoto (1984). A Framework of a Mechanical Translation Between Japanese and English by Analogy Principle. In *Artificial and Human Intelligence*, ed. A. Elithorn and R. Banerji, 173–180. Amsterdam: Elsevier Science Publishers. http://www.mt-archive.info/Nagao-1984.pdf.

Narrative Science (2018). https://narrativescience.com/.

Navas, Eduardo (2012). *Remix Theory: The Aesthetics of Sampling*. Wien: Springer.

Newell, Allen, and Herbert A. Simon (1976). Computer Science as Empirical Inquiry: Symbols and Search. *Communications of the ACM* 19(3): 113–126. https://doi.org/10.1145/360018.360022.

Nilsson, Nils J. (2007). The Physical Symbol System Hypothesis: Status and Prospects. In *50 Years of Artificial Intelligence: Essays Dedicated to the 50th Anniversary of Artificial Intelligence*, ed. Max Lungarella, Fumiya Iida, Josh Bongard, and Rolf Pfeifer, 9–17. Berlin: Springer.

Nilsson, Nils J. (2010). *The Quest for Artificial Intelligence: A History of Ideas and Achievements*. Cambridge: Cambridge University Press.

Nissenbaum, Helen (1996). Accountability in a Computerized Society. *Science and Engineering Ethics* 2(1): 25–42. https://doi.org/10.1007/BF02639315.

Nourbakhsh, Illah (2013). *Robot Futures*. Cambridge: MIT Press.

Nusca, Andrew (2011). How Apple's Siri Really Works. *ZDNet*. https://www.zdnet.com/article/how-apples-siri-really-works/.

Obvious (2018). Obvious Art – Website. http://obvious-art.com.

O'Connell, D. C., S. Kowal, and E. Kaltenbacher (1990). Turn-Taking: A Critical Analysis of the Research Tradition. *Journal of Psycholinguistic Research* 19(6): 345–373. https://doi.org/10.1007/BF01068884.

Okuda, Michael, Denise Okuda, and Debbie Mirek (1994). *The Star Trek Encyclopedia*. New York: Pocket Books.

Oreström, Bingt (1983). *Turn-Taking in English Conversation*. Lund, Sweden: Liber.

Oxford English Dictionary (2017). https://en.oxforddictionaries.com/definition/robot.

The Painting Fool (2017). The Painting Fool. http://www.thepaintingfool. com/.

Parkin, Simon (2015). Rewriting the Rules of Turing's Imitation Game. *MIT Technology Review*. March 17. https://www.technologyreview.com/s/ 535391/rewriting-the-rules-of-turings-imitation-game/.

Pereira, Maria João, Luísa Coheur, Pedro Fialho, and Ricardo Ribeiro (2016). Chatbots' Greetings to Human–Computer Communication. https:// arxiv.org/pdf/1609.06479.pdf.

Peterson, Andrea (2013). On the Internet, No One Knows You're a Bot. And That's a Problem. *Washington Post*, August 13. https://www. washingtonpost.com/news/the-switch/wp/2013/08/13/on-the-internet-no-one-knows-youre-a-bot-and-thats-a-problem/?utm_term=.b4e0dd774 28a.

Pfungst, Oskar (1965). *Clever Hans (The Horse of Mr. von Osten): A Contribution to Experimental Animal and Human Psychology*. New York: Holt, Rinehart & Winston.

Pierce, David (2017). How Apple Finally Made Siri Sound More Human. *Wired*, September 7. https://www.wired.com/story/how-apple-finally-made-siri-sound-more-human/.

Plato (1982). *Plato I: Euthyphro, Apology, Crito, Phaedo, Phaedrus*, trans. H. N. Fowler. Cambridge, MA: Harvard University Press.

Poibeau, Thierry (2017). *Machine Translation*. Cambridge, MA: MIT Press.

Popper, Nathaniel (2016). The Robots Are Coming for Wall Street. *New York Times*, February 25. http://www.nytimes.com/2016/02/28/magazine/ the-robots-are-coming-for-wall-street.html?_r=0.

Prescott, Tony J., and Michael Szollosy (2017). Ethical Principles of Robotics. *Connection Science* 29(2): 119–123. http://dx.doi.org/10.1080/ 09540091.2017.1312800.

Raído, Vanessa Enríquez, and Frank Austermühl (2003). Translation and Localization Tools: Current Developments. In *Speaking in Tongues: Language Across Contexts and Users*, ed. Luis Pérez González, 225–250. València: Universitat de València Press.

Rashid, Tariq (2016). *Make Your Own Neural Network*. CreateSpace Independent Publishing Platform.

Reeves, Byron, and Clifford Nass (1996). *The Media Equation: How People Treat Computers, Television, and New Media Like Real People and Places*. Cambridge: Cambridge University Press.

Ricœur, Paul (2007). *Reflections on the Just*, trans. David Pellauer. Chicago, IL: University of Chicago Press.

Risley, James (2016). Microsoft's Millennial Chatbot Tay.ai Pulled Offline After Internet Teaches Her Racism. *GeekWire*. http://www.geekwire.com/ 2016/even-robot-teens-impressionable-microsofts-tay-ai-pulled-internet-teaches-racism/.

Robins, B., K. Dautenhahn, R. T. Boekhorst, and A. Billard (2005). Robotic Assistants in Therapy and Education of Children with Autism:

Can a Small Humanoid Robot Help Encourage Social Interaction Skills? *Universal Access in the Information Society* 4(2): 105–120. https://doi.org/10.1007/s10209-005-0116-3.

Rosenblatt, Frank (1958). The Perceptron: A Probabilistic Model for Information Storage and Organization in the Brain. *Psychological Review* 65: 386–408. https://doi.org/10.1037/h0042519.

Rosenthal-von der Pütten, Astrid M., Nicole C. Krämer, Laura Hoffmann, Sabrina Sobieraj, and Sabrina C. Eimler (2013). An Experimental Study on Emotional Reactions Towards a Robot. *International Journal of Social Robotics* 5: 17–34. https://doi.org/10.1007/s12369-012-0173-8.

Ross, P. E. (2016). A Google Car Can Qualify as a Legal Driver. *IEEE Spectrum*. http://spectrum.ieee.org/cars-that-think/transportation/self-driving/an-ai-can-legally-be-defined-as-a-cars-driver.

Rumelhart, D., J. McClelland, and The PDP Research Group (1986). *Parallel Distributed Processing: Explorations in the Microstructure of Cognition. Volume 1: Foundations.* Cambridge, MA: MIT Press.

Russell, Bertrand (1992). *A Critical Exposition of the Philosophy of Leibniz.* New York: Routledge.

Šabanović, Selma, Casey C. Bennett, Wan-Ling Chang, and Lesa Huber (2013). PARO Robot Affects Diverse Interaction Modalities in Group Sensory Therapy for Older Adults with Dementia. 2013 IEEE 13th International Conference on Rehabilitation Robotics (ICORR) Seattle, WA, June 24–26. https://doi.org/10.1109/ICORR.2013.6650427.

Sacks, Harvey, Emanuel Schegloff, and Gail Jefferson (1974). A Simplest Systematics for the Organization of Turn-Taking for Conversation. *Language* 50(4): 696–735. https://doi.org/10.2307/412243.

Samuel, Arthur L. (1959). Some Studies in Machine Learning Using the Game of Checkers. *IBM Journal* 3(3): 210–229. https://doi.org/10.1147/rd.33.0210.

Sandoval, Eduardo Benitez, Omar Mubin, and Mohammad Obaid (2014). Human–Robot Interaction and Fiction: A Contradiction. In *Social Robotics: 6th International Conference, ICSR 2014,* Sydney, Australia, October 27–29, ed. Michael Beetz, Benjamin Johnston, and Mary-Anne Williams, 54–63. Cham, Switzerland: Springer.

Sandry, Eleanor (2015a). Re-Evaluating the Form and Communication of Social Robots: The Benefits of Collaborating with Machinelike Robots. *International Journal of Social Robotics* 7(3): 335–346. https://doi.org/10.1007/s12369-014-0278-3.

Sandry, Eleanor (2015b). *Robots and Communication.* New York: Palgrave Macmillan.

Schank, Roger C. (1990). "What is AI Anyway?" In *The Foundations of Artificial Intelligence: A Sourcebook,* ed. Derek Partridge and Yorick Wilks, 3–13. Cambridge: Cambridge University Press.

Scheutz, Matthias (2014). The Inherent Dangers of Unidirectional Emotional Bonds Between Humans and Social Robots. In *Robot Ethics:*

The Ethical and Social Implications of Robotics, ed. Patrick Lin, Keith Abney, and George A. Bekey, 205–221. Cambridge, MA: MIT Press.

Schubert, Klaus (1992). Esperanto as an Intermediate Language for Machine Translation. In *Computers in Translation: A Practical Appraisal*, ed. John Newton, 78–95. New York: Routledge.

Searle, John (1980). Minds, Brains, and Programs. *Behavioral and Brain Sciences* 3(3): 417–457. https://doi.org/10.1017/S0140525X00005756.

Searle, John (1984). *Mind, Brains and Science*. Cambridge, MA: Harvard University Press.

Searle, John (1999). The Chinese Room. In *The MIT Encyclopedia of the Cognitive Sciences*, ed. R. A. Wilson and F. Keil, 115–116. Cambridge, MA: MIT Press.

Shannon, Claude E. (1950). Programming a Computer for Playing Chess. *Philosophical Magazine*, Series 7, 41(314): 256–275. https://doi.org/10.1080/14786445008521796.

Shannon, Claude E., and Warren Weaver (1949). *The Mathematical Theory of Communication*. Urbana: University of Illinois Press.

Sharkey, Noel (2012). Killing Made Easy: From Joysticks to Politics. In *Robot Ethics: The Ethical and Social Implications of Robots*, ed. Keith Abney Patrick Lin and George A. Bekey, 111–128. Cambridge, MA: MIT Press.

Shen, Jonathan, and Ruoming Pang (2017). Tacotron 2: Generating Human-like Speech from Text. *Google AI Blog*. December 19. https://ai.googleblog.com/2017/12/tacotron-2-generating-human-like-speech.html.

Simon, Herbert A., and Allen Newell (1958). Heuristic Problem Solving: The Next Advance in Operations Research. *Operations Research* 6(1): 1–10. https://doi.org/10.1287/opre.6.1.1.

Simonite, Tom (2016). OK Computer, Write Me a Song. *MIT Technology Review*, June 8. https://www.technologyreview.com/s/601642/ok-computer-write-me-a-song/.

Simonite, Tom (2018). When It Comes to Gorillas, Google Photo Remains Blind. *Wired*, January 11. https://www.wired.com/story/when-it-comes-to-gorillas-google-photos-remains-blind/.

Singer, Peter W. (2009). *Wired for War: The Robotics Revolution and Conflict in the Twenty-First Century*. New York: Penguin Books.

Siponen, Mikko (2004). A Pragmatic Evaluation of the Theory of Information Ethics. *Ethics and Information Technology* 6(4): 279–290. https://doi.org/10.1007/s10676-005-6710-5.

Siri Team (2017). Hey Siri: An On-Device DNN-Powered Voice Trigger for Apple's Personal Assistant. *Apple Machine Learning Journal* 1(6), October. https://machinelearning.apple.com/2017/10/01/hey-siri.html.

Skantze, Gabriel (2005). Exploring Human Error Recovery Strategies: Implications for Spoken Dialogue Systems. *Speech Communication* 45: 325–341. https://doi.org/10.1016/j.specom.2004.11.005.

Skantze, Gabriel (2007). *Error Handling in Spoken Dialogue Systems: Managing Uncertainty, Grounding and Miscommunication.* Gothenburg, Sweden: Graduate School of Language and Technology. http://www2.gslt.hum. gu.se/dissertations/skantze.pdf.

Skantze, Gabriel, Anna Hjalmarsson, and Catharine Oertel (2014). Turn-Taking, Feedback and Joint Attention in Situated Human–Robot Interaction. *Speech Communication* 65(1): 50–66. https://doi.org/10.1016/j.specom.2014.05.005.

Smith, S. V. (2015). An NPR Reporter Raced a Machine to Write a News Story. Who Won? *Morning Edition*, May 20. http://www.npr.org/sections/money/2015/05/20/406484294/.

Smolensky, Paul (1990). Connectionism and the Foundations of AI. In *The Foundations of Artificial Intelligence: A Sourcebook*, ed. Derek Partridge and Yorick Wilks, 306–326. Cambridge: Cambridge University Press.

Snow, C. P. (1998). *The Two Cultures.* Cambridge: Cambridge University Press.

SoftBank Robotics (2018). Pepper. https://www.softbankrobotics.com/emea/en/pepper.

Sokolowski, Robert (1988). Natural and Artificial Intelligence. *Daedalus* 117(1): 45–64.

Solaiman, S. M. (2017). Legal Personality of Robots, Corporations, Idols and Chimpanzees: A Quest for Legitimacy. *Artificial Intelligence Law* 25 (2): 155–179. https://doi.org/10.1007/s10506-016-9192-3.

Steffensen, Kenn Nakata (2015). Japan and the Social Sciences: Behind the Headlines. *Times Higher Education*, September 30. https://www.timeshighereducation.com/blog/japan-and-social-sciences-behind-headlines.

Steiner, George (1975). *After Babel.* New York: Oxford University Press.

Sternbach, Rich, and Michael Okuda (1991). *Star Trek Next Generation Technical Manual.* New York: Pocket Books.

Steward, Ian, Debapratim De, and Alex Cole (2015). Technology and People: The Great Job-Creating Machine. Deloitte. https://www2.deloitte.com/content/dam/Deloitte/uk/Documents/ finance/deloitte-uk-technology-and-people.pdf.

Stoyanchev, Svetlana, Alex Liu, and Julia Hirschberg (2014). Towards Natural Clarification Questions in Dialogue Systems. *AISB Symposium on Questions, Discourse and Dialogue* 20. http://doc.gold.ac.uk/aisb50/AISB50-S21/AISB50-S21-Stoyanchev-paper.pdf.

Streeck, Jürgen, and Mark L. Knapp (1992). The Interaction of Visual and Verbal Features in Human Communication. In *Advances in Nonverbal Communication*, ed. F. Poyatos, 3–23. Amsterdam: Benjamins. https://doi.org/10.1075/z.60.06str.

Suchman, Lucy A. (1987). *Plans and Situated Actions: The Problem of Human–Machine Communication.* Cambridge: Cambridge University Press.

Suchman, Lucy A. (2007). *Human–Machine Reconfigurations: Plans and Situated Actions.* Cambridge: Cambridge University Press.

Sullins, John P. (2006). When Is a Robot a Moral Agent? *International Review of Information Ethics* 6(12): 23–30. http://www.i-r-i-e.net/inhalt/006/006_full.pdf.

Sundararajan, Arun (2016). *The Sharing Economy: The End of Employment and the Rise of Crowd-Based Capitalism.* Cambridge, MA: MIT Press.

Tabini, Marco (2013). Inside Siri's Brain: The Challenges of Extending Apple's Virtual Assistant. *MacWorld*, April 8. https://www.macworld.com/article/2033073/inside-siris-brain-the-challenges-of-extending-apples-virtual-assistant.html.

Turing, Alan (1999). Computing Machinery and Intelligence. In *Computer Media and Communication: A Reader*, ed. Paul A. Mayer, 37–58. Oxford: Oxford University Press.

Turing, Alan (2004). Can Automatic Calculating Machines Be Said to Think? In *The Essential Turing*, 487–505. Oxford: Oxford University Press.

Turkle, Sherry (2011). *Alone Together: Why We Expect More from Technology and Less from Each Other.* New York: Basic Books.

Turkle, Sherry, Cynthia Breazeal, Olivia Dasté, and Brian Scassellati (2006). First Encounters with Kismet and Cog. In *Digital Media Transformation in Human Communication*, ed. P. Messaris, 303–330. New York: Peter Lang.

Turner, Karen (2016). Meet "Ross," the Newly Hired Legal Robot. *Washington Post.* May 16. https://www.washingtonpost.com/news/innovations/wp/2016/05/16/meet-ross-the-newly-hired-legal-robot/.

Tzara, Tristan (2016). *Seven Dada Manifestos and Lampisteries*, trans. Barbara Wright. Richmond, UK: Alma Classics.

Ulanoff, Lance (2014). Need to Write 5 Million Stories a Week? Robot Reporters to the Rescue. *Mashable*, July 1. https://mashable.com/2014/07/01/robot-reporters-add-data-to-the-five-ws/#vUyzlnu8agqA.

US Department of Transportation (2017). *Transportation Economic Trends 2017.* https://www.bts.gov/product/transportation-economic-trends.

van de Poel, Ibo, Jessica Nihlén Fahlquist, Neelke Doorn, Sjoerd Zwart, and Lambèr Royakkers (2012). The Problem of Many Hands: Climate Change as an Example. *Science Engineering Ethics* 18(1): 49–67. https://doi.org/10.1007/s11948-011-9276-0.

Verbeek, Peter-Paul (2011). *Moralizing Technology: Understanding and Designing the Morality of Things.* Chicago, IL: University of Chicago Press.

Vincent, Jane (2013). Is the Mobile Phone a Personalized Social Robot? *Intervalla* 1(1):60–70. https://www.fus.edu/intervalla/volume-1-social-robots-and-emotion-transcending-the-boundary-between-humans-and-icts/is-the-mobile-phone-a-personalized-social-robot.

Wada, Kazuyoshi, and Takanori Shibata (2007). Living with Seal Robots: Its Sociopsychological and Physiological Influences on the Elderly at a Care House. *IEEE Transactions on Robotics* 23(5): 972–980. https://doi.org/10.1109/TRO.2007.906261.

Wagenaar, Willem A., and Jop Groeneweg (1987). Accidents at Sea: Multiple Causes and Impossible Consequences. *International Journal of*

Man-Machine Studies 27: 587–598. https://doi.org/10.1016/S0020-7373 (87)80017-2.

Wallace, Michal, and George Dunlop (1997). Eliza, the Rogerian Therapist. Javascript code. http://www.manifestation.com/neurotoys/eliza.php3.

Wallach, Wendell (2008). Implementing Moral Decision Making Faculties in Computers and Robots. *AI & Society* 22: 463–475. https://doi.org/ 10.1007/s00146-007-0093-6.

Wallach, Wendell (2015). *A Dangerous Master: How to Keep Technology from Slipping Beyond Our Control*. New York: Basic Books.

Wallach, Wendell, and Colin Allen (2009). *Moral Machines: Teaching Robots Right from Wrong*. Oxford: Oxford University Press.

Walmsley, Joel (2012). *Mind and Machine*. New York: Palgrave Macmillan.

Weaver, Warren (1949). Translation. The Rockefeller Foundation. http:// www.mt-archive.info/Weaver-1949.pdf.

Weizenbaum, Joseph (1967). Contextual Understanding by Computers. *Communications of the ACM* 10(8): 474–480. https://doi.org/10.1145/363 534.363545.

Weizenbaum, Joseph (1976). *Computer Power and Human Reason: From Judgment to Calculation*. San Francisco, CA: W. H. Freeman.

Westley, B. H., and M. S. MacLean (1957). A Conceptual Model for Communication Research. *Journalism Quarterly* 34(1): 31–38. https://doi.org/ 10.1177/107769905703400103.

White House (2014). Taking Action: Higher Education and Student Loan Debt. http://www.whitehouse.gov/sites/default/files/docs/student_debt_report_ final.pdf.

Wiemann, John M., and Mark L. Knapp (1975). Turn-Taking in Conversations. *Journal of Communication* 25(2): 75-92. https://doi.org/10.1111/j. 1460-2466.1975.tb00582.x.

Wiener, Norbert (1988). *The Human Use of Human Beings: Cybernetics and Society*. Boston, MA: Da Capo Press.

Wiener, Norbert (1996). *Cybernetics: Or Control and Communication in the Animal and the Machine*. Cambridge, MA: MIT Press.

Williams, Jason D., Antoine Raux, and Matthew Henderson (2016). The Dialog State Tracking Challenge Series: A Review. *Dialogue & Discourse* 7(3): 4–33.

Winfield, Alan (2011). Roboethics – For Humans. *New Scientist* 210(2811): 32–33. https://doi.org/10.1016/S0262-4079(11)61052-X.

Winfield, Alan (2012). *Robotics: A Very Short Introduction*. Oxford: Oxford University Press.

Winner, Langdon (1977). *Autonomous Technology: Technics-out-of-Control as a Theme in Political Thought*. Cambridge, MA: MIT Press.

Winograd, Terry (1990). Thinking Machines: Can There Be? Are We? In *The Foundations of Artificial Intelligence: A Sourcebook*, ed. Derek Partridge and Yorick Wilks, 167–189. Cambridge: Cambridge University Press.

Wittgenstein, Ludwig (1981). *Tractatus Logico-Philosophicus*, trans. C. K. Ogden. New York: Routledge.

Wolchover, Natalie (2011). How the Cleverbot Computer Chats Like a Human. *LiveScience*. http://www.livescience.com/15940-cleverbot-computer-chats-human.html.

Wolf, Gary (1996). Channeling McLuhan. *Wired* 4(1), January. http://www.wired.com/wired/archive/4.01/channeling_pr.html.

World Economic Forum (2018) *The Future of Jobs Report 2018*. Centre for the New Economy and Society. http://www3.weforum.org/docs/WEF_Future_of_Jobs_2018.pdf.

Wright, Alex (2015) Algorithmic Authors. *Communications of the ACM* 58(11): 12–14. https://doi.org/10.1145/2820421.

Zeifman, Igal (2017). Bot Traffic Report 2016. *Incapsula*. https://www.incapsula.com/blog/bot-traffic-report-2016.html.

Žižek, Slavoj (2008). *The Sublime Object of Ideology*. London: Verso.

Index